B.D. Nov. 1939

Anna Karenina

Anna Karenina

BY

LEO TOLSTOY

TRANSLATED FROM THE RUSSIAN BY

CONSTANCE GARNETT

WITH

AN INTRODUCTORY ESSAY BY THOMAS MANN

AND ILLUSTRATIONS BY PHILIP REISMAN

VOLUME TWO

RANDOM HOUSE · NEW YORK · 1939

COPYRIGHT, 1939, BY RANDOM HOUSE, INC.

*MANUFACTURED IN THE UNITED STATES OF AMERICA
BY H. WOLFF, NEW YORK*

Part Five

CHAPTER I

Princess Shtcherbatskaya considered that it was out of the question for the wedding to take place before Lent, just five weeks off, since not half the trousseau could possibly be ready by that time. But she could not but agree with Levin that to fix it for after Lent would be putting it off too late, as an old aunt of Prince Shtcherbatsky's was seriously ill and might die, and then the mourning would delay the wedding still longer. And therefore, deciding to divide the trousseau into two parts—a larger and smaller trousseau—the princess consented to have the wedding before Lent. She determined that she would get the smaller part of the trousseau all ready now, and the larger part should be made later, and she was much vexed with Levin because he was incapable of giving her a serious answer to the question whether he agreed to this arrangement or not. The arrangement was the more suitable as, immediately after the wedding, the young people were to go to the country, where the more important part of the trousseau would not be wanted.

Levin still continued in the same delirious condition in which it seemed to him that he and his happiness constituted the chief and sole aim of all existence, and that he need not now think or care about anything, that everything was being done and would be done for him by others. He had not even plans and aims for the future, he left its arrangement to others, knowing that everything would be delightful. His brother Sergey Ivanovitch, Stepan Arkadyevitch, and the princess guided him in doing what he had to do. All he did was to agree entirely with everything suggested to him. His brother raised money for him, the princess advised him to leave Moscow after the wedding. Stepan Arkadyevitch advised him to go abroad. He agreed to everything. "Do what you choose, if it amuses you. I'm happy, and my happiness can be no greater and no less for anything you do," he thought. When he told Kitty of Stepan Arkadyevitch's advice that they should go abroad, he was much surprised that she did not agree to this, and had some definite requirements of her own in regard to their future. She knew Levin had work he loved in the country. She did not, as he saw, understand this work, she did not even care to understand it. But that did not prevent her from regarding it as a matter of great importance. And then she knew their home would be in the country, and she wanted to go, not abroad where she was not going to live, but to the place where their home would be. This definitely expressed purpose astonished Levin. But since he did not care either way, he immediately asked Stepan Arkadyevitch, as though it were his duty, to go down to the country and to arrange everything there to the best of his ability with the taste of which he had so much.

"But I say," Stepan Arkadyevitch said to him one day after he had come back from the country, where he had got everything ready for the young people's arrival, "have you a certificate of having been at confession?"

"No. But what of it?"

"You can't be married without it."

"*Aïe, aïe, aïe!*" cried Levin. "Why, I believe it's nine years since I've taken the sacrament! I never thought of it."

"You're a pretty fellow!" said Stepan Arkadyevitch laughing, "and you call me a Nihilist! But this won't do, you know. You must take the sacrament."

"When? There are four days left now."

Stepan Arkadyevitch arranged this also, and Levin had to go to confession. To Levin, as to any unbeliever who respects the beliefs of others, it was exceedingly disagreeable to be present at and take part in church ceremonies. At this moment, in his present softened state of feeling, sensitive to everything, this inevitable act of hypocrisy was not merely painful to Levin, it seemed to him utterly impossible. Now, in the heyday of his highest glory, his fullest flower, he would have to be a liar or a scoffer. He felt incapable of being either. But though he repeatedly plied Stepan Arkadyevitch with questions as to the possibility of obtaining a certificate without actually communicating, Stepan Arkadyevitch maintained that it was out of the question.

"Besides, what is it to you—two days? And he's an awfully

nice clever old fellow. He'll pull the tooth out for you so gently, you won't notice it."

Standing at the first litany, Levin attempted to revive in himself his youthful recollections of the intense religious emotion he had passed through between the ages of sixteen and seventeen.

But he was at once convinced that it was utterly impossible to him. He attempted to look at it all as an empty custom, having no sort of meaning, like the custom of paying calls. But he felt that he could not do that either. Levin found himself, like the majority of his contemporaries, in the vaguest position in regard to religion. Believe he could not, and at the same time he had no firm conviction that it was all wrong. And consequently, not being able to believe in the significance of what he was doing nor to regard it with indifference as an empty formality, during the whole period of preparing for the sacrament he was conscious of a feeling of discomfort and shame at doing what he did not himself understand, and what, as an inner voice told him, was therefore false and wrong.

During the service he would first listen to the prayers, trying to attach some meaning to them not discordant with his own views; then feeling that he could not understand and must condemn them, he tried not to listen to them, but to attend to the thoughts, observations, and memories which floated through his brain with extreme vividness during this idle time of standing in church.

He had stood through the litany, the evening service and the midnight service, and the next day he got up earlier than usual, and without having tea went at eight o'clock in the morning to the church for the morning service and the confession.

There was no one in the church but a beggar soldier, two old women, and the church officials. A young deacon, whose long back showed in two distinct halves through his thin undercassock, met him, and at once going to a little table at the wall read the exhortation. During the reading, especially at the frequent and rapid repetition of the same words, "Lord, have mercy on us!" which resounded with an echo, Levin felt that thought was shut and sealed up, and that it must not be touched or stirred now or confusion would be the result; and so standing behind the deacon he went on thinking of his own affairs, neither listening nor examining what was said. "It's wonderful what expression there is in her hand," he thought, remembering how they had been sitting the day before at a corner table. They had nothing to talk about, as was almost always the case at this time, and laying her hand on the table she kept opening and shutting it, and laughed herself as she watched her action. He remembered how he had kissed it and then had examined the lines on the pink palm. "Have mercy on us again!" thought Levin, crossing himself, bowing, and looking at the supple spring of the deacon's back bowing before him. "She took my hand then and examined the lines. 'You've got a splendid hand,' she said." And he looked at his own hand and the short hand of the deacon. "Yes, now it will soon be over," he thought. "No, it seems to be beginning again," he thought, listening to the prayers. "No, it's just ending: there he is bowing down to the ground. That's always at the end."

The deacon's hand in a plush cuff accepted a three-rouble note unobtrusively, and the deacon said he would put it down in the register, and his new boots creaking jauntily over the flagstones of the empty church, he went to the altar. A moment later he peeped out thence and beckoned to Levin. Thought, till then locked up, began to stir in Levin's head, but he made haste to drive it away. "It will come right somehow," he thought, and went towards the altar-rails. He went up the steps, and turning to the right saw the priest. The priest, a little old man with a scanty grizzled beard and weary, good-natured eyes, was standing at the altar-rails, turning over the pages of a missal. With a slight bow to Levin he began immediately reading prayers in the official voice.

When he had finished them he bowed down to the ground and turned, facing Levin.

"Christ is present here unseen, receiving your confession," he said, pointing to the crucifix. "Do you believe in all the doctrines of the Holy Apostolic Church?" the priest went on, turning his eyes away from Levin's face and folding his hands under his stole.

"I have doubted, I doubt everything," said Levin in a voice that jarred on himself, and he ceased speaking.

The priest waited a few seconds to see if he would not say more, and closing his eyes he said quickly, with a broad, Vladimirsky accent:

"Doubt is natural to the weakness of mankind, but we must pray that God in His mercy will strengthen us. What are your special sins?" he added, without the slightest interval, as though anxious not to waste time.

"My chief sin is doubt. I have doubts of everything, and for the most part I am in doubt."

"Doubt is natural to the weakness of mankind," the priest repeated the same words. "What do you doubt about principally?"

"I doubt of everything. I sometimes even have doubts of the existence of God," Levin could not help saying, and he was horrified at the impropriety of what he was saying. But Levin's words did not, it seemed, make much impression on the priest.

"What sort of doubt can there be of the existence of God?" he said hurriedly, with a just perceptible smile.

Levin did not speak.

"What doubt can you have of the Creator when you behold His creation?" the priest went on in the rapid customary jargon. "Who has decked the heavenly firmament with its lights? Who has clothed the earth in its beauty? How explain it without the Creator?" he said, looking inquiringly at Levin.

Levin felt that it would be improper to enter upon a metaphysical discussion with the priest, and so he said in reply merely what was a direct answer to the question.

"I don't know," he said.

"You don't know! Then how can you doubt that God created all?" the priest said, with good-humored perplexity.

"I don't understand it at all," said Levin, blushing, and feeling that his words were stupid, and that they could not be anything but stupid in such a position.

"Pray to God and beseech Him. Even the holy fathers had doubts, and prayed to God to strengthen their faith. The devil has great power, and we must resist him. Pray to God, beseech Him. Pray to God," he repeated hurriedly.

The priest paused for some time, as though meditating.

"You're about, I hear, to marry the daughter of my parishioner and son in the spirit, Prince Shtcherbatsky?" he resumed, with a smile. "An excellent young lady."

"Yes," answered Levin, blushing for the priest. "What does he want to ask me about this at confession for?" he thought.

And, as though answering his thought, the priest said to him:

"You are about to enter into holy matrimony, and God may bless you with offspring. Well, what sort of bringing-up can you give your babes if you do not overcome the temptation of the devil, enticing you to infidelity?" he said, with gentle reproachfulness. "If you love your child as a good father, you will not desire only wealth, luxury, honor for your infant; you will be anxious for his salvation, his spiritual enlightenment with the light of truth. Eh? What answer will you make him when the innocent babe asks you: 'Papa! who made all that enchants me in this world—the earth, the waters, the sun, the flowers, the grass?' Can you say to him: 'I don't know'? You cannot but know, since the Lord God in His infinite mercy has revealed it to us. Or your child will ask you: 'What awaits me in the life beyond the tomb?' What will you say to him when you know nothing? How will you answer him? Will you leave him to the allurements of the world and the devil? That's not right," he said, and he stopped, putting his head on one side and looking at Levin with his kindly, gentle eyes.

Levin made no answer this time, not because he did not want to enter upon a discussion with the priest, but because, so far, no one had ever asked him such questions, and when his babes did ask him those questions, it would be time enough to think about answering them.

"You are entering upon a time of life," pursued the priest, "when you must choose your path and keep to it. Pray to God that He may in His mercy aid you and have mercy on you!" he concluded. "Our Lord and God, Jesus Christ, in the abundance and riches of His loving-kindness, forgives this child . . ." and, finishing the prayer of absolution, the priest blessed him and dismissed him.

On getting home that day, Levin had a delightful sense of relief at the awkward position being over and having been got through without his having to tell a lie. Apart from this, there remained a vague memory that what the kind, nice old fellow had said had not been at all so stupid as he had fancied at first, and that there was something in it that must be cleared up.

"Of course, not now," thought Levin, "but some day later on." Levin felt more than ever now that there was something not clear and not clean in his soul, and that, in regard to religion, he was in the same position which he perceived so clearly and disliked in others, and for which he blamed his friend Sviazhsky.

Levin spent that evening with his betrothed at Dolly's, and was in very high spirits. To explain to Stepan Arkadyevitch the state of excitement in which he found himself, he said that he was happy like a dog being trained to jump through a hoop, who, having at last caught the idea, and done what was required of him, whines and wags its tail, and jumps up to the table and the windows in its delight.

CHAPTER II

On the day of the wedding, according to the Russian custom (the princess and Darya Alexandrovna insisted on strictly keeping all the customs), Levin did not see his betrothed, and dined at his hotel with three bachelor friends, casually brought together at his rooms. These were Sergey Ivanovitch, Katavasov, a university friend, now professor of natural science, whom Levin had met in the street and insisted on taking home with him, and Tchirikov, his best man, a Moscow conciliation-board judge, Levin's companion in his bear-hunts. The dinner was a very merry one: Sergey Ivanovitch was in his happiest mood, and was much amused by Katavasov's originality. Katavasov, feeling his originality was appreciated and understood, made the most of it. Tchirikov always gave a lively and good-humored support to conversation of any sort.

"See, now," said Katavasov, drawling his words from a habit acquired in the lecture-room, "what a capable fellow was our friend Konstantin Dmitrievitch. I'm not speaking of present company, for he's absent. At the time he left the university he was fond of science, took an interest in humanity; now one-half of his abilities is devoted to deceiving himself, and the other to justifying the deceit."

"A more determined enemy of matrimony than you I never saw," said Sergey Ivanovitch.

"Oh, no, I'm not an enemy of matrimony. I'm in favor of division of labor. People who can do nothing else ought to rear people while the rest work for their happiness and enlightenment. That's how I look at it. To muddle up two trades is the error of the amateur; I'm not one of their number."

"How happy I shall be when I hear that you're in love!" said Levin. "Please invite me to the wedding."

"I'm in love now."

"Yes, with a cuttlefish! You know," Levin turned to his brother, "Mihail Semyonovitch is writing a work on the digestive organs of the . . ."

"Now, make a muddle of it! It doesn't matter what about. And the fact is, I certainly do love cuttlefish."

"But that's no hindrance to your loving your wife."

"The cuttlefish is no hindrance. The wife is the hindrance."

"Why so?"

"Oh, you'll see! You care about farming, hunting,—well, you'd better look out!"

"Arhip was here to-day; he said there were a lot of elks in Prudno, and two bears," said Tchirikov.

"Well, you must go and get them without me."

"Ah, that's the truth," said Sergey Ivanovitch. "And you may say good-bye to bear-hunting for the future—your wife won't allow it!"

Levin smiled. The picture of his wife not letting him go was so pleasant that he was ready to renounce the delights of looking upon bears forever.

"Still, it's a pity they should get those two bears without you.

Do you remember last time at Hapilovo? That was a delightful hunt!" said Tchirikov.

Levin had not the heart to disillusion him of the notion that there could be something delightful apart from her, and so said nothing.

"There's some sense in this custom of saying good-bye to bachelor life," said Sergey Ivanovitch. "However happy you may be, you must regret your freedom."

"And confess there is a feeling that you want to jump out of the window, like Gogol's bridegroom?"

"Of course there is, but it isn't confessed," said Katavasov, and he broke into loud laughter.

"Oh, well, the window's open. Let's start off this instant to Tver! There's a big she-bear; one can go right up to the lair. Seriously, let's go by the five o'clock! And here let them do what they like," said Tchirikov, smiling.

"Well, now, on my honor," said Levin, smiling, "I can't find in my heart that feeling of regret for my freedom."

"Yes, there's such a chaos in your heart just now that you can't find anything there," said Katavasov. "Wait a bit, when you set it to rights a little, you'll find it!"

"No; if so, I should have felt a little, apart from my feeling" (he could not say love before them) "and happiness, a certain regret at losing my freedom. . . . On the contrary, I am glad at the very loss of my freedom."

"Awful! It's a hopeless case!" said Katavasov. "Well, let's drink to his recovery, or wish that a hundredth part of his dreams may be realized—and that would be happiness such as never has been seen on earth!"

Soon after dinner the guests went away to be in time to be dressed for the wedding.

When he was left alone, and recalled the conversation of these bachelor friends, Levin asked himself: had he in his heart that regret for his freedom of which they had spoken? He smiled at the question. "Freedom! What is freedom for? Happiness is only in loving and wishing her wishes, thinking her thoughts, that is to say, not freedom at all—that's happiness!"

"But do I know her ideas, her wishes, her feelings?" some voice suddenly whispered to him. The smile died away from his face, and he grew thoughtful. And suddenly a strange feeling came upon him. There came over him a dread and doubt—doubt of everything.

"What if she does not love me? What if she's marrying me simply to be married? What if she doesn't see herself what she's doing?" he asked himself. "She may come to her senses, and only when she is being married realize that she does not and cannot love me." And strange, most evil thoughts of her began to come to him. He was jealous of Vronsky, as he had been a year ago, as though the evening he had seen her with Vronsky had been yesterday. He suspected she had not told him everything.

He jumped up quickly. "No, this can't go on!" he said to himself in despair. "I'll go to her; I'll ask her; I'll say for the last time: we are free, and hadn't we better stay so? Anything's better than endless misery, disgrace, unfaithfulness!" With despair in his heart and bitter anger against all men, against himself, against her, he went out of the hotel and drove to her house.

He found her in one of the back rooms. She was sitting on a chest and making some arrangements with her maid, sorting over heaps of dresses of different colors, spread on the backs of chairs and on the floor.

"Ah!" she cried, seeing him, and beaming with delight. "Kostya! Konstantin Dmitrievitch!" (These latter days she used these names almost alternately.) "I didn't expect you! I'm going through my wardrobe to see what's for whom . . ."

"Oh! that's very nice!" he said gloomily, looking at the maid.

"You can go, Dunyasha, I'll call you presently," said Kitty. "Kostya, what's the matter?" she asked, definitely adopting this familiar name as soon as the maid had gone out. She noticed his strange face, agitated and gloomy, and a panic came over her.

"Kitty! I'm in torture. I can't suffer alone," he said with despair in his voice, standing before her and looking imploringly into her eyes. He saw already from her loving, truthful face, that nothing could come of what he had meant to say, but yet he wanted her to reassure him herself. "I've come to say that there's still time. This can all be stopped and set right."

"What? I don't understand. What is the matter?"

"What I have said a thousand times over, and can't help thinking . . . that I'm not worthy of you. You couldn't consent to marry me. Think a little. You've made a mistake. Think it over thoroughly. You can't love me. . . . If . . . better say so," he said, not looking at her. "I shall be wretched. Let people say what they like; anything's better than misery. . . . Far better now while there's still time. . . ."

"I don't understand," she answered, panic-stricken; "you mean you want to give it up . . . don't want it?"

"Yes, if you don't love me."

"You're out of your mind!" she cried, turning crimson with vexation. But his face was so piteous, that she restrained her vexation, and flinging some clothes off an arm-chair, she sat down beside him. "What are you thinking? tell me all."

"I am thinking you can't love me. What can you love me for?"

"My God! what can I do? . . ." she said, and burst into tears.

"Oh! what have I done?" he cried, and kneeling before her, he fell to kissing her hands.

When the princess came into the room five minutes later, she found them completely reconciled. Kitty had not simply assured him that she loved him, but had gone so far—in answer to his question, what she loved him for—as to explain what for. She told him that she loved him because she understood him completely, because she knew what he would like, and because everything he liked was good. And this seemed to him perfectly clear. When the princess came to them, they were sitting side by side on the chest, sorting the dresses and disputing over Kitty's wanting to give Dunyasha the brown dress she had been wearing when Levin proposed to her, while he insisted that that dress must never be given away, but Dunyasha must have the blue one.

"How is it you don't see? She's a brunette, and it won't suit her. . . . I've worked it all out."

Hearing why he had come, the princess was half humorously, half seriously angry with him, and sent him home to dress and not to hinder Kitty's hair-dressing, as Charles the hair-dresser was just coming.

"As it is, she's been eating nothing lately and is losing her looks, and then you must come and upset her with your nonsense," she said to him. "Get along with you, my dear!"

Levin, guilty and shamefaced, but pacified, went back to his hotel. His brother, Darya Alexandrovna, and Stepan Arkadyevitch, all in full dress, were waiting for him to bless him with the holy picture. There was no time to lose. Darya Alexandrovna had to drive home again to fetch her curled and pomaded son, who was to carry the holy pictures after the bride. Then a carriage had to be sent for the best man, and another that would take Sergey Ivanovitch away would have to be sent back. . . . Alto-

gether there were a great many most complicated matters to be considered and arranged. One thing was unmistakable, that there must be no delay, as it was already half-past six.

Nothing special happened at the ceremony of benediction with the holy picture. Stepan Arkadyevitch stood in a comically solemn pose beside his wife, took the holy picture, and telling Levin to bow down to the ground, he blessed him with his kindly, ironical smile, and kissed him three times; Darya Alexandrovna did the same, and immediately was in a hurry to get off, and again plunged into the intricate question of the destinations of the various carriages.

"Come, I'll tell you how we'll manage: you drive in our carriage to fetch him, and Sergey Ivanovitch, if he'll be so good, will drive there and then send his carriage."

"Of course; I shall be delighted."

"We'll come on directly with him. Are your things sent off?" said Stepan Arkadyevitch.

"Yes," answered Levin, and he told Kouzma to put out his clothes for him to dress.

CHAPTER III

A CROWD of people, principally women, was thronging round the church lighted up for the wedding. Those who had not succeeded in getting into the main entrance were crowding about the windows, pushing, wrangling, and peeping through the gratings.

More than twenty carriages had already been drawn up in ranks along the street by the police. A police officer, regardless of the frost, stood at the entrance, gorgeous in his uniform. More carriages were continually driving up, and ladies wearing flowers and carrying their trains, and men taking off their helmets or black hats kept walking into the church. Inside the church both lusters were already lighted, and all the candles before the holy pictures. The gilt on the red ground of the holy picture-stand, and the gilt relief on the pictures, and the silver of the lusters and candlesticks, and the stones of the floor, and the rugs, and the banners above in the choir, and the steps of the altar, and the old blackened books, and the cassocks and surplices—all were flooded with light. On the right side of the warm church, in the crowd of frock coats and white ties, uniforms and broadcloth, velvet, satin, hair and flowers, bare shoulders and arms and long gloves, there was discreet but lively conversation that echoed strangely in the high cupola. Every time there was heard the creak of the opened door the conversation in the crowd died away, and everybody looked round expecting to see the bride and bridegroom come in. But the door had opened more than ten times, and each time it was either a belated guest or guests, who joined the circle of the invited on the right, or a spectator, who had eluded or softened the police officer, and went to join the crowd of outsiders on the left. Both the guests and the outside public had by now passed through all the phases of anticipation.

At first they imagined that the bride and bridegroom would

arrive immediately, and attached no importance at all to their being late. Then they began to look more and more often towards the door, and to talk of whether anything could have happened. Then the long delay began to be positively discomforting, and relations and guests tried to look as if they were not thinking of the bridegroom but were engrossed in conversation.

The head deacon, as though to remind them of the value of his time, coughed impatiently, making the window-panes quiver in their frames. In the choir the bored choristers could be heard trying their voices and blowing their noses. The priest was continually sending first the beadle and then the deacon to find out whether the bridegroom had not come, more and more often he went himself, in a lilac vestment and an embroidered sash, to the side-door, expecting to see the bridegroom. At last one of the ladies, glancing at her watch, said, "It really is strange, though!" and all the guests became uneasy and began loudly expressing their wonder and dissatisfaction. One of the bridegroom's best men went to find out what had happened. Kitty meanwhile had long ago been quite ready, and in her white dress and long veil and wreath of orange blossoms she was standing in the drawing-room of the Shtcherbatskys' house with her sister, Madame Lvova, who was her bridal-mother. She was looking out of the window, and had been for over half an hour anxiously expecting to hear from her best man that her bridegroom was at the church.

Levin meanwhile, in his trousers, but without his coat and waistcoat, was walking to and fro in his room at the hotel, continually putting his head out of the door and looking up and down the corridor. But in the corridor there was no sign of the person he was looking for and he came back in despair, and frantically waving his hands addressed Stepan Arkadyevitch, who was smoking serenely.

"Was ever a man in such a fearful fool's position?" he said.

"Yes, it is stupid," Stepan Arkadyevitch assented, smiling soothingly. "But don't worry, it'll be brought directly."

"No, what is to be done!" said Levin, with smothered fury. "And these fools of open waistcoats! Out of the question!" he said, looking at the crumpled front of his shirt. "And what if the things have been taken on to the railway station!" he roared in desperation.

"Then you must put on mine."

"I ought to have done so long ago, if at all."

"It's not nice to look ridiculous. . . . Wait a bit! it will *come round.*"

The point was that when Levin asked for his evening suit, Kouzma, his old servant, had brought him the coat, waistcoat, and everything that was wanted.

"But the shirt!" cried Levin.

"You've got a shirt on," Kouzma answered, with a placid smile.

Kouzma had not thought of leaving out a clean shirt, and on receiving instructions to pack up everything and send it round to the Shtcherbatskys' house, from which the young people were to set out the same evening, he had done so, packing everything but the dress suit. The shirt worn since the morning was crumpled and out of the question with the fashionable open waistcoat. It was a long way to send to the Shtcherbatskys'. They sent out to buy a shirt. The servant came back; everything was shut up—it was Sunday. They sent to Stepan Arkadyevitch's and brought a shirt—it was impossibly wide and short. They sent finally to the Shtcherbatskys' to unpack the things. The bridegroom was expected at the church while he was pacing up and down his room like a wild beast in a cage, peeping out into the corridor, and with horror and despair recalling what absurd things he had said to Kitty and what she might be thinking now.

At last the guilty Kouzma flew panting into the room with the shirt.

"Only just in time. They were just lifting it into the van," said Kouzma.

Three minutes later Levin ran full speed into the corridor, not looking at his watch for fear of aggravating his sufferings.

"You won't help matters like this," said Stepan Arkadyevitch with a smile, hurrying with more deliberation after him. *"It will come round, it will come round . . . I tell you."*

CHAPTER IV

"THEY'VE come!" "Here he is!" "Which one?" "Rather young, eh?" "Why, my dear soul, she looks more dead than alive!" were the comments in the crowd, when Levin, meeting his bride in the entrance, walked with her into the church.

Stepan Arkadyevitch told his wife the cause of the delay, and the guests were whispering it with smiles to one another. Levin saw nothing and no one; he did not take his eyes off his bride.

Every one said she had lost her looks dreadfully of late, and was not nearly so pretty on her wedding-day as usual; but Levin did not think so. He looked at her hair done up high, with the long white veil and white flowers and the high, stand-up, scolloped collar, that in such a maidenly fashion hid her long neck at the sides and only showed it in front, her strikingly slender figure, and it seemed to him that she looked better than ever—not because these flowers, this veil, this gown from Paris added anything to her beauty; but because, in spite of the elaborate sumptuousness of her attire, the expression of her sweet face, of her eyes, of her lips was still her own characteristic expression of guileless truthfulness.

"I was beginning to think you meant to run away," she said, and smiled to him.

"It's so stupid, what happened to me, I'm ashamed to speak of it!" he said, reddening, and he was obliged to turn to Sergey Ivanovitch, who came up to him.

"This is a pretty story of yours about the shirt!" said Sergey Ivanovitch, shaking his head and smiling.

"Yes, yes!" answered Levin, without an idea of what they were talking about.

"Now, Kostya, you have to decide," said Stepan Arkadyevitch with an air of mock dismay, "a weighty question. You are at this moment just in the humor to appreciate all its gravity. They ask me, are they to light the candles that have been lighted before or candles that have never been lighted? It's a matter of ten roubles," he added, relaxing his lips into a smile. "I have decided, but I was afraid you might not agree."

Levin saw it was a joke, but he could not smile.

"Well, how's it to be then?—unlighted or lighted candles? that's the question."

"Yes, yes, unlighted."

"Oh, I'm very glad. The question's decided!" said Stepan Arkadyevitch, smiling. "How silly men are, though, in this position," he said to Tchirikov, when Levin, after looking absently at him, had moved back to his bride.

"Kitty, mind you're the first to step on the carpet," said Countess Nordston, coming up. "You're a nice person!" she said to Levin.

"Aren't you frightened, eh?" said Marya Dmitrievna, an old aunt.

"Are you cold? You're pale. Stop a minute, stoop down," said Kitty's sister, Madame Lvova, and with her plump, handsome arms she smilingly set straight the flowers on her head.

Dolly came up, tried to say something, but could not speak, cried, and then laughed unnaturally.

Kitty looked at all of them with the same absent eyes as Levin.

Meanwhile the officiating clergy had got into their vestments, and the priest and deacon came out to the lectern, which stood in the forepart of the church. The priest turned to Levin saying something. Levin did not hear what the priest said.

"Take the bride's hand and lead her up," the best man said to Levin.

It was a long while before Levin could make out what was expected of him. For a long time they tried to set him right and made him begin again—because he kept taking Kitty by the wrong arm or with wrong arm—till he understood at last that what he had to do was, without changing his position, to take her right hand in his right hand. When at last he had taken the bride's hand in the correct way, the priest walked a few paces in front of them and stopped at the lectern. The crowd of friends and relations moved after them, with a buzz of talk and a rustle of skirts. Some one stooped down and pulled out the bride's train. The church became so still that the drops of wax could be heard falling from the candles.

The little old priest in his ecclesiastical cap, with his long silvery-gray locks of hair parted behind his ears, was fumbling with something at the lectern, putting out his little old hands from under the heavy silver vestment with the gold cross on the back of it.

Stepan Arkadyevitch approached him cautiously, whispered something, and making a sign to Levin, walked back again.

The priest lighted two candles, wreathed with flowers, and holding them sideways so that the wax dropped slowly from them he turned, facing the bridal pair. The priest was the same old man that had confessed Levin. He looked with weary and melancholy eyes at the bride and bridegroom, sighed, and putting his right hand out from his vestment, blessed the bridegroom with it, and also with a shade of solicitous tenderness laid the crossed fingers on the bowed head of Kitty. Then he gave them the candles, and taking the censer, moved slowly away from them.

"Can it be true?" thought Levin, and he looked round at his bride. Looking down at her he saw her face in profile, and from the scarcely perceptible quiver of her lips and eyelashes he knew she was aware of his eyes upon her. She did not look round, but the high scolloped collar, that reached her little pink ear, trembled faintly. He saw that a sigh was held back in her throat, and the little hand in the long glove shook as it held the candle.

All the fuss of the shirt, of being late, all the talk of friends and relations, their annoyance, his ludicrous position—all suddenly passed away and he was filled with joy and dread.

The handsome, stately head-deacon wearing a silver robe and his curly locks standing out at each side of his head, stepped smartly forward, and lifting his stole on two fingers, stood opposite the priest.

"Blessed be the name of the Lord," the solemn syllables rang out slowly one after another, setting the air quivering with waves of sound.

"Blessed is the name of our God, from the beginning, is now, and ever shall be," the little old priest answered in a submissive, piping voice, still fingering something at the lectern. And the full chorus of the unseen choir rose up, filling the whole church, from the windows to the vaulted roof, with broad waves of melody. It grew stronger, rested for an instant, and slowly died away.

They prayed, as they always do, for peace from on high and for salvation, for the Holy Synod, and for the Tsar; they prayed, too, for the servants of God, Konstantin and Ekaterina, now plighting their troth.

"Vouchsafe to them love made perfect, peace and help, O Lord, we beseech Thee," the whole church seemed to breathe with the voice of the head-deacon.

Levin heard the words, and they impressed him. "How did they guess that it is help, just help that one wants?" he thought, recalling all his fears and doubts of late. "What do I know? what can I do in this fearful business," he thought, "without help? Yes, it is help I want now."

When the deacon had finished the prayer for the Imperial family, the priest turned to the bridal pair with a book: "Eternal God, that joinest together in love them that were separate," he read in a gentle, piping voice: "who hath ordained the union of holy wedlock that cannot be set asunder, Thou who didst bless Isaac and Rebecca and their descendants, according to Thy Holy Covenant; bless Thy servants, Konstantin and Ekaterina, leading them in the path of all good works. For gracious and merciful art Thou, our Lord, and glory be to Thee, the Father, the Son, and the Holy Ghost, now and ever shall be."

"Amen!" the unseen choir sent rolling again upon the air.

" 'Joinest together in love them that were separate.' What deep meaning in those words, and how they correspond with what one feels at this moment," thought Levin. "Is she feeling the same as I?"

And looking round, he met her eyes, and from their expression he concluded that she was understanding it just as he was. But this was a mistake; she almost completely missed the meaning of the words of the service; she had not heard them, in fact. She could not listen to them and take them in, so strong was the one feeling that filled her breast and grew stronger and stronger. That feeling was joy at the completion of the process that for the last month and a half had been going on in her soul, and had during those six weeks been a joy and a torture to her. On the day when in the drawing-room of the house in Arbaty Street she had gone up to him in her brown dress, and given herself to him without a word—on that day, at that hour, there took place in her heart a complete severance from all her old life, and a quite different, new, utterly strange life had begun for her, while the old life was actually going on as before. Those six weeks had for her been a time of the utmost bliss and the utmost misery. All her life, all her desires and hopes were concentrated on this one man, still uncomprehended by her, to whom she was bound by a feeling of alternate attraction and repulsion, even less comprehended than the man himself, and all the while she was going on living in the outward conditions of her old life. Living the old life, she was horrified at herself, at her utter insurmountable callousness to all her own past, to things, to habits, to the people she had loved, who loved her—to her mother, who was wounded by her indifference, to her kind, tender father, till then dearer than all the world. At one moment she was horrified at this indifference, at another she rejoiced at what had brought her to this indifference. She could not frame a thought, not a wish apart from life with this man; but this new life was not yet, and she could not even picture it clearly to herself. There was only anticipation, the dread and joy of the new and the unknown. And now behold—anticipation and uncertainty and remorse at the abandonment of the old life—all was ending, and the new was beginning. This new life could not but have terrors for her inexperience; but, terrible or not, the change had been wrought six weeks before in her soul, and this was merely the final sanction of what had long been completed in her heart.

Turning again to the lectern, the priest with some difficulty took Kitty's little ring, and asking Levin for his hand, put it on the first joint of his finger. "The servant of God, Konstantin, plights his troth to the servant of God, Ekaterina." And putting his big ring on Kitty's touchingly weak, pink little finger, the priest said the same thing.

And the bridal pair tried several times to understand what they had to do, and each time made some mistake and were corrected by the priest in a whisper. At last, having duly performed the ceremony, having signed the rings with the cross, the priest handed Kitty the big ring, and Levin the little one. Again they were puzzled and passed the rings from hand to hand, still without doing what was expected.

Dolly, Tchirikov, and Stepan Arkadyevitch stepped forward to set them right. There was an interval of hesitation, whispering, and smiles; but the expression of solemn emotion on the faces of the betrothed pair did not change: on the contrary, in their perplexity over their hands they looked more grave and deeply moved than before, and the smile with which Stepan Arkadyevitch whispered to them that now they would each put on their own ring died away on his lips. He had a feeling that any smile would jar on them.

"Thou who didst from the beginning create male and female," the priest read after the exchange of rings, "from Thee woman was given to man to be a helpmeet to him, and for the procreation of children. O Lord, our God, who hast poured down the blessings of Thy Truth according to Thy Holy Covenant upon Thy chosen servants, our fathers, from generation to generation, bless Thy servants Konstantin and Ekaterina, and make their troth fast in faith, and union of hearts, and truth, and love. . . ."

Levin felt more and more that all his ideas of marriage, all his dreams of how he would order his life, were mere childishness, and that it was something he had not understood hitherto, and now understood less than ever, though it was being performed upon him. The lump in his throat rose higher and higher, tears that would not be checked came into his eyes.

CHAPTER V

In the church there was all Moscow, all the friends and relations; and during the ceremony of plighting troth, in the brilliantly lighted church, there was an incessant flow of discreetly subdued talk in the circle of gaily dressed women and girls, and men in white ties, frock-coats, and uniforms. The talk was principally kept up by the men, while the women were absorbed in watching every detail of the ceremony, which always means so much to them.

In the little group nearest to the bride were her two sisters:

Dolly, and the other one, the self-possessed beauty, Madame Lvova, who had just arrived from abroad.

"Why is it Marie's in lilac, as bad as black, at a wedding?" said Madame Korsunskaya.

"With her complexion, it's the one salvation," responded Madame Trubetskaya. "I wonder why they had the wedding in the evening? It's like shop-people . . ."

"So much prettier. I was married in the evening too . . ." answered Madame Korsunskaya, and she sighed, remembering how charming she had been that day, and how absurdly in love her husband was, and how different it all was now.

"They say if any one's best man more than ten times, he'll never be married. I wanted to be for the tenth time, but the post was taken," said Count Siniavin to the pretty Princess Tcharskaya, who had designs on him.

Princess Tcharskaya only answered with a smile. She looked at Kitty, thinking how and when she would stand with Count Siniavin in Kitty's place, and how she would remind him then of his joke to-day.

Shtcherbatsky told the old maid of honor, Madame Nikolaeva, that he meant to put the crown on Kitty's chignon for luck.

"She ought not to have worn a chignon," answered Madame Nikolaeva, who had long ago made up her mind that if the elderly widower she was angling for married her, the wedding should be of the simplest. "I don't like such grandeur."

Sergey Ivanovitch was talking to Darya Alexandrovna, jestingly assuring her that the custom of going away after the wedding was becoming common because newly married people always felt a little ashamed of themselves.

"Your brother may feel proud of himself. She's a marvel of sweetness. I believe you're envious."

"Oh, I've got over that, Darya Alexandrovna," he answered, and a melancholy and serious expression suddenly came over his face.

Stepan Arkadyevitch was telling his sister-in-law his joke about divorce.

"The wreath wants setting straight," she answered, not hearing him.

"What a pity she's lost her looks so," Countess Nordston said

to Madame Lvova. "Still he's not worth her little finger, is he?"

"Oh, I like him so—not because he's my future *beau-frère*," answered Madame Lvova. "And how well he's behaving! It's so difficult, too, to look well in such a position, not to be ridiculous. And he's not ridiculous, and not affected; one can see he's moved."

"You expected it, I suppose?"

"Almost. She always cared for him."

"Well, we shall see which of them will step on the rug first. I warned Kitty."

"It will make no difference," said Madame Lvova; "we're all obedient wives; it's in our family."

"Oh, I stepped on the rug before Vassily on purpose. And you, Dolly?"

Dolly stood beside them; she heard them, but she did not answer. She was deeply moved. The tears stood in her eyes, and she could not have spoken without crying. She was rejoicing over Kitty and Levin; going back in thought to her own wedding, she glanced at the radiant figure of Stepan Arkadyevitch, forgot all the present, and remembered only her own innocent love. She recalled not herself only, but all her women-friends and acquaintances. She thought of them on the one day of their triumph, when they had stood like Kitty under the wedding crown, with love and hope and dread in their hearts, renouncing the past, and stepping forward into the mysterious future. Among the brides that came back to her memory, she thought too of her darling Anna, of whose proposed divorce she had just been hearing. And she had stood just as innocent in orange flowers and bridal veil. And now? "It's terribly strange," she said to herself. It was not merely the sisters, the women-friends and female relations of the bride who were following every detail of the ceremony. Women who were quite strangers, mere spectators, were watching it excitedly, holding their breath, in fear of losing a single movement or expression of the bride and bridegroom, and angrily not answering, often not hearing, the remarks of the callous men, who kept making joking or irrelevant observations.

"Why has she been crying? Is she being married against her will?"

"Against her will to a fine fellow like that? A prince, isn't he?"

"Is that her sister in the white satin? Just listen how the deacon booms out, 'and fearing her husband.'"

"Are the choristers from Tchudovo?"

"No, from the Synod."

"I asked the footman. He says he's going to take her home to his country place at once. Awfully rich, they say. That's why she's being married to him."

"No, they're a well-matched pair."

"I say, Marya Vassilievna, you were making out those fly-away crinolines were not being worn. Just look at her in the puce dress—an ambassador's wife they say she is—how her skirt bounces out from side to side!"

"What a pretty dear the bride is—like a lamb decked with flowers! Well, say what you will, we women feel for our sister."

Such were the comments in the crowd of gazing women who had succeeded in slipping in at the church doors.

CHAPTER VI

WHEN the ceremony of plighting troth was over, the beadle spread before the lectern in the middle of the church a piece of pink silken stuff, the choir sang a complicated and elaborate psalm, in which the bass and tenor sang responses to one another, and the priest turning round pointed the bridal pair to the pink silk rug. Though both had often heard a great deal about the saying that the one who steps first on the rug will be the head of the house, neither Levin nor Kitty were capable of recollecting it, as they took the few steps towards it. They did not hear the loud remarks and disputes that followed, some maintaining he had stepped on first, and others that both had stepped on together.

After the customary questions, whether they desired to enter upon matrimony, and whether they were pledged to any one else, and their answers, which sounded strange to themselves, a new ceremony began. Kitty listened to the words of the prayer, trying to make out their meaning, but she could not. The feeling of triumph and radiant happiness flooded her soul more and more as the ceremony went on, and deprived her of all power of attention.

They prayed: "Endow them with continence and fruitfulness, and vouchsafe that their hearts may rejoice looking upon their sons and daughters." They alluded to God's creation of a wife from Adam's rib, "and for this cause a man shall leave father and mother, and cleave unto his wife, and they two shall be one flesh," and that "this is a great mystery"; they prayed that God would make them fruitful and bless them, like Isaac and Rebecca, Joseph, Moses and Zipporah, and that they might look upon their children's children. "That's all splendid," thought Kitty, catching the words, "all that's just as it should be," and a smile of happiness, unconsciously reflected in every one who looked at her, beamed on her radiant face.

"Put it on quite," voices were heard urging when the priest had put on the wedding crowns and Shtcherbatsky, his hand shaking in its three-button glove, held the crown high above her head.

"Put it on!" she whispered, smiling.

Levin looked round at her, and was struck by the joyful radiance on her face, and unconsciously her feeling infected him. He too, like her, felt glad and happy.

They enjoyed hearing the epistle read, and the roll of the head-deacon's voice at the last verse, awaited with such impatience by the outside public. They enjoyed drinking out of the shallow cup of warm red wine and water, and they were still more pleased when the priest, flinging back his stole and taking both their hands in his, led them round the lectern to the accompaniment of bass voices chanting "Glory to God."

Shtcherbatsky and Tchirikov, supporting the crowns and stumbling over the bride's train, smiling too and seeming delighted at something, were at one moment left behind, at the next treading on the bridal pair as the priest came to a halt. The spark of joy kindled in Kitty seemed to have infected every one in the church. It seemed to Levin that the priest and the deacon too wanted to smile just as he did.

Taking the crowns off their heads the priest read the last prayer and congratulated the young people. Levin looked at Kitty, and he had never before seen her look as she did. She was charming with the new radiance of happiness in her face. Levin longed to say something to her, but he did not know whether it was all over. The priest got him out of his difficulty. He smiled his kindly smile and said gently, "Kiss your wife, and you kiss your husband," and took the candles out of their hands.

Levin kissed her smiling lips with timid care, gave her his arm, and with a new strange sense of closeness, walked out of the church. He did not believe, he could not believe, that it was true. It was only when their wondering and timid eyes met that he believed in it, because he felt that they were one.

After supper, the same night, the young people left for the country.

CHAPTER VII

VRONSKY and Anna had been traveling for three months together in Europe. They had visited Venice, Rome, and Naples, and had just arrived at a small Italian town where they meant to stay some time. A handsome head waiter, with thick pomaded hair parted from the neck upwards, an evening coat, a broad white cambric shirt-front, and a bunch of trinkets hanging above his rounded stomach, stood with his hands in the full curve of his pockets, looking contemptuously from under his eyelids while he gave some frigid reply to a gentleman who had stopped him. Catching the sound of footsteps coming from the other side of the entry towards the stair-case, the head waiter turned round, and seeing the Russian count, who had taken their best rooms, he took his hands out of his pockets deferentially, and with a bow informed him that a courier had been, and that the business about the palazzo had been arranged. The steward was prepared to sign the agreement.

"Ah! I'm glad to hear it," said Vronsky. "Is madame at home or not?"

"Madame has been out for a walk but has returned now," answered the waiter.

Vronsky took off his soft, wide-brimmed hat and passed his handkerchief over his heated brow and hair, which had grown half over his ears, and was brushed back covering the bald patch on his head. And glancing casually at the gentleman, who still stood there gazing intently at him, he would have gone on.

"This gentleman is a Russian, and was inquiring after you," said the head waiter.

With mingled feelings of annoyance at never being able to get away from acquaintances anywhere, and longing to find some sort of diversion from the monotony of his life, Vronsky looked once more at the gentleman, who had retreated and stood still again, and at the same moment a light came into the eyes of both.

"Golenishtchev!"

"Vronsky!"

It really was Golenishtchev, a comrade of Vronsky's in the Corps of Pages. In the corps Golenishtchev had belonged to the liberal party; he left the corps without entering the army, and had never taken office under the government. Vronsky and he had gone completely different ways on leaving the corps, and had only met once since.

At that meeting Vronsky perceived that Golenishtchev had taken up a sort of lofty, intellectually liberal line, and was consequently disposed to look down upon Vronsky's interests and calling in life. Hence Vronsky had met him with the chilling and haughty manner he so well knew how to assume, the meaning of which was: "You may like or dislike my way of life, that's a matter of the most perfect indifference to me; you will have to treat me with respect if you want to know me." Golenishtchev had been contemptuously indifferent to the tone taken by Vronsky. This second meeting might have been expected, one would have supposed, to estrange them still more. But now they beamed and exclaimed with delight on recognizing one another. Vronsky would never have expected to be so pleased to see Golenishtchev, but probably he was not himself aware how bored he was. He forgot the disagreeable impression of their last meeting, and with a face of frank delight held out his hand to his old comrade. The same expression of delight replaced the look of uneasiness on Golenishtchev's face.

"How glad I am to meet you!" said Vronsky, showing his strong white teeth in a friendly smile.

"I heard the name Vronsky, but I didn't know which one. I'm very, very glad!"

"Let's go in. Come, tell me what you're doing."

"I've been living here for two years. I'm working."

"Ah!" said Vronsky, with sympathy; "let's go in." And with the habit common with Russians, instead of saying in Russian what he wanted to keep from the servants, he began to speak in French.

"Do you know Madame Karenina? We are traveling together. I am going to see her now," he said in French, carefully scrutinizing Golenishtchev's face.

"Ah! I did not know" (though he did know), Golenishtchev answered carelessly. "Have you been here long?" he added.

"Four days," Vronsky answered, once more scrutinizing his friend's face intently.

"Yes, he's a decent fellow, and will look at the thing properly," Vronsky said to himself, catching the significance of Golenishtchev's face and the change of subject. "I can introduce him to Anna, he looks at it properly."

During those three months that Vronsky had spent abroad with Anna, he had always on meeting new people asked himself how the new person would look at his relations with Anna, and for the most part, in men, he had met with the "proper" way of looking at it. But if he had been asked, and those who looked at it "properly" had been asked, exactly how they did look at it, both he and they would have been greatly puzzled to answer.

In reality, those who in Vronsky's opinion had the "proper" view had no sort of view at all, but behaved in general as well-bred persons do behave in regard to all the complex and insoluble problems with which life is encompassed on all sides; they behaved with propriety, avoiding allusions and unpleasant questions. They assumed an air of fully comprehending the import and force of the situation, of accepting and even approving of it, but of considering it superfluous and uncalled for to put all this into words.

Vronsky at once divined that Golenishtchev was of this class, and therefore was doubly pleased to see him. And in fact, Golenishtchev's manner to Madame Karenina, when he was taken to call on her, was all that Vronsky could have desired. Obviously without the slightest effort he steered clear of all subjects which might lead to embarrassment.

He had never met Anna before, and was struck by her beauty, and still more by the frankness with which she accepted her position. She blushed when Vronsky brought in Golenishtchev, and he was extremely charmed by this childish blush overspreading her candid and handsome face. But what he liked particularly was the way in which at once, as though on purpose that there might be no misunderstanding with an outsider, she called Vronsky simply Alexey, and said they were moving into a house they had just taken, what was here called a palazzo. Golenishtchev liked this direct and simple attitude to her own position. Looking at Anna's manner of simple-hearted, spirited gaiety, and knowing Alexey Alexandrovitch and Vronsky, Golenishtchev fancied that he understood her perfectly. He fancied that he understood what she was utterly unable to understand: how it was that, having made her husband wretched, having abandoned him and her son and lost her good name, she yet felt full of spirits, gaiety, and happiness.

"It's in the guide-book," said Golenishtchev, referring to the palazzo Vronsky had taken. "There's a first-rate Tintoretto there. One of his latest period."

"I tell you what: it's a lovely day, let's go and have another look at it," said Vronsky, addressing Anna.

"I shall be very glad to; I'll go and put on my hat. Would you say it's hot?" she said, stopping short in the door-way and looking inquiringly at Vronsky. And again a vivid flush overspread her face.

Vronsky saw from her eyes that she did not know on what terms he cared to be with Golenishtchev, and so was afraid of not behaving as he would wish.

He looked a long, tender look at her.

"No, not very," he said.

And it seemed to her that she understood everything, most of all, that he was pleased with her; and smiling to him, she walked with her rapid step out at the door.

The friends glanced at one another, and a look of hesitation came into both faces, as though Golenishtchev, unmistakably admiring her, would have liked to say something about her, and could not find the right thing to say, while Vronsky desired and dreaded his doing so.

"Well then," Vronsky began to start a conversation of some sort; "so you're settled here? You're still at the same work, then?" he went on, recalling that he had been told Golenishtchev was writing something.

"Yes, I'm writing the second part of the *Two Elements*," said Golenishtchev, coloring with pleasure at the question—"that is, to be exact, I am not writing it yet; I am preparing, collecting materials. It will be of far wider scope, and will touch on almost all questions. We in Russia refuse to see that we are the heirs of Byzantium," and he launched into a long and heated explanation of his views.

Vronsky at the first moment felt embarrassed at not even knowing of the first part of the *Two Elements*, of which the author spoke as something well known. But as Golenishtchev began to lay down his opinions and Vronsky was able to follow them even without knowing the *Two Elements*, he listened to him with some interest, for Golenishtchev spoke well. But Vronsky was startled and annoyed by the nervous irascibility with which Golenishtchev talked of the subject that engrossed him. As he went on talking, his eyes glittered more and more angrily; he was more and more hurried in his replies to imaginary opponents, and his face grew more and more excited and worried. Remembering Golenishtchev, a thin, lively, good-natured and well-bred boy, always at the head of the class, Vronsky could not make out the reason of his irritability, and he did not like it. What he particularly disliked was that Golenishtchev, a man belonging to a good set, should put himself on a level with some scribbling fellows, with whom he was irritated and angry. Was it worth it? Vronsky disliked it, yet he felt that Golenishtchev was unhappy, and was sorry for him. Unhappiness, almost mental derangement, was visible on his mobile, rather handsome face, while without even noticing Anna's coming in, he went on hurriedly and hotly expressing his views.

When Anna came in in her hat and cape, and her lovely hand rapidly swinging her parasol, and stood beside him, it was with a feeling of relief that Vronsky broke away from the plaintive eyes of Golenishtchev which fastened persistently upon him, and with a fresh rush of love looked at his charming companion, full of life and happiness. Golenishtchev recovered himself with an effort, and at first was dejected and gloomy, but Anna, disposed to feel friendly with every one as she was at that time, soon revived his spirits by her direct and lively manner. After trying various subjects of conversation, she got him upon painting, of which he talked very well, and she listened to him attentively. They walked to the house they had taken, and looked over it.

"I am very glad of one thing," said Anna to Golenishtchev when they were on their way back: "Alexey will have a capital *atelier*. You must certainly take that room," she said to Vronsky in Russian, using the affectionately familiar form as though she saw that Golenishtchev would become intimate with them in their isolation, and that there was no need of reserve before him.

"Do you paint?" said Golenishtchev, turning round quickly to Vronsky.

"Yes, I used to study long ago, and now I have begun to do a little," said Vronsky, reddening.

"He has great talent," said Anna with a delighted smile. "I'm no judge, of course. But good judges have said the same."

CHAPTER VIII

Anna, in that first period of her emancipation and rapid return to health, felt herself unpardonably happy and full of the joy of life. The thought of her husband's unhappiness did not poison her happiness. On one side that memory was too awful to be thought of. On the other side her husband's unhappiness had given her too much happiness to be regretted. The memory of all that had happened after her illness: her reconciliation with her husband, its breakdown, the news of Vronsky's wound, his visit, the preparations for divorce, the departure from her husband's house, the parting from her son—all that seemed to her like a delirious dream, from which she had waked up alone with Vronsky abroad. The thought of the harm caused to her husband aroused in her a feeling like repulsion, and akin to what a drowning man might feel who has shaken off another man clinging to him. That man did drown. It was an evil action, of course, but it was the sole means of escape, and better not to brood over these fearful facts.

One consolatory reflection upon her conduct had occurred to her at the first moment of the final rupture, and when now she recalled all the past, she remembered that one reflection. "I have inevitably made that man wretched," she thought; "but I don't want to profit by his misery. I too am suffering, and shall suffer; I am losing what I prized above everything—I am losing my good name and my son. I have done wrong, and so I don't want happiness, I don't want a divorce, and shall suffer from my shame and the separation from my child." But, however sincerely Anna had meant to suffer, she was not suffering. Shame there was not. With the tact of which both had such a large share, they had succeeded in avoiding Russian ladies abroad, and so had never placed themselves in a false position, and everywhere they had met people who pretended that they perfectly understood their position, far better indeed than they did themselves. Separation from the son she loved—even that did not cause her anguish in these early days. The baby girl—*his* child—was so sweet, and had so won Anna's heart, since she was all that was left her, that Anna rarely thought of her son.

The desire for life, waxing stronger with recovered health, was so intense, and the conditions of life were so new and pleasant, that Anna felt unpardonably happy. The more she got to know Vronsky, the more she loved him. She loved him for himself, and for his love for her. Her complete ownership of him was a continual joy to her. His presence was always sweet to her. All the traits of his character, which she learned to know better and better, were unutterably dear to her. His appearance, changed by his civilian dress, was as fascinating to her as though she were some young girl in love. In everything he said, thought, and did, she saw something particularly noble and elevated. Her adoration of him alarmed her indeed; she sought and could not find in him anything not fine. She dared not show him her sense of her own insignificance beside him. It seemed to her that, knowing this, he might sooner cease to love her; and she dreaded nothing now so much as losing his love, though she had no grounds for fearing it. But she could not help being grateful to him for his attitude to her, and showing that she appreciated it. He, who had in her opinion such a marked aptitude for a political career, in which he would have been certain to play a leading part—he had sacrificed his ambition for her sake, and never betrayed the slightest regret. He was more lovingly respectful to her than ever, and the constant care that she should not feel the awkwardness of her position never deserted him for a single instant. He, so manly a man, never opposed her, had indeed, with her, no will of his own, and was anxious, it seemed, for nothing but to anticipate her wishes. And she could not but appreciate this, even though the very intensity of his solicitude for her, the atmosphere of care with which he surrounded her, sometimes weighed upon her.

Vronsky, meanwhile, in spite of the complete realization of what he had so long desired, was not perfectly happy. He soon felt that the realization of his desires gave him no more than a grain of sand out of the mountain of happiness he had expected. It showed him the mistake men make in picturing to themselves happiness as the realization of their desires. For a time after joining his life to hers, and putting on civilian dress, he had felt all the delight of freedom in general, of which he had known nothing before, and of freedom in his love,—and he was content, but not for long. He was soon aware that there was springing up in his heart a desire for desires—*ennui*. Without conscious intention he began to clutch at every passing caprice, taking it for a desire and an object. Sixteen hours of the day must be occupied in some way, since they were living abroad in complete freedom, outside the conditions of social life which filled up time in Petersburg. As for the amusements of bachelor existence, which had provided Vronsky with entertainment on previous tours abroad, they could not be thought of, since the sole attempt of the sort had led to a sudden attack of depression in Anna, quite out of proportion with the cause—a late supper with bachelor friends. Relations with the society of the place—foreign and Russian—were equally out of the question owing to the irregularity of their position. The inspection of objects of interest, apart from the fact that everything had been seen already, had not for Vronsky, a Russian and a sensible man, the immense significance Englishmen are able to attach to that pursuit.

And just as the hungry stomach eagerly accepts every object

it can get, hoping to find nourishment in it, Vronsky quite unconsciously clutched first at politics, then at new books, and then at pictures.

As he had from a child a taste for painting, and as, not knowing what to spend his money on, he had begun collecting engravings, he came to a stop at painting, began to take interest in it, and concentrated upon it the unoccupied mass of desires which demanded satisfaction.

He had a ready appreciation of art, and probably, with a taste for imitating art, he supposed himself to have the real thing essential for an artist, and after hesitating for some time which style of painting to select—religious, historical, realistic, or genre painting—he set to work to paint. He appreciated all kinds, and could have felt inspired by any one of them; but he had no conception of the possibility of knowing nothing at all of any school of painting, and of being inspired directly by what is within the soul, without caring whether what is painted will belong to any recognized school. Since he knew nothing of this, and drew his inspiration, not directly from life, but indirectly from life embodied in art, his inspiration came very quickly and easily, and as quickly and easily came his success in painting something very similar to the sort of painting he was trying to imitate.

More than any other style he liked the French—graceful and effective—and in that style he began to paint Anna's portrait in Italian costume, and the portrait seemed to him, and to every one who saw it, extremely successful.

CHAPTER IX

The old neglected palazzo, with its lofty carved ceilings and frescoes on the walls, with its floors of mosaic, with its heavy yellow stuff curtains on the windows, with its vases on pedestals, and its open fireplaces, its carved doors and gloomy reception-rooms, hung with pictures—this palazzo did much, by its very appearance after they had moved into it, to confirm in Vronsky the agreeable illusion that he was not so much a Russian country gentleman, a retired army officer, as an enlightened amateur and patron of the arts, himself a modest artist who had renounced the world, his connections, and his ambition for the sake of the woman he loved.

The pose chosen by Vronsky with their removal into the palazzo was completely successful, and having, through Golenishtchev, made acquaintance with a few interesting people, for a time he was satisfied. He painted studies from nature under the guidance of an Italian professor of painting, and studied mediæval Italian life. Mediæval Italian life so fascinated Vronsky that he even wore a hat and flung a cloak over his shoulder in the mediæval style, which, indeed, was extremely becoming to him.

"Here we live, and know nothing of what's going on," Vronsky said to Golenishtchev as he came to see him one morning. "Have you seen Mihailov's picture?" he said, handing him a Russian gazette he had received that morning, and pointing to an article on a Russian artist, living in the very same town, 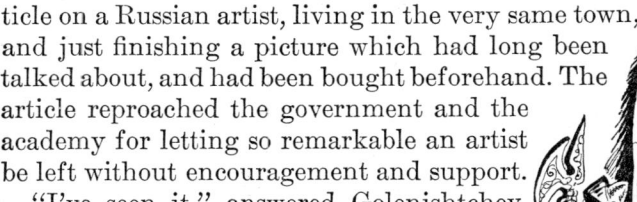 and just finishing a picture which had long been talked about, and had been bought beforehand. The article reproached the government and the academy for letting so remarkable an artist be left without encouragement and support.

"I've seen it," answered Golenishtchev. "Of course, he's not without talent, but it's all in a wrong direction. It's all the Ivanov-Strauss-Renan attitude to Christ and to religious painting."

"What is the subject of the picture?" asked Anna.

"Christ before Pilate. Christ is represented as a Jew with all the realism of the new school."

And the question of the subject of the picture having brought him to one of his favorite theories, Golenishtchev launched forth into a disquisition on it.

"I can't understand how they can fall into such a gross mistake. Christ always has His definite embodiment in the art of the great masters. And therefore, if they want to depict, not God, but a revolutionist or a sage, let them take from history a Socrates, a Franklin, a Charlotte Corday, but not Christ. They take the very figure which cannot be taken for their art, and then . . ."

"And is it true that this Mihailov is in such poverty?" asked Vronsky, thinking that, as a Russian Mæcenas, it was his duty to assist the artist regardless of whether the picture were good or bad.

"I should say not. He's a remarkable portrait-painter. Have you ever seen his portrait of Madame Vassiltchikova? But I believe he doesn't care about painting any more portraits, and so very likely he is in want. I maintain that . . ."

"Couldn't we ask him to paint a portrait of Anna Arkadyevna?" said Vronsky.

"Why mine?" said Anna. "After yours I don't want another portrait. Better have one of Annie" (so she called her baby girl). "Here she is," she added, looking out of the window at the handsome Italian nurse, who was carrying the child out into the garden, and immediately glancing unnoticed at Vronsky. The handsome nurse, from whom Vronsky was painting a head for his picture, was the one hidden grief in Anna's life. He painted with her as his model, admired her beauty and mediævalism, and Anna dared not confess to herself that she was afraid of becoming jealous of this nurse, and was for that reason particularly gracious and condescending both to her and her little son. Vronsky, too, glanced out of the window and into Anna's eyes, and, turning at once to Golenishtchev, he said:

"Do you know this Mihailov?"

"I have met him. But he's a queer fish, and quite without breeding. You know, one of those uncouth new people one's so often coming across nowadays, one of those free-thinkers you know, who are reared *d'emblée* in theories of atheism, scepticism, and materialism. In former days," said Golenishtchev, not observing, or not willing to observe, that both Anna and Vronsky wanted to speak, "in former days the free-thinker was a man who had been brought up in ideas of religion, law, and morality, and only through conflict and struggle came to free-thought; but now there has sprung up a new type of born free-thinkers who grow up without even having heard of principles of morality or of religion, of the existence of authorities, who grow up directly in ideas of negation in everything, that is to say, savages. Well, he's of that class. He's the son, it appears, of some Moscow butler, and has never had any sort of bringing-up. When he got into the academy and made his reputation he tried, as he's no fool, to educate himself. And he turned to what seemed to him the very source of culture—the magazines. In old times, you see, a man who wanted to educate himself—a Frenchman, for instance—would have set to work to study all the classics and theologians and tragedians and historians and philosophers, and, you know, all the intellectual work that came in his way. But in our day he goes straight for the literature of negation, very quickly assimilates all the extracts of the science of negation, and he's ready. And that's not all—twenty years ago he would have found in that literature traces of conflict with authorities, with the creeds of the ages; he would have perceived from this conflict that there was something else; but now he comes at once upon a literature in which the old creeds do not even furnish matter for discussion, but it is stated baldly that there is nothing else—evolution, natural selection, struggle for existence—and that's all. In my article I've . . ."

"I tell you what," said Anna, who had for a long while been exchanging wary glances with Vronsky, and knew that he was not in the least interested in the education of this artist, but was simply absorbed by the idea of assisting him, and ordering a portrait of him; "I tell you what," she said, resolutely interrupting Golenishtchev, who was still talking away, "let's go and see him!"

Golenishtchev recovered his self-possession and readily agreed. But as the artist lived in a remote suburb, it was decided to take the carriage.

An hour later Anna, with Golenishtchev by her side and Vronsky on the front seat of the carriage, facing them, drove up to a new ugly house in the remote suburb. On learning from the porter's wife, who came out to them, that Mihailov saw visitors at his studio, but that at that moment he was in his lodging only a couple of steps off, they sent her to him with their cards, asking permission to see his picture.

CHAPTER X

THE artist Mihailov was, as always, at work when the cards of Count Vronsky and Golenishtchev were brought to him. In the morning he had been working in his studio at his big picture. On getting home he flew into a rage with his wife for not having managed to put off the landlady, who had been asking for money.

"I've said it to you twenty times, don't enter into details. You're fool enough at all times, and when you start explaining things in Italian you're a fool three times as foolish," he said after a long dispute.

"Don't let it run so long; it's not my fault. If I had the money . . ."

"Leave me in peace, for God's sake!" Mihailov shrieked, with tears in his voice, and, stopping his ears, he went off into his working room, the other side of a partition wall, and closed the door after him. "Idiotic woman!" he said to himself, sat down to the table, and, opening a portfolio, he set to work at once with peculiar fervor at a sketch he had begun.

Never did he work with such fervor and success as when things went ill with him, and especially when he quarreled with his wife. "Oh! damn them all!" he thought as he went on working. He was making a sketch for the figure of a man in a violent rage. A sketch had been made before, but he was dissatisfied with it. "No, that one was better . . . where is it?" He went back to his wife, and scowling, and not looking at her, asked his eldest little girl, where was that piece of paper he had given them? The paper with the discarded sketch on it was found, but it was dirty, and spotted with candle-grease. Still, he took the sketch, laid it on his table, and, moving a little away, screwing up his eyes, he fell to gazing at it. All at once he smiled and gesticulated gleefully.

"That's it! that's it!" he said, and, at once picking up the pencil, he began rapidly drawing. The spot of tallow had given the man a new pose.

He had sketched this new pose, when all at once he recalled the face of a shopkeeper of whom he had bought cigars, a vigorous face with a prominent chin, and he sketched this very face, this chin on to the figure of the man. He laughed aloud with delight. The figure from a lifeless imagined thing had become living, and such that it could never be changed. That figure lived, and was clearly and unmistakably defined. The sketch might be corrected in accordance with the requirements of the figure, the legs, indeed, could and must be put differently, and the position of the left hand must be quite altered; the hair too might be thrown back. But in making these corrections he was not altering the figure but simply getting rid of what concealed the figure. He was, as it were, stripping off the wrappings which hindered it from being distinctly seen. Each new feature only brought out the whole figure in all its force and vigor, as it had suddenly come to him from the spot of tallow. He was carefully finishing the figure when the cards were brought him.

"Coming, coming!"

He went in to his wife.

"Come, Sasha, don't be cross!" he said, smiling timidly and affectionately at her. "You were to blame. I was to blame. I'll make it all right." And having made peace with his wife he put on an olive-green overcoat with a velvet collar and a hat, and went towards his studio. The successful figure he had already forgotten. Now he was delighted and excited at the visit of these people of consequence, Russians, who had come in their carriage.

Of his picture, the one that stood now on his easel, he had at the bottom of his heart one conviction—that no one had ever painted a picture like it. He did not believe that his picture was better than all the pictures of Raphael, but he knew that what he tried to convey in that picture, no one ever had conveyed. This he knew positively, and had known a long while, ever since he had begun to paint it. But other people's criticisms, whatever they might be, had yet immense consequence in his eyes, and they agitated him to the depths of his soul. Any remark, the most insignificant, that showed that the critic saw even the tiniest part of what he saw in the picture, agitated him to the depths of his soul. He always attributed to his critics a more profound comprehension than he had himself, and always expected from them something he did not himself see in the picture. And often in their criticisms he fancied that he had found this.

He walked rapidly to the door of his studio, and in spite of his excitement he was struck by the soft light on Anna's figure as she stood in the shade of the entrance listening to Golenishtchev, who was eagerly telling her something, while she evidently wanted to look round at the artist. He was himself unconscious how, as he approached them, he seized on this impression and absorbed it, as he had the chin of the shopkeeper who had sold him the cigars, and put it away somewhere to be brought out when he wanted it. The visitors, not agreeably impressed beforehand by Golenishtchev's account of the artist, were still less so by his personal appearance. Thick-set and of middle height, with nimble movements, with his brown hat, olive-green coat and narrow trousers—though wide trousers had been a long while in fashion,—most of all, with the ordinariness of his broad face, and the combined expression of timidity and anxiety to keep up his dignity, Mihailov made an unpleasant impression.

"Please step in," he said, trying to look indifferent, and going into the passage he took a key out of his pocket and opened the door.

CHAPTER XI

ON ENTERING the studio, Mihailov once more scanned his visitors and noted down in his imagination Vronsky's expression too, and especially his jaws. Although his artistic sense was unceasingly at work collecting materials, although he felt a continually increasing excitement as the moment of criticizing his work drew nearer, he rapidly and subtly formed, from imperceptible signs, a mental image of these three persons.

That fellow (Golenishtchev) was a Russian living here. Mihailov did not remember his surname nor where he had met him, nor what he had said to him. He only remembered his face as he remembered all the faces he had ever seen; but he remembered, too, that it was one of the faces laid by in his memory in the immense class of the falsely consequential and poor in expression. The abundant hair and very open forehead gave an appearance of consequence to the face, which had only one expression—a petty, childish, peevish expression, concentrated just above the bridge of the narrow nose. Vronsky and Madame Karenina must be, Mihailov supposed, distinguished and wealthy Russians, knowing nothing about art, like all those wealthy Russians, but posing as amateurs and connoisseurs. "Most likely they've already looked at all the antiques, and now they're making the round of the studios of the new people, the German humbug, and the cracked Pre-Raphaelite English fellow, and have only come to me to make the point of view complete," he thought. He was well acquainted with the way dilettanti have (the cleverer they were the worse he found them) of looking at the works of contemporary artists with the sole object of being in a position to say that art is a thing of the past, and that the more one sees of the new men the more one sees how inimitable the works of the great old masters have remained. He expected all this; he saw it all in their faces, he saw it in the careless indifference with which they talked among themselves, stared at the lay figures and busts, and walked about in leisurely fashion, waiting for him to uncover his picture. But in spite of this, while he was turning over his studies, pulling up the blinds and taking off the sheet, he was in intense excitement, especially as, in spite of his conviction that all distinguished and wealthy Russians were certain to be beasts and fools, he liked Vronsky, and still more Anna.

"Here, if you please," he said, moving on one side with his nimble gait and pointing to his picture, "it's the exhortation to Pilate. Matthew, chapter xxvii," he said, feeling his lips were beginning to tremble with emotion. He moved away and stood behind them.

For the few seconds during which the visitors were gazing at the picture in silence Mihailov too gazed at it with the indifferent eye of an outsider. For those few seconds he was sure in anticipation that a higher, juster criticism would be uttered by them, by those very visitors whom he had been so despising a moment before. He forgot all he had thought about his picture before during the three years he had been painting it; he forgot all its qualities which had been absolutely certain to him—he saw the picture with their indifferent, new, outside eyes, and saw nothing good in it. He saw in the foreground Pilate's irritated face and the serene face of Christ, and in the background the figures of Pilate's retinue and the face of John watching what was happening. Every face that, with such agony, such blunders and corrections had grown up within him with its special character, every face that had given him such torments and such raptures, and all these faces so many times transposed for the sake of the harmony of the whole, all the shades of color and tones that he had attained with such labor—all of this together seemed to him now, looking at it with their eyes, the merest vulgarity, something that had been done a thousand times over. The face dearest to him, the face of Christ, the center of the picture, which had given him such ecstasy as it unfolded itself to him, was utterly lost to him when he glanced at the picture with their eyes. He saw a well-painted (no, not even that—he distinctly saw now a mass of defects) repetition of those endless Christs of Titian, Raphael, Rubens, and the same soldiers and Pilate. It was all common, poor, and stale, and positively badly painted—weak and unequal. They would be justified in repeating hypocritically civil speeches in the presence of the painter, and pitying him and laughing at him when they were alone again.

The silence (though it lasted no more than a minute) became too intolerable to him. To break it, and to show he was not agitated, he made an effort and addressed Golenishtchev.

"I think I've had the pleasure of meeting you," he said, looking uneasily first at Anna, then at Vronsky, in fear of losing any shade of their expression.

"To be sure! We met at Rossi's, do you remember, at that soirée when that Italian lady recited—the new Rachel?" Golenishtchev answered easily, removing his eyes without the slightest regret from the picture and turning to the artist.

Noticing, however, that Mihailov was expecting a criticism of the picture, he said:

"Your picture has got on a great deal since I saw it last time; and what strikes me particularly now, as it did then, is the figure of Pilate. One so knows the man: a good-natured, capital fellow, but an official through and through, who does not know what it is he's doing. But I fancy . . ."

All Mihailov's mobile face beamed at once; his eyes sparkled. He tried to say something, but he could not speak for excitement, and pretended to be coughing. Low as was his opinion of Golenishtchev's capacity for understanding art, trifling as was the true remark upon the fidelity of the expression of Pilate as an official, and offensive as might have seemed the utterance of so unimportant an observation while nothing was said of more serious points, Mihailov was in an ecstasy of delight at this observation. He had himself thought about Pilate's figure just what Golenishtchev said. The fact that this reflection was but one of millions of reflections, which as Mihailov knew for certain would be true, did not diminish for him the significance of Golenishtchev's remark. His heart warmed to Golenishtchev for this remark, and from a state of depression he suddenly passed to ecstasy. At once the whole of his picture lived before him in all the indescribable complexity of everything living. Mihailov again tried to say that that was how he understood Pilate, but his lips quivered intractably, and he could not pronounce the words. Vronsky and Anna too said something in that subdued voice in which, partly to avoid hurting the artist's feelings and partly to avoid saying out loud something silly—so easily said when talking of art—people usually speak at exhibitions of pictures. Mihailov fancied that the picture had made an impression on them too. He went up to them.

"How marvelous Christ's expression is!" said Anna. Of all she saw she liked that expression most of all, and she felt that it was the center of the picture, and so praise of it would be pleasant to the artist. "One can see that He is pitying Pilate."

This again was one of the million true reflections that could be found in his picture and in the figure of Christ. She said that He was pitying Pilate. In Christ's expression there ought to be indeed an expression of pity, since there is an expression of love, of heavenly peace, of readiness for death, and a sense of the vanity of words. Of course there is the expression of an official in Pilate and of pity in Christ, seeing that one is the incarnation of the fleshly and the other of the spiritual life. All this and much more flashed into Mihailov's thoughts.

"Yes, and how that figure is done—what atmosphere! One can walk round it," said Golenishtchev, unmistakably betraying by this remark that he did not approve of the meaning and idea of the figure.

"Yes, there's a wonderful mastery!" said Vronsky. "How those figures in the background stand out! There you have technique," he said, addressing Golenishtchev, alluding to a conversation between them about Vronsky's despair of attaining this technique.

"Yes, yes, marvelous!" Golenishtchev and Anna assented. In spite of the excited condition in which he was, the sentence about technique had sent a pang to Mihailov's heart, and looking angrily at Vronsky he suddenly scowled. He had often heard this word technique, and was utterly unable to understand what was understood by it. He knew that by this term was understood a mechanical facility for painting or drawing, entirely apart from its subject. He had noticed often that even in actual praise technique was opposed to essential quality, as though one could paint well something that was bad. He knew that a great deal of attention and care was necessary in taking off the coverings, to avoid injuring the creation itself, and to take off all the coverings; but there was no art of painting—no technique of any sort—about it. If to a little child or to his cook were revealed what he saw, it or she would have been able to peel the wrappings off what was seen. And the most experienced and adroit painter could not by mere mechanical facility paint anything if the lines of the subject were not revealed to him first. Besides, he saw that if it came to talking about technique, it was impossible to praise him for it. In all he had painted and repainted he saw faults that hurt his eyes, coming from want of care in taking off the wrappings—faults he could not correct now without spoiling the whole. And in almost all the figures and faces he saw, too, remnants of the wrappings not perfectly removed that spoiled the picture.

"One thing might be said, if you will allow me to make the remark . . ." observed Golenishtchev.

"Oh, I shall be delighted, I beg you," said Mihailov with a forced smile.

"That is, that you make Him the man-god, and not the God-man. But I know that was what you meant to do."

"I cannot paint a Christ that is not in my heart," said Mihailov gloomily.

"Yes; but in that case, if you will allow me to say what I think . . . Your picture is so fine that my observation cannot detract from it, and, besides, it is only my personal opinion. With you it is different. Your very motive is different. But let us take Ivanov. I imagine that if Christ is brought down to the level of an historical character, it would have been better for Ivanov to select some other historical subject, fresh, untouched."

"But if this is the greatest subject presented to art?"

"If one looked one would find others. But the point is that art cannot suffer doubt and discussion. And before the picture of Ivanov the question arises for the believer and the unbeliever alike, 'Is it God, or is it not God?' and the unity of the impression is destroyed."

"Why so? I think that for educated people," said Mihailov, "the question cannot exist."

Golenishtchev did not agree with this, and confounded Mihailov by his support of his first idea of the unity of the impression being essential to art.

Mihailov was greatly perturbed, but he could say nothing in defense of his own idea.

CHAPTER XII

ANNA and Vronsky had long been exchanging glances, regretting their friend's flow of cleverness. At last Vronsky, without waiting for the artist, walked away to another small picture.

"Oh, how exquisite! What a lovely thing! A gem! How exquisite!" they cried with one voice.

"What is it they're so pleased with?" thought Mihailov. He had positively forgotten that picture he had painted three years ago. He had forgotten all the agonies and the ecstasies he had lived through with that picture when for several months it had been the one thought haunting him day and night. He had forgotten, as he always forgot, the pictures he had finished. He did not even like to look at it, and had only brought it out because he was expecting an Englishman who wanted to buy it.

"Oh, that's only an old study," he said.

"How fine!" said Golenishtchev, he too, with unmistakable sincerity, falling under the spell of the picture.

Two boys were angling in the shade of a willow-tree. The elder had just dropped in the hook, and was carefully pulling the float from behind a bush, entirely absorbed in what he was doing. The other, a little younger, was lying in the grass leaning on his elbows, with his tangled, flaxen head in his hands, staring at the water with his dreamy blue eyes. What was he thinking of?

The enthusiasm over this picture stirred some of the old feeling for it in Mihailov, but he feared and disliked this waste of feeling for things past, and so, even though this praise was grateful to him, he tried to draw his visitors away to a third picture.

But Vronsky asked whether the picture was for sale. To Mihailov at that moment, excited by visitors, it was extremely distasteful to speak of money matters.

"It is put up there to be sold," he answered, scowling gloomily.

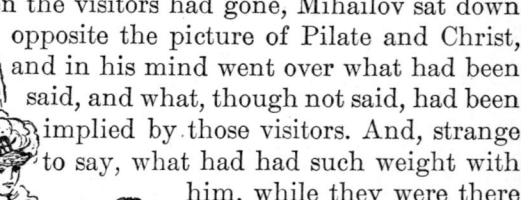

When the visitors had gone, Mihailov sat down opposite the picture of Pilate and Christ, and in his mind went over what had been said, and what, though not said, had been implied by those visitors. And, strange to say, what had had such weight with him, while they were there and while he mentally put himself at their point of view, suddenly lost all importance for him. He began to look at his picture with all his own full artist vision, and was soon in that mood of conviction of the perfectibility, and so of the significance, of his picture—a conviction essential to the most intense fervor, excluding all other interests—in which alone he could work.

Christ's foreshortened leg was not right, though. He took his palette and began to work. As he corrected the leg he looked continually at the figure of John in the background, which his visitors had not even noticed, but which he knew was beyond perfection. When he had finished the leg he wanted to touch that figure, but he felt too much excited for it. He was equally unable to work when he was cold and when he was too much affected and saw everything too much. There was only one stage in the transition from coldness to inspiration, at which work was possible. To-day he was too much agitated. He would have covered the picture, but he stopped, holding the cloth in his hand, and, smiling blissfully, gazed a long while at the figure of John. At last, as it were regretfully tearing himself away, he dropped the cloth, and, exhausted but happy, went home.

Vronsky, Anna, and Golenishtchev, on their way home, were particularly lively and cheerful. They talked of Mihailov and his pictures. The word *talent,* by which they meant an inborn, almost physical, aptitude apart from brain and heart, and in which they tried to find an expression for all the artist had gained from life, recurred particularly often in their talk, as though it were necessary for them to sum up what they had no conception of, though they wanted to talk of it. They said that there was no denying his talent, but that his talent could not develop for want of education—the common defect of our Russian artists. But the picture of the boys had imprinted itself on their memories, and they were continually coming back to it. "What an exquisite thing! How he has succeeded in it, and how simply! He doesn't even comprehend how good it is. Yes, I mustn't let it slip; I must buy it," said Vronsky.

CHAPTER XIII

Mihailov sold Vronsky his picture, and agreed to paint a portrait of Anna. On the day fixed he came and began the work. From the fifth sitting the portrait impressed every one, especially Vronsky, not only by its resemblance, but by its characteristic beauty. It was strange how Mihailov could have discovered just her characteristic beauty. "One needs to know and love her as I have loved her to discover the very sweetest expression of her soul," Vronsky thought, though it was only from this portrait that he had himself learned this sweetest expression of her soul. But the expression was so true that he, and others too, fancied they had long known it.

"I have been struggling on for ever so long without doing anything," he said of his own portrait of her, "and he just looked and painted it. That's where technique comes in."

"That will come," was the consoling reassurance given him by Golenishtchev, in whose view Vronsky had both talent, and what was most important, culture, giving him a wider outlook on art. Golenishtchev's faith in Vronsky's talent was propped up by his own need of Vronsky's sympathy and approval for his own articles and ideas, and he felt that the praise and support must be mutual.

In another man's house, and especially in Vronsky's palazzo, Mihailov was quite a different man from what he was in his studio. He behaved with hostile courtesy, as though he were afraid of coming closer to people he did not respect. He called Vronsky "your excellency," and notwithstanding Anna's and Vronsky's invitations, he would never stay to dinner, nor come except for the sittings. Anna was even more friendly to him than to other people, and was very grateful for her portrait. Vronsky was more than cordial with him, and was obviously interested to know the artist's opinion of his picture. Golenishtchev never let slip an opportunity of instilling sound ideas about art into Mihailov. But Mihailov remained equally chilly to all of them. Anna was aware from his eyes that he liked looking at her, but he avoided conversation with her. Vronsky's talk about his painting he met with stubborn silence, and he was as stubbornly silent when he was shown Vronsky's picture. He was unmistakably bored by Golenishtchev's conversation, and he did not attempt to oppose him.

Altogether Mihailov, with his reserved and disagreeable, as it were, hostile attitude, was quite disliked by them as they got to know him better; and they were glad when the sittings were over, and they were left with a magnificent portrait in their possession, and he gave up coming. Golenishtchev was the first to give expression to an idea that had occurred to all of them, which was that Mihailov was simply jealous of Vronsky.

"Not envious, let us say, since he has *talent;* but it annoys him that a wealthy man of the highest society, and a count, too (you know they all detest a title), can, without any particular trouble, do as well, if not better, than he who has devoted all his life to it. And more than all, it's a question of culture, which he is without."

Vronsky defended Mihailov, but at the bottom of his heart he believed it, because in his view a man of a different, lower world would be sure to be envious.

Anna's portrait—the same subject painted from nature both by him and by Mihailov—ought to have shown Vronsky the difference between him and Mihailov; but he did not see it. Only after Mihailov's portrait was painted he left off painting his portrait of Anna, deciding that it was now not needed. His picture of mediæval life he went on with. And he himself, and Golenishtchev, and still more Anna, thought it very good, because it was far more like the celebrated pictures they knew than Mihailov's picture.

Mihailov meanwhile, although Anna's portrait greatly fascinated him, was even more glad than they were when the sittings were over, and he had no longer to listen to Golenishtchev's disquisitions upon art, and could forget about Vronsky's painting. He knew that Vronsky could not be prevented from amusing himself with painting; he knew that he and all dilettanti had a perfect right to paint what they liked, but it was distasteful to him. A man could not be prevented from making himself a big wax doll, and kissing it. But if the man were to come with the doll and sit before a man in love, and began caressing his doll as the lover caressed the woman he loved, it would be distasteful to the lover. Just such a distasteful sensation was what Mihailov felt at the sight of Vronsky's painting: he felt it both ludicrous and irritating, both pitiable and offensive.

Vronsky's interest in painting and the Middle Ages did not last long. He had enough taste for painting to be unable to finish his picture. The picture came to a standstill. He was vaguely aware that its defects, inconspicuous at first, would be glaring if he were to go on with it. The same experience befell him as Golenishtchev, who felt that he had nothing to say, and continually deceived himself with the theory that his idea was not yet mature, that he was working it out and collecting materials. This exasperated and tortured Golenishtchev, but Vronsky was incapable of deceiving and torturing himself, and even more incapable of exasperation. With his characteristic decision, without explanation or apology, he simply ceased working at painting.

But without this occupation, the life of Vronsky and of Anna, who wondered at his loss of interest in it, struck them as intolerably tedious in an Italian town. The palazzo suddenly seemed so obtrusively old and dirty, the spots on the curtains, the cracks in the floors, the broken plaster on the cornices became so disagreeably obvious, and the everlasting sameness of Golenishtchev, and the Italian professor and the German traveler became so wearisome, that they had to make some change. They resolved to go to Russia, to the country. In Petersburg Vronsky intended to arrange a partition of the land with his brother, while Anna meant to see her son. The summer they intended to spend on Vronsky's great family estate.

CHAPTER XIV

LEVIN had been married three months. He was happy, but not at all in the way he had expected to be. At every step he found his former dreams disappointed, and new, unexpected surprises of happiness. He was happy; but on entering upon family life he saw at every step that it was utterly different from what he had imagined. At every step he experienced what a man would experience who, after admiring the smooth, happy course of a little boat on a lake, should get himself into that little boat. He saw that it was not all sitting still, floating smoothly; that one had to think too, not for an instant to forget where one was floating; and that there was water under one, and that one must row; and that his unaccustomed hands would be sore; and that it was only to look at it that was easy; but that doing it, though very delightful, was very difficult.

As a bachelor, when he had watched other people's married life, seen the petty cares, the squabbles, the jealousy, he had only smiled contemptuously in his heart. In his future married life there could be, he was convinced, nothing of that sort; even the external forms, indeed, he fancied, must be utterly unlike the life of others in everything. And all of a sudden, instead of his life with his wife being made on an individual pattern, it was, on the contrary, entirely made up of the pettiest details, which he had so despised before, but which now, by no will of his own, had gained an extraordinary importance that it was useless to contend against. And Levin saw that the organization of all these details was by no means so easy as he had fancied before. Although Levin believed himself to have the most exact conceptions of domestic life, unconsciously, like all men, he pictured domestic life as the happiest enjoyment of love, with nothing to hinder and no petty cares to distract. He ought, as he conceived the position, to do his work, and to find repose from it in the happiness of love. She ought to be beloved, and nothing more. But, like all men, he forgot that she too would want work. And he was surprised that she, his poetic, exquisite Kitty, could, not merely in the first weeks, but even in the first days of their married life, think, remember, and busy herself about table-cloths, and furniture, about mattresses for visitors, about a tray, about the cook, and the dinner, and so on. While they were still engaged, he had been struck by the definiteness with which she had declined the tour abroad and decided to go into the country, as though she knew of something she wanted, and could still think of something outside her love. This had jarred upon him then, and now her trivial cares and anxieties jarred upon him several times. But he saw that this was essential for her. And, loving her as he did, though he did not understand the reason of them, and jeered at these domestic pursuits, he could not help admiring them. He jeered at the way in which she arranged the furniture they had brought from Moscow; rearranged their room; hung up curtains; prepared rooms for visitors; a room for Dolly; saw after an abode for her new maid; ordered dinner of the old cook; came into collision with Agafea Mihalovna, taking from her the charge of the stores. He saw how the old cook smiled, admiring her, and listening to her inexperienced, impossible orders, how mournfully and tenderly Agafea Mihalovna shook her head over the young mistress's new arrangements. He saw that Kitty was extraordinarily sweet when, laughing and crying, she came to tell him that her maid, Masha, was used to looking upon her as her young lady, and so no one obeyed her. It seemed to him sweet, but strange, and he thought it would have been better without this.

He did not know how great a sense of change she was experiencing; she, who at home had sometimes wanted some favorite dish, or sweets, without the possibility of getting either, now could order what she liked, buy pounds of sweets, spend as much money as she liked, and order any puddings she pleased.

She was dreaming with delight now of Dolly's coming to them with her children, especially because she would order for the children their favorite puddings and Dolly would appreciate all her new housekeeping. She did not know herself why and wherefore, but the arranging of her house had an irresistible attraction for her. Instinctively feeling the approach of spring, and knowing that there would be days of rough weather too, she built her nest as best she could, and was in haste at the same time to build it and to learn how to do it.

This care for domestic details in Kitty, so opposed to Levin's ideal of exalted happiness, was at first one of the disappointments; and this sweet care of her household, the aim of which he did not understand, but could not help loving, was one of the new happy surprises.

Another disappointment and happy surprise came in their quarrels. Levin could never have conceived that between him and his wife any relations could arise other than tender, respectful and loving, and all at once in the very early days they quarreled, so that she said he did not care for her, that he cared for no one but himself, burst into tears, and wrung her arms.

This first quarrel arose from Levin's having gone out to a new farmhouse and having been away half an hour too long, because he had tried to get home by a short cut and had lost his way. He drove home thinking of nothing but her, of her love, of his own happiness, and the nearer he drew to home, the warmer was his tenderness for her. He ran into the room with the same feeling, with an even stronger feeling than he had had when he reached the Shtcherbatskys' house to make his offer. And suddenly he was met by a lowering expression he had never seen in her. He would have kissed her; she pushed him away.

"What is it?"

"You've been enjoying yourself," she began, trying to be calm and spiteful. But as soon as she opened her mouth, a stream of reproach, of senseless jealousy, of all that had been torturing her during that half-hour which she had spent sitting motionless at the window, burst from her. It was only then, for the first time, that he clearly understood what he had not understood when he led her out of the church after the wedding. He felt now that he was not simply close to her, but that he did not know where he ended and she began. He felt this from the agonizing sensation of division that he experienced at that instant. He was offended for the first instant, but the very same second he felt that he could not be offended by her, that she was himself. He felt for the first moment as a man feels when, having suddenly received a violent blow from behind, he turns round, angry and eager to avenge himself, to look for his antagonist, and finds that it is he himself who has accidentally struck himself, that there is no one to be angry with, and that he must put up with and try to soothe the pain.

Never afterwards did he feel it with such intensity, but this first time he could not for a long while get over it. His natural feeling urged him to defend himself, to prove to her she was wrong; but to prove her wrong would mean irritating her still more and making the rupture greater that was the cause of all his suffering. One habitual feeling impelled him to get rid of the blame and to pass it on her. Another feeling, even stronger, impelled him as quickly as possible to smooth over the rupture without letting it grow greater. To remain under such undeserved reproach was wretched, but to make her suffer by justifying himself was worse still. Like a man half-awake in an agony of pain, he wanted to tear out, to fling away the aching place, and coming to his senses, he felt that the aching place was himself. He could do nothing but try to help the aching place to bear it, and this he tried to do.

They made peace. She, recognizing that she was wrong, though she did not say so, became tenderer to him, and they experienced new, redoubled happiness in their love. But that did not prevent such quarrels from happening again, and exceedingly often too, on the most unexpected and trivial grounds. These quarrels frequently arose from the fact that they did not yet know what was of importance to each other and that all this early period they were both often in a bad temper. When one was in a good temper, and the other in a bad temper, the peace was not broken; but when both happened to be in an ill-humor, quarrels sprang up from such incomprehensibly trifling causes, that they could never remember afterwards what they had quarreled about. It is true that when they were both in a good temper their enjoyment of life was redoubled. But still this first period of their married life was a difficult time for them.

During all this early time they had a peculiarly vivid sense of tension, as it were, a tugging in opposite directions of the chain by which they were bound. Altogether their honeymoon—that is to say, the month after their wedding—from which from tradition Levin expected so much, was not merely not a time of sweetness, but remained in the memories of both as the bitterest and most humiliating period in their lives. They both alike tried in later life to blot out from their memories all the monstrous, shameful incidents of that morbid period, when both were rarely in a normal frame of mind, both were rarely quite themselves.

It was only in the third month of their married life, after their return from Moscow, where they had been staying for a month, that their life began to go more smoothly.

CHAPTER XV

THEY had just come back from Moscow, and were glad to be alone. He was sitting at the writing-table in his study, writing. She, wearing the dark lilac dress she had worn during the first days of their married life, and put on again to-day, a dress particularly remembered and loved by him, was sitting on the sofa, the same old-fashioned leather sofa which had always stood in the study in Levin's father's and grandfather's days. She was sewing at *broderie anglaise*. He thought and wrote, never losing the happy consciousness of her presence. His work, both on the land and on the book, in which the principles of the new land system were to be laid down, had not been abandoned; but just as formerly these pursuits and ideas had seemed to him petty and trivial in comparison with the darkness that overspread all life, now they seemed as unimportant and petty in comparison with the life that lay before him suffused with the brilliant light of happiness. He went on with his work, but he felt now that the center of gravity of his attention had passed to something else, and that consequently he looked at his work quite differently and more clearly. Formerly this work had been for him an escape from life. Formerly he had felt that without this work his life would be too gloomy. Now these pursuits were necessary for him that life might not be too uniformly bright. Taking up his manuscript, reading through what he had written, he found with pleasure that the work was worth his working at. Many of his old ideas seemed to him superfluous and extreme, but many blanks became distinct to him when he reviewed the whole thing in his memory. He was writing now a new chapter on the causes of the present disastrous condition of agriculture in Russia. He maintained that the poverty of Russia arises not merely from the anomalous distribution of landed property and misdirected reforms, but that what had contributed of late years to this result was the civilization from without abnormally grafted upon Russia, especially facilities of communication, as railways, leading to centralization in towns, the development of luxury, and the consequent development of manufactures, credit and its accompaniment of speculation—all to the detriment of agriculture. It seemed to him that in a normal development of wealth in a state all these phenomena would arise only when a considerable amount of labor had been put into agriculture, when it had come under regular, or at least definite, conditions; that the wealth of a country ought to increase proportionally, and especially in such a way that other sources of wealth should not outstrip agriculture; that in harmony with a certain stage of agriculture there should be means of communication corresponding to it, and that in our unsettled condition of the land, railways, called into being by political and not by economic needs, were premature, and instead of promoting agriculture, as was expected of them, they were competing with agriculture and promoting the development of manufactures and credit, and so arresting its progress; and that just as the one-sided and premature development of one organ in an animal would hinder its general development, so in the general development of wealth in Russia, credit, facilities of communication, manufacturing activity, indubitably necessary in Europe, where they had arisen in their proper time, had with us only done harm, by throwing into the background the chief question calling for settlement— the question of the organization of agriculture.

While he was writing his ideas she was thinking how unnaturally cordial her husband had been to young Prince Tcharsky, who had, with great want of tact, flirted with her the day before they left Moscow. "He's jealous," she thought. "Goodness! how sweet and silly he is! He's jealous of me! If he knew that I think no more of them than of Piotr the cook," she thought, looking at his head and red neck with a feeling of possession strange to herself. "Though it's a pity to take him from his work (but he has plenty of time!), I must look at his face; will he feel I'm looking at him? I wish he'd turn round . . . I'll *will* him to!" and she opened her eyes wide, as though to intensify the influence of her gaze.

"Yes, they draw away all the sap and give a false appearance of prosperity," he muttered, stopping to write, and, feeling that she was looking at him and smiling, he looked round.

"Well?" he queried, smiling, and getting up.

"He looked round," she thought.

"It's nothing; I wanted you to look round," she said, watching him, and trying to guess whether he was vexed at being interrupted or not.

"How happy we are alone together!—I am, that is," he said, going up to her with a radiant smile of happiness.

"I'm just as happy. I'll never go anywhere, especially not to Moscow."

"And what were you thinking about?"

"I? I was thinking . . . No, no, go along, go on writing; don't break off," she said, pursing up her lips, "and I must cut out these little holes now, do you see?"

She took up her scissors and began cutting them out.

"No; tell me, what was it?" he said, sitting down beside her and watching the tiny scissors moving round.

"Oh! what was I thinking about? I was thinking about Moscow, about the back of your head."

"Why should I, of all people, have such happiness! It's unnatural, too good," he said, kissing her hand.

"I feel quite the opposite; the better things are, the more natural it seems to me."

"And you've got a little curl loose," he said, carefully turning her head round.

"A little curl, oh yes. No, no, we are busy at our work!"

Work did not progress further, and they darted apart from one another like culprits when Kouzma came in to announce that tea was ready.

"Have they come from the town?" Levin asked Kouzma.

"They've just come; they're unpacking the things."

"Come quickly," she said to him as she went out of the study, "or else I shall read your letters without you."

Left alone, after putting his manuscripts together in the new portfolio bought by her, he washed his hands at the new washstand with the elegant fittings, that had all made their appearance with her. Levin smiled at his own thoughts, and shook his head disapprovingly at those thoughts; a feeling akin to remorse fretted him. There was something shameful, effeminate, Capuan, as he called it to himself, in his present mode of life. "It's not right to go on like this," he thought. "It'll soon be three months, and I'm doing next to nothing. To-day, almost for the first time, I set to work seriously, and what happened? I did nothing but begin and throw it aside. Even my ordinary pursuits I have almost given up. On the land I scarcely walk or drive about at all to look after things. Either I am loath to leave her, or I see she's dull alone. And I used to think that, before marriage, life was nothing much, somehow didn't count, but that after marriage, life began in earnest. And here almost three months have passed, and I have spent my time so idly and unprofitably. No, this won't do; I must begin. Of course, it's not her fault. She's not to blame in any way. I ought myself to be firmer, to maintain my masculine independence of action; or else I shall get into such ways, and she'll get used to them too. . . . Of course she's not to blame," he told himself.

But it is hard for anyone who is dissatisfied not to blame some one else, and especially the person nearest of all to them, for the ground of his dissatisfaction. And it vaguely came into Levin's mind that she herself was not to blame (she could not be to blame for anything), but what was to blame was her education, too superficial and frivolous. ("That fool Tcharsky: she wanted, I know, to stop him, but didn't know how to.") "Yes, apart from her interest in the house (that she has), apart from dress and *broderie anglaise*, she has no serious interests. No interest in her work, in the estate, in the peasants, nor in music, though she's rather good at it, nor in reading. She does nothing, and is perfectly satisfied." Levin, in his heart, censured this, and did not as yet understand that she was preparing for that period of activity which was to come for her when she would at once be the wife of her husband and mistress of the house, and would bear, and nurse, and bring up children. He knew not that she was instinctively aware of this, and preparing herself for this time of terrible toil, did not reproach herself for the moments of carelessness and happiness in her love that she enjoyed now while gaily building her nest for the future.

CHAPTER XVI

When Levin went up-stairs, his wife was sitting near the new silver samovar behind the new tea-service, and, having settled old Agafea Mihalovna at a little table with a full cup of tea, was reading a letter from Dolly, with whom they were in continual and frequent correspondence.

"You see, your good lady's settled me here, told me to sit a bit with her," said Agafea Mihalovna, smiling affectionately at Kitty.

In these words of Agafea Mihalovna, Levin read the final act of the drama which had been enacted of late between her and Kitty. He saw that, in spite of Agafea Mihalovna's feelings being hurt by a new mistress taking the reins of government out of her hands, Kitty had yet conquered her and made her love her.

"Here, I opened your letter too," said Kitty, handing him an illiterate letter. "It's from that woman, I think, your brother's . . ." she said. "I did not read it through. This is from my people and from Dolly. Fancy! Dolly took Tanya and Grisha to a children's ball at the Sarmatskys': Tanya was a French marquise."

But Levin did not hear her. Flushing, he took the letter from Marya Nikolaevna, his brother's former mistress, and began to read it. This was the second letter he had received from Marya Nikolaevna. In the first letter, Marya Nikolaevna wrote that his brother had sent her away for no fault of hers, and, with touching simplicity, added that though she was in want again, she asked for nothing, and wished for nothing, but was only tormented by the thought that Nikolay Dmitrievitch would come to grief without her, owing to the weak state of his health, and begged his brother to look after him. Now she wrote quite differently. She had found Nikolay Dmitrievitch, had again made it up with him in Moscow, and had moved with him to a provincial town, where he had received a post in the government service. But that he had quarreled with the head official, and was on his way back to Moscow, only he had been taken so ill on the road that it was doubtful if he would ever leave his bed again, she wrote. "It's always of you he has talked, and, besides, he has no more money left."

"Read this; Dolly writes about you," Kitty was beginning, with a smile; but she stopped suddenly, noticing the changed expression on her husband's face.

"What is it? What's the matter?"

"She writes to me that Nikolay, my brother, is at death's door. I shall go to him."

Kitty's face changed at once. Thoughts of Tanya as a marquise, of Dolly, all had vanished.

"When are you going?" she said.

"To-morrow."

"And I will go with you, can I?" she said.

"Kitty! What are you thinking of?" he said reproachfully.

"How do you mean?" offended that he should seem to take her suggestion unwillingly and with vexation. "Why shouldn't I go? I shan't be in your way. I . . ."

"I'm going because my brother is dying," said Levin. "Why should you . . ."

"Why? For the same reason as you."

"And, at a moment of such gravity for me, she only thinks of of her being dull by herself," thought Levin. And this lack of candor in a matter of such gravity infuriated him.

"It's out of the question," he said sternly.

Agafea Mihalovna, seeing that it was coming to a quarrel, gently put down her cup and withdrew. Kitty did not even notice her. The tone in which her husband had said the last words wounded her, especially because he evidently did not believe what she had said.

"I tell you, that if you go, I shall come with you; I shall certainly come," she said hastily and wrathfully. "Why out of the question? Why do you say it's out of the question?"

"Because it'll be going God knows where, by all sorts of roads and to all sorts of hotels. You would be a hindrance to me," said Levin, trying to be cool.

"Not at all. I don't want anything. Where you can go, I can. . . ."

"Well, for one thing then, because this woman's there whom you can't meet."

"I don't know and don't care to know who's there and what. I know that my husband's brother is dying and my husband is going to him, and I go with my husband too. . . ."

"Kitty! Don't get angry. But just think a little: this is a matter of such importance that I can't bear to think that you should bring in a feeling of weakness, of dislike to being left alone. Come, you'll be dull alone, so go and stay at Moscow a little."

"There, you always ascribe base, vile motives to me," she said with tears of wounded pride and fury. "I didn't mean, it wasn't weakness, it wasn't . . . I feel that it's my duty to be with my husband when he's in trouble, but you try on purpose to hurt me, you try on purpose not to understand. . . ."

"No; this is awful! To be such a slave!" cried Levin, getting up, and unable to restrain his anger any longer. But at the same second he felt that he was beating himself.

"Then why did you marry? You could have been free. Why

did you, if you regret it?" she said, getting up and running away into the drawing-room.

When he went to her, she was sobbing.

He began to speak, trying to find words not to dissuade but simply to soothe her. But she did not heed him, and would not agree to anything. He bent down to her and took her hand, which resisted him. He kissed her hand, kissed her hair, kissed her hand again—still she was silent. But when he took her face in both his hands and said "Kitty!" she suddenly recovered herself, and began to cry, and they were reconciled.

It was decided that they should go together the next day. Levin told his wife that he believed she wanted to go simply in order to be of use, agreed that Marya Nikolaevna's being with his brother did not make her going improper, but he set off at the bottom of his heart dissatisfied both with her and with himself. He was dissatisfied with her for being unable to make up her mind to let him go when it was necessary (and how strange it was for him to think that he, so lately hardly daring to believe in such happiness as that she could love him—now was unhappy because she loved him too much!), and he was dissatisfied with himself for not showing more strength of will. Even greater was the feeling of disagreement at the bottom of his heart as to her not needing to consider the woman who was with his brother, and he thought with horror of all the contingencies they might meet with. The mere idea of his wife, his Kitty, being in the same room with a common wench, set him shuddering with horror and loathing.

CHAPTER XVII

THE hotel of the provincial town where Nikolay Levin was lying ill was one of those provincial hotels which are constructed on the newest model of modern improvements, with the best intentions of cleanliness, comfort, and even elegance, but owing to the public that patronizes them, are with astounding rapidity transformed into filthy taverns with a pretension of modern improvement that only makes them worse than the old-fashioned, honestly filthy hotels. This hotel had already reached that stage, and the soldier in a filthy uniform smoking in the entry, supposed to stand for a hall-porter, and the cast-iron, slippery, dark, and disagreeable staircase, and the free and easy waiter in a filthy frock coat, and the common dining-room with a dusty bouquet of wax flowers adorning the table, and filth, dust, and disorder everywhere, and at the same time the sort of modern up-to-date self-complacent railway uneasiness of this hotel, aroused a most painful feeling in Levin after their fresh young life, especially because the impression of falsity made by the hotel was so out of keeping with what awaited them.

As is invariably the case, after they had been asked at what price they wanted rooms, it appeared that there was not one decent room for them; one decent room had been taken by the inspector of railroads, another by a lawyer from Moscow, a third by Princess Astafieva from the country. There remained only one filthy room, next to which they promised that another should be empty by the evening. Feeling angry with his wife because what he had expected had come to pass, which was that at the moment of arrival, when his heart throbbed with emotion and anxiety to know how his brother was getting on, he should have to be seeing after her, instead of rushing straight to his brother, Levin conducted her to the room assigned them.

"Go, do go!" she said, looking at him with timid and guilty eyes.

He went out of the door without a word, and at once stumbled over Marya Nikolaevna, who had heard of his arrival and had not dared to go in to see him. She was just the same as when he saw her in Moscow; the same woolen gown, and bare arms and neck, and the same good-naturedly stupid, pockmarked face, only a little plumper.

"Well, how is he? how is he?"

"Very bad. He can't get up. He has kept expecting you. He . . . Are you . . . with your wife?"

Levin did not for the first moment understand what it was confused her, but she immediately enlightened him.

"I'll go away. I'll go down to the kitchen," she brought out. "Nikolay Dmitrievitch will be delighted. He heard about it, and knows your lady, and remembers her abroad."

Levin realized that she meant his wife, and did not know what answer to make.

"Come along, come along to him!" he said.

But as soon as he moved, the door of his room opened and Kitty peeped out. Levin crimsoned both from shame and anger with his wife, who had put herself and him in such a difficult position; but Marya Nikolaevna crimsoned still more. She positively shrank together and flushed to the point of tears, and clutching the ends of her apron in both hands, twisted them in her red fingers without knowing what to say and what to do.

For the first instant Levin saw an expression of eager curiosity in the eyes with which Kitty looked at this awful woman, so incomprehensible to her; but it lasted only a single instant.

"Well! how is he?" she turned to her husband and then to her.

"But one can't go on talking in the passage like this!" Levin said, looking angrily at a gentleman who walked jauntily at that instant across the corridor, as though about his affairs.

"Well then, come in," said Kitty, turning to Marya Nikolaevna, who had recovered herself, but noticing her husband's face of dismay, "or go on; go, and then come for me," she said, and went back into the room.

Levin went to his brother's room. He had not in the least expected what he saw and felt in his brother's room. He had expected to find him in the same state of self-deception which he had heard was so frequent with the consumptive, and which had struck him so much during his brother's visit in the autumn. He had expected to find the physical signs of the approach of death more marked — greater weakness, greater emaciation, but still almost the same condition of things. He had expected himself to feel the same

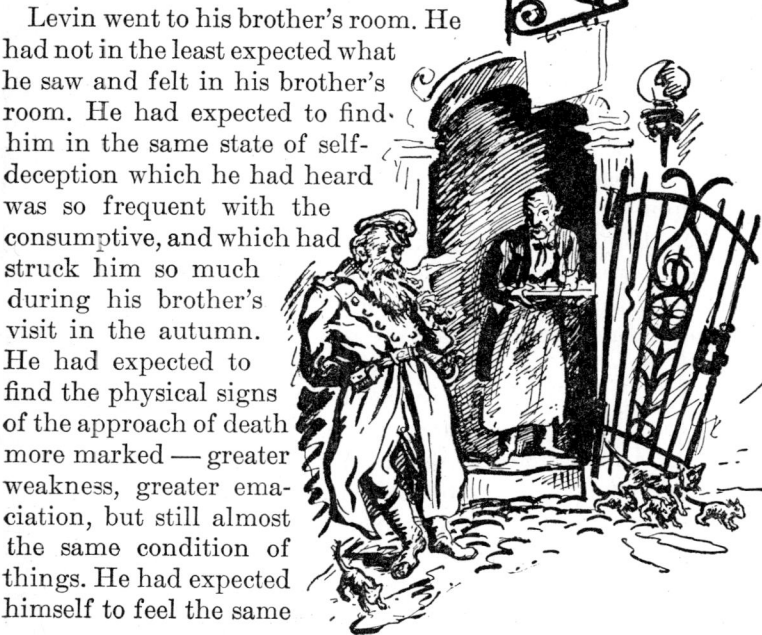

distress at the loss of the brother he loved and the same horror in face of death as he had felt then, only in a greater degree. And he had prepared himself for this; but he found something utterly different.

In a little dirty room with the painted panels of its walls filthy with spittle, and conversation audible through the thin partition from the next room, in a stifling atmosphere saturated with impurities, on a bedstead moved away from the wall, there lay covered with a quilt, a body. One arm of this body was above the quilt, and the wrist, huge as a rake-handle, was attached, inconceivably it seemed, to the thin, long bone of the arm smooth from the beginning to the middle. The head lay sideways on the pillow. Levin could see the scanty locks wet with sweat on the temples and tense, transparent-looking forehead.

"It cannot be that that fearful body was my brother Nikolay?" thought Levin. But he went closer, saw the face, and doubt became impossible. In spite of the terrible change in the face, Levin had only to glance at those eager eyes raised at his approach, only to catch the faint movement of the mouth under the sticky mustache, to realize the terrible truth that this death-like body was his living brother.

The glittering eyes looked sternly and reproachfully at his brother as he drew near. And immediately this glance established a living relationship between living men. Levin immediately felt the reproach in the eyes fixed on him, and felt remorse at his own happiness.

When Konstantin took him by the hand, Nikolay smiled. The smile was faint, scarcely perceptible, and in spite of the smile the stern expression of the eyes was unchanged.

"You did not expect to find me like this," he articulated with effort.

"Yes . . . no," said Levin, hesitating over his words. "How was it you didn't let me know before, that is, at the time of my wedding? I made inquiries in all directions."

He had to talk so as not to be silent, and he did not know what to say, especially as his brother made no reply, and simply stared without dropping his eyes, and evidently penetrated to the inner meaning of each word. Levin told his brother that his wife had come with him. Nikolay expressed pleasure, but said he was afraid of frightening her by his condition. A silence followed. Suddenly Nikolay stirred, and began to say something. Levin expected something of peculiar gravity and importance from the expression of his face, but Nikolay began speaking of his health. He found fault with the doctor, regretting he had not a celebrated Moscow doctor. Levin saw that he still hoped.

Seizing the first moment of silence, Levin got up, anxious to escape, if only for an instant, from his agonizing emotion, and said that he would go and fetch his wife.

"Very well, and I'll tell her to tidy up here. It's dirty and stinking here, I expect. Marya! clear up the room," the sick man said with effort. "Oh, and when you've cleared up, go away yourself," he added, looking inquiringly at his brother.

Levin made no answer. Going out into the corridor, he stopped short. He had said he would fetch his wife, but now, taking stock of the emotion he was feeling, he decided that he would try on the contrary to persuade her not to go in to the sick man. "Why should she suffer as I am suffering?" he thought.

"Well, how is he?" Kitty asked with a frightened face.

"Oh, it's awful, it's awful! What did you come for?" said Levin.

Kitty was silent for a few seconds, looking timidly and ruefully at her husband; then she went up and took him by the elbow with both hands.

"Kostya! take me to him; it will be easier for us to bear it together. You only take me, take me to him, please, and go away," she said. "You must understand that for me to see you, and not to see him, is far more painful. There I might be a help to you and to him. Please, let me!" she besought her husband, as though the happiness of her life depended on it.

Levin was obliged to agree, and regaining his composure, and completely forgetting about Marya Nikolaevna by now, he went again in to his brother with Kitty.

Stepping lightly, and continually glancing at her husband, showing him a valorous and sympathetic face, Kitty went into the sick-room, and, turning without haste, noiselessly closed the door. With inaudible steps she went quickly to the sick man's bedside, and going up so that he had not to turn his head, she immediately clasped in her fresh young hand the skeleton of his huge hand, pressed it, and began speaking with that soft eagerness, sympathetic and not jarring, which is peculiar to women.

"We have met, though we were not acquainted, at Soden," she said. "You never thought I was to be your sister?"

"You would not have recognized me?" he said, with a radiant smile at her entrance.

"Yes, I should. What a good thing you let us know! Not a day has passed that Kostya has not mentioned you, and been anxious."

But the sick man's interest did not last long.

Before she had finished speaking, there had come back into his face the stern, reproachful expression of the dying man's envy of the living.

"I am afraid you are not quite comfortable here," she said, turning away from his fixed stare, and looking about the room. "We must ask about another room," she said to her husband, "so that we might be nearer."

CHAPTER XVIII

LEVIN could not look calmly at his brother; he could not himself be natural and calm in his presence. When he went in to the sick man, his eyes and his attention were unconsciously dimmed, and he did not see and did not distinguish the details of his brother's position. He smelt the awful odor, saw the dirt, disorder, and miserable condition, and heard the groans, and felt that nothing could be done to help. It never entered his head to analyze the details of the sick man's situation, to consider how that body was lying under the quilt, how those emaciated legs and thighs and spine were lying huddled up, and whether they could not be made more comfortable, whether anything could not be done to make things, if not better, at least less bad. It made his blood run cold when he began to think of all these details. He was absolutely convinced that nothing could be done to prolong his brother's life or to relieve his suffering. But a sense of his regarding all aid as out of the question was felt by the sick man, and exasperated him. And this made it still more painful for Levin. To be in the sick-room was agony to him, not to be there still worse. And he was continually, on various pretexts, going out of the room, and coming in again, because he was unable to remain alone.

But Kitty thought, and felt, and acted quite differently. On seeing the sick man, she pitied him. And pity in her womanly heart did not arouse at all that feeling of horror and loathing that it aroused in her husband, but a desire to act, to find out all the details of his state, and to remedy them. And since she had not the slightest doubt that it was her duty to help him, she had no doubt either that it was possible, and immediately set to work. The very details, the mere thought of which reduced her husband to terror, immediately engaged her attention. She sent for the doctor, sent to the chemist's, set the maid who had come with her and Marya Nikolaevna to sweep and dust and scrub; she herself washed up something, washed out something else, laid something under the quilt. Something was by her directions brought into the sick-room, something else was carried out. She herself went several times to her room, regardless of the men she met in the corridor, got out and brought in sheets, pillow-cases, towels, and shirts.

The waiter who was busy with a party of engineers dining in the dining-hall, came several times with an irate countenance in answer to her summons, and could not avoid carrying out her orders, as she gave them with such gracious insistence that there was no evading her. Levin did not approve of all this; he did not believe it would be of any good to the patient. Above all, he feared the patient would be angry at it. But the sick man, though he seemed and was indifferent about it, was not angry, but

only abashed, and on the whole as it were interested in what she was doing with him. Coming back from the doctor to whom Kitty had sent him, Levin, on opening the door, came upon the sick man at the instant when, by Kitty's directions, they were changing his linen. The long white ridge of his spine, with the huge, prominent shoulderblades and jutting ribs and vertebræ, was bare, and Marya Nikolaevna and the waiter were struggling with the sleeve of the night-shirt, and could not get the long, limp arm into it. Kitty, hurriedly closing the door after Levin, was not looking that way; but the sick man groaned, and she moved rapidly towards him.

"Make haste," she said.

"Oh, don't you come," said the sick man angrily. "I'll do it myself. . . ."

"What say?" queried Marya Nikolaevna. But Kitty heard and saw he was ashamed and uncomfortable at being naked before her.

"I'm not looking, I'm not looking!" she said, putting the arm in. "Marya Nikolaevna, you come this side, you do it," she added.

"Please go for me, there's a little bottle in my small bag," she said, turning to her husband, "you know, in the side pocket; bring it, please, and meanwhile they'll finish clearing up here."

Returning with the bottle, Levin found the sick man settled comfortably and everything about him completely changed. The heavy smell was replaced by the smell of aromatic vinegar, which Kitty with pouting lips and puffed-out, rosy cheeks was squirting through a little pipe. There was no dust visible anywhere, a rug was laid by the bedside. On the table stood medicine bottles and decanters tidily arranged, and the linen needed was folded up there, and Kitty's *broderie anglaise*. On the other table by the patient's bed there were candles and drink and powders. The sick man himself, washed and combed, lay in clean sheets on high raised pillows, in a clean night-shirt with a white collar about his astoundingly thin neck, and with a new expression of hope looked fixedly at Kitty.

The doctor brought by Levin, and found by him at the club, was not the one who had been attending Nikolay Levin, as the patient was dissatisfied with him. The new doctor took up a stethoscope and sounded the patient, shook his head, prescribed medicine, and with extreme minuteness explained first how to take the medicine and then what diet was to be kept to. He advised eggs, raw or hardly cooked, and seltzer water, with warm milk at a certain temperature. When the doctor had gone away the sick man said something to his brother, of which Levin could distinguish only the last words: "Your Katya." By the expression with which he gazed at her, Levin saw that he was praising her. He called indeed to Katya, as he called her.

"I'm much better already," he said. "Why, with you I should have got well long ago. How nice it is!" he took her hand and drew it towards his lips, but as though afraid she would dislike it he changed his mind, let it go, and only stroked it. Kitty took his hand in both hers and pressed it.

"Now turn me over on the left side and go to bed," he said.

No one could make out what he said but Kitty; she alone understood. She understood because she was all the while mentally keeping watch on what he needed.

"On the other side," she said to her husband, "he always sleeps on that side. Turn him over, it's so disagreeable calling the servants. I'm not strong enough. Can you?" she said to Marya Nikolaevna.

"I'm afraid not," answered Marya Nikolaevna.

Terrible as it was to Levin to put his arms round that terrible body, to take hold of that under the quilt, of which he preferred to know nothing, under his wife's influence he made his resolute face that she knew so well, and putting his arms into the bed took hold of the body, but in spite of his own strength he was struck by the strange heaviness of those powerless limbs. While he was turning him over, conscious of the huge emaciated arm about his neck, Kitty swiftly and noiselessly turned the pillow, beat it up and settled in it the sick man's head, smoothing back his hair, which was sticking again to his moist brow.

The sick man kept his brother's hand in his own. Levin felt that he meant to do something with his hand and was pulling it somewhere. Levin yielded with a sinking heart: yes, he drew it to his mouth and kissed it. Levin, shaking with sobs and unable to articulate a word, went out of the room.

CHAPTER XIX

"Thou hast hid these things from the wise and prudent, and hast revealed them unto babes." So Levin thought about his wife as he talked to her that evening.

Levin thought of the text, not because he considered himself "wise and prudent." He did not so consider himself, but he could not help knowing that he had more intellect than his wife and Agafea Mihalovna, and he could not help knowing that when he thought of death, he thought with all the force of his intellect. He knew too that the brains of many great men, whose thoughts he had read, had brooded over death and yet knew not a hundredth part of what his wife and Agafea Mihalovna knew about it. Different as those two women were, Agafea Mihalovna and Katya, as his brother Nikolay had called her, and as Levin particularly liked to call her now, they were quite alike in this. Both knew, without a shade of doubt, what sort of thing life was and what was death, and though neither of them could have answered, and would even not have understood the questions that presented themselves to Levin, both had no doubt of the significance of this event, and were precisely alike in their way of looking at it, which they shared with millions of people. The proof that they knew for a certainty the nature of death lay in the fact that they knew without a second of hesitation how to deal with the dying, and were not frightened of them. Levin and other men like him, though they could have said a great deal about death, obviously did not know this since they were afraid of death, and were absolutely at a loss what to do when people were dying. If Levin had been alone now with his brother Nikolay, he would have looked at him with terror, and with still greater terror waited, and would not have known what else to do.

More than that, he did not know what to say, how to look, how to move. To talk of outside things seemed to him shocking, impossible, to talk of death and depressing subjects—also impossible. To be silent, also impossible. "If I look at him he will think I am studying him, I am afraid; if I don't look at him, he'll think I'm thinking of other things. If I walk on tiptoe, he will be vexed; to tread firmly, I'm ashamed." Kitty evidently did not think of herself, and had no time to think about herself: she was thinking about him because she knew something, and all went well. She told him about herself even and about her wedding, and smiled and sympathized with him and petted him, and talked of cases of recovery and all went well; so then she must know. The proof that her behavior and Agafea Mihalovna's was not instinctive, animal, irrational, was that apart from the physical treatment, the relief of suffering, both Agafea Mihalovna and Kitty required for the dying man something else more important than the physical treatment, and something which had nothing in common with physical conditions. Agafea Mihalovna, speaking of the man just dead, had said: "Well, thank God, he took the sacrament and received absolution; God grant each one of us such a death." Katya in just the same way, besides all her care about linen, bed-sores, drink, found time the very first day to persuade the sick man of the necessity of taking the sacrament and receiving absolution.

On getting back from the sick-room to their own two rooms for the night, Levin sat with hanging head not knowing what to do. Not to speak of supper, of preparing for bed, of considering what they were going to do, he could not even talk to his wife; he was ashamed to. Kitty, on the contrary, was more active than usual. She was even livelier than usual. She ordered supper to be brought, herself unpacked their things, and herself helped to make the beds, and did not even forget to sprinkle them with Persian powder. She showed that alertness, that swiftness of reflection which comes out in men before a battle, in conflict, in the dangerous and decisive moments of life—those moments when a man shows once and for all his value, and that all his past has not been wasted but has been a preparation for these moments.

Everything went rapidly in her hands, and before it was twelve o'clock all their things were arranged cleanly and tidily in her rooms, in such a way that the hotel rooms seemed like home: the beds were made, brushes, combs, looking-glasses were put out, table-napkins were spread.

Levin felt that it was unpardonable to eat, to sleep, to talk even now, and it seemed to him that every movement he made was unseemly. She arranged the brushes, but she did it all so that there was nothing shocking in it.

They could neither of them eat, however, and for a long while they could not sleep, and did not even go to bed.

"I am very glad I persuaded him to receive extreme unction to-morrow," she said, sitting in her dressing-jacket before her folding looking-glass, combing her soft, fragrant hair with a fine comb. "I have never seen it, but I know, mamma has told me, there are prayers said for recovery."

"Do you suppose he can possibly recover?" said Levin, watching a slender tress at the back of her round little head that was continually hidden when she passed the comb through the front.

"I asked the doctor; he said he couldn't live more than three days. But can they be sure? I'm very glad, anyway, that I persuaded him," she said, looking askance at her husband through her hair. "Anything is possible," she added with that peculiar, rather sly expression that was always in her face when she spoke of religion.

Since their conversation about religion when they were engaged neither of them had ever started a discussion of the subject, but she performed all the ceremonies of going to church, saying her prayers, and so on, always with the unvarying conviction that this ought to be so. In spite of his assertion to the contrary, she was firmly persuaded that he was as much a Christian as she, and indeed a far better one; and all that he said about it was simply one of his absurd masculine freaks, just as he would say about her *broderie anglaise,* that good people patch holes but that she cut them on purpose, and so on.

"Yes, you see this woman, Marya Nikolaevna, did not know how to manage all this," said Levin. "And . . . I must own I'm very, very glad you came. You are such purity that . . ." He took her hand and did not kiss it (to kiss her hand in such closeness to death seemed to him improper); he merely squeezed it with a penitent air, looking at her brightening eyes.

"It would have been miserable for you to be alone," she said, and lifting her hands which hid her cheeks flushing with pleasure, twisted her coil of hair on the nape of her neck and pinned it there. "No," she went on, "she did not know how. . . . Luckily, I learned a lot at Soden."

"Surely there are not people there so ill?"

"Worse."

"What's so awful to me is that I can't see him as he was when he was young. You would not believe how charming he was as a youth, but I did not understand him then."

"I can quite, quite believe it. How I feel that we might have been friends!" she said; and, distressed at what she had said, she looked round at her husband, and tears came into her eyes.

"Yes, *might have been*," he said mournfully. "He's just one of those people of whom they say they're not for this world."

"But we have many days before us; we must go to bed," said Kitty, glancing at her tiny watch.

CHAPTER XX

THE next day the sick man received the sacrament and extreme unction. During the ceremony Nikolay Levin prayed fervently. His great eyes, fastened on the holy image that was set out on a card-table covered with a colored napkin, expressed such passionate prayer and hope that it was awful to Levin to see it. Levin knew that this passionate prayer and hope would only make him feel more bitterly parting from the life he so loved. Levin knew his brother and the workings of his intellect: he knew that his unbelief came not from life being easier for him without faith, but had grown up because step by step the contemporary scientific interpretation of natural phenomena crushed out the possibility of faith; and so he knew that his present return was not a legitimate one, brought about by way of the same working of his intellect, but simply a temporary, interested return to faith in a desperate hope of recovery. Levin knew too that Kitty had strengthened his hope by accounts of the marvelous recoveries she had heard of. Levin knew all this; and it was agonizingly painful to him to behold the supplicating, hopeful eyes and the emaciated wrist, lifted with difficulty, making the sign of the cross on the tense brow, and the prominent shoulders and hollow, gasping chest, which one could not feel consistent with the life the sick man was praying for. During the sacrament Levin did what he, an unbeliever, had done a thousand times. He said, addressing God, "If Thou dost exist, make this man to recover" (of course this same thing has been repeated many times), "and Thou wilt save him and me."

After extreme unction the sick man became suddenly much better. He did not cough once in the course of an hour, smiled, kissed Kitty's hand, thanking her with tears, and said he was comfortable, free from pain, and that he felt strong and had an appetite. He even raised himself when his soup was brought, and asked for a cutlet as well. Hopelessly ill as he was, obvious as it was at the first glance that he could not recover, Levin and Kitty were for that hour both in the same state of excitement, happy, though fearful of being mistaken.

"Is he better?"

"Yes, much."

"It's wonderful."

"There's nothing wonderful in it."

"Anyway, he's better," they said in a whisper, smiling to one another.

This self-deception was not of long duration. The sick man fell into a quiet sleep, but he was waked up half an hour later by his cough. And all at once every hope vanished in those about him and in himself. The reality of his suffering crushed all hopes in Levin and Kitty and in the sick man himself, leaving no doubt, no memory even of past hopes.

Without referring to what he had believed in half an hour before, as though ashamed even to recall it, he asked for iodine to inhale in a bottle covered with perforated paper. Levin gave him the bottle, and the same look of passionate hope with which he had taken the sacrament was now fastened on his brother, demanding from him the confirmation of the doctor's words that inhaling iodine worked wonders.

"Is Katya not here?" he gasped, looking round while Levin reluctantly assented to the doctor's words. "No; so I can say it. . . . It was for her sake I went through that farce. She's so sweet; but you and I can't deceive ourselves. This is what I be-

lieve in," he said, and, squeezing the bottle in his bony hand, he began breathing over it.

At eight o'clock in the evening Levin and his wife were drinking tea in their room, when Marya Nikolaevna ran in to them breathlessly. She was pale, and her lips were quivering. "He is dying!" she whispered. "I'm afraid he will die this minute."

Both of them ran to him. He was sitting raised up with one elbow on the bed, his long back bent, and his head hanging low.

"How do you feel?" Levin asked in a whisper, after a silence.

"I feel I'm setting off," Nikolay said with difficulty, but with extreme distinctness, screwing the words out of himself. He did not raise his head, but simply turned his eyes upwards, without their reaching his brother's face. "Katya, go away!" he added.

Levin jumped up, and with a peremptory whisper made her go out.

"I'm setting off," he said again.

"Why do you think so?" said Levin, so as to say something.

"Because I'm setting off," he repeated, as though he had a liking for the phrase. "It's the end."

Marya Nikolaevna went up to him.

"You had better lie down; you'd be easier," she said.

"I shall lie down soon enough," he pronounced slowly, "when I'm dead," he said sarcastically, wrathfully. "Well, you can lay me down if you like."

Levin laid his brother on his back, sat down beside him, and gazed at his face, holding his breath. The dying man lay with closed eyes, but the muscles twitched from time to time on his forehead, as with one thinking deeply and intensely. Levin involuntarily thought with him of what it was that was happening to him now, but in spite of all his mental efforts to go along with him he saw by the expression of that calm, stern face that for the dying man all was growing clearer and clearer that was still as dark as ever for Levin.

"Yes, yes, so," the dying man articulated slowly at intervals. "Wait a little." He was silent. "Right!" he pronounced all at once reassuringly, as though all were solved for him. "O Lord!" he murmured, and sighed deeply.

Marya Nikolaevna felt his feet. "They're getting cold," she whispered.

For a long while, a very long while it seemed to Levin, the sick man lay motionless. But he was still alive, and from time to time he sighed. Levin by now was exhausted from mental strain. He felt that, with no mental effort, could he understand what it was that was *right*. He could not even think of the problem of death itself, but with no will of his own thoughts kept coming to him of what he had to do next; closing the dead man's eyes, dressing him, ordering the coffin. And, strange to say, he felt utterly cold, and was not conscious of sorrow nor of loss, less still of pity for his brother. If he had any feeling for his brother at that moment, it was envy for the knowledge the dying man had now that he could not have.

A long time more he sat over him so, continually expecting the end. But the end did not come. The door opened and Kitty appeared. Levin got up to stop her. But at the moment he was getting up, he caught the sound of the dying man stirring.

"Don't go away," said Nikolay and held out his hand. Levin gave him his, and angrily waved to his wife to go away.

With the dying man's hand in his hand, he sat for half an hour, an hour, another hour. He did not think of death at all now. He wondered what Kitty was doing; who lived in the next room; whether the doctor lived in a house of his own. He longed for food and for sleep. He cautiously drew away his hand and felt the feet. The feet were cold, but the sick man was still breathing. Levin tried again to move away on tiptoe, but the sick man stirred again and said: "Don't go."

. . . . .

The dawn came; the sick man's condition was unchanged. Levin stealthily withdrew his hand, and without looking at the dying man, went off to his own room and went to sleep. When he woke up, instead of news of his brother's death which he expected, he learned that the sick man had returned to his earlier condition. He had begun sitting up again, coughing, had begun eating again, talking again, and again had ceased to talk of death, again had begun to express hope of his recovery, and had become more irritable and gloomier than ever. No one, neither his brother nor Kitty, could soothe him. He was angry with every one, and said nasty things to every one, reproached every one for his sufferings, and insisted that they should get him a celebrated doctor from Moscow. To all inquiries made him as to how he felt, he made the same answer with an expression of vindictive reproachfulness, "I'm suffering horribly, intolerably!"

The sick man was suffering more and more, especially from bedsores, which it was impossible now to remedy, and grew more and more angry with every one about him, blaming them for everything, and especially for not having brought him a doctor from Moscow. Kitty tried in every possible way to relieve him, to soothe him; but it was all in vain, and Levin saw that she herself was exhausted both physically and morally, though she would not admit it. The sense of death, which had been evoked in all by his taking leave of life on the night when he had sent for his brother, was broken up. Every one knew that he must inevitably die soon, that he was half dead already. Every one wished for nothing but that he should die as soon as possible, and every one, concealing this, gave him medicines, tried to find remedies and doctors, and deceived him and themselves and each other. All this was falsehood, disgusting, irreverent deceit. And owing to the bent of his character, and because he loved the dying man more than any one else did, Levin was most painfully conscious of this deceit.

Levin, who had long been possessed by the idea of reconciling his brothers, at least in face of death, had written to his brother, Sergey Ivanovitch, and having received an answer from him, he read this letter to the sick man. Sergey Ivanovitch wrote that he could not come himself, and in touching terms he begged his brother's forgiveness.

The sick man said nothing.

"What am I to write to him?" said Levin. "I hope you are not angry with him?"

"No, not the least!" Nikolay answered, vexed at the question. "Tell him to send me a doctor."

Three more days of agony followed; the sick man was still in the same condition. The sense of longing for his death was felt by every one now at the mere sight of him, by the waiters and the hotel-keeper and all the people staying in the hotel, and the doctor and Marya Nikolaevna and Levin and Kitty. The sick man alone did not express this feeling, but on the contrary was furious at their not getting him doctors, and went on taking medicine and talking of life. Only at rare moments, when the opium gave him an instant's relief from the never-ceasing pain, he would sometimes, half asleep, utter what was ever more intense in his heart than in all the others: "Oh, if it were only the end!" or: "When will it be over?"

His sufferings, steadily growing more intense, did their work and prepared him for death. There was no position in which he was not in pain, there was not a minute in which he was unconscious of it, not a limb, not a part of his body that did not ache and cause him agony. Even the memories, the impressions, the thoughts of this body awakened in him now the same aversion as the body itself. The sight of other people, their remarks, his own reminiscences, everything was for him a source of agony. Those about him felt this, and instinctively did not allow themselves to move freely, to talk, to express their wishes before him. All his life was merged in the one feeling of suffering and desire to be rid of it.

There was evidently coming over him that revulsion that would make him look upon death as the goal of his desires, as happiness. Hitherto each individual desire, aroused by suffering or privation, such as hunger, fatigue, thirst, had been satisfied by some bodily function giving pleasure. But now no physical craving or suffering received relief, and the effort to relieve them only caused fresh suffering. And so all desires were merged in one—the desire to be rid of all his sufferings and their source, the body. But he had no words to express this desire of deliverance, and so he did not speak of it, and from habit asked for the satisfaction of desires which could not now be satisfied. "Turn me over on the other side," he would say, and immediately after he would ask to be turned back again as before. "Give me some broth. Take away the broth. Talk of something: why are you silent?" And directly they began to talk he would close his eyes, and would show weariness, indifference, and loathing.

On the tenth day from their arrival at the town, Kitty was unwell. She suffered from headache and sickness, and she could not get up all the morning.

The doctor opined that the indisposition arose from fatigue and excitement, and prescribed rest.

After dinner, however, Kitty got up and went as usual with her work to the sick man. He looked at her sternly when she came in, and smiled contemptuously when she said she had been unwell. That day he was continually blowing his nose, and groaning piteously.

"How do you feel?" she asked him.

"Worse," he articulated with difficulty. "In pain!"

"In pain, where?"

"Everywhere."

"It will be over to-day, you will see," said Marya Nikolaevna. Though it was said in a whisper, the sick man, whose hearing Levin had noticed was very keen, must have heard. Levin said hush to her, and looked round at the sick man. Nikolay had heard; but these words produced no effect on him. His eyes had still the same intense, reproachful look.

"Why do you think so?" Levin asked her, when she had followed him into the corridor.

"He has begun picking at himself," said Marya Nikolaevna.

"How do you mean?"

"Like this," she said, tugging at the folds of her woolen skirt. Levin noticed, indeed, that all that day the patient pulled at himself, as it were, trying to snatch something away.

Marya Nikolaevna's prediction came true. Towards night the sick man was not able to lift his hands, and could only gaze before him with the same intensely concentrated expression in his eyes. Even when his brother or Kitty bent over him, so that he could see them, he looked just the same. Kitty sent for the priest to read the prayer for the dying.

While the priest was reading it, the dying man did not show any sign of life; his eyes were closed. Levin, Kitty, and Marya Nikolaevna stood at the bedside. The priest had not quite finished reading the prayer when the dying man stretched, sighed, and opened his eyes. The priest, on finishing the prayer, put the cross to the cold forehead, then slowly returned it to the stand, and after standing for two minutes more in silence, he touched the huge, bloodless hand that was turning cold.

"He is gone," said the priest, and would have moved away; but suddenly there was a faint stir in the mustaches of the dead man that seemed glued together, and quite distinctly in the hush they heard from the bottom of the chest the sharply defined sounds:

"Not quite . . . soon."

And a minute later the face brightened, a smile came out under the mustaches, and the women who had gathered round began carefully laying out the corpse.

The sight of his brother, and the nearness of death, revived in Levin that sense of horror in face of the insoluble enigma, together with the nearness and inevitability of death, that had come upon him that autumn evening when his brother had come to him. This feeling was now even stronger than before; even less than before did he feel capable of apprehending the meaning of death, and its inevitability rose up before him more terrible than ever. But now, thanks to his wife's presence, that feeling did not reduce him to despair. In spite of death, he felt the need of life and love. He felt that love saved him from despair, and that this love, under the menace of despair, had become still stronger and purer. The one mystery of death, still unsolved, had scarcely passed before his eyes, when another mystery had arisen, as insoluble, urging him to love and to life.

The doctor confirmed his suppositions in regard to Kitty. Her indisposition was a symptom that she was with child.

CHAPTER XXI

From the moment when Alexey Alexandrovitch understood from his interviews with Betsy and with Stepan Arkadyevitch that all that was expected of him was to leave his wife in peace, without burdening her with his presence, and that his wife herself desired this, he felt so distraught that he could come to no decision of himself; he did not know himself what he wanted now, and putting himself in the hands of those who were so pleased to interest themselves in his affairs, he met everything with unqualified assent. It was only when Anna had left his house, and the English governess sent to ask him whether she should dine with him or separately, that for the first time he clearly comprehended his position, and was appalled by it. Most difficult of all in this position was the fact that he could not in any way connect and reconcile his past with what was now. It was not the past when he had lived happily with his wife that troubled him. The transition from that past to a knowledge of his wife's unfaithfulness he had lived through miserably already; that state was painful, but he could understand it. If his wife had then, on declaring to him her unfaithfulness, left him, he would have been wounded, unhappy, but he would not have been in the hopeless position—incomprehensible to himself—in which he felt himself now. He could not now reconcile his immediate past, his tenderness, his love for his sick wife, and for the other man's child with what was now the case, that is with the fact that, as it were, in return for all this he now found himself alone, put to shame, a laughing-stock, needed by no one, and despised by every one.

For the first two days after his wife's departure Alexey Alexandrovitch received applicants for assistance and his chief secretary, drove to the committee, and went down to dinner in the dining-room as usual. Without giving himself a reason for what he was doing, he strained every nerve of his being for those two days, simply to preserve an appearance of composure, and even of indifference. Answering inquiries about the disposition of Anna Arkadyevna's rooms and belongings, he had exercised immense self-control to appear like a man in whose eyes what had occurred was not unforeseen nor out of the ordinary course of events, and he attained his aim: no one could have detected in him signs of despair. But on the second day after her departure, when Korney gave him a bill from a fashionable draper's shop, which Anna had forgotten to pay, and announced that the clerk from the shop was waiting, Alexey Alexandrovitch told him to show the clerk up.

"Excuse me, your excellency, for venturing to trouble you. But if you direct us to apply to her excellency, would you graciously oblige us with her address?"

Alexey Alexandrovitch pondered, as it seemed to the clerk, and all at once, turning round, he sat down to the table. Letting his head sink into his hands, he sat for a long while in that position, several times attempted to speak and stopped short. Korney, perceiving his master's emotion, asked the clerk to call another time. Left alone, Alexey Alexandrovitch recognized that he had not the strength to keep up the line of firmness and composure any longer. He gave orders for the carriage that was awaiting him to be taken back, and for no one to be admitted, and he did not go down to dinner.

He felt that he could not endure the weight of universal contempt and exasperation, which he had distinctly seen in the face of the clerk and of Korney, and every one, without exception, whom he had met during those two days. He felt that he could not turn aside from himself the hatred of men, because that hatred did not come from his being bad (in that case he could have tried to be better), but from his being shamefully and repulsively unhappy. He knew that for this, for the very fact that his heart was torn with grief, they would be merciless to him. He felt that men would crush him as dogs strangle a torn dog yelping with pain. He knew that his sole means of security against people was to hide his wounds from them, and instinctively he tried to do this for two days, but now he felt incapable of keeping up the unequal struggle.

His despair was even intensified by the consciousness that he was utterly alone in his sorrow. In all Petersburg there was not a human being to whom he could express what he was feeling, who would feel for him, not as a high official, not as a member of society, but simply as a suffering man; indeed he had not such a one in the whole world.

Alexey Alexandrovitch grew up an orphan. There were two brothers. They did not remember their father, and their mother died when Alexey Alexandrovitch was ten years old. The property was a small one. Their uncle, Karenin, a government official of high standing, at one time a favorite of the late Tsar, had brought them up.

On completing his high school and university courses with medals, Alexey Alexandrovitch had, with his uncle's aid, immediately started in a prominent position in the service, and from that time forward he had devoted himself exclusively to political ambition. In the high school and the university, and afterwards in the service, Alexey Alexandrovitch had never formed a close friendship with any one. His brother had been the person nearest to his heart, but he had a post in the Ministry of Foreign Affairs, and was always abroad, where he had died shortly after Alexey Alexandrovitch's marriage.

While he was governor of a province, Anna's aunt, a wealthy provincial lady, had thrown him—middle-aged as he was, though young for a governor—with her niece, and had succeeded in putting him in such a position that he had either to declare himself or to leave the town. Alexey Alexandrovitch was not long in hesitation. There were at the time as many reasons for the step as against it, and there was no over-balancing consideration to outweigh his invariable rule of abstaining when in doubt. But Anna's aunt had through a common acquaintance insinuated that he had already compromised the girl, and that he was in honor bound to make her an offer. He made the offer, and concentrated on his betrothed and his wife all the feeling of which he was capable.

The attachment he felt to Anna precluded in his heart every need of intimate relations with others. And now among all his acquaintances he had not one friend. He had plenty of so-called connections, but no friendships. Alexey Alexandrovitch had plenty of people whom he could invite to dinner, to whose sympathy he could appeal in any public affair he was concerned about, whose interest he could reckon upon for any one he wished to help, with whom he could candidly discuss other people's business and affairs of state. But his relations with these people were confined to one clearly defined channel, and had a certain routine from which it was impossible to depart. There was one man, a comrade of his at the university, with whom he had made friends later, and with whom he could have spoken of a personal sorrow; but this friend had a post in the Department of Education in a remote part of Russia. Of the people in Petersburg the most intimate and most possible were his chief secretary and his doctor.

Mihail Vassilievitch Sludin, the chief secretary, was a straightforward, intelligent, good-hearted, and conscientious man, and Alexey Alexandrovitch was aware of his personal good-will. But their five years of official work together seemed to have put a barrier between them that cut off warmer relations.

After signing the papers brought him, Alexey Alexandrovitch had sat for a long while in silence, glancing at Mihail Vassilievitch, and several times he attempted to speak, but could not. He had already prepared the phrase: "You have heard of my trouble?" But he ended by saying, as usual: "So you'll get this ready for me?" and with that dismissed him.

The other person was the doctor, who had also a kindly feeling for him; but there had long existed a taciturn understanding between them that both were weighed down by work, and always in a hurry.

Of his women-friends, foremost amongst them Countess Lidia Ivanovna, Alexey Alexandrovitch never thought. All women, simply as women, were terrible and distasteful to him.

CHAPTER XXII

ALEXEY ALEXANDROVITCH had forgotten the Countess Lidia Ivanovna, but she had not forgotten him. At the bitterest moment of his lonely despair she came to him, and without waiting to be announced, walked straight into his study. She found him as he was sitting with his head in both hands.

"*J'ai forcé la consigne,*" she said, walking in with rapid steps and breathing hard with excitement and rapid exercise. "I have heard all! Alexey Alexandrovitch! Dear friend!" she went on, warmly squeezing his hand in both of hers and gazing with her fine pensive eyes into his.

Alexey Alexandrovitch, frowning, got up, and disengaging his hand, moved her a chair.

"Won't you sit down, countess? I'm seeing no one because I'm unwell, countess," he said, and his lips twitched.

"Dear friend!" repeated Countess Lidia Ivanovna, never taking her eyes off his, and suddenly her eyebrows rose at the inner corners, describing a triangle on her forehead, her ugly yellow face became still uglier, but Alexey Alexandrovitch felt that she was sorry for him and was preparing to cry. And he too was softened; he snatched her plump hand and proceeded to kiss it.

"Dear friend!" she said in a voice breaking with emotion. "You ought not to give way to grief. Your sorrow is a great one, but you ought to find consolation."

"I am crushed, I am annihilated, I am no longer a man!" said

Alexey Alexandrovitch, letting go her hand, but still gazing into her brimming eyes. "My position is so awful because I can find nowhere, I cannot find within me strength to support me."

"You will find support; seek it—not in me, though I beseech you to believe in my friendship," she said, with a sigh. "Our support is love, that love that He has vouchsafed us. His burden is light," she said, with the look of ecstasy Alexey Alexandrovitch knew so well. "He will be your support and your succor."

Although there was in these words a flavor of that sentimental emotion at her own lofty feelings, and that new mystical fervor which had lately gained ground in Petersburg, and which seemed to Alexey Alexandrovitch disproportionate, still it was pleasant to him to hear this now.

"I am weak. I am crushed. I foresaw nothing, and now I understand nothing."

"Dear friend," repeated Lidia Ivanovna.

"It's not the loss of what I have not now, it's not that!" pursued Alexey Alexandrovitch. "I do not grieve for that. But I cannot help feeling humiliated before other people for the position I am placed in. It is wrong, but I can't help it, I can't help it."

"Not you it was performed that noble act of forgiveness, at which I was moved to ecstasy, and every one else too, but He, working within your heart," said Countess Lidia Ivanovna, raising her eyes rapturously, "and so you cannot be ashamed of your act."

Alexey Alexandrovitch knitted his brows, and crooking his hands, he cracked his fingers.

"One must know all the facts," he said in his thin voice. "A man's strength has its limits, countess, and I have reached my limits. The whole day I have had to be making arrangements, arrangements about household matters arising" (he emphasized the word *arising*) "from my new, solitary position. The servants, the governess, the accounts . . . These pinpricks have stabbed me to the heart, and I have not the strength to bear it. At dinner . . . yesterday, I was almost getting up from the dinner-table. I could not bear the way my son looked at me. He did not ask me the meaning of it all, but he wanted to ask, and I could not bear the look in his eyes. He was afraid to look at me, but that is not all. . . ." Alexey Alexandrovitch would have referred to the bill that had been brought him, but his voice shook, and he stopped. That bill on blue paper, for a hat and ribbons, he could not recall without a rush of self-pity.

"I understand, dear friend," said Lidia Ivanovna. "I understand it all. Succor and comfort you will find not in me, though I have come only to aid you if I can. If I could take from off you all these petty, humiliating cares . . . I understand that a woman's word, a woman's superintendence is needed. You will intrust it to me?"

Silently and gratefully Alexey Alexandrovitch pressed her hand.

"Together we will take care of Seryozha. Practical affairs are not my strong point. But I will set to work. I will be your housekeeper. Don't thank me. I do it not from myself . . ."

"I cannot help thanking you."

"But, dear friend, do not give way to the feeling of which you spoke—being ashamed of what is the Christian's highest glory: *he who humbles himself shall be exalted.* And you cannot thank me. You must thank Him, and pray to Him for succor. In Him alone we find peace, consolation, salvation, and love," she said, and turning her eyes heavenwards, she began praying, as Alexey Alexandrovitch gathered from her silence.

Alexey Alexandrovitch listened to her now, and those expressions which had seemed to him, if not distasteful, at least exaggerated, now seemed to him natural and consolatory. Alexey Alexandrovitch had disliked this new enthusiastic fervor. He was a believer, who was interested in religion primarily in its political aspect, and the new doctrine which ventured upon several new interpretations, just because it paved the way to discussion and analysis, was in principle disagreeable to him. He had hitherto taken up a cold and even antagonistic attitude to this new doctrine, and with Countess Lidia Ivanovna, who had been carried away by it, he had never argued, but by silence had assiduously parried her attempts to provoke him into argument. Now for the first time he heard her words with pleasure, and did not inwardly oppose them.

"I am very, very grateful to you, both for your deeds and for your words," he said, when she had finished praying.

Countess Lidia Ivanovna once more pressed both her friend's hands.

"Now I will enter upon my duties," she said with a smile after a pause, as she wiped away the traces of tears. "I am going to Seryozha. Only in the last extremity I shall apply to you." And she got up and went out.

Countess Lidia Ivanovna went into Seryozha's part of the house, and dropping tears on the scared child's cheeks, she told him that his father was a saint and his mother was dead.

Countess Lidia Ivanovna kept her promise. She did actually take upon herself the care of the organization and management of Alexey Alexandrovitch's household. But she had not overstated the case when saying that practical affairs were not her strong point. All her arrangements had to be modified because they could not be carried out, and they were modified by Korney, Alexey Alexandrovitch's valet, who, though no one was aware of the fact, now managed Karenin's household, and quietly and discreetly reported to his master while he was dressing all it was necessary for him to know. But Lidia Ivanovna's help was none the less real; she gave Alexey Alexandrovitch moral support in the consciousness of her love and respect for him, and still more, as it was soothing to her to believe, in that she almost turned him to Christianity—that is, from an indifferent and apathetic believer she turned him into an ardent and steadfast adherent of the new interpretation of Christian doctrine, which had been gaining ground of late in Petersburg. It was easy for Alexey Alexandrovitch to believe in this teaching. Alexey Alexandrovitch, like Lidia Ivanovna indeed, and others who shared their views, was completely devoid of vividness of imagination, that spiritual faculty in virtue of which the conceptions evoked by the imagination become so vivid that they must needs be in harmony with other conceptions, and with actual fact. He saw nothing impossible and inconceivable in the idea that death, though existing for unbelievers, did not exist for him, and that, as he was possessed of the most perfect faith, of the measure of which he was himself the judge, therefore there was no sin in his soul, and he was experiencing complete salvation here on earth.

It is true that the erroneousness and shallowness of this conception of his faith was dimly perceptible to Alexey Alexandrovitch, and he knew that when, without the slightest idea that his forgiveness was the action of a higher power, he had surrendered directly to the feeling of forgiveness, he had felt more happiness than now when he was thinking every instant that Christ was in his heart, and that in signing official papers he was doing His will. But for Alexey Alexandrovitch it was a necessity to think in that way; it was such a necessity for him in his humiliation to have some elevated standpoint, however imaginary, from which, looked down upon by all, he could look down on others, that he clung, as to his one salvation, to his delusion of salvation.

CHAPTER XXIII

The Countess Lidia Ivanovna had, as a very young and sentimental girl, been married to a wealthy man of high rank, an extremely good-natured, jovial, and extremely dissipated rake. Two months after marriage her husband abandoned her, and her impassioned protestations of affection he met with a sarcasm and even hostility that people knowing the count's good heart, and seeing no defects in the sentimental Lidia, were at loss to explain. Though they were divorced and lived apart, yet whenever the husband met the wife, he invariably behaved to her with the same malignant irony, the cause of which was incomprehensible.

Countess Lidia Ivanovna had long given up being in love with her husband, but from that time she had never given up being in love with some one. She was in love with several people at once, both men and women; she had been in love with almost every one who had been particularly distinguished in any way. She was in love with all the new princes and princesses who married into the imperial family; she had been in love with a high dignitary of the Church, a vicar, and a parish priest; she had been in love with a journalist, three Slavophils, with Komissarov, with a minister, a doctor, an English missionary and Karenin. All these passions constantly waning or growing more ardent, did not prevent her from keeping up the most extended and complicated relations with the court and fashionable society. But from the time that after Karenin's trouble she took him under her special protection, from the time that she set to work in Karenin's household looking after his welfare, she felt that all her other attachments were not the real thing, and that she was now genuinely in love, and with no one but Karenin. The feeling she now experienced for him seemed to her stronger than any of her former feelings. Analyzing her feeling, and comparing it with former passions, she distinctly perceived that she would not have been in love with Komissarov if he had not saved the life of the Tsar, that she would not have been in love with Ristitch-Kudzhitsky if there had been no Slavonic question, but that she loved Karenin for himself, for his lofty, uncomprehended soul, for the sweet—to her—high notes of his voice, for his drawling intonation, his weary eyes, his character, and his soft white hands with their swollen veins. She was not simply overjoyed at meeting him, but she sought in his face signs of the impression she was making on him. She tried to please him, not by her words only, but in her whole person. For his sake it was that she now lavished more care on her dress than before. She caught herself in reveries on what might have been, if she had not been married and he had been free. She blushed with emotion when he came into the room, she could not repress a smile of rapture when he said anything amiable to her.

For several days now Countess Lidia Ivanovna had been in a state of intense excitement. She had learned that Anna and Vronsky were in Petersburg. Alexey Alexandrovitch must be saved from seeing her, he must be saved even from the torturing knowledge that that awful woman was in the same town with him, and that he might meet her any minute.

Lidia Ivanovna made inquiries through her friends as to what those *infamous people,* as she called Anna and Vronsky, intended doing, and she endeavored so to guide every movement of her friend during those days that he could not come across them. The young adjutant, an acquaintance of Vronsky, through whom she obtained her information, and who hoped through Countess Lidia Ivanovna to obtain a concession, told her that they had finished their business and were going away next day. Lidia Ivanovna had already begun to calm down, when the next morning a note was brought her, the handwriting of which she recognized with horror. It was the handwriting of Anna Karenina. The envelope was of paper as thick as bark; on the oblong yellow paper there was a huge monogram, and the letter smelt of agreeable scent.

"Who brought it?"

"A commissionaire from the hotel."

It was some time before Countess Lidia Ivanovna could sit down to read the letter. Her excitement brought on an attack of asthma, to which she was subject. When she had recovered her composure, she read the following letter in French:

Madame la Comtesse,

"The Christian feelings with which your heart is filled give me the, I feel, unpardonable boldness to write to you. I am miserable at being separated from my son. I entreat permission to see him once before my departure. Forgive me for recalling myself to your memory. I apply to you and not to Alexey Alexandrovitch, simply because I do not wish to cause that generous man to suffer in remembering me. Knowing your friendship for him, I know you will understand me. Could you send Seryozha to me, or should I come to the house at some fixed hour, or will you let me know when and where I could see him away from home? I do not anticipate a refusal, knowing the magnanimity of him with whom it rests. You cannot conceive the craving I have to see him, and so cannot conceive the gratitude your help will arouse in me."

Anna.

Everything in this letter exasperated Countess Lidia Ivanovna: its contents and the allusion to magnanimity, and especially its free and easy—as she considered—tone.

"Say that there is no answer," said Countess Lidia Ivanovna, and immediately opening her blotting-book, she wrote to Alexey Alexandrovitch that she hoped to see him at one o'clock at the levee.

"I must talk with you of a grave and painful subject. There we will arrange where to meet. Best of all at my house, where I will order tea *as you like it.* Urgent. He lays the cross, but He gives the strength to bear it," she added, so as to give him some slight preparation. Countess Lidia Ivanovna usually wrote some two or three letters a day to Alexey Alexandrovitch. She enjoyed that form of communication, which gave opportunity for a refinement and air of mystery not afforded by their personal interviews.

CHAPTER XXIV

THE levee was drawing to a close. People met as they were going away, and gossiped of the latest news, of the newly bestowed honors and the changes in the positions of the higher functionaries.

"If only Countess Marya Borissovna were Minister of War, and Princess Vatkovskaya were Commander-in-Chief," said a gray-headed, little old man in a gold-embroidered uniform, addressing a tall, handsome maid of honor who had questioned him about the new appointments.

"And me among the adjutants," said the maid of honor, smiling.

"You have an appointment already. You're over the ecclesiastical department. And your assistant's Karenin."

"Good-day, prince!" said the little old man to a man who came up to him.

"What were you saying of Karenin?" said the prince.

"He and Putyatov have received the Alexander Nevsky."

"I thought he had it already."

"No. Just look at him," said the little old man, pointing with his embroidered hat to Karenin in a court uniform with the new red ribbon across his shoulders, standing in the doorway of the hall with an influential member of the Imperial Council. "Pleased and happy as a brass farthing," he added, stopping to shake hands with a handsome gentleman of the bedchamber of colossal proportions.

"No; he's looking older," said the gentleman of the bedchamber.

"From overwork. He's always drawing up projects nowadays. He won't let a poor devil go nowadays till he's explained it all to him under heads."

"Looking older, did you say? *Il fait des passions.* I believe Countess Lidia Ivanovna's jealous now of his wife."

"Oh, come now, please don't say any harm of Countess Lidia Ivanovna."

"Why, is there any harm in her being in love with Karenin?"

"But is it true Madame Karenina's here?"

"Well, not here in the palace, but in Petersburg. I met her yesterday with Alexey Vronsky, *bras dessus, bras dessous*, in the Morsky."

"*C'est un homme qui n'a pas* . . ." the gentleman of the bedchamber was beginning, but he stopped to make room, bowing, for a member of the Imperial family to pass.

Thus people talked incessantly of Alexey Alexandrovitch, finding fault with him and laughing at him, while he, blocking up the way of the member of the Imperial Council he had captured, was explaining to him point by point his new financial project, never interrupting his discourse for an instant for fear he should escape.

Almost at the same time that his wife left Alexey Alexandrovitch there had come to him that bitterest moment in the life of an official—the moment when his upward career comes to a full stop. This full stop had arrived and every one perceived it, but Alexey Alexandrovitch himself was not yet aware that his career was over. Whether it was due to his feud with Stremov, or his misfortune with his wife, or simply that Alexey Alexandrovitch had reached his destined limits, it had become evident to every one in the course of that year that his career was at an end. He still filled a position of consequence, he sat on many commissions and committees, but he was a man whose day was over, and from whom nothing was expected. Whatever he said, whatever he proposed, was heard as though it were something long familiar, and the very thing that was not needed. But Alexey Alexandrovitch was not aware of this, and, on the contrary, being cut off from direct participation in governmental activity, he saw more clearly than ever the errors and defects in the action of others, and thought it his duty to point out means for their correction. Shortly after his separation from his wife, he began writing his first note on the new judicial procedure, the first of the endless series of notes he was destined to write in the future.

Alexey Alexandrovitch did not merely fail to observe his hopeless position in the official world, he was not merely free from anxiety on this head, he was positively more satisfied than ever with his own activity.

"He that is unmarried careth for the things that belong to the Lord, how he may please the Lord: But he that is married careth for the things that are of the world, how he may please his wife," says the Apostle Paul, and Alexey Alexandrovitch, who was now guided in every action by Scripture, often recalled this text. It seemed to him that ever since he had been left without a wife, he had in these very projects of reform been serving the Lord more zealously than before.

The unmistakable impatience of the member of the Council trying to get away from him did not trouble Alexey Alexandrovitch; he gave up his exposition only when the member of the Council, seizing his chance when one of the Imperial family was passing, slipped away from him.

Left alone, Alexey Alexandrovitch looked down, collecting his thoughts, then looked casually about him and walked towards the door, where he hoped to meet Countess Lidia Ivanovna.

"And how strong they all are, how sound physically," thought Alexey Alexandrovitch, looking at the powerfully built gentleman of the bedchamber with his well-combed, perfumed whiskers, and at the red neck of the prince, pinched by his tight uniform. He had to pass them on his way. "Truly is it said that all the world is evil," he thought, with another sidelong glance at the calves of the gentleman of the bedchamber.

Moving forward deliberately, Alexey Alexandrovitch bowed with his customary air of weariness and dignity to the gentleman who had been talking about him, and looking towards the door, his eyes sought Countess Lidia Ivanovna.

"Ah! Alexey Alexandrovitch!" said the little old man, with a malicious light in his eyes, at the moment when Karenin was on a level with them, and was nodding with a frigid gesture, "I haven't congratulated you yet," said the old man, pointing to his newly received ribbon.

"Thank you," answered Alexey Alexandrovitch. "What an *exquisite* day to-day," he added, laying emphasis in his peculiar way on the word *exquisite*.

That they laughed at him he was well aware, but he did not

expect anything but hostility from them; he was used to that by now.

Catching sight of the yellow shoulders of Lidia Ivanovna jutting out above her corset, and her fine pensive eyes bidding him to her, Alexey Alexandrovitch smiled, revealing untarnished white teeth, and went towards her.

Lidia Ivanovna's dress had cost her great pains, as indeed all her dresses had done of late. Her aim in dress was now quite the reverse of that she had pursued thirty years before. Then her desire had been to adorn herself with something, and the more adorned the better. Now, on the contrary, she was perforce decked out in a way so inconsistent with her age and her figure, that her one anxiety was to contrive that the contrast between these adornments and her own exterior should not be too appalling. And as far as Alexey Alexandrovitch was concerned she succeeded, and was in his eyes attractive. For him she was the one island not only of good-will to him, but of love in the midst of the sea of hostility and jeering that surrounded him.

Passing through rows of ironical eyes, he was drawn as naturally to her loving glance as a plant to the sun.

"I congratulate you," she said to him, her eyes on his ribbon.

Suppressing a smile of pleasure, he shrugged his shoulders, closing his eyes, as though to say that that could not be a source of joy to him. Countess Lidia Ivanovna was very well aware that it was one of his chief sources of satisfaction, though he never admitted it.

"How is our angel?" said Countess Lidia Ivanovna, meaning Seryozha.

"I can't say I was quite pleased with him," said Alexey Alexandrovitch, raising his eyebrows and opening his eyes. "And Sitnikov is not satisfied with him." (Sitnikov was the tutor to whom Seryozha's secular education had been intrusted.) "As I have mentioned to you, there's a sort of coldness in him towards the most important questions which ought to touch the heart of every man and every child. . . ." Alexey Alexandrovitch began expounding his views on the sole question that interested him besides the service—the education of his son.

When Alexey Alexandrovitch with Lidia Ivanovna's help had been brought back anew to life and activity, he felt it his duty to undertake the education of the son left on his hands. Having never before taken any interest in educational questions, Alexey Alexandrovitch devoted some time to the theoretical study of the subject. After reading several books on anthropology, education, and didactics, Alexey Alexandrovitch drew up a plan of education, and engaging the best tutor in Petersburg to superintend it, he set to work, and the subject continually absorbed him.

"Yes, but the heart. I see in him his father's heart, and with such a heart a child cannot go far wrong," said Lidia Ivanovna with enthusiasm.

"Yes, perhaps . . . As for me, I do my duty. It's all I can do."

"You're coming to me," said Countess Lidia Ivanovna, after a pause; "we have to speak of a subject painful for you. I would give anything to have spared you certain memories, but others are not of the same mind. I have received a letter from *her*. *She* is here in Petersburg."

Alexey Alexandrovitch shuddered at the allusion to his wife, but immediately his face assumed the deathlike rigidity which expressed utter helplessness in the matter.

"I was expecting it," he said.

Countess Lidia Ivanovna looked at him ecstatically, and tears of rapture at the greatness of his soul came into her eyes.

CHAPTER XXV

When Alexey Alexandrovitch came into the Countess Lidia Ivanovna's snug little boudoir, decorated with old china and hung with portraits, the lady herself had not yet made her appearance.

She was changing her dress.

A cloth was laid on a round table, and on it stood a china tea-service and a silver spirit-lamp and tea-kettle. Alexey Alexandrovitch looked idly about at the endless familiar portraits which adorned the room, and sitting down to the table, he opened a New Testament lying upon it. The rustle of the countess's silk skirt drew his attention off.

"Well now, we can sit quietly," said Countess Lidia Ivanovna, slipping hurriedly with an agitated smile between the table and the sofa, "and talk over our tea."

After some words of preparation, Countess Lidia Ivanovna, breathing hard and flushing crimson, gave into Alexey Alexandrovitch's hands the letter she had received.

After reading the letter, he sat a long while in silence.

"I don't think I have the right to refuse her," he said, timidly lifting his eyes.

"Dear friend, you never see evil in any one!"

"On the contrary, I see that all is evil. But whether it is just . . ."

His face showed irresolution, and a seeking for counsel, support, and guidance in a matter he did not understand.

"No," Countess Lidia Ivanovna interrupted him; "there are limits to everything. I can understand immorality," she said, not quite truthfully, since she never could understand that which leads women to immorality; "but I don't understand cruelty: to whom? to you! How can she stay in the town where you are? No, the longer one lives the more one learns. And I'm learning to understand your loftiness and her baseness."

"Who is to throw a stone?" said Alexey Alexandrovitch, unmistakably pleased with the part he had to play. "I have forgiven all, and so I cannot deprive her of what is exacted by love in her—by her love for her son. . . ."

"But is that love, my friend? Is it sincere? Admitting that you have forgiven—that you forgive—have we the right to work on the feelings of that angel? He looks on her as dead. He prays for her, and beseeches God to have mercy on her sins. And it is better so. But now what will he think?"

"I had not thought of that," said Alexey Alexandrovitch, evidently agreeing.

Countess Lidia Ivanovna hid her face in her hands and was silent. She was praying.

"If you ask my advice," she said, having finished her prayer and uncovered her face, "I do not advise you to do this. Do you suppose I don't see how you are suffering, how this has torn open your wounds? But supposing that, as always, you don't think of yourself, what can it lead to?—to fresh suffering for you, to torture for the child. If there were a trace of humanity left in her, she ought not to wish for it herself. No, I have no hesitation in saying I advise not, and if you will intrust it to me, I will write to her."

And Alexey Alexandrovitch consented, and Countess Lidia Ivanovna sent the following letter in French:

DEAR MADAME,

"*To be reminded of you might have results for your son in leading to questions on his part which could not be answered without implanting in the child's soul a spirit of censure towards what should be for him sacred, and therefore I beg you to interpret your husband's refusal in the spirit of Christian love. I pray to Almighty God to have mercy on you.*"

COUNTESS LIDIA.

This letter attained the secret object which Countess Lidia Ivanovna had concealed from herself. It wounded Anna to the quick.

For his part, Alexey Alexandrovitch, on returning home from Lidia Ivanovna's, could not all that day concentrate himself on his usual pursuits, and find that spiritual peace of one saved and believing which he had felt of late.

The thought of his wife, who had so greatly sinned against him, and towards whom he had been so saintly, as Countess Lidia

Ivanovna had so justly told him, ought not to have troubled him; but he was not easy; he could not understand the book he was reading; he could not drive away harassing recollections of his relations with her, of the mistake which, as it now seemed, he had made in regard to her. The memory of how he had received her confession of infidelity on their way home from the races (especially that he had insisted only on the observance of external decorum, and had not sent a challenge) tortured him like a remorse. He was tortured too by the thought of the letter he had written her; and most of all, his forgiveness, which nobody wanted, and his care of the other man's child made his heart burn with shame and remorse.

And just the same feeling of shame and regret he felt now, as he reviewed all his past with her, recalling the awkward words in which, after long wavering, he had made her an offer.

"But how have I been to blame?" he said to himself. And this question always excited another question in him—whether they felt differently, did their loving and marrying differently, these Vronskys and Oblonskys . . . these gentlemen of the bedchamber, with their fine calves. And there passed before his mind a whole series of these mettlesome, vigorous, self-confident men, who always and everywhere drew his inquisitive attention in spite of himself. He tried to dispel these thoughts, he tried to persuade himself that he was not living for this transient life, but for the life of eternity, and that there was peace and love in his heart.

But the fact that he had in this transient, trivial life made, as it seemed to him, a few trivial mistakes tortured him as though the eternal salvation in which he believed had no existence. But this temptation did not last long, and soon there was reëstablished once more in Alexey Alexandrovitch's soul the peace and the elevation by virtue of which he could forget what he did not want to remember.

CHAPTER XXVI

"Well, Kapitonitch?" said Seryozha, coming back rosy and good-humored from his walk the day before his birthday, and giving his overcoat to the tall old hall-porter, who smiled down at the little person from the height of his long figure. "Well, has the bandaged clerk been here to-day? Did papa see him?"

"He saw him. The minute the chief secretary came out, I announced him," said the hall-porter with a good-humored wink. "Here, I'll take it off."

"Seryozha!" said the tutor, stopping in the doorway leading to the inner rooms. "Take it off yourself." But Seryozha, though he heard his tutor's feeble voice, did not pay attention to it. He stood keeping hold of the hall-porter's belt, and gazing into his face.

"Well, and did papa do what he wanted for him?"

The hall-porter nodded his head affirmatively. The clerk with his face tied up, who had already been seven times to ask some favor of Alexey Alexandrovitch, interested both Seryozha and the hall-porter. Seryozha had come upon him in the hall, and had heard him plaintively beg the hall-porter to announce him, saying that he and his children had death staring them in the face.

Since then Seryozha, having met him a second time in the hall, took great interest in him.

"Well, was he very glad?" he asked.

"Glad? I should think so! Almost dancing as he walked away."

"And has anything been left?" asked Seryozha, after a pause.

"Come, sir," said the hall-porter; then with a shake of his head he whispered, "Something from the countess."

Seryozha understood at once that what the hall-porter was speaking of was a present from Countess Lidia Ivanovna for his birthday.

"What do you say? Where?"

"Korney took it to your papa. A fine plaything it must be too!"

"How big? Like this?"

"Rather small, but a fine thing."

"A book."

"No, a thing. Run along, run along, Vassily Lukitch is calling you," said the porter, hearing the tutor's steps approaching, and carefully taking away from his belt the little hand in the glove half pulled off, he signed with his head towards the tutor.

"Vassily Lukitch, in a tiny minute!" answered Seryozha with that gay and loving smile which always won over the conscientious Vassily Lukitch.

Seryozha was too happy, everything was too delightful for him to be able to help sharing with his friend the porter the family good fortune of which he had heard during his walk in the public gardens from Lidia Ivanovna's niece. This piece of good news seemed to him particularly important from its coming at the same time with the gladness of the bandaged clerk and his own gladness at toys having come for him. It seemed to Seryozha that this was a day on which every one ought to be glad and happy.

"You know papa's received the Alexander Nevsky to-day?"

"To be sure I do! People have been already to congratulate him."

"And is he glad?"

"Glad at the Tsar's gracious favor! I should think so! It's a proof he's deserved it," said the porter severely and seriously.

Seryozha fell to dreaming, gazing up at the face of the porter, which he had thoroughly studied in every detail, especially the chin that hung down between the gray whiskers, never seen by any one but Seryozha, who saw him only from below.

"Well, and has your daughter been to see you lately?"

The porter's daughter was a ballet-dancer.

"When is she to come on week-days? They've their lessons to learn too. And you've your lesson, sir; run along."

On coming into the room, Seryozha, instead of sitting down to his lessons, told his tutor of his supposition that what had been brought him must be a machine. "What do you think?" he inquired.

But Vassily Lukitch was thinking of nothing but the necessity of learning the grammar lesson for the teacher, who was coming at two.

"No, do just tell me, Vassily Lukitch," he asked suddenly,

when he was seated at their work-table with the book in his hands, "what is greater than the Alexander Nevsky? You know papa's received the Alexander Nevsky?"

Vassily Lukitch replied that the Vladimir was greater than the Alexander Nevsky.

"And higher still?"

"Well, highest of all is the Andrey Pervozvanny."

"And higher than the Andrey?"

"I don't know."

"What, you don't know?" and Seryozha, leaning on his elbows, sank into deep meditation.

His meditations were of the most complex and diverse character. He imagined his father's having suddenly been presented with both the Vladimir and the Andrey to-day, and in consequence being much better tempered at his lesson, and dreamed how, when he was grown up, he would himself receive all the orders, and what they might invent higher than the Andrey. Directly any higher order were invented, he would win it. They would make a higher one still, and he would immediately win that too.

The time passed in such meditations, and when the teacher came, the lesson about the adverbs of place and time and manner of action was not ready, and the teacher was not only displeased, but hurt. This touched Seryozha. He felt he was not to blame for not having learned the lesson; however much he tried, he was utterly unable to do that. As long as the teacher was explaining to him, he believed him and seemed to comprehend, but as soon as he was left alone, he was positively unable to recollect and to understand that the short and familiar word "suddenly" is an adverb of manner of action. Still he was sorry that he had disappointed the teacher.

He chose a moment when the teacher was looking in silence at the book.

"Mihail Ivanitch, when is your birthday?" he asked, all of a sudden.

"You'd much better be thinking about your work. Birthdays are of no importance to a rational being. It's a day like any other on which one has to do one's work."

Seryozha looked intently at the teacher, at his scanty beard, at his spectacles, which had slipped down below the ridge on his nose, and fell into so deep a reverie that he heard nothing of what the teacher was explaining to him. He knew that the teacher did not think what he said, he felt it from the tone in which it was said. "But why have they all agreed to speak just in the same manner always the dreariest and most useless stuff? Why does he keep me off; why doesn't he love me?" he asked himself mournfully, and could not think of an answer.

CHAPTER XXVII

AFTER the lesson with the grammar teacher came his father's lesson. While waiting for his father, Seryozha sat at the table playing with a penknife, and fell to dreaming. Among Seryozha's favorite occupations was searching for his mother during his walks. He did not believe in death generally, and in her death in particular, in spite of what Lidia Ivanovna had told him and his father had confirmed, and it was just because of that, and after he had been told she was dead, that he had begun looking for her when out for a walk. Every woman of full, graceful figure with dark hair was his mother. At the sight of such a woman such a feeling of tenderness was stirred within him that his breath failed him, and tears came into his eyes. And he was on the tiptoe of expectation that she would come up to him, would lift her veil. All her face would be visible, she would smile, she would hug him, he would sniff her fragrance, feel the softness of her arms, and cry with happiness, just as he had one evening lain on her lap while she tickled him, and he laughed and bit her white, ring-covered fingers. Later, when he accidentally learned from his old nurse that his mother was not dead, and his father and Lidia Ivanovna had explained to him that she was dead to him because she was wicked (which he could not possibly believe, because he loved her), he went on seeking her and expecting her in the same way. That day in the public gardens there had been a lady in a lilac veil, whom he had watched with a throbbing heart, believing it to be she as she came towards them along the path. The lady had not come up to them, but had disappeared somewhere. That day, more intensely than ever, Seryozha felt a rush of love for her, and now, waiting for his father, he forgot everything, and cut all round the edge of the table with his penknife, staring straight before him with sparkling eyes and dreaming of her.

"Here is your papa!" said Vassily Lukitch, rousing him.

Seryozha jumped up and went up to his father, and kissing his hand, looked at him intently, trying to discover signs of his joy at receiving the Alexander Nevsky.

"Did you have a nice walk?" said Alexey Alexandrovitch, sitting down in his easy-chair, pulling the volume of the Old Testament to him and opening it. Although Alexey Alexandrovitch had more than once told Seryozha that every Christian ought to know Scripture history thoroughly, he often referred to the Bible himself during the lesson, and Seryozha observed this.

"Yes, it was very nice indeed, papa," said Seryozha, sitting sideways on his chair and rocking it, which was forbidden. "I saw Nadinka" (Nadinka was a niece of Lidia Ivanovna's who was being brought up in her house). "She told me you'd been given a new star. Are you glad, papa?"

"First of all, don't rock your chair, please," said Alexey Alexandrovitch. "And secondly, it's not the reward that's precious, but the work itself. And I could have wished you understood that. If you now are going to work, to study in order to win a reward, then the work will seem hard to you; but when you work" (Alexey Alexandrovitch, as he spoke, thought of how he had been sustained by a sense of duty through the wearisome labor of the morning, consisting of signing one hundred and eighty papers), "loving your work, you will find your reward in it."

Seryozha's eyes, that had been shining with gaiety and tenderness, grew dull and dropped before his father's gaze. This was the same long-familiar tone his father always took with him, and Seryozha had learned by now to fall in with it. His father always talked to him—so Seryozha felt—as though he were addressing some boy of his own imagination, one of those boys that exist in books, utterly unlike himself. And Seryozha always tried with his father to act being the story-book boy.

"You understand that, I hope?" said his father.

"Yes, papa," answered Seryozha, acting the part of the imaginary boy.

The lesson consisted of learning by heart several verses out of the Gospel and the repetition of the beginning of the Old Testament. The verses from the Gospel Seryozha knew fairly well, but at the moment when he was saying them he became so absorbed in watching the sharply protruding, bony knobbiness of his father's forehead, that he lost the thread, and he transposed the end of one verse and the beginning of another. So it was evident to Alexey Alexandrovitch that he did not understand what he was saying, and that irritated him.

He frowned, and began explaining what Seryozha had heard many times before and never could remember, because he understood it too well, just as that "suddenly" is an adverb of manner of action. Seryozha looked with scared eyes at his father, and could think of nothing but whether his father would make him repeat what he had said, as he sometimes did. And this thought so alarmed Seryozha that he now understood nothing. But his father did not make him repeat it, and passed on to the lesson out of the Old Testament. Seryozha recounted the events themselves well enough, but when he had to answer questions as to what certain events prefigured, he knew nothing, though he had already been punished over this lesson. The passage at which he was utterly unable to say anything, and began fidgeting and cutting the table and swinging his chair, was where he had to repeat the patriarchs before the Flood. He did not know one of them, except

Enoch, who had been taken up alive to heaven. Last time he had remembered their names, but now he had forgotten them utterly, chiefly because Enoch was the personage he liked best in the whole of the Old Testament, and Enoch's translation to heaven was connected in his mind with a whole long train of thought, in which he became absorbed now while he gazed with fascinated eyes at his father's watch-chain and a half-unbuttoned button on his waistcoat.

In death, of which they talked to him so often, Seryozha disbelieved entirely. He did not believe that those he loved could die, above all that he himself would die. That was to him something utterly inconceivable and impossible. But he had been told that all men die; he had asked people, indeed, whom he trusted, and they too, had confirmed it; his old nurse, too, said the same, though reluctantly. But Enoch had not died, and so it followed that every one did not die. "And why cannot any one else so serve God and be taken alive to heaven?" thought Seryozha. Bad people, that is those Seryozha did not like, they might die, but the good might all be like Enoch.

"Well, what are the names of the patriarchs?"

"Enoch, Enos—"

"But you have said that already. This is bad, Seryozha, very bad. If you don't try to learn what is more necessary than anything for a Christian," said his father, getting up, "whatever can interest you? I am displeased with you, and Pyotr Ignatitch" (this was the most important of his teachers) "is displeased with you. . . . I shall have to punish you."

His father and his teacher were both displeased with Seryozha, and he certainly did learn his lessons very badly. But still it could not be said he was a stupid boy. On the contrary, he was far cleverer than the boys his teacher held up as examples to Seryozha. In his father's opinion, he did not want to learn what he was taught. In reality he could not learn that. He could not, because the claims of his own soul were more binding on him than those claims his father and his teacher made upon him. Those claims were in opposition, and he was in direct conflict with his education. He was nine years old; he was a child; but he knew his own soul, it was precious to him, he guarded it as the eyelid guards the eye, and without the key of love he let no one into his soul. His teachers complained that he would not learn, while his soul was brimming over with thirst for knowledge. And he learned from Kapitonitch, from his nurse, from Nadinka, from Vassily Lukitch, but not from his teachers. The spring his father and his teachers reckoned upon to turn their mill-wheels had long dried up at the source, but its waters did their work in another channel.

His father punished Seryozha by not letting him go to see Nadinka, Lidia Ivanovna's niece; but this punishment turned out happily for Seryozha. Vassily Lukitch was in a good humor, and showed him how to make windmills. The whole evening passed over this work and in dreaming how to make a windmill on which he could turn himself—clutching at the sails or tying himself on and whirling round. Of his mother Seryozha did not think all the evening, but when he had gone to bed, he suddenly remembered her, and prayed in his own words that his mother to-morrow for his birthday might leave off hiding herself and come to him.

"Vassily Lukitch, do you know what I prayed for to-night extra besides the regular things?"

"That you might learn your lessons better?"

"No."

"Toys?"

"No. You'll never guess. A splendid thing; but it's a secret! When it comes to pass I'll tell you. Can't you guess?"

"No, I can't guess. You tell me," said Vassily Lukitch with a smile, which was rare with him. "Come, lie down, I'm putting out the candle."

"Without the candle I can see better what I see and what I prayed for. There! I was almost telling the secret!" said Seryozha, laughing gaily.

When the candle was taken away, Seryozha heard and felt his mother. She stood over him, and with loving eyes caressed him. But then came windmills, a knife, everything began to be mixed up, and he fell asleep.

CHAPTER XXVIII

On arriving in Petersburg, Vronsky and Anna stayed at one of the best hotels; Vronsky apart in a lower story, Anna above with her child, its nurse, and her maid, in a large suite of four rooms.

On the day of his arrival Vronsky went to his brother's. There he found his mother, who had come from Moscow on business. His mother and sister-in-law greeted him as usual: they asked him about his stay abroad, and talked of their common acquaintances, but did not let drop a single word in allusion to his connection with Anna. His brother came the next morning to see Vronsky, and of his own accord asked him about her, and Alexey Vronsky told him directly that he looked upon his connection with Madame Karenina as marriage; that he hoped to arrange a divorce, and then to marry her, and until then he considered her as much a wife as any other wife, and he begged him to tell their mother and his wife so.

"If the world disapproves, I don't care," said Vronsky; "but if my relations want to be on terms of relationship with me, they will have to be on the same terms with my wife."

The elder brother, who had always a respect for his younger brother's judgment, could not well tell whether he was right or not till the world had decided the question; for his part he had nothing against it, and with Alexey he went up to see Anna.

Before his brother, as before every one, Vronsky addressed Anna with a certain formality, treating her as he might a very intimate friend, but it was understood that his brother knew their real relations, and they talked about Anna's going to Vronsky's estate.

In spite of all his social experience Vronsky was, in consequence of the new position in which he was placed, laboring under a strange misapprehension. One would have thought he must have understood that society was closed for him and Anna; but now some vague ideas had sprung up in his brain that this was only the case in old-fashioned days, and that now with the rapidity of modern progress (he had unconsciously become by now a partisan of every sort of progress) the views of society had changed, and that the question whether they would be received in society was not a foregone conclusion. "Of course," he thought, "she would not be received at court, but intimate friends can and must look at it in the proper light." One may sit for several hours at a stretch with one's legs crossed in the same position, if one knows that there's nothing to prevent one's changing one's position; but if a man knows that he must remain sitting so with crossed legs, then cramps come on, the legs begin to twitch and to strain towards the spot to which one would like to draw them. This was what Vronsky was experiencing in regard to the world. Though at the bottom of his heart he knew that the world was shut on them, he put it to the test whether the world had not changed by now and would not receive them. But he very quickly perceived that though the world was open for him personally, it was closed for Anna. Just as in the game of cat and mouse, the hands raised for him were dropped to bar the way for Anna.

One of the first ladies of Petersburg society whom Vronsky saw was his cousin Betsy.

"At last!" she greeted him joyfully. "And Anna? How glad I am! Where are you stopping? I can fancy after your delightful travels you must find our poor Petersburg horrid. I can fancy your honeymoon in Rome. How about the divorce? Is that all over?"

Vronsky noticed that Betsy's enthusiasm waned when she learned that no divorce had as yet taken place.

"People will throw stones at me, I know," she said, "but I shall come and see Anna; yes, I shall certainly come. You won't be here long, I suppose?"

And she did certainly come to see Anna the same day, but her tone was not at all the same as in former days. She unmistakably prided herself on her courage, and wished Anna to appreciate the fidelity of her friendship. She only stayed ten minutes, talking of society gossip, and on leaving she said:

"You've never told me when the divorce is to be? Supposing I'm ready to fling my cap over the mill, other starchy people will give you the cold shoulder until you're married. And that's so simple nowadays. *Ça se fait.* So you're going on Friday? Sorry we shan't see each other again."

From Betsy's tone Vronsky might have grasped what he had to expect from the world; but he made another effort in his own family. His mother he did not reckon upon. He knew that his mother, who had been so enthusiastic over Anna at their first acquaintance, would have no mercy on her now for having ruined her son's career. But he had more hope of Varya, his brother's wife. He fancied she would not throw stones, and would go simply and directly to see Anna, and would receive her in her own house.

The day after his arrival Vronsky went to her, and finding her alone, expressed his wishes directly.

"You know, Alexey," she said after hearing him, "how fond I am of you, and how ready I am to do anything for you; but I have not spoken, because I knew I could be of no use to you and to Anna Arkadyevna," she said, articulating the name "Anna Arkadyevna" with particular care. "Don't suppose, please, that I judge her. Never; perhaps in her place I should have done the same. I don't and can't enter into that," she said, glancing timidly at his gloomy face. "But one must call things by their names. You want me to go and see her, to ask her here, and to rehabilitate her in society; but do understand that *I cannot* do so. I have daughters growing up, and I must live in the world for my husband's sake. Well, I'm ready to come and see Anna Arkadyevna: she will understand that I can't ask her here, or I should have to do so in such a way that she would not meet people who look at things differently; that would offend her. I can't raise her . . ."

"Oh, I don't regard her as fallen more than hundreds of women you do receive!" Vronsky interrupted her still more gloomily, and he got up in silence, understanding that his sister-in-law's decision was not to be shaken.

"Alexey! don't be angry with me. Please understand that I'm not to blame," began Varya, looking at him with a timid smile.

"I'm not angry with you," he said still as gloomily; "but I'm sorry in two ways. I'm sorry, too, that this means breaking up our friendship—if not breaking up, at least weakening it. You will understand that for me, too, it cannot be otherwise."

And with that he left her.

Vronsky knew that further efforts were useless, and that he had to spend these few days in Petersburg as though in a strange town, avoiding every sort of relation with his own old circle in order not to be exposed to the annoyances and humiliations which were so intolerable to him. One of the most unpleasant features of his position in Petersburg was that Alexey Alexandrovitch and his name seemed to meet him everywhere. He could not begin to talk of anything without the conversation turning on Alexey Alexandrovitch, he could not go anywhere without risk of meeting him. So at least it seemed to Vronsky, just as it seems to a man with a sore finger that he is continually, as though on purpose, grazing his sore finger on everything.

Their stay in Petersburg was the more painful to Vronsky that he perceived all the time a sort of new mood that he could not understand in Anna. At one time she would seem in love with him, and then she would become cold, irritable, and impenetrable. She was worrying over something, and keeping something back from him, and did not seem to notice the humiliations which poisoned his existence, and for her, with her delicate intuition, must have been still more unbearable.

CHAPTER XXIX

One of Anna's objects in coming back to Russia had been to see her son. From the day she left Italy the thought of it had never ceased to agitate her. And as she got nearer to Petersburg, the delight and importance of this meeting grew ever greater in her imagination. She did not even put to herself the question how to arrange it. It seemed to her natural and simple to see her son when she should be in the same town with him. But on her arrival in Petersburg she was suddenly made distinctly aware of her present position in society, and she grasped the fact that to arrange this meeting was no easy matter.

She had now been two days in Petersburg. The thought of her son never left her for a single instant, but she had not yet seen him. To go straight to the house, where she might meet Alexey Alexandrovitch, that she felt she had no right to do. She might be refused admittance and insulted. To write and so enter into relations with her husband—that it made her miserable to think of doing; she could only be at peace when she did not think of her husband. To get a glimpse of her son out walking, finding out where and when he went out, was not enough for her; she had so looked forward to this meeting, she had so much she must say to him, she so longed to embrace him, to kiss him. Seryozha's old nurse might be a help to her and show her what to do. But the nurse was not now living in Alexey Alexandrovitch's house. In this uncertainty, and in efforts to find the nurse, two days had slipped by.

Hearing of the close intimacy between Alexey Alexandrovitch and Countess Lidia Ivanovna, Anna decided on the third day to write to her a letter, which cost her great pains, and in which she intentionally said that permission to see her son must depend on her husband's generosity. She knew that if the letter were shown to her husband, he would keep up his character of magnanimity, and would not refuse her request.

The commissionaire who took the letter had brought her back the most cruel and unexpected answer, that there was no answer. She had never felt so humiliated as at the moment when, sending for the commissionaire, she heard from him the exact account of how he had waited, and how afterwards he had been told there was no answer. Anna felt humiliated, insulted, but she saw that from her point of view Countess Lidia Ivanovna was right. Her suffering was the more poignant that she had to bear it in solitude. She could not and would not share it with Vronsky. She knew that to him, although he was the primary cause of her distress, the question of her seeing her son would seem a matter of very little consequence. She knew that he would never be capable of understanding all the depth of her suffering, that for his cool tone at any allusion to it she would begin to hate him. And she dreaded that more than anything in the world, and so she hid from him everything that related to her son. Spending the whole day at home she considered ways of seeing her son, and had reached a decision to write to her husband. She was just composing this letter when she was handed the letter from Lidia

Ivanovna. The countess's silence had subdued and depressed her, but the letter, all that she read between the lines in it, so exasperated her, this malice was so revolting beside her passionate, legitimate tenderness for her son, that she turned against other people and left off blaming herself.

"This coldness—this pretense of feeling!" she said to herself. "They must needs insult me and torture the child, and I am to submit to it! Not on any consideration! She is worse than I am. I don't lie, anyway." And she decided on the spot that next day, Seryozha's birthday, she would go straight to her husband's house, bribe or deceive the servants, but at any cost see her son and overturn the hideous deception with which they were encompassing the unhappy child.

She went to a toy-shop, bought toys and thought over a plan of action. She would go early in the morning at eight o'clock, when Alexey Alexandrovitch would be certain not to be up. She would have money in her hand to give the hall-porter and the footman, so that they should let her in, and not raising her veil, she would say that she had come from Seryozha's godfather to congratulate him, and that she had been charged to leave the toys at his bedside. She had prepared everything but the words she should say to her son. Often as she had dreamed of it, she could never think of anything.

The next day, at eight o'clock in the morning, Anna got out of a hired sledge and rang at the front entrance of her former home.

"Run and see what's wanted. Some lady," said Kapitonitch, who, not yet dressed, in his overcoat and goloshes, had peeped out of the window and seen a lady in a veil standing close up to the door. His assistant, a lad Anna did not know, had no sooner opened the door to her than she came in, and pulling a three-rouble note out of her muff put it hurriedly into his hand.

"Seryozha—Sergey Alexeitch," she said, and was going on. Scrutinizing the note, the porter's assistant stopped her at the second glass-door.

"Whom do you want?" he asked.

She did not hear his words and made no answer.

Noticing the embarrassment of the unknown lady, Kapitonitch went out to her, opened the second door for her, and asked her what she was pleased to want.

"From Prince Skorodumov for Sergey Alexeitch," she said.

"His honor's not up yet," said the porter, looking at her attentively.

Anna had not anticipated that the absolutely unchanged hall of the house where she had lived for nine years would so greatly affect her. Memories sweet and painful rose one after another in her heart, and for a moment she forgot what she was here for.

"Would you kindly wait?" said Kapitonitch, taking off her fur cloak.

As he took off the cloak, Kapitonitch glanced at her face, recognized her, and made her a low bow in silence.

"Please walk in, your excellency," he said to her.

She tried to say something, but her voice refused to utter any sound; with a guilty and imploring glance at the old man she went with light, swift steps up the stairs. Bent double, and his goloshes catching in the steps, Kapitonitch ran after her, trying to overtake her.

"The tutor's there; maybe he's not dressed. I'll let him know."

Anna still mounted the familiar staircase, not understanding what the old man was saying.

"This way, to the left, if you please. Excuse its not being tidy. His honor's in the old parlor now," the hall-porter said, panting. "Excuse me, wait a little, your excellency; I'll just see," he said, and overtaking her, he opened the high door and disappeared behind it. Anna stood still waiting. "He's only just awake," said the hall-porter, coming out. And at the very instant the porter said this, Anna caught the sound of a childish yawn. From the sound of this yawn alone she knew her son and seemed to see him living before her eyes.

"Let me in; go away!" she said, and went in through the high doorway. On the right of the door stood a bed, and sitting up in the bed was the boy. His little body bent forward with his nightshirt unbuttoned, he was stretching and still yawning. The instant his lips came together they curved into a blissfully sleepy smile, and with that smile he slowly and deliciously rolled back again.

"Seryozha!" she whispered, going noiselessly up to him.

When she was parted from him, and all this latter time when she had been feeling a fresh rush of love for him, she had pictured him as he was at four years old, when she had loved him most of all. Now he was not even the same as when she had left him; he was still further from the four-year-old baby, more grown and thinner. How thin his face was, how short his hair was! What long hands! How he had changed since she left him! But it was he with his head, his lips, his soft neck and broad little shoulders.

"Seryozha!" she repeated just in the child's ear.

He raised himself again on his elbow, turned his tangled head from side to side as though looking for something, and opened his eyes. Slowly and inquiringly he looked for several seconds at his mother standing motionless before him, then all at once he smiled a blissful smile, and shutting his eyes, rolled not backwards but towards her into her arms.

"Seryozha! my darling boy!" she said, breathing hard and putting her arms round his plump little body. "Mother!" he said, wriggling about in her arms so as to touch her hands with different parts of him.

Smiling sleepily still with closed eyes, he flung his fat little arms round her shoulders, rolled towards her, with the delicious sleepy warmth and fragrance that is only found in children, and began rubbing his face against her neck and shoulders.

"I know," he said, opening his eyes; "it's my birthday to-day. I knew you'd come. I'll get up directly."

And saying that he dropped asleep.

Anna looked at him hungrily; she saw how he had grown and changed in her absence. She knew, and did not know, the bare legs so long now, that were thrust out below the quilt, those short-cropped curls on his neck in which she had so often kissed him. She touched all this and could say nothing; tears choked her.

"What are you crying for, mother?" he said, waking completely up. "Mother, what are you crying for?" he cried in a tearful voice.

"I won't cry . . . I'm crying for joy. It's so long since I've seen you. I won't, I won't," she said, gulping down her tears and turning away. "Come, it's time for you to dress now," she added, after a pause, and, never letting go his hands, she sat down by his bedside on the chair, where his clothes were put ready for him.

"How do you dress without me? How . . ." she tried to begin talking simply and cheerfully, but she could not, and again she turned away.

"I don't have a cold bath, papa didn't order it. And you've not seen Vassily Lukitch? He'll come in soon. Why, you're sitting on my clothes!"

And Seryozha went off into a peal of laughter. She looked at him and smiled.

"Mother, darling, sweet one!" he shouted, flinging himself on her again and hugging her. It was as though only now, on seeing her smile, he fully grasped what had happened.

"I don't want that on," he said, taking off her hat. And as it were, seeing her afresh without her hat, he fell to kissing her again.

"But what did you think about me? You didn't think I was dead?"

"I never believed it."

"You didn't believe it, my sweet?"

"I knew, I knew!" he repeated his favorite phrase, and snatching the hand that was stroking his hair, he pressed the open palm to his mouth and kissed it.

CHAPTER XXX

MEANWHILE Vassily Lukitch had not at first understood who this lady was, and had learned from their conversation that it was no other person than the mother who had left her husband, and whom he had not seen, as he had entered the house after her departure. He was in doubt whether to go in or not, or whether to communicate with Alexey Alexandrovitch. Reflecting finally that his duty was to get Seryozha up at the hour fixed, and that it was therefore not his business to consider who was there, the mother or any one else, but simply to do his duty, he finished dressing, went to the door and opened it.

But the embraces of the mother and child, the sound of their voices, and what they were saying, made him change his mind.

He shook his head, and with a sigh he closed the door. "I'll wait another ten minutes," he said to himself, clearing his throat and wiping away tears.

Among the servants of the household there was intense excitement all this time. All had heard that their mistress had come, and that Kapitonitch had let her in, and that she was even now in the nursery, and that their master always went in person to the nursery at nine o'clock, and every one fully comprehended that it was impossible for the husband and wife to meet, and that they must prevent it. Korney, the valet, going down to the hall-porter's room, asked who had let her in, and how it was he had done so, and ascertaining that Kapitonitch had admitted her and shown her up, he gave the old man a talking-to. The hall-porter was doggedly silent, but when Korney told him he ought to be sent away, Kapitonitch darted up to him, and waving his hands in Korney's face, began:

"Oh yes, to be sure you'd not have let her in! After ten years' service, and never a word but of kindness, and there you'd up and say, 'Be off, go along, get away with you!' Oh yes, you're a shrewd one at politics, I dare say! You don't need to be taught how to swindle the master, and to filch fur coats!"

"Soldier!" said Korney contemptuously, and he turned to the nurse who was coming in. "Here, what do you think, Marya

Efimovna: he let her in without a word to any one," Korney said addressing her. "Alexey Alexandrovitch will be down immediately—and go into the nursery!"

"A pretty business, a pretty business!" said the nurse. "You, Korney Vassilievitch, you'd best keep him some way or other, the master, while I'll run and get her away somehow. A pretty business!"

When the nurse went into the nursery, Seryozha was telling his mother how he and Nadinka had had a fall in sledging downhill, and had turned over three times. She was listening to the sound of his voice, watching his face and the play of expression on it, touching his hand, but she did not follow what he was saying. She must go, she must leave him,—this was the only thing she was thinking and feeling. She heard the steps of Vassily Lukitch coming up to the door and coughing; she heard, too, the steps of the nurse as she came near; but she sat like one turned to stone, incapable of beginning to speak or to get up.

"Mistress, darling!" began the nurse, going up to Anna and kissing her hands and shoulders. "God has brought joy indeed to our boy on his birthday. You aren't changed one bit."

"Oh, nurse dear, I didn't know you were in the house," said Anna, rousing herself for a moment.

"I'm not living here, I'm living with my daughter. I came for the birthday, Anna Arkadyevna, darling!"

The nurse suddenly burst into tears, and began kissing her hand again.

Seryozha, with radiant eyes and smiles, holding his mother by one hand and his nurse by the other, pattered on the rug with his fat little bare feet. The tenderness shown by his beloved nurse to his mother threw him into an ecstasy.

"Mother! She often comes to see me, and when she comes . . ." he was beginning, but he stopped, noticing that the nurse was saying something in a whisper to his mother, and that in his mother's face there was a look of dread and something like shame, which was so strangely unbecoming to her.

She went up to him.

"My sweet!" she said.

She could not say *good-bye,* but the expression on her face said it, and he understood. "Darling, darling Kootik!" she used the name by which she had called him when he was little, "you won't forget me? You . . ." but she could not say more.

How often afterwards she thought of words she might have said. But now she did not know how to say it, and could say nothing. But Seryozha knew all she wanted to say to him. He understood that she was unhappy and loved him. He understood even what the nurse had whispered. He had caught the words "always at nine o'clock," and he knew that this was said of his father, and that his father and mother could not meet. That he understood, but one thing he could not understand—why there should be a look of dread and shame in her face? . . . She was not in fault, but she was afraid of him and ashamed of something. He would have liked to put a question that would have set at rest this doubt, but he did not dare; he saw that she was miserable, and he felt for her. Silently he pressed close to her and whispered, "Don't go yet. He won't come just yet."

The mother held him away from her to see what he was thinking, what to say to him, and in his frightened face she read not only that he was speaking of his father, but, as it were, asking her what he ought to think about his father.

"Seryozha, my darling," she said, "love him; he's better and kinder than I am, and I have done him wrong. When you grow up you will judge."

"There's no one better than you! . . ." he cried in despair through his tears, and, clutching her by the shoulders, he began squeezing her with all his force to him, his arms trembling with the strain.

"My sweet, my little one!" said Anna, and she cried as weakly and childishly as he.

At that moment the door opened. Vassily Lukitch came in.

At the other door there was the sound of steps, and the nurse in a scared whisper said, "He's coming," and gave Anna her hat.

Seryozha sank onto the bed and sobbed, hiding his face in his hands. Anna removed his hands, once more kissed his wet face, and with rapid steps went to the door. Alexey Alexandrovitch walked in, meeting her. Seeing her, he stopped short and bowed his head.

Although she had just said he was better and kinder than she, in the rapid glance she flung at him, taking in his whole figure in all its details, feelings of repulsion and hatred for him and jealousy over her son took possession of her. With a swift gesture she put down her veil, and, quickening her pace, almost ran out of the room.

She had not time to undo, and so carried back with her, the parcel of toys she had chosen the day before in a toy-shop with such love and sorrow.

CHAPTER XXXI

INTENSELY as Anna had longed to see her son, and long as she had been thinking of it and preparing herself for it, she had not in the least expected that seeing him would affect her so deeply. On getting back to her lonely rooms in the hotel she could not for a long while understand why she was there. "Yes, it's all over, and I am again alone," she said to herself, and without taking off her hat she sat down in a low chair by the hearth. Fixing her eyes on a bronze clock standing on a table between the windows, she tried to think.

The French maid brought from abroad came in to suggest she should dress. She gazed at her wonderingly and said, "Presently." A footman offered her coffee. "Later on," she said.

The Italian nurse, after having taken the baby out in her best, came in with her, and brought her to Anna. The plump, well-fed little baby, on seeing her mother, as she always did, held out her fat little hands, and with a smile on her toothless mouth, began, like a fish with a float, bobbing her fingers up and down the starched folds of her embroidered skirt, making them rustle. It was impossible not to smile, not to kiss the baby, impossible not to hold out a finger for her to clutch, crowing and prancing all over; impossible not to offer her a lip which she sucked into her little mouth by way of a kiss. And all this Anna did, and took her in her arms and made her dance, and kissed her fresh little cheek and bare little elbows; but at the sight of this child it was plainer than ever to her that the feeling she had for her could not be called love in comparison with what she felt for Seryozha. Everything in this baby was charming, but for some reason all this did not go deep to her heart. On her first child, though the child of an unloved father, had been concentrated all the love that had never found satisfaction. Her baby girl had been born in the most painful circumstances and had not had a hundredth part of the care and thought which had been concentrated on her first child. Besides, in the little girl everything was still in the future, while Seryozha was by now almost a personality, and a personality dearly loved. In him there was a conflict of thought and feeling; he understood her, he loved her, he judged her, she thought, recalling his words and his eyes. And she was forever—not physically only but spiritually—divided from him, and it was impossible to set this right.

She gave the baby back to the nurse, let her go, and opened the locket in which there was Seryozha's portrait when he was almost of the same age as the girl. She got up, and, taking off her hat, took up from a little table an album in which there were photographs of her son at different ages. She wanted to compare them, and began taking them out of the album. She took them all out except one, the latest and best photograph. In it he was in a white smock, sitting astride a chair, with frowning eyes and smiling lips. It was his best, most characteristic expression. With her little supple hands, her white, delicate fingers, that moved with a peculiar intensity to-day, she pulled at a corner of the photograph, but the photograph had caught somewhere, and she could not get it out. There was no paper-knife on the table, and so, pulling out the photograph that was next to her son's (it was a photograph of Vronsky taken at Rome in a round hat and with long hair), she used it to push out her son's photograph. "Oh, here is he!" she said, glancing at the portrait of Vronsky, and she suddenly recalled that he was the cause of her present misery. She had not once thought of him all the morning. But now, coming all at once upon that manly, noble face, so familiar and so dear to her, she felt a sudden rush of love for him.

"But where is he? How is it he leaves me alone in my misery?" she thought all at once with a feeling of reproach, forgetting she had herself kept from him everything concerning her son. She sent to ask him to come to her immediately; with a throbbing heart she awaited him, rehearsing to herself the words in which she would tell him all, and the expressions of love with which he would console her. The messenger returned with the answer that he had a visitor with him, but that he would come immediately, and that he asked whether she would let him bring with him Prince Yashvin, who had just arrived in Petersburg. "He's not coming alone, and since dinner yesterday he has not seen me," she thought; "he's not coming so that I could tell him everything, but coming with Yashvin." And all at once a strange idea came to her: what if he had ceased to love her?

And going over the events of the last few days, it seemed to her that she saw in everything a confirmation of this terrible idea. The fact that he had not dined at home yesterday, and the fact that he had insisted on their taking separate sets of rooms at Petersburg, and that even now he was not coming to her alone, as though he were trying to avoid meeting her face to face.

"But he ought to tell me so. I must know that it is so. If I knew it, then I know what I should do," she said to herself, utterly unable to picture to herself the position she would be in if she were convinced of his not caring for her. She thought he had ceased to love her, she felt close upon despair, and consequently she felt exceptionally alert. She rang for her maid and went to her dressing-room. As she dressed, she took more care over her appearance than she had done all those days, as though he might, if he had grown cold to her, fall in love with her again because she had dressed and arranged her hair in the way most becoming to her.

She heard the bell ring before she was ready. When she went into the drawing-room it was not he, but Yashvin, who met her eyes. Vronsky was looking through the photographs of her son, which she had forgotten on the table, and he made no haste to look round at her.

"We have met already," she said, putting her little hand into the huge hand of Yashvin, whose bashfulness was so queerly out of keeping with his immense frame and coarse face. "We met last year at the races. Give them to me," she said, with a rapid movement snatching from Vronsky the photographs of her son, and glancing significantly at him with flashing eyes. "Were the races good this year? Instead of them I saw the races in the Corso in Rome. But you don't care for life abroad," she said with a cordial smile. "I know you and all your tastes, though I have seen so little of you."

"I'm awfully sorry for that, for my tastes are mostly bad," said Yashvin, gnawing at his left mustache.

Having talked a little while, and noticing that Vronsky glanced at the clock, Yashvin asked her whether she would be staying much longer in Petersburg, and unbending his huge figure reached after his cap.

"Not long, I think," she said hesitatingly, glancing at Vronsky.

"So then we shan't meet again?"

"Come and dine with me," said Anna resolutely, angry it seemed with herself for her embarrassment, but flushing as she always did when she defined her position before a fresh person. "The dinner here is not good, but at least you will see him. There is no one of his old friends in the regiment Alexey cares for as he does for you."

"Delighted," said Yashvin with a smile, from which Vronsky could see that he liked Anna very much.

Yashvin said good-bye and went away; Vronsky stayed behind.

"Are you going too?" she said to him.

"I'm late already," he answered. "Run along! I'll catch you up in a moment," he called to Yashvin.

She took him by the hand, and without taking her eyes off him, gazed at him while she ransacked her mind for the words to say that would keep him.

"Wait a minute, there's something I want to say to you," and taking his broad hand she pressed it on her neck. "Oh, was it right my asking him to dinner?"

"You did quite right," he said with a serene smile that showed his even teeth, and he kissed her hand.

"Alexey, you have not changed to me?" she said, pressing his hand in both of hers. "Alexey, I am miserable here. When are we going away?"

"Soon, soon. You wouldn't believe how disagreeable our way of living here is to me too," he said, and he drew away his hand.

"Well, go, go!" she said in a tone of offense, and she walked quickly away from him.

CHAPTER XXXII

When Vronsky returned home, Anna was not yet home. Soon after he had left, some lady, so they told him, had come to see her, and she had gone out with her. That she had gone out without leaving word where she was going, that she had not yet come back, and that all the morning she had been going about somewhere without a word to him—all this, together with the strange look of excitement in her face in the morning, and the recollection of the hostile tone with which she had before Yashvin almost snatched her son's photographs out of his hands, made him serious. He decided he absolutely must speak openly with her. And he waited for her in her drawing-room. But Anna did not return alone, but brought with her her old unmarried aunt, Princess Oblonskaya. This was the lady who had come in the morning, and with whom Anna had gone out shopping. Anna appeared not to notice Vronsky's worried and inquiring expression, and began a lively account of her morning's shopping. He saw that there was something working within her; in her flashing eyes, when they rested for a moment on him, there was an intense concentration, and in her words and movements there was that nervous rapidity and grace which, during the early period of their intimacy, had so fascinated him, but which now so disturbed and alarmed him.

The dinner was laid for four. All were gathered together and about to go into the little dining-room when Tushkevitch made his appearance with a message from Princess Betsy. Princess Betsy begged her to excuse her not having come to say good-bye; she had been indisposed, but begged Anna to come to her between half-past six and nine o'clock. Vronsky glanced at Anna at the precise limit of time, so suggestive of steps having been taken that she should meet no one; but Anna appeared not to notice it.

"Very sorry that I can't come just between half-past six and nine," she said with a faint smile.

"The princess will be very sorry."

"And so am I."

"You're going, no doubt, to hear Patti?" said Tushkevitch.

"Patti? You suggest the idea to me. I would go if it were possible to get a box."

"I can get one," Tushkevitch offered his services.

"I should be very, very grateful to you," said Anna. "But won't you dine with us?"

Vronsky gave a hardly perceptible shrug. He was at a complete loss to understand what Anna was about. What had she brought the old Princess Oblonskaya home for, what had she made Tushkevitch stay to dinner for, and, most amazing of all, why was she sending him for a box? Could she possibly think in her position of going to Patti's benefit, where all the circle of her acquaintances would be? He looked at her with serious eyes, but she responded with that defiant, half-mirthful, half-desperate look, the meaning of which he could not comprehend. At dinner Anna was in aggressively high spirits—she almost flirted both with Tushkevitch and with Yashvin. When they got up from dinner and Tushkevitch had gone to get a box at the opera, Yashvin went to smoke, and Vronsky went down with him to his own rooms. After sitting there for some time he ran upstairs. Anna was already dressed in a low-necked gown of light silk and velvet that she had had made in Paris, and with costly white lace on her head, framing her face, and particularly becoming, showing up her dazzling beauty.

"Are you really going to the theater?" he said, trying not to look at her.

"Why do you ask with such alarm?" she said, wounded again at his not looking at her. "Why shouldn't I go?"

She appeared not to understand the motive of his words.

"Oh, of course, there's no reason whatever," he said, frowning.

"That's just what I say," she said, willfully refusing to see the irony of his tone, and quietly turning back her long, perfumed glove.

"Anna, for God's sake! what is the matter with you?" he said, appealing to her exactly as once her husband had done.

"I don't understand what you are asking."

"You know that it's out of the question to go."

"Why so? I'm not going alone. Princess Varvara has gone to dress, she is going with me."

He shrugged his shoulders with an air of perplexity and despair.

"But do you mean to say you don't know? . . ." he began.

"But I don't care to know!" she almost shrieked. "I don't care to. Do I regret what I have done? No, no, no! If it were all to do again from the beginning, it would be the same. For us, for you and for me, there is only one thing that matters, whether we love each other. Other people we need not consider. Why are we living here apart and not seeing each other? Why can't I go? I love you, and I don't care for anything," she said in Russian, glancing at him with a peculiar gleam in her eyes that he could not understand. "If you have not changed to me, why don't you look at me?"

He looked at her. He saw all the beauty of her face and full dress, always so becoming to her. But now her beauty and elegance were just what irritated him.

"My feeling cannot change, you know, but I beg you, I entreat you," he said again in French, with a note of tender supplication in his voice, but with coldness in his eyes.

She did not hear his words, but she saw the coldness of his eyes, and answered with irritation:

"And I beg you to explain why I should not go."

"Because it might cause you . . ." He hesitated.

"I don't understand. Yashvin *n'est pas compromettant,* and Princess Varvara is no worse than others. Oh, here she is!"

CHAPTER XXXIII

VRONSKY for the first time experienced a feeling of anger against Anna, almost a hatred for her willfully refusing to understand her own position. This feeling was aggravated by his being unable to tell her plainly the cause of his anger. If he had told her directly what he was thinking, he would have said:

"In that dress, with a princess only too well known to every one, to show yourself at the theater is equivalent not merely to acknowledging your position as a fallen woman, but is flinging down a challenge to society, that is to say, cutting yourself off from it forever."

He could not say that to her. "But how can she fail to see it, and what is going on in her?" he said to himself. He felt at the same time that his respect for her was diminished while his sense of her beauty was intensified.

He went back scowling to his rooms, and sitting down beside Yashvin, who, with his long legs stretched out on a chair, was drinking brandy and seltzer water, he ordered a glass of the same for himself.

"You were talking of Lankovsky's Powerful. That's a fine horse, and I would advise you to buy him," said Yashvin, glancing at his comrade's gloomy face. "His hind-quarters aren't quite first-rate, but the legs and head—one couldn't wish for anything better."

"I think I will take him," answered Vronsky.

Their conversation about horses interested him, but he did not for an instant forget Anna, and could not help listening to the sound of steps in the corridor and looking at the clock on the chimney-piece.

"Anna Arkadyevna gave orders to announce that she has gone to the theater."

Yashvin, tipping another glass of brandy into the bubbling water, drank it and got up, buttoning his coat.

"Well, let's go," he said, faintly smiling under his mustache, and showing by this smile that he knew the cause of Vronsky's gloominess, and did not attach any significance to it.

"I'm not going," Vronsky answered gloomily.

"Well, I must, I promised to. Good-bye, then. If you do, come to the stalls; you can take Kruzin's stall," added Yashvin as he went out.

"No, I'm busy."

"A wife is a care, but it's worse when she's not a wife," thought Yashvin, as he walked out of the hotel.

Vronsky, left alone, got up from his chair and began pacing up and down the room.

"And what's to-day? The fourth night. . . . Yegor and his wife are there, and my mother, most likely. Of course all Petersburg's there. Now she's gone in, taken off her cloak and come into the light. Tushkevitch, Yashvin, Princess Varvara," he pictured them to himself. . . . "What about me? Either that I'm frightened or have given up to Tushkevitch the right to protect her? From every point of view—stupid, stupid! . . . And why is she putting me in such a position?" he said with a gesture of despair.

With that gesture he knocked against the table, on which there was standing the seltzer water and the decanter of brandy, and almost upset it. He tried to catch it, let it slip, and angrily kicked the table over and rang.

"If you care to be in my service," he said to the valet who came in, "you had better remember your duties. This shouldn't be here. You ought to have cleared away."

The valet, conscious of his own innocence, would have defended himself, but glancing at his master, he saw from his face that the only thing to do was to be silent, and hurriedly threading his way in and out, dropped down on the carpet and began gathering up the whole and broken glasses and bottles.

"That's not your duty; send the waiter to clear away, and get my dress-coat out."

. . . . . .

Vronsky went into the theater at half-past eight. The performance was in full swing. The little old box-keeper, recognizing Vronsky as he helped him off with his fur coat, called him "Your Excellency," and suggested he should not take a number but should simply call Fyodor. In the brightly lighted corridor there was no one but the box-opener and two attendants with fur cloaks on their arms listening at the doors. Through the closed doors came the sounds of the discreet *staccato* accompaniment of the orchestra, and a single female voice rendering distinctly a musical phrase. The door opened to let the box-opener slip through, and the phrase drawing to the end reached Vronsky's hearing clearly. But the doors were closed again at once, and Vronsky did not hear the end of the phrase and the cadence of the accompaniment, though he knew from the thunder of applause that it was over. When he entered the hall, brilliantly lighted with chandeliers and gas jets, the noise was still going on. On the stage the singer, bowing and smiling, with bare shoulders flashing with diamonds, was, with the help of the tenor who had given her his arm, gathering up the bouquets that were flying awkwardly over the footlights. Then she went up to a gentleman with glossy pomaded hair parted down the center, who was stretching across the footlights holding out something to her, and all the public in the stalls as well as in the boxes was in excitement, craning forward, shouting and clapping. The conductor in his high chair assisted in passing the offering, and straightened his white tie. Vronsky walked into the middle of the stalls, and, standing still, began looking about him. That day less than ever was his attention turned upon the familar, habitual surroundings, the stage, the noise, all the familiar, uninteresting, parti-colored herd of spectators in the packed theater.

There were, as always, the same ladies of some sort with officers of some sort in the back of the boxes; the same gaily dressed women—God knows who—and uniforms and black coats; the same dirty crowd in the upper gallery; and among the crowd, in the boxes and in the front rows, were some forty of the *real* people. And to those oases Vronsky at once directed his attention, and with them he entered at once into relation.

The act was over when he went in, and so he did not go straight to his brother's box, but going up to the first row of stalls stopped at the footlights with Serpuhovskoy, who, standing with one knee raised and his heel on the footlights, caught sight of him in the distance and beckoned to him, smiling.

Vronsky had not yet seen Anna. He purposely avoided looking in her direction. But he knew by the direction of people's eyes where she was. He looked round discreetly, but he was not seeking her; expecting the worst, his eyes sought for Alexey Alexandrovitch. To his relief Alexey Alexandrovitch was not in the theater that evening.

"How little of the military man there is left in you!" Serpuhovskoy was saying to him. "A diplomat, an artist, something of that sort, one would say."

"Yes, it was like going back home when I put on a black coat," answered Vronsky, smiling and slowly taking out his opera-glass.

"Well, I'll own I envy you there. When I come back from abroad and put on this," he touched his epaulets, "I regret my freedom."

Serpuhovskoy had long given up all hope of Vronsky's career, but he liked him as before, and was now particularly cordial to him.

"What a pity you were not in time for the first act!"

Vronsky, listening with one ear, moved his opera-glass from the stalls and scanned the boxes. Near a lady in a turban and a bald old man, who seemed to wave angrily in the moving opera-glass, Vronsky suddenly caught sight of Anna's head, proud, strikingly beautiful, and smiling in the frame of lace. She was in the fifth box, twenty paces from him. She was sitting in front, and slightly turning, was saying something to Yashvin. The setting of her head on her handsome, broad shoulders, and the restrained excitement and brilliance of her eyes and her whole face reminded him of her just as he had seen her at the ball in Moscow. But he felt utterly different towards her beauty now. In his feeling for her now there was no element of mystery, and so her beauty, though it attracted him even more intensely than before, gave him now a sense of injury. She was not looking in his direction, but Vronsky felt that she had seen him already.

When Vronsky turned the opera-glass again in that direction, he noticed that Princess Varvara was particularly red, and kept laughing unnaturally and looking round at the next box. Anna, folding her fan and tapping it on the red velvet, was gazing away and did not see, and obviously did not wish to see, what was taking place in the next box. Yashvin's face wore the expression which was common when he was losing at cards. Scowling, he sucked the left end of his mustache further and further into his mouth, and cast sidelong glances at the next box.

In that box on the left were the Kartasovs. Vronsky knew them, and knew that Anna was acquainted with them. Madame

Kartasova, a thin little woman, was standing up in her box, and, her back turned upon Anna, she was putting on a mantle that her husband was holding for her. Her face was pale and angry, and she was talking excitedly. Kartasov, a fat, bald man, was continually looking round at Anna, while he attempted to soothe his wife. When the wife had gone out, the husband lingered a long while, and tried to catch Anna's eye, obviously anxious to bow to her. But Anna, with unmistakable intention, avoided noticing him, and talked to Yashvin, whose cropped head was bent down to her. Kartasov went out without making his salutation, and the box was left empty.

Vronsky could not understand exactly what had passed between the Kartasovs and Anna, but he saw that something humiliating for Anna had happened. He knew this both from what he had seen, and most of all from the face of Anna, who, he could see, was taxing every nerve to carry through the part she had taken up. And in maintaining this attitude of external composure she was completely successful. Any one who did not know her and her circle, who had not heard all the utterances of the women expressive of commiseration, indignation, and amazement, that she should show herself in society, and show herself so conspicuously with her lace and her beauty, would have admired the serenity and loveliness of this woman without a suspicion that she was undergoing the sensations of a man in the stocks.

Knowing that something had happened, but not knowing precisely what, Vronsky felt a thrill of agonizing anxiety, and hoping to find out something, he went towards his brother's box. Purposely choosing the way round furthest from Anna's box, he jostled as he came out against the colonel of his old regiment talking to two acquaintances. Vronsky heard the name of Madame Karenina, and noticed how the colonel hastened to address Vronsky loudly by name, with a meaning glance at his companions.

"Ah, Vronsky! When are you coming to the regiment? We can't let you off without a supper. You're one of the old set," said the colonel of his regiment.

"I can't stop, awfully sorry, another time," said Vronsky, and he ran up-stairs towards his brother's box.

The old countess, Vronsky's mother, with her steel-gray curls, was in his brother's box. Varya with the young Princess Sorokina met him in the corridor.

Leaving the Princess Sorokina with her mother, Varya held out her hand to her brother-in-law, and began immediately to speak of what interested him. She was more excited than he had ever seen her.

"I think it's mean and hateful, and Madame Kartasova had no right to do it. Madame Karenina . . ." she began.

"But what is it? I don't know."

"What? you've not heard?"

"You know I should be the last person to hear of it."

"There isn't a more spiteful creature than that Madame Kartasova!"

"But what did she do?"

"My husband told me. . . . She has insulted Madame Karenina. Her husband began talking to her across the box, and Madame Kartasova made a scene. She said something aloud, he says, something insulting, and went away."

"Count, your maman is asking for you," said the young Princess Sorokina, peeping out of the door of the box.

"I've been expecting you all the while," said his mother, smiling sarcastically. "You were nowhere to be seen."

Her son saw that she could not suppress a smile of delight.

"Good-evening, maman. I have come to you," he said coldly.

"Why aren't you going to *faire la cour à Madame Karenina?*" she went on, when Princess Sorokina had moved away. *"Elle fait sensation. On oublie la Patti pour elle."*

"Maman, I have asked you not to say anything to me of that," he answered, scowling.

"I'm only saying what every one's saying."

Vronsky made no reply, and saying a few words to Princess Sorokina, he went away. At the door he met his brother.

"Ah, Alexey!" said his brother. "How disgusting! Idiot of a woman, nothing else. . . . I wanted to go straight to her. Let's go together."

Vronsky did not hear him. With rapid steps he went downstairs; he felt that he must do something, but he did not know what. Anger with her for having put herself and him in such a false position, together with pity for her suffering, filled his heart. He went down, and made straight for Anna's box. At her box stood Stremov, talking to her.

"There are no more tenors. *Le moule en est brisé!*"

Vronsky bowed to her and stopped to greet Stremov.

"You came in late, I think, and have missed the best song," Anna said to Vronsky, glancing ironically, he thought, at him.

"I am a poor judge of music," he said, looking sternly at her.

"Like Prince Yashvin," she said smiling, "who considers that Patti sings too loud."

"Thank you," she said, her little hand in its long glove taking the playbill Vronsky picked up, and suddenly at that instant her lovely face quivered. She got up and went into the interior of the box.

Noticing in the next act that her box was empty, Vronsky, rousing indignant "hushes" in the silent audience, went out in the middle of a solo and drove home.

Anna was already at home. When Vronsky went up to her, she was in the same dress as she had worn at the theater. She was sitting in the first armchair against the wall, looking straight before her. She looked at him, and at once resumed her former position.

"Anna," he said.

"You, you are to blame for everything!" she cried, with tears of despair and hatred in her voice, getting up.

"I begged, I implored you not to go; I knew it would be unpleasant. . . ."

"Unpleasant!" she cried—"hideous! As long as I live I shall never forget it. She said it was a disgrace to sit beside me."

"A silly woman's chatter," he said: "but why risk it, why provoke? . . ."

"I hate your calm. You ought not to have brought me to this. If you had loved me . . ."

"Anna! How does the question of my love come in?"

"Oh, if you loved me, as I love, if you were tortured as I am! . . ." she said, looking at him with an expression of terror.

He was sorry for her, and angry notwithstanding. He assured her of his love because he saw that this was the only means of

soothing her, and he did not reproach her in words, but in his heart he reproached her.

And the asseverations of his love, which seemed to him so vulgar that he was ashamed to utter them, she drank in eagerly, and gradually became calmer. The next day, completely reconciled, they left for the country.

Part Six

CHAPTER I

Darya Alexandrovna spent the summer with her children at Pokrovskoe, at her sister Kitty Levin's. The house on her own estate was quite in ruins, and Levin and his wife had persuaded her to spend the summer with them. Stepan Arkadyevitch greatly approved of the arrangement. He said he was very sorry his official duties prevented him from spending the summer in the country with his family, which would have been the greatest happiness for him; and remaining in Moscow, he came down to the country from time to time for a day or two. Besides the Oblonskys, with all their children and their governess, the old princess too came to stay that summer with the Levins, as she considered it her duty to watch over her inexperienced daughter in her *interesting condition*. Moreover, Varenka, Kitty's friend abroad, kept her promise to come to Kitty when she was married, and stayed with her friend. All of these were friends or relations of Levin's wife. And though he liked them all, he rather regretted his own Levin world and ways, which was smothered by this influx of the "Shtcherbatsky element," as he called it to himself. Of his own relations there stayed with him only Sergey Ivanovitch, but he too was a man of the Koznishev and not the Levin stamp, so that the Levin spirit was utterly obliterated.

In the Levins' house, so long deserted, there were now so many people that almost all the rooms were occupied, and almost every day it happened that the old princess, sitting down to table, counted them all over, and put the thirteenth grandson or granddaughter at a separate table. And Kitty, with her careful housekeeping, had no little trouble to get all the chickens, turkeys, and geese, of which so many were needed to satisfy the summer appetites of the visitors and children.

The whole family were sitting at dinner. Dolly's children, with their governess and Varenka, were making plans for going to look for mushrooms. Sergey Ivanovitch, who was looked up to by all the party for his intellect and learning, with a respect that almost amounted to awe, surprised every one by joining in the conversation about mushrooms.

"Take me with you. I am very fond of picking mushrooms," he said, looking at Varenka; "I think it's a very nice occupation."

"Oh, we shall be delighted," answered Varenka, coloring a little. Kitty exchanged meaning glances with Dolly. The proposal of the learned and intellectual Sergey Ivanovitch to go looking for mushrooms with Varenka confirmed certain theories of Kitty's with which her mind had been very busy of late. She made haste to address some remark to her mother, so that her look should not be noticed. After dinner Sergey Ivanovitch sat with his cup of coffee at the drawing-room window, and while he took part in a conversation he had begun with his brother, he watched the door through which the children would start on the mushroom-picking expedition. Levin was sitting in the window near his brother.

Kitty stood beside her husband, evidently awaiting the end of a conversation that had no interest for her, in order to tell him something.

"You have changed in many respects since your marriage, and for the better," said Sergey Ivanovitch, smiling to Kitty, and obviously little interested in the conversation, "but you have remained true to your passion for defending the most paradoxical theories."

"Katya, it's not good for you to stand," her husband said to her, putting a chair for her and looking significantly at her.

"Oh, and there's no time either," added Sergey Ivanovitch, seeing the children running out.

At the head of them all Tanya galloped sideways, in her tightly-drawn stockings, and waving a basket and Sergey Ivanovitch's hat, she ran straight up to him.

Boldly running up to Sergey Ivanovitch with shining eyes, so like her father's fine eyes, she handed him his hat and made as though she would put it on for him, softening her freedom by a shy and friendly smile.

"Varenka's waiting," she said, carefully putting his hat on, seeing from Sergey Ivanovitch's smile that she might do so.

Varenka was standing at the door, dressed in a yellow print gown, with a white kerchief on her head.

"I'm coming, I'm coming, Varvara Andreevna," said Sergey Ivanovitch, finishing his cup of coffee, and putting into their separate pockets his handkerchief and cigar-case.

"And how sweet my Varenka is! eh?" said Kitty to her husband, as soon as Sergey Ivanovitch rose. She spoke so that Sergey Ivanovitch could hear, and it was clear that she meant him to do so. "And how good-looking she is—such a refined beauty! Varenka!" Kitty shouted. "Shall you be in the mill copse? We'll come out to you."

"You certainly forget your condition, Kitty," said the old princess, hurriedly coming out at the door. "You mustn't shout like that."

Varenka, hearing Kitty's voice and her mother's reprimand, went with light, rapid steps up to Kitty. The rapidity of her movement, her flushed and eager face, everything betrayed that something out of the common was going on in her. Kitty knew what this was, and had been watching her intently. She called Varenka at that moment merely in order mentally to give her a blessing for the important event which, as Kitty fancied, was bound to come to pass that day after dinner in the wood.

"Varenka, I should be very happy if a certain something were to happen," she whispered as she kissed her.

"And are you coming with us?" Varenka said to Levin in confusion, pretending not to have heard what had been said.

"I am coming, but only as far as the thrashing-floor, and there I shall stop."

"Why, what do you want there?" said Kitty.

"I must go to have a look at the new wagons, and to check the invoice," said Levin; "and where will you be?"

"On the terrace."

CHAPTER II

On the terrace were assembled all the ladies of the party. They always liked sitting there after dinner, and that day they had work to do there too. Besides the sewing and knitting of baby-clothes, with which all of them were busy, that afternoon jam was being made on the terrace by a method new to Agafea Mihalovna, without the addition of water. Kitty had introduced this new method, which had been in use in her home. Agafea Mihalovna, to whom the task of jam-making had always been intrusted, considering that what had been done in the Levin household could not be amiss, had nevertheless put water with the strawberries, maintaining that the jam could not be made without it. She had been caught in the act, and was now making jam before every one, and it was to be proved to her conclusively that jam could be very well made without water.

Agafea Mihalovna, her face heated and angry, her hair untidy, and her thin arms bare to the elbows, was turning the preserving-pan over the charcoal stove, looking darkly at the raspberries and devoutly hoping they would stick and not cook properly. The princess, conscious that Agafea Mihalovna's wrath must be chiefly directed against her, as the person responsible for the raspberry jam-making, tried to appear to be absorbed in other things and not interested in the jam, talked of other matters, but cast stealthy glances in the direction of the stove.

"I always buy my maids' dresses myself, of some cheap material," the princess said, continuing the previous conversation. "Isn't it time to skim it, my dear?" she added, addressing Agafea Mihalovna. "There's not the slightest need for you to do it, and it's hot for you," she said, stopping Kitty.

"I'll do it," said Dolly, and getting up, she carefully passed the spoon over the frothing sugar, and from time to time shook off the clinging jam from the spoon by knocking it on a plate that was covered with yellow-red scum and blood-colored syrup. "How they'll enjoy this at tea-time!" she thought of her children, remembering how she herself as a child had wondered how it was the grown-up people did not eat what was best of all—the scum of the jam.

"Stiva says it's much better to give money." Dolly took up meanwhile the weighty subject under discussion, what presents should be made to servants. "But . . ."

"Money's out of the question!" the princess and Kitty exclaimed with one voice. "They appreciate a present . . ."

"Well, last year, for instance, I bought our Matrona Semyenovna, not a poplin, but something of that sort," said the princess.

"I remember she was wearing it on your nameday."

"A charming pattern—so simple and refined,—I should have liked it myself, if she hadn't had it. Something like Varenka's. So pretty and inexpensive."

"Well, now I think it's done," said Dolly, dropping the syrup from the spoon.

"When it sets as it drops, it's ready. Cook it a little longer, Agafea Mihalovna."

"The flies!" said Agafea Mihalovna angrily. "It'll be just the same," she added.

"Ah! how sweet it is! don't frighten it!" Kitty said suddenly, looking at a sparrow that had settled on the step and was pecking at the center of a raspberry.

"Yes, but you keep a little further from the stove," said her mother.

"*A propos de Varenka,*" said Kitty, speaking in French, as they had been doing all the while, so that Agafea Mihalovna should not understand them, "you know, mamma, I somehow expect things to be settled to-day. You know what I mean. How splendid it would be!"

"But what a famous matchmaker she is!" said Dolly. "How carefully and cleverly she throws them together! . . ."

"No; tell me, mamma, what do you think?"

"Why, what is one to think? He" (*he* meant Sergey Ivanovitch) "might at any time have been a match for any one in Russia; now, of course, he's not quite a young man, still I know ever so many girls would be glad to marry him even now. . . . She's a very nice girl, but he might . . ."

"Oh, no, mamma, do understand why, for him and for her too, nothing better could be imagined. In the first place, she's charming!" said Kitty, crooking one of her fingers.

"He thinks her very attractive, that's certain," assented Dolly.

"Then he occupies such a position in society that he has no need to look for either fortune or position in his wife. All he needs is a good, sweet wife—a restful one."

"Well, with her he would certainly be restful," Dolly assented.

"Thirdly, that she should love him. And so it is . . . that is, it would be so splendid! . . . I look forward to seeing them coming out of the forest—and everything settled. I shall see at once by their eyes. I should be so delighted! What do you think, Dolly?"

"But don't excite yourself. It's not at all the thing for you to be excited," said her mother.

"Oh, I'm not excited, mamma. I fancy he will make her an offer to-day."

"Ah, that's so strange, how and when a man makes an offer! . . . There is a sort of barrier, and all at once it's broken down," said Dolly, smiling pensively and recalling her past with Stepan Arkadyevitch.

"Mamma, how did papa make you an offer?" Kitty asked suddenly.

"There was nothing out of the way, it was very simple," answered the princess, but her face beamed all over at the recollection.

"Oh, but how was it? You loved him, anyway, before you were allowed to speak?"

Kitty felt a peculiar pleasure in being able now to talk to her mother on equal terms about those questions of such paramount interest in a woman's life.

"Of course I did; he had come to stay with us in the country."

"But how was it settled between you, mamma?"

"You imagine, I dare say, that you invented something quite new? It's always just the same: it was settled by the eyes, by smiles . . ."

"How nicely you said that, mamma! It's just by the eyes, by smiles that it's done," Dolly assented.

"But what words did he say?"

"What did Kostya say to you?"

"He wrote it in chalk. It was wonderful. . . . How long ago it seems!" she said.

And the three women all fell to musing on the same thing. Kitty was the first to break the silence. She remembered all that last winter before her marriage, and her passion for Vronsky.

"There's one thing . . . that old love-affair of Varenka's," she said, a natural chain of ideas bringing her to this point. "I should have liked to say something to Sergey Ivanovitch, to prepare him. They're all—all men, I mean," she added, "awfully jealous over our past."

"Not all," said Dolly. "You judge by your own husband. It makes him miserable even now to remember Vronsky. Eh? that's true, isn't it?"

"Yes," Kitty answered, a pensive smile in her eyes.

"But I really don't know," the mother put in in defense of her motherly care of her daughter, "what there was in your past that could worry him? That Vronsky paid you attentions—that happens to every girl."

"Oh, yes, but we didn't mean that," Kitty said, flushing a little.

"No, let me speak," her mother went on, "why, you yourself would not let me have a talk to Vronsky. Don't you remember?"

"Oh, mamma!" said Kitty, with an expression of suffering.

"There's no keeping you young people in check nowadays. . . . Your friendship could not have gone beyond what was suitable. I should myself have called upon him to explain himself. But, my darling, it's not right for you to be agitated. Please remember that, and calm yourself."

"I'm perfectly calm, maman."

"How happy it was for Kitty that Anna came then," said Dolly, "and how unhappy for her. It turned out quite the opposite," she said, struck by her own ideas. "Then Anna was so happy, and Kitty thought herself unhappy. Now it is just the opposite. I often think of her."

"A nice person to think about! Horrid, repulsive woman—no heart," said her mother, who could not forget that Kitty had married not Vronsky, but Levin.

"What do you want to talk of it for?" Kitty said with annoyance. "I never think about it, and I don't want to think of it . . . And I don't want to think of it," she said, catching the sound of her husband's well-known step on the steps of the terrace.

"What's that you don't want to think about?" inquired Levin, coming on to the terrace.

But no one answered him, and he did not repeat the question.

"I'm sorry I've broken in on your feminine parliament," he said, looking round on every one discontentedly, and perceiving that they had been talking of something which they would not talk about before him.

For a second he felt that he was sharing the feeling of Agafea Mihalovna, vexation at their making jam without water, and altogether at the outside Shtcherbatsky element. He smiled, however, and went up to Kitty.

"Well, how are you?" he asked her, looking at her with the expression with which every one looked at her now.

"Oh, very well," said Kitty, smiling, "and how have things gone with you?"

"The wagons held three times as much as the old carts did. Well, are we going for the children? I've ordered the horses to be put in."

"What! you want to take Kitty in the wagonette?" her mother said reproachfully.

"Yes, at a walking-pace, princess."

Levin never called the princess "maman" as men often do call their mothers-in-law, and the princess disliked his not doing so. But though he liked and respected the princess, Levin could not call her so without a sense of profaning his feeling for his dead mother.

"Come with us, maman," said Kitty.

"I don't like to see such imprudence."

"Well, I'll walk then, I'm so well." Kitty got up and went to her husband and took his hand.

"You may be well, but everything in moderation," said the princess.

"Well, Agafea Mihalovna, is the jam done?" said Levin, smiling to Agafea Mihalovna, and trying to cheer her up. "Is it all right in the new way?"

"I suppose it's all right. For our notions it's boiled too long."

"It'll be all the better, Agafea Mihalovna, it won't mildew, even though our ice has begun to thaw already, so that we've no cool cellar to store it," said Kitty, at once divining her husband's motive, and addressing the old housekeeper with the same feeling; "but your pickle's so good, that mamma says she never tasted any like it," she added, smiling, and putting her kerchief straight.

Agafea Mihalovna looked angrily at Kitty.

"You needn't try to console me, mistress. I need only to look at you with him, and I feel happy," she said, and something in the rough familiarity of that *with him* touched Kitty.

"Come along with us to look for mushrooms, you will show us the best places." Agafea Mihalovna smiled and shook her head, as though to say: "I should like to be angry with you too, but I can't."

"Do it, please, by my receipt," said the princess; "put some paper over the jam, and moisten it with a little rum, and without even ice, it will never go mildewy."

CHAPTER III

KITTY was particularly glad of a chance of being alone with her husband, for she had noticed the shade of mortification that had passed over his face—always so quick to reflect every feeling—at the moment when he had come onto the terrace and asked what they were talking of, and had got no answer.

When they had set off on foot ahead of the others, and had come out of sight of the house onto the beaten dusty road, marked with rusty wheels and sprinkled with grains of corn, she clung faster to his arm and pressed it closer to her. He had quite forgotten the momentary unpleasant impression, and alone with her he felt, now that the thought of her approaching motherhood was never for a moment absent from his mind, a new and delicious bliss, quite pure from all alloy of sense, in the being near to the woman he loved. There was no need of speech, yet he longed to hear the sound of her voice, which like her eyes had changed since she had been with child. In her voice, as in her eyes, there was that softness and gravity which is found in people continually concentrated on some cherished pursuit.

"So you're not tired? Lean more on me," said he.

"No, I'm so glad of a chance of being alone with you, and I must own, though I'm happy with them, I do regret our winter evenings alone."

"That was good, but this is even better. Both are better," he said, squeezing her hand.

"Do you know what we were talking about when you came in?"

"About jam?"

"Oh, yes, about jam too; but afterwards, about how men make offers."

"Ah!" said Levin, listening more to the sound of her voice than to the words she was saying, and all the while paying attention to the road, which passed now through the forest, and avoiding places where she might make a false step.

"And about Sergey Ivanovitch and Varenka. You've noticed? . . . I'm very anxious for it," she went on. "What do you think about it?" And she peeped into his face.

"I don't know what to think," Levin answered, smiling. "Sergey seems very strange to me in that way. I told you, you know . . ."

"Yes, that he was in love with that girl who died. . . ."

"That was when I was a child; I know about it from hearsay and tradition. I remember him then. He was wonderfully sweet. But I've watched him since with women; he is friendly, some of them he likes, but one feels that to him they're simply people, not women."

"Yes, but now with Varenka . . . I fancy there's something . . ."

"Perhaps there is . . . But one has to know him . . . He's a peculiar, wonderful person. He lives a spiritual life only. He's too pure, too exalted a nature."

"Why? Would this lower him, then?"

"No, but he's so used to a spiritual life that he can't reconcile himself with actual fact, and Varenka is after all fact."

Levin had grown used by now to uttering his thought boldly, without taking the trouble of clothing it in exact language. He knew that his wife, in such moments of loving tenderness as now, would understand what he meant to say from a hint, and she did understand him.

"Yes, but there's not so much of that actual fact about her as about me. I can see that he would never have cared for me. She is altogether spiritual."

"Oh, no, he is so fond of you, and I am always so glad when my people like you. . . ."

"Yes, he's very nice to me; but . . ."

"It's not as it was with poor Nikolay . . . you really cared for each other," Levin finished. "Why not speak of him?" he added. "I sometimes blame myself for not; it ends in one's forgetting. Ah, how terrible and dear he was! . . . Yes, what were we talking about?" Levin said, after a pause.

"You think he can't fall in love," said Kitty, translating into her own language.

"It's not so much that he can't fall in love," Levin said, smiling, "but he has not the weakness necessary. . . . I've always envied him, and even now, when I'm so happy, I still envy him."

"You envy him for not being able to fall in love?"

"I envy him for being better than I," said Levin. "He does not live for himself. His whole life is subordinated to his duty. And that's why he can be calm and contented."

"And you?" Kitty asked, with an ironical and loving smile.

She could never have explained the chain of thought that made her smile; but the last link in it was that her husband, in exalting his brother and abasing himself, was not quite sincere. Kitty knew that this insincerity came from his love for his brother, from his sense of shame at being too happy, and above all from his unflagging craving to be better—she loved it in him, and so she smiled.

"And you? What are you dissatisfied with?" she asked, with the same smile.

Her disbelief in his self-dissatisfaction delighted him, and unconsciously he tried to draw her into giving utterance to the grounds of her disbelief.

"I am happy, but dissatisfied with myself. . . ." he said.

"Why, how can you be dissatisfied with yourself if you are happy?"

"Well, how shall I say? . . . In my heart I really care for nothing whatever but that you should not stumble—see? Oh, but really you mustn't skip about like that!" he cried, breaking off to scold her for too agile a movement in stepping over a branch that lay in the path. "But when I think about myself, and compare myself with others, especially with my brother, I feel I'm a poor creature."

"But in what way?" Kitty pursued with the same smile. "Don't you too work for others? What about your co-operative settlement, and your work on the estate, and your book? . . ."

"Oh, but I feel, and particularly just now—it's your fault," he said, pressing her hand—"that all that doesn't count. I do it in a way half-heartedly. If I could care for all that as I care for you! . . . Instead of that, I do it in these days like a task that is set me."

"Well, what would you say about papa?" asked Kitty. "Is he a poor creature then, as he does nothing for the public good?"

"He?—no! But then one must have the simplicity, the straightforwardness, the goodness of your father: and I haven't got that. I do nothing, and I fret about it. It's all your doing. Before there was you—and *this* too," he added with a glance towards her waist that she understood—"I put all my energies into work; now I can't, and I'm ashamed; I do it just as though it were a task set me, I'm pretending. . . ."

"Well, but would you like to change this minute with Sergey Ivanovitch?" said Kitty. "Would you like to do this work for the general good, and to love the task set you, as he does, and nothing else?"

"Of course not," said Levin. "But I'm so happy that I don't understand anything. So you think he'll make her an offer to-day?" he added after a brief silence.

"I think so, and I don't think so. Only, I'm awfully anxious for it. Here, wait a minute." She stooped down and picked a wild camomile at the edge of the path. "Come, count: he does propose, he doesn't," she said, giving him the flower.

"He does, he doesn't," said Levin, tearing off the white petals.

"No, no!" Kitty, snatching at his hand, stopped him. She had been watching his fingers with interest. "You picked off two."

"Oh, but see, this little one shan't count to make up," said Levin, tearing off a little half-grown petal. "Here's the wagonette overtaking us."

"Aren't you tired, Kitty?" called the princess.

"Not in the least."

"If you are you can get in, as the horses are quiet and walking."

But it was not worth while to get in, they were quite near the place, and all walked on together.

CHAPTER IV

Varenka, with her white kerchief on her black hair, surrounded by the children, gaily and good-humoredly looking after them, and at the same time visibly excited at the possibility of receiving a declaration from the man she cared for, was very attractive. Sergey Ivanovitch walked beside her, and never left off admiring her. Looking at her, he recalled all the delightful things he had heard from her lips, all the good he knew about her, and became more and more conscious that the feeling he had for her was something special that he had felt long, long ago, and only once, in his early youth. The feeling of happiness in being near her continually grew, and at last reached such a point that, as he put a huge, slender-stalked agaric fungus in her basket, he looked straight into her face, and noticing the flush of glad and alarmed excitement that overspread her face, he was confused himself, and smiled to her in silence a smile that said too much.

"If so," he said to himself, "I ought to think it over and make up my mind, and not give way like a boy to the impulse of a moment."

"I'm going to pick by myself apart from all the rest, or else my efforts will make no show," he said, and he left the edge of the forest where they were walking on low silky grass between old birch-trees standing far apart, and went more into the heart of the wood, where between the white birch-trunks there were gray trunks of aspen and dark bushes of hazel. Walking some forty paces away, Sergey Ivanovitch, knowing he was out of sight, stood still behind a bushy spindle-tree in full flower with its rosy red catkins. It was perfectly still all round him. Only overhead in the birches under which he stood, the flies, like a swarm of bees, buzzed unceasingly, and from time to time the children's voices were floated across to him. All at once he heard, not far from the edge of the wood, the sound of Varenka's contralto voice, calling Grisha, and a smile of delight passed over Sergey Ivanovitch's face. Conscious of this smile, he shook his head disapprovingly at his own condition, and taking out a cigar, he began lighting it. For a long while he could not get a match to light against the trunk of a birch-tree. The soft scales of the white bark rubbed off the phosphorus, and the light went out. At last one of the matches burned, and the fragrant cigar smoke, hovering uncertainly in flat, wide coils, stretched away forwards and upwards over a bush under the overhanging branches of a birch-tree. Watching the streak of smoke, Sergey Ivanovitch walked gently on, deliberating on his position.

"Why not?" he thought. "If it were only a passing fancy or a passion, if it were only this attraction—this mutual attraction (I can call it a *mutual* attraction), but I felt that it was in contradiction with the whole bent of my life—if I felt that in giving way to this attraction I should be false to my vocation and my duty . . . but it's not so. The only thing I can say against it is that, when I lost Marie, I said to myself that I would remain faithful to her memory. That's the only thing I can say against my feeling. . . . That's a great thing," Sergey Ivanovitch said to himself, feeling at the same time that this consideration had not the slightest importance for him personally, but would only perhaps detract from his romantic character in the eyes of others. "But apart from that, however much I searched, I should never find anything to say against my feeling. If I were choosing by considerations of suitability alone, I could not have found anything better."

However many women and girls he thought of whom he knew, he could not think of a girl who united to such a degree all, positively all, the qualities he would wish to see in his wife. She had all the charm and freshness of youth, but she was not a child; and if she loved him, she loved him consciously as a woman ought to love; that was one thing. Another point: she was not only far from being worldly, but had an unmistakable distaste for worldly society, and at the same time she knew the world, and had all the ways of a woman of the best society, which were absolutely essential to Sergey Ivanovitch's conception of the woman who was to share his life. Thirdly: she was religious, and not like a child, unconsciously religious and good, as Kitty, for example, was, but her life was founded on religious principles. Even in trifling matters, Sergey Ivanovitch found in her all that he wanted in his wife: she was poor and alone in the world, so she would not bring with her a mass of relations and their influence into her husband's house, as he saw now in Kitty's case. She would owe everything to her husband, which was what he had always desired too for his future family life. And this girl, who united all these qualities, loved him. He was a modest man, but he could not help seeing it. And he loved her. There was one consideration against it—his age. But he came of a long-lived family, he had not a single gray hair, no one would have taken him for forty, and he remembered Varenka's saying that it was only in Russia that men of fifty thought themselves old, and that in France a man of fifty considers himself *dans la force de l'age,* while a man of forty is *un jeune homme.* But what did the mere reckoning of years matter when he felt as young in heart as he had been twenty years ago? Was it not youth to feel as he felt now, when coming from the other side to the edge of the wood he saw in the glowing light of the slanting sunbeams the gracious figure of Varenka in her yellow gown with her basket, walking lightly by the trunk of an old birch-tree, and when this impression of the sight of Varenka blended so harmoniously with the beauty of the view, of the yellow oatfield lying bathed in the slanting sunshine, and beyond it the distant ancient forest flecked with yellow and melting into the blue of the distance? His heart throbbed joyously. A softened feeling came over him. He felt that he had made up his mind. Varenka, who had just crouched down to pick a mushroom, rose with a supple movement and looked round. Flinging away the cigar, Sergey Ivanovitch advanced with resolute steps towards her.

CHAPTER V

"Varvara Andreevna, when I was very young, I set before myself the ideal of the woman I loved and should be happy to call my wife. I have lived through a long life, and now for the first time I have met what I sought—in you. I love you, and offer you my hand."

Sergey Ivanovitch was saying this to himself while he was ten paces from Varvara. Kneeling down, with her hands over the mushrooms to guard them from Grisha, she was calling little Masha.

"Come here, little ones! There are so many!" she was saying in her sweet, deep voice.

Seeing Sergey Ivanovitch approaching, she did not get up and did not change her position, but everything told him that she felt his presence and was glad of it.

"Well, did you find some?" she asked from under the white kerchief, turning her handsome, gently smiling face to him.

"Not one," said Sergey Ivanovitch. "Did you?"

She did not answer, busy with the children who thronged about her.

"That one too, near the twig," she pointed out to little Masha a little fungus, split in half across its rosy cap by the dry grass from under which it thrust itself. Varenka got up while Masha picked the fungus, breaking it into two white halves. "This brings back my childhood," she added, moving apart from the children beside Sergey Ivanovitch.

They walked on for some steps in silence. Varenka saw that he wanted to speak; she guessed of what, and felt faint with joy and panic. They had walked so far away that no one could hear them now, but still he did not begin to speak. It would have been better for Varenka to be silent. After a silence it would have been easier for them to say what they wanted to say than after talking about mushrooms. But against her own will, as it were accidentally, Varenka said:

"So you found nothing? In the middle of the wood there are always fewer, though." Sergey Ivanovitch sighed and made no answer. He was annoyed that she had spoken about the mushrooms. He wanted to bring her back to the first words she had uttered about her childhood; but after a pause of some length, as though against his own will, he made an observation in response to her last words.

"I have heard that the white edible funguses are found principally at the edge of the wood, though I can't tell them apart."

Some minutes more passed, they moved still further away from the children, and were quite alone. Varenka's heart throbbed so that she heard it beating, and felt that she was turning red and pale and red again.

To be the wife of a man like Koznishev, after her position with Madame Stahl, was to her imagination the height of happiness. Besides, she was almost certain that she was in love with him. And this moment it would have to be decided. She felt frightened. She dreaded both his speaking and his not speaking.

Now or never it must be said—that Sergey Ivanovitch felt too. Everything in the expression, the flushed cheeks and the downcast eyes of Varenka betrayed a painful suspense. Sergey Ivanovitch saw it and felt sorry for her. He felt even that to say nothing now would be a slight to her. Rapidly in his own mind he ran over all the arguments in support of his decision. He even said over to himself the words in which he meant to put his offer, but instead of those words, some utterly unexpected reflection that occurred to him made him ask:

"What is the difference between the 'birch' mushroom and the 'white' mushroom?"

Varenka's lips quivered with emotion as she answered:

"In the top part there is scarcely any difference, it's in the stalk."

And as soon as these words were uttered, both he and she felt that it was over, that what was to have been said would not be said; and their emotion, which had up to then been continually growing more intense, began to subside.

"The birch mushroom's stalk suggests a dark man's chin after two days without shaving," said Sergey Ivanovitch, speaking quite calmly now.

"Yes, that's true," answered Varenka smiling, and unconsciously the direction of their walk changed. They began to turn towards the children. Varenka felt both sore and ashamed; at the same time she had a sense of relief.

When he had got home again and went over the whole subject, Sergey Ivanovitch thought his previous decision had been a mistaken one. He could not be false to the memory of Marie.

"Gently, children, gently!" Levin shouted quite angrily to the children, standing before his wife to protect her when the crowd of children flew with shrieks of delight to meet them.

Behind the children Sergey Ivanovitch and Varenka walked out of the wood. Kitty had no need to ask Varenka; she saw from the calm and somewhat crestfallen faces of both that her plans had not come off.

"Well?" her husband questioned her as they were going home again.

"It doesn't bite," said Kitty, her smile and manner of speaking recalling her father, a likeness Levin often noticed with pleasure.

"How doesn't bite?"

"I'll show you," she said, taking her husband's hand, lifting it to her mouth, and just faintly brushing it with closed lips. "Like a kiss on a priest's hand."

"Which didn't it bite with?" he said, laughing.

"Both. But it should have been like this . . ."

"There are some peasants coming . . ."

"Oh, they didn't see."

CHAPTER VI

DURING the time of the children's tea the grown-up people sat in the balcony and talked as though nothing had happened though they all, especially Sergey Ivanovitch and Varenka, were very well aware that there had happened an event which, though negative, was of very great importance. They both had the same feeling, rather like that of a schoolboy after an examination, which has left him in the same class or shut him out of the school forever. Every one present, feeling too that something had happened, talked eagerly about extraneous subjects. Levin and Kitty were particularly happy and conscious of their love that evening. And their happiness in their love seemed to imply a disagreeable slur on those who would have liked to feel the same and could not—and they felt a prick of conscience.

"Mark my words, Alexander will not come," said the old princess.

That evening they were expecting Stepan Arkadyevitch to come down by train, and the old prince had written that possibly he might come too.

"And I know why," the princess went on; "he says that young people ought to be left alone for a while at first."

"But papa has left us alone. We've never seen him," said Kitty. "Besides, we're not young people!—we're old, married people by now."

"Only if he doesn't come, I shall say good-bye to you children," said the princess, sighing mournfully.

"What nonsense, mamma!" both the daughters fell upon her at once.

"How do you suppose he is feeling? Why, now . . ."

And suddenly there was an unexpected quiver in the princess's voice. Her daughters were silent, and looked at one another. "Maman always finds something to be miserable about," they said in that glance. They did not know that happy as the princess was in her daughter's house, and useful as she felt herself to be there, she had been extremely miserable, both on her own account and her husband's, ever since they had married their last and favorite daughter, and the old home had been left empty.

"What is it, Agafea Mihalovna?" Kitty asked suddenly of Agafea Mihalovna, who was standing with a mysterious air, and a face full of meaning.

"About supper."

"Well, that's right," said Dolly; "you go and arrange about it, and I'll go and hear Grisha repeat his lesson, or else he will have nothing done all day."

"That's my lesson! No, Dolly, I'm going," said Levin, jumping up.

Grisha, who was by now at a high school, had to go over the lessons of the term in the summer holidays. Darya Alexandrovna, who had been studying Latin with her son in Moscow before, had made it a rule on coming to the Levins' to go over with him, at least once a day, the most difficult lessons of Latin and arithmetic. Levin had offered to take her place, but the mother, having once overheard Levin's lesson, and noticing that it was not given exactly as the teacher in Moscow had given it, said resolutely, though with much embarrassment and anxiety not to mortify Levin, that they must keep strictly to the book as the teacher had done, and that she had better undertake it again herself. Levin was amazed both at Stepan Arkadyevitch, who, by neglecting his duty, threw upon the mother the supervision of studies of which she had no comprehension, and at the teachers for teaching the children so badly. But he promised his sister-in-law to give the lessons exactly as she wished. And he went on teaching Grisha, not in his own way, but by the book, and so took little interest in it, and often forgot the hour of the lesson. So it had been to-day.

"No, I'm going, Dolly, you sit still," he said. "We'll do it all properly, like the book. Only when Stiva comes, and we go out shooting, then we shall have to miss it."

And Levin went to Grisha.

Varenka was saying the same thing to Kitty. Even in the happy, well-ordered household of the Levins Varenka had succeeded in making herself useful.

"I'll see to the supper, you sit still," she said, and got up to go to Agafea Mihalovna.

"Yes, yes, most likely they've not been able to get chickens. If so, ours . . ."

"Agafea Mihalovna and I will see about it," and Varenka vanished with her.

"What a nice girl!" said the princess.

"Not nice, maman; she's an exquisite girl; there's no one else like her."

"So you are expecting Stepan Arkadyevitch to-day?" said

Sergey Ivanovitch, evidently not disposed to pursue the conversation about Varenka. "It would be difficult to find two sons-in-law more unlike than yours," he said with a subtle smile. "One all movement, only living in society, like a fish in water; the other our Kostya, lively, alert, quick in everything, but as soon as he is in society, he either sinks into apathy, or struggles helplessly like a fish on land."

"Yes, he's very heedless," said the princess, addressing Sergey Ivanovitch. "I've been meaning, indeed, to ask you to tell him that it's out of the question for her" (she indicated Kitty) "to stay here; that she positively must come to Moscow. He talks of getting a doctor down . . ."

"Maman, he'll do everything; he has agreed to everything," Kitty said, angry with her mother for appealing to Sergey Ivanovitch to judge in such a matter.

In the middle of their conversation they heard the snorting of horses and the sound of wheels on the gravel. Dolly had not time to get up to go and meet her husband, when from the window of the room below, where Grisha was having his lesson, Levin leaped out and helped Grisha out after him.

"It's Stiva!" Levin shouted from under the balcony. "We've finished, Dolly, don't be afraid!" he added, and started running like a boy to meet the carriage.

"*Is ea id, ejus, ejus, ejus!*" shouted Grisha, skipping along the avenue.

"And some one else too! Papa, of course!" cried Levin, stopping at the entrance of the avenue. "Kitty, don't come down the steep staircase, go round."

But Levin had been mistaken in taking the person sitting in the carriage for the old prince. As he got nearer to the carriage he saw beside Stepan Arkadyevitch not the prince but a handsome, stout young man in a Scotch cap, with long ends of ribbon behind. This was Vassenka Veslovsky, a distant cousin of the Shtcherbatskys, a brilliant young gentleman in Petersburg and Moscow society. "A capital fellow, and a keen sportsman," as Stepan Arkadyevitch said, introducing him.

Not a whit abashed by the disappointment caused by his having come in place of the old prince, Veslovsky greeted Levin gaily, claiming acquaintance with him in the past, and snatching up Grisha into the carriage, lifted him over the pointer that Stepan Arkadyevitch had brought with him.

Levin did not get into the carriage, but walked behind. He was rather vexed at the non-arrival of the old prince, whom he liked more and more the more he saw of him, and also at the arrival of this Vassenka Veslovsky, a quite uncongenial and superfluous person. He seemed to him still more uncongenial and superfluous when, on approaching the steps where the whole party, children and grown-up, were gathered together in much excitement, Levin saw Vassenka Veslovsky, with a particularly warm and gallant air, kissing Kitty's hand.

"Your wife and I are cousins and very old friends," said Vassenka Veslovsky, once more shaking Levin's hand with great warmth.

"Well, are there plenty of birds?" Stepan Arkadyevitch said to Levin, hardly leaving time for every one to utter their greetings. "We've come with the most savage intentions. Why, maman, they've not been in Moscow since! Look, Tanya, here's something for you! Get it, please, it's in the carriage, behind!" he talked in all directions. "How pretty you've grown, Dolly," he said to his wife, once more kissing her hand, holding it in one of his, and patting it with the other.

Levin, who a minute before had been in the happiest frame of mind, now looked darkly at every one, and everything displeased him.

"Who was it he kissed yesterday with those lips?" he thought, looking at Stepan Arkadyevitch's tender demonstrations to his wife. He looked at Dolly, and he did not like her either.

"She doesn't believe in his love. So what is she so pleased about? Revolting!" thought Levin.

He looked at the princess, who had been so dear to him a minute before, and he did not like the manner in which she welcomed this Vassenka, with his ribbons, just as though she were in her own house.

Even Sergey Ivanovitch, who had come out too onto the steps, seemed to him unpleasant with the show of cordiality with which he met Stepan Arkadyevitch, though Levin knew that his brother neither liked nor respected Oblonsky.

And Varenka, even she seemed hateful, with her air *sainte nitouche* making the acquaintance of this gentleman, while all the while she was thinking of nothing but getting married.

And more hateful than any one was Kitty for falling in with the tone of gaiety with which this gentleman regarded his visit in the country, as though it were a holiday for himself and every one else. And, above all, unpleasant was that particular smile with which she responded to his smile.

Noisily talking, they all went into the house; but as soon as they were all seated, Levin turned and went out.

Kitty saw something was wrong with her husband. She tried to seize a moment to speak to him alone, but he made haste to get away from her, saying he was wanted at the counting-house. It was long since his own work on the estate had seemed to him so important as at that moment. "It's all holiday for them," he thought; "but these are no holiday matters, they won't wait, and there's no living without them."

CHAPTER VII

LEVIN came back to the house only when they sent to summon him to supper. On the stairs were standing Kitty and Agafea Mihalovna, consulting about wines for supper.

"But why are you making all this fuss? Have what we usually do."

"No, Stiva doesn't drink . . . Kostya, stop, what's the matter?" Kitty began, hurrying after him, but he strode ruthlessly away to the dining-room without waiting for her, and at once joined in the lively general conversation which was being maintained there by Vassenka Veslovsky and Stepan Arkadyevitch.

"Well, what do you say, are we going shooting to-morrow?" said Stepan Arkadyevitch.

"Please, do let's go," said Veslovsky, moving to another chair, where he sat down sideways, with one fat leg crossed under him.

"I shall be delighted, we will go. And have you had any shooting yet this year?" said Levin to Veslovsky, looking intently at his leg, but speaking with that forced amiability that Kitty knew so well in him, and that was so out of keeping with him. "I can't answer for our finding grouse, but there are plenty of snipe. Only we ought to start early. You're not tired? Aren't you tired, Stiva?"

"Me tired? I've never been tired yet. Suppose we stay up all night. Let's go for a walk!"

"Yes, really, let's not go to bed at all! Capital!" Veslovsky chimed in.

"Oh, we all know you can do without sleep, and keep other people up too," Dolly said to her husband, with that faint note of irony in her voice which she almost always had now with her husband. "But to my thinking, it's time for bed now. . . . I'm going, I don't want supper."

"No, do stay a little, Dolly," said Stepan Arkadyevitch, going round to her side behind the table where they were having supper. "I've so much still to tell you."

"Nothing really, I suppose."

"Do you know Veslovsky has been at Anna's, and he's going to them again? You know they're hardly fifty miles from you, and I too must certainly go over there. Veslovsky, come here!"

Vassenka crossed over to the ladies, and sat down beside Kitty.

"Ah, do tell me, please; you have stayed with her? How was she?" Darya Alexandrovna appealed to him.

Levin was left at the other end of the table, and though never pausing in his conversation with the princess and Varenka, he saw that there was an eager and mysterious conversation going on between Stepan Arkadyevitch, Dolly, Kitty, and Veslovsky. And that was not all. He saw on his wife's face an expression of real feeling as she gazed with fixed eyes on the handsome face of Vassenka, who was telling them something with great animation.

"It's exceedingly nice at their place," Veslovsky was telling them about Vronsky and Anna. "I can't, of course, take it upon myself to judge, but in their house you feel the real feeling of home."

"What do they intend doing?"

"I believe they think of going to Moscow."

"How jolly it would be for us all to go over to them together! When are you going there?" Stepan Arkadyevitch asked Vassenka.

"I'm spending July there."

"Will you go?" Stepan Arkadyevitch said to his wife.

"I've been wanting to a long while; I shall certainly go," said Dolly. "I am sorry for her, and I know her. She's a splendid woman. I will go alone, when you go back, and then I shall be in no one's way. And it will be better indeed without you."

"To be sure," said Stepan Arkadyevitch. "And you, Kitty?"

"I? Why should I go?" Kitty said, flushing all over, and she glanced round at her husband.

"Do you know Anna Arkadyevna, then?" Veslovsky asked her. "She's a very fascinating woman."

"Yes," she answered Veslovsky, crimsoning still more. She got up and walked across to her husband.

"Are you going shooting, then, to-morrow?" she said.

His jealousy had in these few moments, especially at the flush that had overspread her cheeks while she was talking to Veslovsky, gone far indeed. Now as he heard her words, he construed them in his own fashion. Strange as it was to him afterwards to recall it, it seemed to him at the moment clear that in asking whether he was going shooting, all she cared to know was whether he would give that pleasure to Vassenka Veslovsky, with whom, as he fancied, she was in love.

"Yes, I'm going," he answered her in an unnatural voice, disagreeable to himself.

"No, better spend the day here to-morrow, or Dolly won't see anything of her husband, and set off the day after," said Kitty.

The motive of Kitty's words was interpreted by Levin thus: "Don't separate me from *him*. I don't care about *your* going, but do let me enjoy the society of this delightful young man."

"Oh, if you wish, we'll stay here to-morrow," Levin answered, with peculiar amiability.

Vassenka meanwhile, utterly unsuspecting the misery his presence had occasioned, got up from the table after Kitty, and watching her with smiling and admiring eyes, he followed her.

Levin saw that look. He turned white, and for a minute he could hardly breathe. "How dare he look at my wife like that!" was the feeling that boiled within him.

"To-morrow, then? Do, please, let us go," said Vassenka, sitting down on a chair, and again crossing his leg as his habit was.

Levin's jealousy went further still. Already he saw himself a deceived husband, looked upon by his wife and her lover as simply necessary to provide them with the conveniences and pleasures of life. . . . But in spite of that he made polite and hospitable inquiries of Vassenka about his shooting, his gun, and his boots, and agreed to go shooting next day.

Happily for Levin, the old princess cut short his agonies by getting up herself and advising Kitty to go to bed. But even at this point Levin could not escape another agony. As he said good-night to his hostess, Vassenka would again have kissed her hand, but Kitty, reddening, drew back her hand and said with a naïve bluntness, for which the old princess scolded her afterwards:

"We don't like that fashion."

In Levin's eyes she was to blame for having allowed such relations to arise, and still more to blame for showing so awkwardly that she did not like them.

"Why, how can one want to go to bed!" said Stepan Arkadyevitch, who, after drinking several glasses of wine at supper, was now in his most charming and sentimental humor. "Look, Kitty," he said, pointing to the moon, which had just risen behind the lime-trees—"how exquisite! Veslovsky, this is the time for a serenade. You know, he has a splendid voice; we practised songs together along the road. He has brought some lovely songs with him, two new ones. Varvara Andreevna and he must sing some duets."

When the party had broken up, Stepan Arkadyevitch walked a long while about the avenue with Veslovsky; their voices could be heard singing one of the new songs.

Levin hearing these voices sat scowling in an easy-chair in his wife's bedroom, and maintained an obstinate silence when she asked him what was wrong. But when at last with a timid glance she hazarded the question: "Was there perhaps something you disliked about Veslovsky?"—it all burst out, and he told her all. He was humiliated himself at what he was saying, and that exasperated him all the more.

He stood facing her with his eyes glittering menacingly under his scowling brows, and he squeezed his strong arms across his chest, as though he were straining every nerve to hold himself in. The expression of his face would have been grim, and even cruel, if it had not at the same time had a look of suffering which touched her. His jaws were twitching, and his voice kept breaking.

"You must understand that I'm not jealous, that's a nasty word. I can't be jealous, and believe that. . . . I can't say what I feel, but this is awful. . . . I'm not jealous, but I'm wounded, humiliated that anybody dare think, that anybody dare look at you with eyes like that."

"Eyes like what?" said Kitty, trying as conscientiously as possible to recall every word and gesture of that evening and every shade implied in them.

At the very bottom of her heart she did think there had been something precisely at the moment when he had crossed over after her to the other end of the table; but she dared not own it even to herself, and would have been even more unable to bring herself to say so to him, and so increase his suffering.

"And what can there possibly be attractive about me as I am now? . . ."

"Ah!" he cried, clutching at his head, "you shouldn't say that! . . . If you had been attractive then . . ."

"Oh, no, Kostya, oh, wait a minute, oh, do listen!" she said, looking at him with an expression of pained commiseration. "Why, what can you be thinking about! When for me there's no one in the world, no one, no one! . . . Would you like me never to see any one?"

For the first minute she had been offended at his jealousy; she was angry that the slightest amusement, even the most innocent, should be forbidden her; but now she would readily have sacrificed, not merely such trifles, but everything, for his peace of mind, to save him from the agony he was suffering.

"You must understand the horror and comedy of my position," he went on in a desperate whisper; "that he's in my house, that he's done nothing improper positively except his free and easy airs and the way he sits on his legs. He thinks it's the best possible form, and so I'm obliged to be civil to him."

"But, Kostya, you're exaggerating," said Kitty, at the bottom of her heart rejoicing at the depth of his love for her, shown now in his jealousy.

"The most awful part of it all is that you're just as you always are, and especially now when to me you're something sacred, and we're so happy, so particularly happy—and all of a sudden a little wretch . . . He's not a little wretch; why should I abuse him? I have nothing to do with him. But why should my, and your, happiness . . ."

"Do you know, I understand now what it's all come from," Kitty was beginning.

"Well, what? what?"

"I saw how you looked while we were talking at supper."

"Well, well!" Levin said in dismay.

She told him what they had been talking about. And as she told him, she was breathless with emotion. Levin was silent for a space, then he scanned her pale and distressed face, and suddenly he clutched at his head.

"Katya, I've been worrying you! Darling, forgive me! It's madness! Katya, I'm a criminal. And how could you be so distressed at such idiocy?"

"Oh, I was sorry for you."

"For me? for me? How mad I am! . . . But why make you miserable? It's awful to think that any outsider can shatter our happiness."

"It's humiliating too, of course."

"Oh, then I'll keep him here all the summer, and will overwhelm him with civility," said Levin, kissing her hands. "You shall see. To-morrow . . . Oh, yes, we are going to-morrow."

CHAPTER VIII

NEXT day, before the ladies were up, the wagonette and a trap for the shooting-party were at the door, and Laska, aware since early morning that they were going shooting, after much whining and darting to and fro, had sat herself down in the wagonette beside the coachman, and, disapproving of the delay, was excitedly watching the door from which the sportsmen still did not come out. The first to come out was Vassenka Veslovsky, in new high boots that reached half-way up his thick thighs, in a green blouse, with a new Russian leather cartridge-belt, and in his Scotch cap with ribbons, with a brand-new English gun without a sling. Laska flew up to him, welcomed him, and jumping up, asked him in her own way whether the others were coming soon, but getting no answer from him, she returned to her post of observation and sank into repose again, her head on one side, and one ear pricked up to listen. At last the door opened with a creak, and Stepan Arkadyevitch's spot-and-tan pointer Krak flew out, running round and round and turning over in the air. Stepan Arkadyevitch himself followed with a gun in his hand and a cigar in his mouth.

"Good dog, good dog, Krak!" he cried encouragingly to the dog, who put his paws up on his chest, catching at his game-bag. Stepan Arkadyevitch was dressed in rough leggings and spats, in torn trousers and a short coat. On his head there was a wreck of a hat of indefinite form, but his gun of a new patent was a perfect gem, and his game-bag and cartridge-belt, though worn, were of the very best quality.

Vassenka Veslovsky had had no notion before that it was truly *chic* for a sportsman to be in tatters, but to have his shooting outfit of the best quality. He saw it now as he looked at Stepan Arkadyevitch, radiant in his rags, graceful, well-fed, and joyous, a typical Russian nobleman. And he made up his mind that next time he went shooting he would certainly adopt the same get-up.

"Well, and what about our host?" he asked.

"A young wife," said Stepan Arkadyevitch, smiling.

"Yes, and such a charming one!"

"He came down dressed. No doubt he's run up to her again."

Stepan Arkadyevitch guessed right. Levin had run up again to his wife to ask her once more if she forgave him for his idiocy yesterday, and, moreover, to beg her for Christ's sake to be more careful. The great thing was for her to keep away from the children—they might any minute push against her. Then he had once more to hear her declare that she was not angry with him for going away for two days, and to beg her to be sure to send him a note next morning by a servant on horseback, to write him, if it were but two words only, to let him know that all was well with her.

Kitty was distressed, as she always was, at parting for a couple of days from her husband, but when she saw his eager figure, looking big and strong in his shooting-boots and his white blouse, and a sort of sportsman elation and excitement incomprehensible to her, she forgot her own chagrin for the sake of his pleasure, and said good-bye to him cheerfully.

"Pardon, gentlemen!" he said, running out onto the steps. "Have you put the lunch in? Why is the chestnut on the right? Well, it doesn't matter. Laska, down; go and lie down!"

"Put it with the herd of oxen," he said to the herdsman, who was waiting for him at the steps with some question. "Excuse me, here comes another villain."

Levin jumped out of the wagonette, in which he had already taken his seat, to meet the carpenter, who came towards the steps with a rule in his hand.

"You didn't come to the counting-house yesterday, and now you're detaining me. Well, what is it?"

"Would your honor let me make another turning? It's only three steps to add. And we make it just fit at the same time. It will be much more convenient."

"You should have listened to me," Levin answered with annoyance. "I said: Put the lines and then fit in the steps. Now there's no setting it right. Do as I told you, and make a new staircase."

The point was that in the lodge that was being built the carpenter had spoiled the staircase, fitting it together without calculating the space it was to fill, so that the steps were all sloping when it was put in place. Now the carpenter wanted keeping the same staircase, to add three steps.

"It will be much better."

"But where's your staircase coming out with its three steps?"

"Why, upon my word, sir," the carpenter said with a contemptuous smile. "It comes out right at the very spot. It starts, so to speak," he said, with a persuasive gesture; "it comes down, and comes down, and comes out."

"But three steps will add to the length too . . . where is it to come out?"

"Why, to be sure, it'll start from the bottom and go up and go up, and come out so," the carpenter said obstinately and convincingly.

"It'll reach the ceiling and the wall."

"Upon my word! Why, it'll go up, and up, and come out like this."

Levin took out a ramrod and began sketching him the staircase in the dust.

"There, do you see?"

"As your honor likes," said the carpenter, with a sudden gleam in his eyes, obviously understanding the thing at last. "It seems it'll be best to make a new one."

"Well, then, do it as you're told," Levin shouted, seating himself in the wagonette. "Down! Hold the dogs, Philip!"

Levin felt now at leaving behind all his family and household cares such an eager sense of joy in life and expectation that he was not disposed to talk. Besides that, he had that feeling of concentrated excitement that every sportsman experiences as he approaches the scene of action. If he had anything on his mind at that moment, it was only the doubt whether they would start anything in the Kolpensky marsh, whether Laska would show to advantage in comparison with Krak, and whether he would shoot well that day himself. Not to disgrace himself before a new spectator—not to be outdone by Oblonsky—that too was a thought that crossed his brain.

Oblonsky was feeling the same, and he too was not talkative. Vassenka Veslovsky kept up alone a ceaseless flow of cheerful chatter. As he listened to him now, Levin felt ashamed to think how unfair he had been to him the day before. Vassenka was really a nice fellow, simple, good-hearted, and very good-humored. If Levin had met him before he was married, he would have made friends with him. Levin rather disliked his holiday attitude to life and a sort of free and easy assumption of elegance. It was as though he assumed a high degree of importance in himself that could not be disputed, because he had long nails and a stylish cap, and everything else to correspond; but this could be forgiven for the sake of his good nature and good breeding. Levin liked him for his good education, for speaking French and English with such an excellent accent, and for being a man of his world.

Vassenka was extremely delighted with the left horse, a horse of the Don steppes. He kept praising him enthusiastically. "How fine it must be galloping over the steppes on a steppe horse! Eh?

isn't it?" he said. He had imagined riding on a steppe horse as something wild and romantic, and it turned out nothing of the sort. But his simplicity, particularly in conjunction with his good looks, his amiable smile, and the grace of his movements, was very attractive. Either because his nature was sympathetic to Levin, or because Levin was trying to atone for his sins of the previous evening by seeing nothing but what was good in him, anyway he liked his society.

After they had driven over two miles from home, Veslovsky all at once felt for a cigar and his pocketbook, and did not know whether he had lost them or left them on the table. In the pocketbook there were thirty-seven pounds, and so the matter could not be left in uncertainty.

"Do you know what, Levin, I'll gallop home on that left tracehorse. That will be splendid. Eh?" he said, preparing to get out.

"No, why should you?" answered Levin, calculating that Vassenka could hardly weigh less than seventeen stone. "I'll send the coachman."

The coachman rode back on the trace-horse, and Levin himself drove the remaining pair.

CHAPTER IX

"WELL, now what's our plan of campaign? Tell us all about it," said Stepan Arkadyevitch.

"Our plan is this. Now we're driving to Gvozdyov. In Gvozdyov there's a grouse marsh on this side, and beyond Gvozdyov come some magnificent snipe marshes where there are grouse too. It's hot now, and we'll get there—it's fifteen miles or so—towards evening and have some evening shooting; we'll spend the night there and go on to-morrow to the bigger moors."

"And is there nothing on the way?"

"Yes; but we'll reserve ourselves; besides it's hot. There are two nice little places, but I doubt there being anything to shoot."

Levin would himself have liked to go into these little places, but they were near home; he could shoot them over any time, and they were only little places—there would hardly be room for three to shoot. And so, with some insincerity, he said that he doubted there being anything to shoot. When they reached a little marsh Levin would have driven by, but Stepan Arkadyevitch, with the experienced eye of a sportsman, at once detected reeds visible from the road.

"Shan't we try that?" he said, pointing to the little marsh.

"Levin, do, please! how delightful!" Vassenka Veslovsky began begging, and Levin could but consent.

Before they had time to stop, the dogs had flown one before the other into the marsh.

"Krak! Laska! . . ."

The dogs came back.

"There won't be room for three. I'll stay here," said Levin, hoping they would find nothing but peewits, who had been startled by the dogs, and turning over in their flight, were plaintively wailing over the marsh.

"No! Come along, Levin, let's go together!" Veslovsky called.

"Really, there's not room. Laska, back, Laska! You won't want another dog, will you?"

Levin remained with the wagonette, and looked enviously at the sportsmen. They walked right across the marsh. Except little birds and peewits, of which Vassenka killed one, there was nothing in the marsh.

"Come, you see now that it was not that I grudged the marsh," said Levin, "only it's wasting time."

"Oh, no, it was jolly all the same. Did you see us?" said Vassenka Veslovsky, clambering awkwardly into the wagonette with his gun and his peewit in his hands. "How splendidly I shot this bird! Didn't I? Well, shall we soon be getting to the real place?"

The horses started off suddenly, Levin knocked his head against the stock of some one's gun, and there was the report of a shot. The gun did actually go off first, but that was how it seemed to Levin. It appeared that Vassenka Veslovsky had pulled only one trigger, and had left the other hammer still cocked. The charge flew into the ground without doing harm to any one. Stepan Arkadyevitch shook his head and laughed reprovingly at Veslovsky. But Levin had not the heart to reprove him. In the first place, any reproach would have seemed to be called forth by the danger he had incurred and the bump that

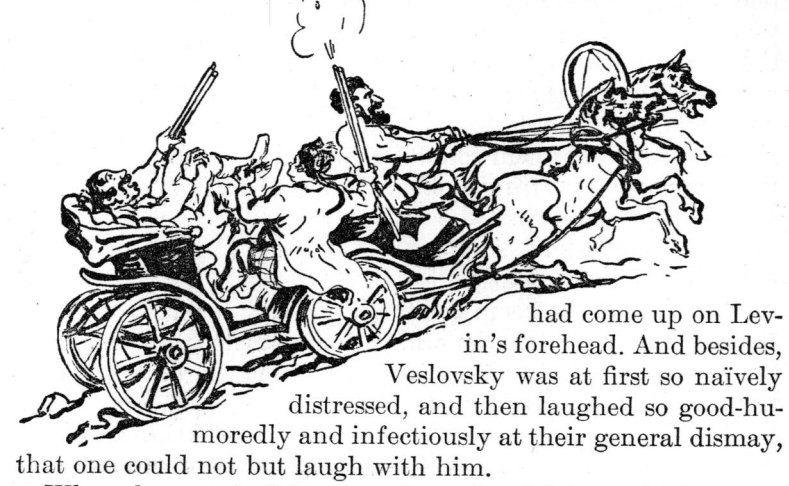

had come up on Levin's forehead. And besides, Veslovsky was at first so naïvely distressed, and then laughed so good-humoredly and infectiously at their general dismay, that one could not but laugh with him.

When they reached the second marsh, which was fairly large, and would inevitably take some time to shoot over, Levin tried to persuade them to pass it by. But Veslovsky again overpersuaded him. Again, as the marsh was narrow, Levin, like a good host, remained with the carriage.

Krak made straight for some clumps of sedge. Vassenka Veslovsky was the first to run after the dog. Before Stepan Arkadyevitch had time to come up, a grouse flew out. Veslovsky missed it and it flew into an unmown meadow. This grouse was left for Veslovsky to follow up. Krak found it again and pointed, and Veslovsky shot it and went back to the carriage. "Now you go and I'll stay with the horses," he said.

Levin had begun to feel the pangs of a sportsman's envy. He handed the reins to Veslovsky and walked into the marsh.

Laska, who had been plaintively whining and fretting against the injustice of her treatment, flew straight ahead to a hopeful place that Levin knew well, and that Krak had not yet come upon.

"Why don't you stop her?" shouted Stepan Arkadyevitch.

"She won't scare them," answered Levin, sympathizing with his bitch's pleasure and hurrying after her.

As she came nearer and nearer to the familiar breeding-places there was more and more earnestness in Laska's exploration. A little marsh bird did not divert her attention for more than an instant. She made one circuit round the clump of reeds, was beginning a second, and suddenly quivered with excitement and became motionless.

"Come, come, Stiva!" shouted Levin, feeling his heart beginning to beat more violently; and all of a sudden, as though some sort of shutter had been drawn back from his straining ears, all sounds, confused but loud, began to beat on his hearing, losing all sense of distance. He heard the steps of Stepan Arkadyevitch, mistaking them for the tramp of the horses in the distance; he heard the brittle sound of the twigs on which he had trodden, taking this sound for the flying of a grouse. He heard too, not far behind him, a splashing in the water, which he could not explain to himself.

Picking his steps, he moved up to the dog.

"Fetch it!"

Not a grouse but a snipe flew up from beside the dog. Levin had lifted his gun, but at the very instant when he was taking aim, the sound of splashing grew louder, came closer, and was joined with the sound of Veslovsky's voice, shouting something with strange loudness. Levin saw he had his gun pointed behind the snipe, but still he fired.

When he had made sure he had missed, Levin looked round and saw the horses and the wagonette not on the road but in the marsh.

Veslovsky, eager to see the shooting, had driven into the marsh, and got the horses stuck in the mud.

"Damn the fellow!" Levin said to himself, as he went back to the carriage that had sunk in the mire. "What did you drive in for?" he said to him dryly, and calling the coachman, he began pulling the horses out.

Levin was vexed both at being hindered from shooting and at his horses getting stuck in the mud, and still more at the fact that neither Stepan Arkadyevitch nor Veslovsky helped him and the coachman to unharness the horses and get them out, since neither of them had the slightest notion of harnessing. Without vouchsafing a syllable in reply to Vassenka's protestations that it had been quite dry there, Levin worked in silence with the coachman at extricating the horses. But then, as he got warm at the work and saw how assiduously Veslovsky was tugging at the wagonette by one of the mud-guards, so that he broke it indeed, Levin blamed himself for having under the influence of yesterday's feelings been too cold to Veslovsky, and tried to be particularly genial so as to smooth over his chilliness. When everything had been put right, and the carriage had been brought back to the road, Levin had the lunch served.

"*Bon appétit—bonne conscience! Ce poulet va tomber jusqu'au fond de mes bottes,*" Vassenka, who had recovered his spirits, quoted the French saying as he finished his second chicken. "Well, now our troubles are over, now everything's going to go well. Only, to atone for my sins, I'm bound to sit on the box. That's so? eh? No, no! I'll be your Automedon. You shall see how I'll get you along," he answered, not letting go the rein, when Levin begged him to let the coachman drive. "No, I must atone for my sins, and I'm very comfortable on the box." And he drove.

Levin was a little afraid he would exhaust the horses, especially the chestnut, whom he did not know how to hold in; but unconsciously he fell under the influence of his gaiety and listened to the songs he sang all the way on the box, or the descriptions and representations he gave of driving in the English fashion, four-in-hand; and it was in the very best of spirits that after lunch they drove to the Gvozdyov marsh.

CHAPTER X

VASSENKA drove the horses so smartly that they reached the marsh too early, while it was still hot.

As they drew near this more important marsh, the chief aim of their expedition, Levin could not help considering how he could get rid of Vassenka and be free in his movements. Stepan Arkadyevitch evidently had the same desire, and on his face Levin saw the look of anxiety always present in a true sportsman when beginning shooting, together with a certain good-humored slyness peculiar to him.

"How shall we go? It's a splendid marsh, I see, and there are hawks," said Stepan Arkadyevitch, pointing to two great birds hovering over the reeds. "Where there are hawks, there is sure to be game."

"Now, gentlemen," said Levin, pulling up his boots and examining the lock of his gun with rather a gloomy expression, "do you see those reeds?" He pointed to an oasis of blackish green in the huge half-mown wet meadow that stretched along the right bank of the river. "The marsh begins here, straight in front of us, do you see—where it is greener? From here it runs to the right where the horses are; there are breeding-places there, and grouse, and all round those reeds as far as that alder, and right up to the mill. Over there, do you see, where the pools are? That's the best place. There I once shot seventeen snipe. We'll separate with the dogs and go in different directions, and then meet over there at the mill."

"Well, which shall go to left and which to right?" asked Stepan Arkadyevitch. "It's wider to the right; you two go that way and I'll take the left," he said with apparent carelessness.

"Capital! we'll make the bigger bag! Yes, come along, come along!" Vassenka exclaimed.

Levin could do nothing but agree, and they divided.

As soon as they entered the marsh, the two dogs began hunting about together and made towards the green, slime-covered pool. Levin knew Laska's method, wary and indefinite; he knew the place too and expected a whole covey of snipe.

"Veslovsky, beside me, walk beside me!" he said in a faint voice to his companion splashing in the water behind him. Levin could not help feeling an interest in the direction his gun was pointed, after that casual shot near the Kolpensky marsh.

"Oh, I won't get in your way, don't trouble about me."

But Levin could not help troubling, and recalled Kitty's words at parting: "Mind you don't shoot one another." The dogs came nearer and nearer, passed each other, each pursuing its own scent. The expectation of snipe was so intense that to Levin the squelching sound of his own heel, as he drew it up out of the mire, seemed to be the call of a snipe, and he clutched and pressed the lock of his gun.

"Bang! bang!" sounded almost in his ear. Vassenka had fired

at a flock of ducks which was hovering over the marsh and flying at that moment towards the sportsmen, far out of range. Before Levin had time to look round, there was the whir of one snipe, another, a third, and some eight more rose one after another.

Stepan Arkadyevitch hit one at the very moment when it was beginning its zigzag movements, and the snipe fell in a heap into the mud. Oblonsky aimed deliberately at another, still flying low in the reeds, and together with the report of the shot, that snipe too fell, and it could be seen fluttering out where the sedge had been cut, its unhurt wing showing white beneath.

Levin was not so lucky: he aimed at his first bird too low, and missed; he aimed at it again, just as it was rising, but at that instant another snipe flew up at his very feet, distracting him so that he missed again.

While they were loading their guns, another snipe rose, and Veslovsky, who had had time to load again, sent two charges of small-shot into the water. Stepan Arkadyevitch picked up his snipe, and with sparkling eyes looked at Levin.

"Well, now let us separate," said Stepan Arkadyevitch, and limping on his left foot, holding his gun in readiness and whistling to his dog, he walked off in one direction. Levin and Veslovsky walked in the other.

It always happened with Levin that when his first shots were a failure he got hot and out of temper, and shot badly the whole day. So it was that day. The snipe showed themselves in numbers. They kept flying up from just under the dogs, from under the sportsmen's legs, and Levin might have retrieved his ill-luck. But the more he shot, the more he felt disgraced in the eyes of Veslovsky, who kept popping away merrily and indiscriminately, killing nothing, and not in the slightest abashed by his ill-success. Levin, in feverish haste, could not restrain himself, got more and more out of temper, and ended by shooting almost without a hope of hitting. Laska, indeed, seemed to understand this. She began looking more languidly, and gazed back at the sportsmen, as it were, with perplexity or reproach in her eyes. Shots followed shots in rapid succession. The smoke of the powder hung about the sportsmen, while in the great roomy net of the game-bag there were only three light little snipe. And of these one had been killed by Veslovsky alone, and one by both of them together. Meanwhile from the other side of the marsh came the sound of Stepan Arkadyevitch's shots, not frequent, but, as Levin fancied, well-directed, for almost after each they heard "Krak, Krak, *apporte!*"

This excited Levin still more. The snipe were floating continually in the air over the reeds. Their whirring wings close to the earth, and their harsh cries high in the air, could be heard on all sides; the snipe that had risen first and flown up into the air, settled again before the sportsmen. Instead of two hawks there were now dozens of them hovering with shrill cries over the marsh.

After walking through the larger half of the marsh, Levin and Veslovsky reached the place where the peasants' mowing-grass was divided into long strips reaching to the reeds, marked off in one place by the trampled grass, in another by a path mown through it. Half of these strips had already been mown.

Though there was not so much hope of finding birds in the uncut part as the cut part, Levin had promised Stepan Arkadyevitch to meet him, and so he walked on with his companion through the cut and uncut patches.

"Hi, sportsmen!" shouted one of a group of peasants, sitting on an unharnessed cart; "come and have some lunch with us! Have a drop of wine!"

Levin looked round.

"Come along, it's all right!" shouted a good-humored-looking bearded peasant with a red face, showing his white teeth in a grin, and holding up a greenish bottle that flashed in the sunlight.

"*Qu'est-ce qu'ils disent?*" asked Veslovsky.

"They invite you to have some vodka. Most likely they've been dividing the meadow into lots. I should have some," said Levin, not without some guile, hoping Veslovsky would be tempted by the vodka, and would go away to them.

"Why do they offer it?"

"Oh, they're merry-making. Really, you should join them. You would be interested."

"*Allons, c'est curieux.*"

"You go, you go, you'll find the way to the mill!" cried Levin, and looking round he perceived with satisfaction that Veslovsky, bent and stumbling with weariness, holding his gun out at arm's length, was making his way out of the marsh towards the peasants.

"You come too!" the peasants shouted to Levin. "Never fear! You taste our cake!"

Levin felt a strong inclination to drink a little vodka and to eat some bread. He was exhausted, and felt it a great effort to drag his staggering legs out of the mire, and for a minute he hesitated. But Laska was setting. And immediately all his weariness vanished, and he walked lightly through the swamp towards the dog. A snipe flew up at his feet; he fired and killed it. Laska still pointed.—"Fetch it!" Another bird flew up close to the dog. Levin fired. But it was an unlucky day for him; he missed it, and when he went to look for the one he had shot, he could not find that either. He wandered all about the reeds, but Laska did not believe he had shot it, and when he sent her to find it, she pretended to hunt for it, but did not really. And in the absence of Vassenka, on whom Levin threw the blame of his failure, things went no better. There were plenty of snipe still, but Levin made one miss after another.

The slanting rays of the sun were still hot; his clothes, soaked through with perspiration, stuck to his body; his left boot full of water weighed heavily on his leg and squeaked at every step; the sweat ran in drops down his powder-grimed face, his mouth was full of the bitter taste, his nose of the smell of powder and stagnant water, his ears were ringing with the incessant whir of the snipe; he could not touch the stock of his gun, it was so hot; his heart beat with short, rapid throbs; his hands shook with excitement, and his weary legs stumbled and staggered over the hillocks and in the swamp, but still he walked on and still he shot. At last, after a disgraceful miss, he flung his gun and his hat on the ground.

"No, I must control myself," he said to himself. Picking up his gun and his hat, he called Laska, and went out of the swamp. When he got on to dry ground he sat down, pulled off his boot and emptied it, then walked to the marsh, drank some stagnant-tasting water, moistened his burning hot gun, and washed his face and hands. Feeling refreshed, he went back to the spot where a snipe had settled, firmly resolved to keep cool.

He tried to be calm, but it was the same again. His finger pressed the cock before he had taken a good aim at the bird. It got worse and worse.

He had only five birds in his game-bag when he walked out of the marsh towards the alders where he was to rejoin Stepan Arkadyevitch.

Before he caught sight of Stepan Arkadyevitch he saw his dog. Krak darted out from behind the twisted root of an alder, black all over with the stinking mire of the marsh, and with the air of a conqueror sniffed at Laska. Behind Krak there came into view in the shade of the alder-tree the shapely figure of Stepan Arkadyevitch. He came to meet him, red and perspiring, with unbuttoned neckband, still limping in the same way.

"Well? You have been popping away!" he said, smiling good-humoredly.

"How have you got on?" queried Levin. But there was no need to ask, for he had already seen the full game-bag.

"Oh, pretty fair."

He had fourteen birds.

"A splendid marsh! I've no doubt Veslovsky got in your way. It's awkward too, shooting with one dog," said Stepan Arkadyevitch, to soften his triumph.

CHAPTER XI

WHEN Levin and Stepan Arkadyevitch reached the peasant's hut where Levin always used to stay, Veslovsky was already there. He was sitting in the middle of the hut, clinging with both hands to the bench from which he was being pulled by a soldier, the brother of the peasant's wife, who was helping him off with his miry boots. Veslovsky was laughing his infectious, good-humored laugh.

"I've only just come. *Ils ont été charmants.* Just fancy they gave me drink, fed me! Such bread, it was exquisite! *Délicieux!*

And the vodka, I never tasted any better. And they would not take a penny for anything. And they kept saying: 'Excuse our homely ways.' "

"What should they take anything for? They were entertaining you, to be sure. Do you suppose they keep vodka for sale?" said the soldier, succeeding at last in pulling the soaked boot off the blackened stocking.

In spite of the dirtiness of the hut, which was all muddied by their boots and the filthy dogs licking themselves clean, and the smell of marsh mud and powder that filled the room, and the absence of knives and forks, the party drank their tea and ate their supper with a relish only known to sportsmen. Washed and clean, they went into a hay-barn swept ready for them, where the coachman had been making up beds for the gentlemen.

Though it was dusk, not one of them wanted to go to sleep.

After wavering among reminiscences and anecdotes of guns, of dogs, and of former shooting-parties, the conversation rested on a topic that interested all of them. After Vassenka had several times over expressed his appreciation of this delightful sleeping-place among the fragrant hay, this delightful broken cart (he supposed it to be broken because the shafts had been taken out), of the good-nature of the peasants that had treated him to vodka, of the dogs who lay at the feet of their respective masters, Oblonsky began telling them of a delightful shooting-party at Malthus's, where he had stayed the previous summer.

Malthus was a well-known capitalist, who had made his money by speculation in railway shares. Stepan Arkadyevitch described what grouse moors this Malthus had bought in the Tver province, and how they were preserved, and of the carriages and dog-carts in which the shooting-party had been driven, and the luncheon pavilion that had been rigged up at the marsh.

"I don't understand you," said Levin, sitting up in the hay; "how is it such people don't disgust you? I can understand a lunch with Lafitte is all very pleasant, but don't you dislike just that very sumptuousness? All these people, just like our spirit monopolists in old days, get their money in a way that gains them the contempt of every one. They don't care for their contempt, and then they use their dishonest gains to buy off the contempt they have deserved."

"Perfectly true!" chimed in Vassenka Veslovsky. "Perfectly! Oblonsky, of course, goes out of *bonhomie*, but other people say: 'Well, Oblonsky stays with them.' . . ."

"Not a bit of it." Levin could hear that Oblonsky was smiling as he spoke. "I simply don't consider him more dishonest than any other wealthy merchant or nobleman. They've all made their money alike—by their work and their intelligence."

"Oh, by what work? Do you call it work to get hold of concessions and speculate with them?"

"Of course it's work. Work in this sense, that if it were not for him and others like him, there would have been no railways."

"But that's not work, like the work of a peasant or a learned profession."

"Granted, but it's work in the sense that his activity produces a result—the railways. But of course you think the railways useless."

"No, that's another question; I am prepared to admit that they're useful. But all profit that is out of proportion to the labor expended is dishonest."

"But who is to define what is proportionate?"

"Making profit by dishonest means, by trickery," said Levin, conscious that he could not draw a distinct line between honesty and dishonesty. "Such as banking, for instance," he went on. "It's an evil—the amassing of huge fortunes without labor, just the same thing as with the spirit monopolies, it's only the form that's changed. *Le roi est mort, vive le roi.* No sooner were the spirit monopolies abolished than the railways came up, and banking companies; that, too, is profit without work."

"Yes, that may all be very true and clever. . . . Lie down, Krak!" Stepan Arkadyevitch called to his dog, who was scratching and turning over all the hay. He was obviously convinced of the correctness of his position, and so talked serenely and without haste. "But you have not drawn the line between honest and dishonest work. That I receive a bigger salary than my chief clerk, though he knows more about the work than I do—that's dishonest, I suppose?"

"I can't say."

"Well, but I can tell you: your receiving some five thousand, let's say, for your work on the land, while our host, the peasant here, however hard he works, can never get more than fifty roubles, is just as dishonest as my earning more than my chief clerk, and Malthus getting more than a station-master. No, quite the contrary; I see that society takes up a sort of antagonistic attitude to these people, which is utterly baseless, and I fancy there's envy at the bottom of it. . . ."

"No, that's unfair," said Veslovsky; "how could envy come in? There is something not nice about that sort of business."

"You say," Levin went on, "that it's unjust for me to receive five thousand, while the peasant has fifty; that's true. It is unfair, and I feel it, but . . ."

"It really is. Why is it we spend our time riding, drinking, shooting, doing nothing, while they are forever at work?" said Vassenka Veslovsky, obviously for the first time in his life reflecting on the question, and consequently considering it with perfect sincerity.

"Yes, you feel it, but you don't give him your property," said Stepan Arkadyevitch, intentionally, as it seemed, provoking Levin.

There had arisen of late something like a secret antagonism between the two brothers-in-law; as though, since they had married sisters, a kind of rivalry had sprung up between them as to which was ordering his life best, and now this hostility showed itself in the conversation, as it began to take a personal note.

"I don't give it away, because no one demands that from me, and if I wanted to, I could not give it away," answered Levin, "and have no one to give it to."

"Give it to this peasant, he would not refuse it."

"Yes, but how am I to give it up? Am I to go to him and make a deed of conveyance?"

"I don't know; but if you are convinced that you have no right . . ."

"I'm not at all convinced. On the contrary, I feel I have no right to give it up, that I have duties both to the land and to my family."

"No, excuse me, but if you consider this inequality is unjust, why is it you don't act accordingly? . . ."

"Well, I do act negatively on that idea, so far as not trying to increase the difference of position existing between him and me."

"No, excuse me, that's a paradox."

"Yes, there's something of a sophistry about that," Veslovsky agreed. "Ah! our host; so you're not asleep yet?" he said to the peasant who came into the barn, opening the creaking door. "How is it you're not asleep?"

"No, how's one to sleep! I thought our gentlemen would be asleep, but I heard them chattering. I want to get a hook from here. She won't bite?" he added, stepping cautiously with his bare feet.

"And where are you going to sleep?"

"We are going out for the night with the beasts."

"Ah, what a night!" said Veslovsky, looking out at the edge of the hut and the unharnessed wagonette that could be seen in the faint light of the evening glow in the great frame of the open doors. "But listen, there are women's voices singing, and, on my word, not badly too. Who's that singing, my friend?"

"That's the maids from hard by here."

"Let's go, let's have a walk! We shan't go to sleep, you know. Oblonsky, come along!"

"If one could only do both, lie here and go," answered Oblonsky, stretching. "It's capital lying here."

"Well, I shall go by myself," said Veslovsky, getting up eagerly, and putting on his shoes and stockings. "Good-bye, gentlemen. If it's fun, I'll fetch you. You've treated me to some good sport, and I won't forget you."

"He really is a capital fellow, isn't he?" said Stepan Arkadyevitch, when Veslovsky had gone out and the peasant had closed the door after him.

"Yes, capital," answered Levin, still thinking of the subject of their conversation just before. It seemed to him that he had clearly expressed his thoughts and feelings to the best of his capacity, and yet both of them, straightforward men and not fools, had said with one voice that he was comforting himself with sophistries. This disconcerted him.

"It's just this, my dear boy. One must do one of two things: either admit that the existing order of society is just, and then stick up for one's rights in it; or acknowledge that you are enjoying unjust privileges, as I do, and then enjoy them and be satisfied."

"No, if it were unjust, you could not enjoy these advantages and be satisfied—at least I could not. The great thing for me is to feel that I'm not to blame."

"What do you say, why not go after all?" said Stepan Arkadyevitch, evidently weary of the strain of thought. "We shan't go to sleep, you know. Come, let's go!"

Levin did not answer. What they had said in the conversation, that he acted justly only in a negative sense, absorbed his thoughts. "Can it be that it's only possible to be just negatively?" he was asking himself.

"How strong the smell of the fresh hay is, though," said Stepan Arkadyevitch, getting up. "There's not a chance of sleeping. Vassenka has been getting up some fun there. Do you hear the laughing and his voice? Hadn't we better go? Come along!"

"No, I'm not coming," answered Levin.

"Surely that's not a matter of principle too," said Stepan Arkadyevitch, smiling, as he felt about in the dark for his cap.

"It's not a matter of principle, but why should I go?"

"But do you know you are preparing trouble for yourself," said Stepan Arkadyevitch, finding his cap and getting up.

"How so?"

"Do you suppose I don't see the line you've taken up with your wife? I heard how it's a question of the greatest consequence, whether or not you're to be away for a couple of days' shooting. That's all very well as an idyllic episode, but for your whole life that won't answer. A man must be independent; he has his masculine interests. A man has to be manly," said Oblonsky, opening the door.

"In what way? To go running after servant-girls?" said Levin.

"Why not, if it amuses him? *Ça ne tire pas à conséquence.* It won't do my wife any harm, and it'll amuse me. The great thing is to respect the sanctity of the home. There should be nothing in the home. But don't tie your own hands."

"Perhaps so," said Levin dryly, and he turned on his side. "To-morrow, early, I want to go shooting, and I won't wake any one, and shall set off at daybreak."

"*Messieurs, venez vite!*" they heard the voice of Veslovsky coming back. "*Charmante!* I've made such a discovery. *Charmante!* a perfect Gretchen, and I've already made friends with her. Really, exceedingly pretty," he declared in a tone of approval, as though she had been made pretty entirely on his account, and he was expressing his satisfaction with the entertainment that had been provided for him.

Levin pretended to be asleep, while Oblonsky, putting on his slippers, and lighting a cigar, walked out of the barn, and soon their voices were lost.

For a long while Levin could not get to sleep. He heard the horses munching hay, then he heard the peasant and his elder boy getting ready for the night, and going off for the nightwatch with the beasts, then he heard the soldier arranging his bed on the other side of the barn, with his nephew, the younger son of their peasant host. He heard the boy in his shrill little voice telling his uncle what he thought about the dogs, who seemed to him huge and terrible creatures, and asking what the dogs were going to hunt next day, and the soldier in a husky, sleepy voice, telling him the sportsmen were going in the morning to the marsh, and would shoot with their guns; and then, to check the boy's questions, he said, "Go to sleep, Vaska; go to sleep, or you'll catch it," and soon after he began snoring himself, and everything was still. He could only hear the snort of the horses, and the guttural cry of a snipe.

"Is it really only negative?" he repeated to himself. "Well, what of it? It's not my fault." And he began thinking about the next day.

"To-morrow I'll go out early, and I'll make a point of keeping cool. There are lots of snipe; and there are grouse too. When I come back there'll be the note from Kitty. Yes, Stiva may be right, I'm not manly with her, I'm tied to her apron-strings. . . . Well, it can't be helped! Negative again. . . ."

Half asleep, he heard the laughter and mirthful talk of Veslovsky and Stepan Arkadyevitch. For an instant he opened his eyes: the moon was up, and in the open doorway, brightly lighted up by the moonlight, they were standing talking. Stepan Arkadyevitch was saying something of the freshness of one girl, comparing her to a freshly peeled nut, and Veslovsky with his infectious laugh was repeating some words, probably said to him by a peasant: "Ah, you do your best to get round her!" Levin, half asleep, said:

"Gentlemen, to-morrow before daylight!" and fell asleep.

CHAPTER XII

WAKING up at earliest dawn, Levin tried to wake his companions. Vassenka, lying on his stomach, with one leg in a stocking thrust out, was sleeping so soundly that he could elicit no response. Oblonsky, half asleep, declined to get up so early. Even Laska, who was asleep, curled up in the hay, got up unwillingly, and lazily stretched out and straightened her hindlegs one after the other. Getting on his boots and stockings, taking his gun, and carefully opening the creaking door of the barn, Levin went out into the road. The coachmen were sleeping in their carriages, the horses were dozing. Only one was lazily eating oats, dipping its nose into the manger. It was still gray out-of-doors.

"Why are you up so early, my dear?" the old woman, their hostess, said, coming out of the hut and addressing him affectionately as an old friend.

"Going shooting, granny. Do I go this way to the marsh?"

"Straight out at the back; by our thrashing-floor, my dear, and hemp-patches; there's a little footpath." Stepping carefully with her sunburnt, bare feet, the old woman conducted Levin, and moved back the fence for him by the thrashing-floor.

"Straight on and you'll come to the marsh. Our lads drove the cattle there yesterday evening."

Laska ran eagerly forward along the little path. Levin followed her with a light, rapid step, continually looking at the sky. He hoped the sun would not be up before he reached the marsh. But the sun did not delay. The moon, which had been bright when he went out, by now shone only like a crescent of quicksilver. The pink flush of dawn, which one could not help seeing before, now had to be sought to be discerned at all. What were before undefined, vague blurs in the distant countryside could now be distinctly seen. They were sheaves of rye. The dew, not visible till the sun was up, wetted Levin's legs and his blouse above his belt in the high-growing, fragrant hemp-patch, from which the pollen had already fallen out. In the transparent stillness of morning the smallest sounds were audible. A bee flew by Levin's ear with the whizzing sound of a bullet. He looked carefully, and saw a second and a third. They were all flying from the beehives behind the hedge, and they disappeared over the

hemp-patch in the direction of the marsh. The path led straight to the marsh. The marsh could be recognized by the mist which rose from it, thicker in one place and thinner in another, so that the reeds and willow-bushes swayed like islands in this mist. At the edge of the marsh and the road, peasant boys and men, who had been herding for the night, were lying, and in the dawn all were asleep under their coats. Not far from them were three hobbled horses. One of them clanked a chain. Laska walked beside her master, pressing a little forward and looking round. Passing the sleeping peasants and reaching the first reeds, Levin examined his pistols and let his dog off. One of the horses, a sleek, dark-brown three-year-old, seeing the dog, started away, switched its tail and snorted. The other horses too were frightened, and splashing through the water with their hobbled legs, and drawing their hoofs out of the thick mud with a squelching sound, they bounded out of the marsh. Laska stopped, looking ironically at the horses and inquiringly at Levin. Levin patted Laska, and whistled as a sign that she might begin.

Laska ran joyfully and anxiously through the slush that swayed under her.

Running into the marsh among the familiar scents of roots, marsh plants, and slime, and the extraneous smell of horse dung, Laska detected at once a smell that pervaded the whole marsh, the scent of that strong-smelling bird that always excited her more than any other. Here and there among the moss and marsh plants this scent was very strong, but it was impossible to determine in which direction it grew stronger or fainter. To find the direction, she had to go further away from the wind. Not feeling the motion of her legs, Laska bounded with a stiff gallop, so that at each bound she could stop short, to the right, away from the wind that blew from the east before sunrise, and turned facing the wind. Sniffing in the air with dilated nostrils, she felt at once that not their tracks only but they themselves were here before her, and not one, but many. Laska slackened her speed. They were here, but where precisely she could not yet determine. To find the very spot, she began to make a circle, when suddenly her master's voice drew her off. "Laska! here?" he asked, pointing her to a different direction. She stopped, asking him if she had better not go on doing as she had begun. But he repeated his command in an angry voice, pointing to a spot covered with water, where there could not be anything. She obeyed him, pretending she was looking, so as to please him, went round it, and went back to her former position, and was at once aware of the scent again. Now when he was not hindering her, she knew what to do, and without looking at what was under her feet, and to her vexation stumbling over a high stump into the water, but righting herself with her strong, supple legs, she began making the circle which was to make all clear to her. The scent of them reached her, stronger and stronger, and more and more defined, and all at once it became perfectly clear to her that one of them was here, behind this tuft of reeds, five paces in front of her; she stopped, and her whole body was still and rigid. On her short legs she could see nothing in front of her, but by the scent she knew it was sitting not more than five paces off. She stood still, feeling more and more concious of it, and enjoying it in anticipation. Her tail was stretched straight and tense, and only wagging at the extreme end. Her mouth was slightly open, her ears raised. One ear had been turned wrong side out as she ran up, and she breathed heavily but warily, and still more warily looked round, but more with her eyes than her head, to her master. He was coming along with the face she knew so well, though the eyes were always terrible to her. He stumbled over the stump as he came, and moved, as she thought, extraordinarily slowly. She thought he came slowly, but he was running.

Noticing Laska's special attitude as she crouched on the ground, as it were, scratching big prints with her hind paws, and with her mouth slightly open, Levin knew she was pointing at grouse, and with an inward prayer for luck, especially with the first bird, he ran up to her. Coming quite close up to her, he could from his height look beyond her, and he saw with his eyes what she was seeing with her nose. In a space between two little thickets, to a couple of yards' distance, he could see a grouse. Turning its head, it was listening. Then lightly preening and folding its wings, it disappeared round a corner with a clumsy wag of its tail.

"Fetch it, fetch it!" shouted Levin, giving Laska a shove from behind.

"But I can't go," thought Laska. "Where am I to go? From here I feel them, but if I move forward I shall know nothing of where they are or who they are." But then he shoved her with his knee, and in an excited whisper said, "Fetch it, Laska."

"Well, if that's what he wishes, I'll do it, but I can't answer for myself now," she thought, and darted forward as fast as her legs would carry her between the thick bushes. She scented nothing now; she could only see and hear, without understanding anything.

Ten paces from her former place a grouse rose with a guttural cry and the peculiar round sound of its wings. And immediately after the shot it splashed heavily with its white breast on the wet mire. Another bird did not linger, but rose behind Levin without the dog. When Levin turned towards it, it was already some way off. But his shot caught it. Flying twenty paces further, the second grouse rose upwards, and whirling round like a ball, dropped heavily on a dry place.

"Come, this is going to be some good!" thought Levin, packing the warm and fat grouse into his game-bag. "Eh, Laska, will it be good?"

When Levin, after loading his gun, moved on, the sun had fully risen, though unseen behind the storm-clouds. The moon had lost all of its luster, and was like a white cloud in the sky. Not a single star could be seen. The sedge, silvery with dew before, now shone like gold. The stagnant pools were all like amber. The blue of the grass had changed to yellow-green. The marsh-birds twittered and swarmed about the brook and upon the bushes that glittered with dew and cast long shadows. A hawk woke up and settled on a haycock, turning its head from side to side and looking discontentedly at the marsh. Crows were flying about the field, and a bare-legged boy was driving the horses to an old man, who had got up from under his long coat and was combing his hair. The smoke from the gun was white as milk over the green of the grass.

One of the boys ran up to Levin.

"Uncle, there were ducks here yesterday!" he shouted to him, and he walked a little way off behind him.

And Levin was doubly pleased, in sight of the boy, who expressed his approval, at killing three snipe, one after another, straight off.

CHAPTER XIII

THE SPORTSMAN'S saying, that if the first beast or the first bird is not missed, the day will be lucky, turned out correct.

At ten o'clock Levin, weary, hungry, and happy after a tramp of twenty miles, returned to his night's lodging with nineteen head of fine game and one duck, which he tied to his belt, as it would not go into the game-bag. His companions had long been awake, and had had time to get hungry and have breakfast.

"Wait a bit, wait a bit, I know there are nineteen," said Levin, counting a second time over the grouse and snipe, that looked so much less important now, bent and dry and blood-stained, with heads crooked aside, than they did when they were flying.

The number was verified, and Stepan Arkadyevitch's envy pleased Levin. He was pleased too on returning to find the man sent by Kitty with a note was already there.

"I am perfectly well and happy. If you were uneasy about me, you can feel easier than ever. I've a new bodyguard, Marya Vlasyevna,"—this was the midwife, a new and important personage in Levin's domestic life. "She has come to have a look at me. She found me perfectly well, and we have kept her till you are back. All are happy and well, and please, don't be in a hurry to come back, but, if the sport is good, stay another day."

These two pleasures, his lucky shooting and the letter from his wife, were so great that two slightly disagreeable incidents passed lightly over Levin. One was that the chestnut tracehorse, who had been unmistakably overworked on the previous day, was off his feed and out of sorts. The coachman said he was "Overdriven yesterday, Konstantin Dmitrievitch," he said. "Yes, indeed! driving ten miles with no sense!"

The other unpleasant incident, which for the first minute destroyed his good-humor, though later he laughed at it a great deal, was to find that of all the provisions Kitty had provided in such abundance that one would have thought there was enough for a week, nothing was left. On his way back, tired and hungry from shooting, Levin had so distinct a vision of meat-pies that as he approached the hut he seemed to smell and taste them, as Laska had smelt the game, and he immediately told Philip to give him some. It appeared that there were no pies left, nor even any chicken.

"Well, this fellow's appetite!" said Stepan Arkadyevitch, laughing and pointing at Vassenka Veslovsky. "I never suffer from loss of appetite, but he's really marvelous! . . ."

"Well, it can't be helped," said Levin, looking gloomily at Veslovsky. "Well, Philip, give me some beef, then."

"The beef's been eaten, and the bones given to the dogs," answered Philip.

Levin was so hurt that he said, in a tone of vexation, "You might have left me something!" and he felt ready to cry.

"Then put away the game," he said in a shaking voice to Philip, trying not to look at Vassenka, "and cover them with some nettles. And you might at least ask for some milk for me."

But when he had drunk some milk, he felt ashamed immediately at having shown his annoyance to a stranger, and he began to laugh at his hungry mortification.

In the evening they went shooting again, and Veslovsky had several successful shots, and in the night they drove home.

Their homeward journey was as lively as their drive out had been. Veslovsky sang songs and related with enjoyment his adventures with the peasants, who had regaled him with vodka, and said to him, "Excuse our homely ways," and his night's adventures with kiss-in-the-ring and the servant-girl and the peasant, who had asked him was he married, and on learning that he was not, said to him, "Well, mind you don't run after other men's wives—you'd better get one of your own." These words had particularly amused Veslovsky.

"Altogether, I've enjoyed our outing awfully. And you, Levin?"

"I have, very much," Levin said quite sincerely. It was particularly delightful to him to have got rid of the hostility he had been feeling towards Vassenka Veslovsky at home, and to feel instead the most friendly disposition to him.

CHAPTER XIV

NEXT day at ten o'clock Levin, who had already gone his rounds, knocked at the room where Vassenka had been put for the night.

"*Entrez!*" Veslovsky called to him. "Excuse me, I've only just finished my ablutions," he said, smiling, standing before him in his underclothes only.

"Don't mind me, please." Levin sat down in the window. "Have you slept well?"

"Like the dead. What sort of day is it for shooting?"

"What will you take, tea or coffee?"

"Neither. I'll wait till lunch. I'm really ashamed. I suppose the ladies are down? A walk now would be capital. You show me your horses."

After walking about the garden, visiting the stable, and even doing some gymnastic exercises together on the parallel bars, Levin returned to the house with his guest, and went with him into the drawing-room.

"We had splendid shooting, and so many delightful experiences!" said Veslovsky, going up to Kitty, who was sitting at the samovar. "What a pity ladies are cut off from these delights!"

"Well, I suppose he must say something to the lady of the house," Levin said to himself. Again he fancied something in the smile, in the all-conquering air with which their guest addressed Kitty. . . .

The princess, sitting on the other side of the table with Marya Vlasyevna and Stepan Arkadyevitch, called Levin to her side, and began to talk to him about moving to Moscow for Kitty's confinement, and getting ready rooms for them. Just as Levin had disliked all the trivial preparations for his wedding, as derogatory to the grandeur of the event, now he felt still more offensive the preparations for the approaching birth, the date of which they reckoned, it seemed, on their fingers. He tried to turn a deaf ear to these discussions of the best patterns of long clothes for the coming baby; tried to turn away and avoid seeing the mysterious, endless strips of knitting, the triangles of linen, and so on, to which Dolly attached special importance. The birth of a son (he was certain it would be a son) which was promised him, but which he still could not believe in—so marvelous it seemed—presented itself to his mind, on one hand, as a happiness so immense, and therefore so incredible; on the other, as an event so mysterious, that this assumption of a definite knowledge of what would be, and consequent preparation for it, as for something ordinary that did happen to people, jarred on him as confusing and humiliating.

But the princess did not understand his feelings, and put down his reluctance to think and talk about it to carelessness and indifference, and so she gave him no peace. She had commissioned Stepan Arkadyevitch to look at a flat, and now she called Levin up.

"I know nothing about it, princess. Do as you think fit," he said.

"You must decide when you will move."

"I really don't know. I know millions of children are born away from Moscow, and doctors . . . why . . ."

"But if so . . ."

"Oh, no, as Kitty wishes."

"We can't talk to Kitty about it! Do you want me to frighten her? Why, this spring Natalia Golitzina died from having an ignorant doctor."

"I will do just what you say," he said gloomily.

The princess began talking to him, but he did not hear her. Though the conversation with the princess had indeed jarred upon him, he was gloomy, not on account of that conversation, but from what he saw at the samovar.

"No, it's impossible," he thought, glancing now and then at Vassenka bending over Kitty, telling her something with his charming smile, and at her, flushed and disturbed.

There was something not nice in Vassenka's attitude, in his eyes, in his smile. Levin even saw something not nice in Kitty's attitude and look. And again the light died away in his eyes. Again, as before, all of a sudden, without the slightest transition, he felt cast down from a pinnacle of happiness, peace, and dignity, into an abyss of despair, rage, and humiliation. Again everything and every one had become hateful to him.

"You do just as you think best, princess," he said again, looking round.

"Heavy is the cap of Monomach," Stepan Arkadyevitch said playfully, hinting, evidently, not simply at the princess's conversation, but at the cause of Levin's agitation, which he had noticed.

"How late you are to-day, Dolly!"

Every one got up to greet Darya Alexandrovna. Vassenka only rose for an instant, and with the lack of courtesy to ladies characteristic of the modern young man, he scarcely bowed, and resumed his conversation again, laughing at something.

"I've been worried about Masha. She did not sleep well, and is dreadfully tiresome to-day," said Dolly.

The conversation Vassenka had started with Kitty was running on the same lines as on the previous evening, discussing Anna, and whether love is to be put higher than worldly considerations. Kitty disliked the conversation, and she was disturbed both by the subject and the tone in which it was conducted, and also by the knowledge of the effect it would have on her husband. But she was too simple and innocent to know how to cut short this conversation, or even to conceal the superficial pleasure afforded her by the young man's very obvious admiration. She wanted to stop it, but she did not know what to do. Whatever she did she knew would be observed by her husband, and the worst interpretation put on it. And, in fact, when she asked Dolly what was wrong with Masha, and Vassenka, waiting till this uninteresting conversation was over, began to gaze indifferently at Dolly, the question struck Levin as an unnatural and disgusting piece of hypocrisy.

"What do you say, shall we go and look for mushrooms to-day?" said Dolly.

"By all means, please, and I shall come too," said Kitty, and she blushed. She wanted from politeness to ask Vassenka whether he would come, and she did not ask him. "Where are you going, Kostya?" she asked her husband with a guilty face, as he passed by her with a resolute step. This guilty air confirmed all his suspicions.

"The mechanician came when I was away; I haven't seen him yet," he said, not looking at her.

He went down-stairs, but before he had time to leave his study he heard his wife's familiar footsteps running with reckless speed to him.

"What do you want?" he said to her shortly. "We are busy."

"I beg your pardon," she said to the German mechanician; "I want a few words with my husband."

The German would have left the room, but Levin said to him: "Don't disturb yourself."

"The train is at three?" queried the German. "I mustn't be late."

Levin did not answer him, but walked out himself with his wife.

"Well, what have you to say to me?" he said to her in French.

He did not look her in the face, and did not care to see that she in her condition was trembling all over, and had a piteous, crushed look.

"I . . . I want to say that we can't go on like this; that this is misery . . ." she said.

"The servants are here at the sideboard," he said angrily; "don't make a scene."

"Well, let's go in here!"

They were standing in the passage. Kitty would have gone into the next room, but there the English governess was giving Tanya a lesson.

"Well, come into the garden."

In the garden they came upon a peasant weeding the path. And no longer considering that the peasant could see her tear-stained and his agitated face, that they looked like people fleeing from some disaster, they went on with rapid steps, feeling that they must speak out and clear up misunderstandings, must be alone together, and so get rid of the misery they were both feeling.

"We can't go on like this! It's misery! I am wretched; you are wretched. What for?" she said, when they had at last reached a solitary garden-seat at a turn in the lime-tree avenue.

"But tell me one thing: was there in his tone anything unseemly, not nice, humiliatingly horrible?" he said, standing before her again in the same position with his clenched fists on his chest, as he had stood before her that night.

"Yes," she said in a shaking voice; "but, Kostya, surely you see I'm not to blame? All the morning I've been trying to take a tone . . . but such people . . . Why did he come? How happy we were!" she said, breathless with the sobs that shook her.

Although nothing had been pursuing them, and there was nothing to run away from, and they could not possibly have found anything very delightful on that garden-seat, the gardener saw with astonishment that they passed him on their way home with comforted and radiant faces.

CHAPTER XV

AFTER escorting his wife up-stairs, Levin went to Dolly's part of the house. Darya Alexandrovna, for her part, was in great distress too that day. She was walking about the room, talking angrily to a little girl, who stood in the corner roaring.

"And you shall stand all day in the corner, and have your dinner all alone, and not see one of your dolls, and I won't make you a new frock," she said, not knowing how to punish her.

"Oh, she is a disgusting child!" she turned to Levin. "Where does she get such wicked propensities?"

"Why, what has she done?" Levin said without much interest, for he had wanted to ask her advice, and so was annoyed that he had come at an unlucky moment.

"Grisha and she went into the raspberries, and there . . . I can't tell you really what she did. It's a thousand pities Miss Elliot's not with us. This one sees to nothing—she's a machine . . . *Figurez-vous que la petite? . . .*"

And Darya Alexandrovna described Masha's crime.

"That proves nothing; it's not a question of evil propensities at all, it's simply mischief," Levin assured her.

"But you are upset about something? What have you come for?" asked Dolly. "What's going on there?"

And in the tone of her question Levin heard that it would be easy for him to say what he had meant to say.

"I've not been in there, I've been alone in the garden with Kitty. We've had a quarrel for the second time since . . . Stiva came."

Dolly looked at him with her shrewd, comprehending eyes.

"Come, tell me, honor bright, has there been . . . not in Kitty, but in that gentleman's behavior, a tone which might be unpleasant—not unpleasant, but horrible, offensive to a husband?"

"You mean, how shall I say . . . Stay, stay in the corner!" she said to Masha, who, detecting a faint smile in her mother's face, had been turning round. "The opinion of the world would be that he is behaving as young men do behave. *Il fait la cour à une jeune et jolie femme,* and a husband who's a man of the world should only be flattered by it."

"Yes, yes," said Levin gloomily; "but you noticed it?"

"Not only I, but Stiva noticed it. Just after breakfast he said to me in so many words, *Je crois que Veslovsky fait un petit brin de cour à Kitty.*"

"Well, that's all right then; now I'm satisfied. I'll send him away," said Levin.

"What do you mean! Are you crazy?" Dolly cried in horror; "nonsense, Kostya, only think!" she said, laughing. "You can go now to Fanny," she said to Masha. "No, if you wish it, I'll speak to Stiva. He'll take him away. He can say you're expecting visitors. Altogether he doesn't fit into the house."

"No, no, I'll do it myself."

"But you'll quarrel with him?"

"Not a bit. I shall so enjoy it," Levin said, his eyes flashing with real enjoyment. "Come, forgive her, Dolly, she won't do it again," he said of the little sinner, who had not gone to Fanny, but was standing irresolutely before her mother, waiting and looking up from under her brows to catch her mother's eye.

The mother glanced at her. The child broke into sobs, hid her face on her mother's lap, and Dolly laid her thin, tender hand on her head.

"And what is there in common between us and him?" thought Levin, and he went off to look for Veslovsky.

As he passed through the passage he gave orders for the carriage to be got ready to drive to the station.

"The spring was broken yesterday," said the footman.

"Well, the covered trap, then, and make haste. Where's the visitor?"

"The gentleman's gone to his room."

Levin came upon Veslovsky at the moment when the latter, having unpacked his things from his trunk, and laid out some new songs, was putting on his gaiters to go out riding.

Whether there was something exceptional in Levin's face, or that Vassenka was himself conscious that *ce petit brin de cour* he was making was out of place in this family, but he was somewhat (as much as a young man in society can be) disconcerted at Levin's entrance.

"You ride in gaiters?"

"Yes, it's much cleaner," said Vassenka, putting his fat leg on a chair, fastening the bottom hook, and smiling with simplehearted good-humor.

He was undoubtedly a good-natured fellow, and Levin felt

sorry for him and ashamed of himself, as his host, when he saw the shy look on Vassenka's face.

On the table lay a piece of stick which they had broken together that morning, trying their strength. Levin took the fragment in his hands and began smashing it up, breaking bits off the stick, not knowing how to begin.

"I wanted . . ." He paused, but suddenly, remembering Kitty and everything that had happened, he said, looking him resolutely in the face: "I have ordered the horses to be put-to for you."

"How so?" Vassenka began in surprise. "To drive where?"

"For you to drive to the station," Levin said gloomily.

"Are you going away, or has something happened?"

"It happens that I expect visitors," said Levin, his strong fingers more and more rapidly breaking off the ends of the split stick. "And I'm not expecting visitors, and nothing has happened, but I beg you to go away. You can explain my rudeness as you like."

Vassenka drew himself up.

"I beg you to explain . . ." he said with dignity, understanding at last.

"I can't explain," Levin said softly and deliberately, trying to control the trembling of his jaw; "and you'd better not ask."

And as the split ends were all broken off, Levin clutched the thick ends in his finger, broke the stick in two, and carefully caught the end as it fell.

Probably the sight of those nervous fingers, of the muscles he had proved that morning at gymnastics, of the glittering eyes, the soft voice, and quivering jaws, convinced Vassenka better than any words. He bowed, shrugging his shoulders, and smiling contemptuously.

"Can I not see Oblonsky?"

The shrug and the smile did not irritate Levin.

"What else was there for him to do?" he thought.

"I'll send him to you at once."

"What madness is this?" Stepan Arkadyevitch said when, after hearing from his friend that he was being turned out of the house, he found Levin in the garden, where he was walking about waiting for his guest's departure. *"Mais c'est ridicule!* What fly has stung you? *Mais c'est du dernier ridicule!* What did you think, if a young man . . ."

But the place where Levin had been stung was evidently still sore, for he turned pale again, when Stepan Arkadyevitch would have enlarged on the reason, and he himself cut him short.

"Please don't go into it! I can't help it. I feel ashamed of how I'm treating you and him. But it won't be, I imagine, a great grief to him to go, and his presence was distasteful to me and to my wife."

"But it's insulting to him! *Et puis c'est ridicule."*

"And to me it's both insulting and distressing! And I'm not in fault in any way, and there's no need for me to suffer."

"Well, this I didn't expect of you! *On peut être jaloux, mais à ce point, c'est du dernier ridicule!"*

Levin turned quickly, and walked away from him into the depths of the avenue, and he went on walking up and down alone. Soon he heard the rumble of the trap, and saw from behind the trees how Vassenka, sitting in the hay (unluckily there was no seat in the trap) in his Scotch cap, was driven along the avenue, jolting up and down over the ruts.

"What's this?" Levin thought, when a footman ran out of the house and stopped the trap. It was the mechanician, whom Levin had totally forgotten. The mechanician, bowing low, said something to Veslovsky, then clambered into the trap, and they drove off together.

Stepan Arkadyevitch and the princess were much upset by Levin's action. And he himself felt not only in the highest degree *ridicule,* but also utterly guilty and disgraced. But remembering what sufferings he and his wife had been through, when he asked himself how he should act another time, he answered that he should do just the same again.

In spite of all this, towards the end of that day, every one except the princess, who could not pardon Levin's action, became extraordinarily lively and good-humored, like children after a punishment or grown-up people after a dreary, ceremonious reception, so that by the evening Vassenka's dismissal was spoken of, in the absence of the princess, as though it were some remote event. And Dolly, who had inherited her father's gift of humorous story-telling, made Varenka helpless with laughter as she related for the third and fourth time, always with fresh humorous additions, how she had only just put on her new shoes for the benefit of the visitor, and on going into the drawing-room, heard suddenly the rumble of the trap. And who should be in the trap but Vassenka himself, with his Scotch cap, and his songs and his gaiters, and all, sitting in the hay.

"If only you'd ordered out the carriage! But no! and then I hear: 'Stop!' Oh, I thought they've relented. I look out, and behold a fat German being sat down by him and driving away . . . And my new shoes all for nothing! . . ."

CHAPTER XVI

DARYA ALEXANDROVNA carried out her intention and went to see Anna. She was sorry to annoy her sister and to do anything Levin disliked. She quite understood how right the Levins were in not wishing to have anything to do with Vronsky. But she felt she must go and see Anna, and show her that her feelings could not be changed, in spite of the change in her position. That she might be independent of the Levins in this expedition,

Darya Alexandrovna sent to the village to hire horses for the drive; but Levin learning of it went to her to protest.

"What makes you suppose that I dislike your going? But, even if I did dislike it, I should still more dislike your not taking my horses," he said. "You never told me that you were going for certain. Hiring horses in the village is disagreeable to me, and, what's of more importance, they'll undertake the job and never get you there. I have horses. And if you don't want to wound me, you'll take mine."

Darya Alexandrovna had to consent, and on the day fixed Levin had ready for his sister-in-law a set of four horses and relays, getting them together from the farm- and saddle-horses —not at all a smart-looking set, but capable of taking Darya Alexandrovna the whole distance in a single day. At that moment, when horses were wanted for the princess, who was going, and for the midwife, it was a difficult matter for Levin to make up the number, but the duties of hospitality would not let him allow Darya Alexandrovna to hire horses when staying in his house. Moreover, he was well aware that the twenty roubles that would be asked for the journey were a serious matter for her; Darya Alexandrovna's pecuniary affairs, which were in a very unsatisfactory state, were taken to heart by the Levins as if they were their own.

Darya Alexandrovna, by Levin's advice, started before daybreak. The road was good, the carriage comfortable, the horses trotted along merrily, and on the box, besides the coachman, sat the counting-house clerk, whom Levin was sending instead of a groom for greater security. Darya Alexandrovna dozed and waked up only on reaching the inn where the horses were to be changed.

After drinking tea at the same well-to-do peasant's with whom Levin had stayed on the way to Sviazhsky's, and chatting with the women about their children, and with the old man about Count Vronsky, whom the latter praised very highly, Darya Alexandrovna, at ten o'clock, went on again. At home, looking after her children, she had no time to think. So now, after this journey of four hours, all the thoughts she had suppressed before rushed swarming into her brain, and she thought over all her life as she never had before, and from the most different points of view. Her thoughts seemed strange even to herself. At first she thought about the children, about whom she was uneasy, although the princess and Kitty (she reckoned more upon her) had promised to look after them. "If only Masha does not begin her naughty tricks, if Grisha isn't kicked by a horse, and Lily's stomach isn't upset again!" she thought. But these questions of the present were succeeded by questions of the immediate future. She began thinking how she had to get a new flat in Moscow for the coming winter, to renew the drawing-room furniture, and to make her elder girl a cloak. Then questions of the more remote future occurred to her: how she was to place her children in the world. "The girls are all right," she thought; "but the boys?"

"It's very well that I'm teaching Grisha, but of course that's only because I am free myself now, I'm not with child. Stiva, of course, there's no counting on. And with the help of good-natured friends I can bring them up; but if there's another baby coming? . . ." And the thought struck her how untruly it was said that the curse laid on woman was that in sorrow she should bring forth children.

"The birth itself, that's nothing; but the months of carrying the child—that's what's so intolerable," she thought, picturing to herself her last pregnancy, and the death of the last baby. And she recalled the conversation she had just had with the young woman at the inn. On being asked whether she had any children, the handsome young woman had answered cheerfully:

"I had a girl baby, but God set me free; I buried her last Lent."

"Well, did you grieve very much for her?" asked Darya Alexandrovna.

"Why grieve? The old man has grandchildren enough as it is. It was only a trouble. No working, nor nothing. Only a tie."

This answer had struck Darya Alexandrovna as revolting in spite of the good-natured and pleasing face of the young woman; but now she could not help recalling these words. In those cynical words there was indeed a grain of truth.

"Yes, altogether," thought Darya Alexandrovna, looking back over her whole existence during those fifteen years of her married life, "pregnancy, sickness, mental incapacity, indifference to everything, and most of all—hideousness. Kitty, young and pretty as she is, even Kitty has lost her looks; and I when I'm with child become hideous, I know it. The birth, the agony, the hideous agonies, that last moment . . . then the nursing, the sleepless nights, the fearful pains. . . ."

Darya Alexandrovna shuddered at the mere recollection of the pain from sore breasts which she had suffered with almost every child. "Then the children's illnesses, that everlasting apprehension; then bringing them up; evil propensities" (she thought of little Masha's crime among the raspberries), "education, Latin—it's all so incomprehensible and difficult. And on the top of it all, the death of these children." And there rose again before her imagination the cruel memory, that always tore her mother's heart, of the death of her last little baby, who had died of croup; his funeral, the callous indifference of all at the little pink coffin, and her own torn heart, and her lonely anguish at the sight of the pale little brow with its projecting temples, and the open, wondering little mouth seen in the coffin at the moment when it was being covered with the little pink lid with a cross braided on it.

"And all this, what's it for? What is to come of it all? That I'm wasting my life, never having a moment's peace, either with child, or nursing a child, forever irritable, peevish, wretched myself and worrying others, repulsive to my husband, while the children are growing up unhappy, badly educated and penniless. Even now, if it weren't for spending the summer at the Levins', I don't know how we should be managing to live. Of course Kostya and Kitty have so much tact that we don't feel it; but it can't go on. They'll have children, they won't be able to keep us; it's a drag on them as it is. How is papa, who has hardly anything left for himself, to help us? So that I can't even bring the children up by myself, and may find it hard with the help of other people, at the cost of humiliation. Why, even if we suppose the greatest good luck, that the children don't die, and I bring them up somehow. At the very best they'll simply be decent people. That's all I can hope for. And to gain simply that —what agonies, what toil! . . . One's whole life ruined!" Again she recalled what the young peasant woman had said, and again she was revolted at the thought; but she could not help admitting that there was a grain of brutal truth in the words.

"Is it far now, Mihail?" Darya Alexandrovna asked the counting-house clerk, to turn her mind from thoughts that were frightening her.

"From this village, they say, it's five miles." The carriage drove along the village street and onto a bridge. On the bridge was a crowd of peasant women with coils of ties for the sheaves on their shoulders, gaily and noisily chattering. They stood still on the bridge, staring inquisitively at the carriage. All the faces turned to Darya Alexandrovna looked to her healthy and happy, making her envious of their enjoyment of life. "They're all living, they're all enjoying life," Darya Alexandrovna still mused when she had passed the peasant women and was driving uphill again at a trot, seated comfortably on the soft springs of the old carriage, "while I, let out, as it were from prison, from the world of worries that fret me to death, am only looking about me now for an instant. They all live; those peasant women and my sister Natalia and Varenka and Anna, whom I am going to see—all, but not I.

"And they attack Anna. What for? am I any better? I have, anyway, a husband I love—not as I should like to love him, still I do love him, while Anna never loved hers. How is she to blame? She wants to live. God has put that in our hearts. Very likely I should have done the same. Even to this day I don't feel sure I did right in listening to her at that terrible time when she came to me in Moscow. I ought then to have cast off my husband and have begun my life fresh. I might have loved and have been loved in reality. And is it any better as it is? I don't respect him. He's necessary to me," she thought about her husband, "and I put up with him. Is that any better? At that time I could still have been admired, I had beauty left me still," Darya Alexandrovna pursued her thoughts, and she would have liked to look at herself in the looking-glass. She had a traveling looking-glass in her hand-bag, and she wanted to take it out; but looking at the backs of the coachman and the swaying counting-house clerk, she felt that she would be ashamed if either of them were to look round, and she did not take out the glass.

But without looking in the glass, she thought that even now it was not too late; and she thought of Sergey Ivanovitch, who was always particularly attentive to her, of Stiva's good-hearted friend, Turovtsin, who had helped her nurse her children through the scarlatina, and was in love with her. And there was some one else, a quite young man, who—her husband had told her it as a joke—thought her more beautiful than either of her sisters. And the most passionate and impossible romances rose before Darya Alexandrovna's imagination. "Anna did quite right, and certainly I shall never reproach her for it. She is happy, she makes another person happy, and she's not broken down as I am, but most likely just as she always was, bright, clever, open to every impression," thought Darya Alexandrovna, —and a sly smile curved her lips, for, as she pondered on Anna's love-affair, Darya Alexandrovna constructed on parallel lines an almost identical love-affair for herself, with an imaginary composite figure, the ideal man who was in love with her. She, like Anna, confessed the whole affair to her husband. And the amazement and perplexity of Stepan Arkadyevitch at this avowal made her smile.

In such day-dreams she reached the turning of the highroad that led to Vozdvizhenskoe.

CHAPTER XVII

The coachman pulled up his four horses and looked round to the right, to a field of rye, where some peasants were sitting on a cart. The counting-house clerk was just going to jump down, but on second thoughts he shouted peremptorily to the peasants instead, and beckoned to them to come up. The wind, that seemed to blow as they drove, dropped when the carriage stood still; gadflies settled on the steaming horses that angrily shook them off. The metallic clank of a whetstone against a scythe, that came to them from the cart, ceased. One of the peasants got up and came towards the carriage.

"Well, you are slow!" the counting-house clerk shouted angrily to the peasant who was stepping slowly with his bare feet over the ruts of the rough dry road. "Come along, do!"

A curly-headed old man with a bit of bast tied round his hair, and his bent back dark with perspiration, came towards the carriage, quickening his steps, and took hold of the mud-guard with his sunburnt hand.

"Vozdvizhenskoe, the manor-house? the count's?" he repeated; "go on to the end of this track. Then turn to the left. Straight along the avenue and you'll come right upon it. But whom do you want? The count himself?"

"Well, are they at home, my good man?" Darya Alexandrovna said vaguely, not knowing how to ask about Anna, even of this peasant.

"At home for sure," said the peasant, shifting from one bare foot to the other, and leaving a distinct print of five toes and a heel in the dust. "Sure to be at home," he repeated, evidently eager to talk. "Only yesterday visitors arrived. There's a sight of visitors come. What do you want?" He turned round and called to a lad, who was shouting something to him from the cart. "Oh! They all rode by here not long since, to look at a reaping-machine. They'll be home by now. And who will you be belonging to? . . ."

"We've come a long way," said the coachman, climbing onto the box. "So it's not far?"

"I tell you, it's just here. As soon as you get out . . ." he said, keeping hold all the while of the carriage.

A healthy-looking, broad-shouldered young fellow came up too.

"What, is it laborers they want for the harvest?" he asked.

"I don't know, my boy."

"So you keep to the left, and you'll come right on it," said the peasant, unmistakably loth to let the travelers go, and eager to converse.

The coachman started the horses, but they were only just turning off when the peasant shouted: "Stop! Hi, friend! Stop!" called the two voices. The coachman stopped.

"They're coming! They're yonder!" shouted the peasant. "See what a turn-out!" he said, pointing to four persons on horseback, and two in a *char-à-banc,* coming along the road.

They were Vronsky with a jockey, Veslovsky and Anna on horseback, and Princess Varvara and Sviazhsky in the *char-à-banc.* They had gone out to look at the working of a new reaping-machine.

When the carriage stopped, the party on horseback were coming at a walking-pace. Anna was in front beside Veslovsky. Anna, quietly walking her horse, a sturdy English cob with cropped mane and short tail, her beautiful head with her black hair straying loose under her high hat, her full shoulders, her slender waist in her black riding-habit, and all the ease and grace of her deportment, impressed Dolly.

For the first minute it seemed to her unsuitable for Anna to be on horseback. The conception of riding on horseback for a lady was, in Darya Alexandrovna's mind, associated with ideas of youthful flirtation and frivolity, which, in her opinion, was unbecoming in Anna's position. But when she had scrutinized her, seeing her closer, she was at once reconciled to her riding. In spite of her elegance, everything was so simple, quiet, and dignified in the attitude, the dress and the movements of Anna, that nothing could have been more natural.

Beside Anna, on a hot-looking gray cavalry-horse, was Vassenka Veslovsky in his Scotch cap with floating ribbons, his stout legs stretched out in front, obviously pleased with his own appearance. Darya Alexandrovna could not suppress a good-humored smile as she recognized him. Behind rode Vronsky on a dark bay mare, obviously heated from galloping. He was holding her in, pulling at the reins.

After him rode a little man in the dress of a jockey. Sviazhsky and Princess Varvara in a new *char-à-banc* with a big, raven-black trotting-horse, overtook the party on horseback.

Anna's face suddenly beamed with a joyful smile at the instant when, in the little figure huddled in a corner of the old carriage, she recognized Dolly. She uttered a cry, started in the saddle, and set her horse into a gallop. On reaching the carriage she jumped off without assistance, and holding up her riding-habit, she ran up to greet Dolly.

"I thought it was you and dared not think it. How delightful! You can't fancy how glad I am!" she said, at one moment pressing her face against Dolly and kissing her, and at the next holding her off and examining her with a smile.

"Here's a delightful surprise, Alexey!" she said, looking round at Vronsky, who had dismounted, and was walking towards them.

Vronsky, taking off his tall gray hat, went up to Dolly.

"You wouldn't believe how glad we are to see you," he said, giving peculiar significance to the words, and showing his strong white teeth in a smile.

Vassenka Veslovsky, without getting off his horse, took off his cap and greeted the visitor by gleefully waving the ribbons over his head.

"That's Princess Varvara," Anna said in reply to a glance of inquiry from Dolly as the *char-à-banc* drove up.

"Ah!" said Darya Alexandrovna, and unconsciously her face betrayed her dissatisfaction.

Princess Varvara was her husband's aunt, and she had long known her, and did not respect her. She knew that Princess Varvara had passed her whole life toadying on her rich relations, but that she should now be sponging on Vronsky, a man who was nothing to her, mortified Dolly on account of her kinship with her husband. Anna noticed Dolly's expression, and was disconcerted by it. She blushed, dropped her riding-habit, and stumbled over it.

Darya Alexandrovna went up to the *char-à-banc* and coldly greeted Princess Varvara. Sviazhsky too she knew. He inquired how his queer friend with the young wife was, and running his eyes over the ill-matched horses and the carriage with its patched mud-guards, proposed to the ladies that they should get into the *char-à-banc*.

"And I'll get into this vehicle," he said. "The horse is quiet, and the princess drives capitally."

"No, stay as you were," said Anna, coming up, "and we'll go in the carriage," and taking Dolly's arm, she drew her away.

Darya Alexandrovna's eyes were fairly dazzled by the elegant carriage of a pattern she had never seen before, the splendid horses, and the elegant and gorgeous people surrounding her. But what struck her most of all was the change that had taken place in Anna, whom she knew so well and loved. Any other woman, a less close observer, not knowing Anna before, or not having thought as Darya Alexandrovna had been thinking on the road, would not have noticed anything special in Anna. But now Dolly was struck by that temporary beauty, which is only found in women during the moments of love, and which she saw now in Anna's face. Everything in her face, the clearly marked dimples in her cheeks and chin, the line of her lips, the smile which, as it were, fluttered about her face, the brilliance of her eyes, the grace and rapidity of her movements, the fulness of the notes of her voice, even the manner in which, with a sort of angry friendliness, she answered Veslovsky when he asked permission to get on her cob, so as to teach it to gallop with the right leg foremost—it was all peculiarly fascinating, and it seemed as if she were herself aware of it, and rejoicing in it.

When both the women were seated in the carriage, a sudden embarrassment came over both of them. Anna was disconcerted by the intent look of inquiry Dolly fixed upon her. Dolly was embarrassed because after Sviazhsky's phrase about "this vehicle," she could not help feeling ashamed of the dirty old carriage in which Anna was sitting with her. The coachman Philip and the counting-house clerk were experiencing the same sensation. The counting-house clerk, to conceal his confusion, busied himself settling the ladies, but Philip the coachman became sullen, and was bracing himself not to be overawed in future by this external superiority. He smiled ironically, looking at the raven horse, and was already deciding in his own mind that this smart trotter in the *char-à-banc* was only good for *promenade,* and wouldn't do thirty miles straight off in the heat.

The peasants had all got up from the cart and were inquisitively and mirthfully staring at the meeting of the friends, making their comments on it.

"They're pleased, too; haven't seen each other for a long while," said the curly-headed old man with the bast round his hair.

"I say, Uncle Gerasim, if we could take that raven horse now, to cart the corn, that 'ud be quick work!"

"Look-ee! Is that a woman in breeches?" said one of them, pointing to Vassenka Veslovsky sitting in a side-saddle.

"Nay, a man! See how smartly he's going it!"

"Eh, lads! seems we're not going to sleep, then?"

"What chance of sleep to-day!" said the old man, with a sidelong look at the sun. "Midday's past, look-ee! Get your hooks, and come along!"

CHAPTER XVIII

ANNA looked at Dolly's thin, care-worn face, with its wrinkles filled with dust from the road, and she was on the point of saying what she was thinking, that is, that Dolly had got thinner. But, conscious that she herself had grown handsomer, and that Dolly's eyes were telling her so, she sighed and began to speak about herself.

"You are looking at me," she said, "and wondering how I can be happy in my position? Well! it's shameful to confess, but I . . . I'm inexcusably happy. Something magical has happened to me, like a dream, when you're frightened, panic-stricken, and all of a sudden you wake up and all the horrors are no more. I have waked up. I have lived through the misery, the dread, and now for a long while past, especially since we've been here, I've been so happy! . . ." she said, with a timid smile of inquiry looking at Dolly.

"How glad I am!" said Dolly smiling, involuntarily speaking more coldly than she wanted to. "I'm very glad for you. Why haven't you written to me?"

"Why? . . . Because I hadn't the courage. . . . You forget my position . . ."

"To me? Hadn't the courage? If you knew how I . . . I look at . . ."

Darya Alexandrovna wanted to express her thoughts of the morning, but for some reason it seemed to her now out of place to do so.

"But of that we'll talk later. What's this, what are all these buildings?" she asked, wanting to change the conversation and pointing to the red and green roofs that came into view behind the green hedges of acacia and lilac. "Quite a little town."

But Anna did not answer.

"No, no! How do you look at my position, what do you think of it?" she asked.

"I consider . . ." Darya Alexandrovna was beginning, but at that instant Vassenka Veslovsky, having brought the cob to gallop with the right leg foremost, galloped past them, bumping heavily up and down in his short jacket on the chamois leather of the side-saddle. "He's doing it, Anna Arkadyevna!" he shouted.

Anna did not even glance at him; but again it seemed to Darya Alexandrovna out of place to enter upon such a long conversation in the carriage, and so she cut short her thought.

"I don't think anything," she said, "but I always loved you, and if one loves any one, one loves the whole person, just as they are and not as one would like them to be. . . ."

Anna, taking her eyes off her friend's face and dropping her eyelids (this was a new habit Dolly had not seen in her before), pondered, trying to penetrate the full significance of the words. And obviously interpreting them as she would have wished, she glanced at Dolly.

"If you had any sins," she said, "they would all be forgiven you for your coming to see me and these words."

And Dolly saw that the tears stood in her eyes. She pressed Anna's hand in silence.

"Well, what are these buildings? How many there are of them!" After a moment's silence she repeated her question.

"These are the servants' houses, barns, and stables," answered Anna. "And there the park begins. It had all gone to ruin, but Alexey had everything renewed. He is very fond of this place, and, what I never expected, he has become intensely interested in looking after it. But his is such a rich nature! Whatever he takes up, he does splendidly. So far from being bored by it, he works with passionate interest. He—with his temperament as I know it—he has become careful and businesslike, a first-rate manager, he positively reckons every penny in his management of the land. But only in that. When it's a question of tens of thousands, he doesn't think of money." She spoke with that gleefully sly smile with which women often talk of the secret characteristics only known to them—of those they love. "Do you see that big building? that's the new hospital. I believe it will cost over a hundred thousand; that's his hobby just now. And do you know how it all came about? The peasants asked him for some meadowland, I think it was, at a cheaper rate, and he refused, and I accused him of being miserly. Of course it was not really because of that, but everything together, he began this hospital to prove, do you see, that he was not miserly about money. *C'est une petitesse,* if you like, but I love him all the more for it. And now you'll see the house in a moment. It was his grandfather's house, and he has had nothing changed outside."

"How beautiful!" said Dolly, looking with involuntary admiration at the handsome house with columns, standing out among the different-colored greens of the old trees in the garden.

"Isn't it fine? And from the house, from the top, the view is wonderful."

They drove into a courtyard strewn with gravel and bright with flowers, in which two laborers were at work putting an edging of stones round the light mould of a flower-bed, and drew up in a covered entry.

"Ah, they're here already!" said Anna, looking at the saddle-horses, which were just being led away from the steps. "It is a nice horse, isn't it? It's my cob; my favorite. Lead him here and bring me some sugar. Where is the count?" she inquired of two smart footmen who darted out. "Ah, there he is!" she said seeing Vronsky coming to meet her with Veslovsky.

"Where are you going to put the princess?" said Vronsky in French, addressing Anna, and without waiting for a reply, he once more greeted Darya Alexandrovna, and this time he kissed her hand. "I think the big balcony room."

"Oh, no, that's too far off! Better in the corner room, we shall see each other more. Come, let's go up," said Anna, as she gave her favorite horse the sugar the footman had brought her.

"Et vous oubliez votre devoir," she said to Veslovsky, who came out too on the steps.

"Pardon, j'en ai tout plein les poches," he answered, smiling, putting his fingers in his waistcoat pocket.

"Mais vous venez trop tard," she said, rubbing her handkerchief on her hand, which the horse had made wet in taking the sugar.

Anna turned to Dolly. "You can stay some time? For one day only? That's impossible!"

"I promised to be back, and the children . . ." said Dolly, feeling embarrassed both because she had to get her bag out of the carriage, and because she knew her face must be covered with dust.

"No, Dolly, darling! . . . Well, we'll see. Come along, come along!" and Anna led Dolly to her room.

That room was not the smart guest-chamber Vronsky had suggested, but the one of which Anna had said that Dolly would excuse it. And this room, for which excuse was needed, was more full of luxury than any in which Dolly had ever stayed, a luxury that reminded her of the best hotels abroad.

"Well, darling, how happy I am!" Anna said, sitting down in her riding-habit for a moment beside Dolly. "Tell me about all of you. Stiva I had only a glimpse of, and he cannot tell one about the children. How is my favorite, Tanya? Quite a big girl, I expect?"

"Yes, she's very tall," Darya Alexandrovna answered shortly, surprised herself that she should respond so coolly about her children. "We are having a delightful stay at the Levins'," she added.

"Oh, if I had known," said Anna, "that you do not despise me! . . . You might have all come to us. Stiva's an old friend and a great friend of Alexey's, you know," she added, and suddenly she blushed.

"Yes, but we are all . . ." Dolly answered in confusion.

"But in my delight I'm talking nonsense. The one thing, darling, is that I am so glad to have you!" said Anna, kissing her again. "You haven't told me yet how and what you think about me, and I keep wanting to know. But I'm glad you will see me as I am. The chief thing I shouldn't like would be for people to imagine I want to prove anything. I don't want to prove anything; I merely want to live, to do no one harm but myself. I have the right to do that, haven't I? But it is a big subject, and we'll talk over everything properly later. Now I'll go and dress and send a maid to you."

CHAPTER XIX

Left alone, Darya Alexandrovna, with a good housewife's eye, scanned her room. All she had seen in entering the house and walking through it, and all she saw now in her room, gave her an impression of wealth and sumptuousness and of that modern European luxury of which she had only read in English novels, but had never seen in Russia and in the country. Everything was new from the new French hangings on the walls to the carpet which covered the whole floor. The bed had a spring mattress, and a special sort of bolster and silk pillow-cases on the little pillows. The marble wash-stand, the dressing-table, the little sofa, the tables, the bronze clock on the chimneypiece, the window-curtains and the portières were all new and expensive.

The smart maid, who came in to offer her services, with her hair done up high, and a gown more fashionable than Dolly's, was as new and expensive as the whole room. Darya Alexandrovna liked her neatness, her deferential and obliging manners, but she felt ill at ease with her. She felt ashamed of her seeing the patched dressing-jacket that had unluckily been packed by mistake for her. She was ashamed of the very patches and darned places of which she had been so proud at home. At home it had been so clear that for six dressing-jackets there would be needed twenty-four yards of nainsook at sixteen pence the yard, which was a matter of thirty shillings besides the cutting-out and making, and these thirty shillings had been saved. But before the maid she felt, if not exactly ashamed, at least uncomfortable.

Darya Alexandrovna had a great sense of relief when Annushka, whom she had known for years, walked in. The smart maid was sent for to go to her mistress, and Annushka remained with Darya Alexandrovna.

Annushka was obviously much pleased at that lady's arrival, and began to chatter away without a pause. Dolly observed that she was longing to express her opinion in regard to her mistress's position, especially as to the love and devotion of the count to Anna Arkadyevna, but Dolly carefully interrupted her whenever she began to speak about this.

"I grew up with Anna Arkadyevna; my lady's dearer to me than anything. Well, it's not for us to judge. And, to be sure, there seems so much love . . ."

"Kindly pour out the water for me to wash now, please," Darya Alexandrovna cut her short.

"Certainly. We've two women kept specially for washing small things, but most of the linen's done by machinery. The count goes into everything himself. Ah, what a husband! . . ."

Dolly was glad when Anna came in, and by her entrance put a stop to Annushka's gossip.

Anna had put on a very simple batiste gown. Dolly scrutinized that simple gown attentively. She knew what it meant, and the price at which such simplicity was obtained.

"An old friend," said Anna of Annushka.

Anna was not embarrassed now. She was perfectly composed and at ease. Dolly saw that she had now completely recovered from the impression her arrival had made on her, and had assumed that superficial, careless tone which, as it were, closed the door on that compartment in which her deeper feelings and ideas were kept.

"Well, Anna, and how is your little girl?" asked Dolly.

"Annie?" (This was what she called her little daughter Anna.) "Very well. She has got on wonderfully. Would you like to see her? Come, I'll show her to you. We had a terrible bother," she began telling her, "over nurses. We had an Italian wet-nurse. A good creature, but so stupid! We wanted to get rid of her, but the baby is so used to her that we've gone on keeping her still."

"But how have you managed? . . ." Dolly was beginning a question as to what name the little girl would have; but noticing a sudden frown on Anna's face, she changed the drift of her question.

"How did you manage? have you weaned her yet?"

But Anna had understood.

"You didn't mean to ask that? You meant to ask about her surname. Yes? That worries Alexey. She has no name—that is, she's a Karenin," said Anna, dropping her eyelids till nothing could be seen but the eyelashes meeting. "But we'll talk about all that later," her face suddenly brightening. "Come, I'll show you her. *Elle est très gentille.* She crawls now."

In the nursery the luxury which had impressed Dolly in the whole house struck her still more. There were little go-carts ordered from England, and appliances for learning to walk, and a sofa after the fashion of a billiard-table, purposely constructed for crawling, and swings and baths, all of special pattern, and

modern. They were all English, solid, and of good make, and obviously very expensive. The room was large, and very light and lofty.

When they went in, the baby, with nothing on but her little smock, was sitting in a little elbow-chair at the table, having her dinner of broth, which she was spilling all over her little chest. The baby was being fed, and the Russian nursery-maid was evidently sharing her meal. Neither the wet-nurse nor the head-nurse were there; they were in the next room, from which came the sound of their conversation in the queer French, which was their only means of communication.

Hearing Anna's voice, a smart, tall, English nurse with a disagreeable face and a dissolute expression walked in at the door, hurriedly shaking her fair curls, and immediately began to defend herself though Anna had not found fault with her. At every word Anna said the English nurse said hurriedly several times, "Yes, my lady."

The rosy baby with her black eyebrows and hair, her sturdy red little body with tight goose-flesh skin, delighted Darya Alexandrovna in spite of the cross expression with which she stared at the stranger. She positively envied the baby's healthy appearance. She was delighted, too, at the baby's crawling. Not one of her own children had crawled like that. When the baby was put on the carpet and its little dress tucked up behind, it was wonderfully charming. Looking round like some little wild animal at the grown-up big people with her bright black eyes, she smiled, unmistakably pleased at their admiring her, and holding her legs sideways, she pressed vigorously on her arms, and rapidly drew her whole back up after, and then made another step forward with her little arms.

But the whole atmosphere of the nursery, and especially the English nurse, Darya Alexandrovna did not like at all. It was only on the supposition that no good nurse would have entered so irregular a household as Anna's that Darya Alexandrovna could explain to herself how Anna with her insight into people could take such an unprepossessing, disreputable-looking woman as nurse to her child.

Besides, from a few words that were dropped, Darya Alexandrovna saw at once that Anna, the two nurses and the child had no common existence, and that the mother's visit was something exceptional. Anna wanted to get the baby her plaything, and could not find it.

Most amazing of all was the fact that on being asked how many teeth the baby had, Anna answered wrong, and knew nothing about the two last teeth.

"I sometimes feel sorry I'm so superfluous here," said Anna, going out of the nursery and holding up her skirt so as to escape the plaything standing in the doorway. "It was very different with my first child."

"I expected it to be the other way," said Darya Alexandrovna shyly.

"Oh, no! By the way, do you know I saw Seryozha?" said Anna, screwing up her eyes, as though looking at something far away. "But we'll talk about that later. You wouldn't believe it, I'm like a hungry beggar-woman when a full dinner is set before her, and she does not know what to begin on first. The dinner is you, and the talks I have before me with you, which I could never have with any one else; and I don't know which subject to begin upon first. *Mais je ne vous ferai grâce de rien.* I must have everything out with you."

"Oh, I ought to give you a sketch of the company you will meet with us," she began. "I'll begin with the ladies. Princess Varvara—you know her, and I know your opinion and Stiva's about her. Stiva says the whole aim of her existence is to prove her superiority over Auntie Katerina Pavlovna: that's all true; but she's a good-natured woman, and I am so grateful to her. In Petersburg there was a moment when a chaperon was absolutely essential for me. Then she turned up. But really she is good-natured. She did a great deal to alleviate my position. I see you don't understand all the difficulty of my position . . . there in Petersburg," she added. "Here I'm perfectly at ease and happy. Well, of that later on, though. Then Sviazhsky—he's the marshal of the district, and he's a very good sort of a man, but he wants to get something out of Alexey. You understand, with his property, now that we are settled in the country, Alexey can exercise great influence. Then there's Tushkevitch—you have seen him, you know—Betsy's admirer. Now he's been thrown over and he's come to see us. As Alexey says, he's one of those people who are very pleasant if one accepts them for what they try to appear to be, *et puis il est comme il faut,* as Princess Varvara says. Then Veslovsky . . . you know him. A very nice boy," she said, and a sly smile curved her lips. "What's this wild story about him and the Levins? Veslovsky told Alexey about it, and we don't believe it. *Il est très gentil et naïf,"* she said again with the same smile. "Men need occupation, and Alexey needs a circle, so I value all these people. We have to have the house lively and gay, so that Alexey may not long for any novelty. Then you'll see the steward—a German, a very good fellow, and he understands his work. Alexey has a very high opinion of him. Then the doctor, a young man, not quite a Nihilist perhaps, but you know, eats with his knife . . . but a very good doctor. Then the architect . . . *Une petite cour."*

CHAPTER XX

"Here's Dolly for you, princess, you were so anxious to see her," said Anna, coming out with Darya Alexandrovna onto the stone terrace where Princess Varvara was sitting in the shade at an embroidery frame, working at a cover for Count Alexey Kirillovitch's easy-chair. "She says she doesn't want anything before dinner, but please order some lunch for her, and I'll go and look for Alexey and bring them all in."

Princess Varvara gave Dolly a cordial and rather patronizing reception, and began at once explaining to her that she was living with Anna because she had always cared more for her than her sister Katerina Pavlovna, the aunt that had brought Anna up, and that now, when every one had abandoned Anna, she thought it her duty to help her in this most difficult period of transition.

"Her husband will give her a divorce, and then I shall go back to my solitude; but now I can be of use, and I am doing my duty, however difficult it may be for me—not like some other people. And how sweet it is of you, how right of you to have come! They live like the best of married couples; it's for God to judge them, not for us. And didn't Biryuzovsky and Madame

Avenieva . . . and Sam Nikandrov, and Vassiliev and Madame Mamonova, and Liza Neptunova . . . Did no one say anything about them? And it has ended by their being received by every one. And then, *c'est un intérieur si joli, si comme il faut. Tout-à-fait à l'anglaise. On se réunit le matin au breakfast, et puis on se sépare.* Every one does as he pleases till dinner-time. Dinner at seven o'clock. Stiva did very rightly to send you. He needs their support. You know that through his mother and brother he can do anything. And then they do so much good. He didn't tell you about his hospital? *Ce sera admirable*—everything from Paris."

Their conversation was interrupted by Anna, who had found the men of the party in the billiard-room, and returned with them to the terrace. There was still a long time before the dinner-hour, it was exquisite weather, and so several different methods of spending the next two hours were proposed. There were very many methods of passing the time at Vozdvizhenskoe, and these were all unlike those in use at Pokrovskoe.

"*Une partie de lawn-tennis,*" Veslovsky proposed, with his handsome smile. "We'll be partners again, Anna Arkadyevna."

"No, it's too hot; better stroll about the garden and have a row in the boat, show Darya Alexandrovna the river-banks," Vronsky proposed.

"I agree to anything," said Sviazhsky.

"I imagine that what Dolly would like best would be a stroll—wouldn't you? And then the boat, perhaps," said Anna.

So it was decided. Veslovsky and Tushkevitch went off to the bathing-place, promising to get the boat ready and to wait there for them.

They walked along the path in two couples, Anna with Sviazhsky, and Dolly with Vronsky. Dolly was a little embarrassed and anxious in the new surroundings in which she found herself. Abstractly, theoretically, she did not merely justify, she positively approved of Anna's conduct. As is indeed not unfrequent with women of unimpeachable virtue, weary of the monotony of respectable existence, at a distance she not only excused illicit love, she positively envied it. Besides, she loved Anna with all her heart. But seeing Anna in actual lfe among these strangers, with this fashionable tone that was so new to

Darya Alexandrovna, she felt ill at ease. What she disliked particularly was seeing Princess Varvara ready to overlook everything for the sake of the comforts she enjoyed.

As a general principle, abstractly, Dolly approved of Anna's action; but to see the man for whose sake her action had been taken was disagreeable to her. Moreover, she had never liked Vronsky. She thought him very proud, and saw nothing in him of which he could be proud except his wealth. But against her own will, here in his own house, he overawed her more than ever, and she could not be at ease with him. She felt with him the same feeling she had had with the maid about her dressing-jacket. Just as with the maid she had felt not exactly ashamed, but embarrassed at her darns, so she felt with him not exactly ashamed, but embarrassed at herself.

Dolly was ill at ease, and tried to find a subject of conversation. Even though she supposed that, through his pride, praise of his house and garden would be sure to be disagreeable to him, she did all the same tell him how much she liked his house.

"Yes, it's a very fine building, and in the good old-fashioned style," he said.

"I like so much the court in front of the steps. Was that always so?"

"Oh, no!" he said, and his face beamed with pleasure. "If you could only have seen that court last spring!"

And he began, at first rather diffidently, but more and more carried away by the subject as he went on, to draw her attention to the various details of the decoration of his house and garden. It was evident that, having devoted a great deal of trouble to improve and beautify his home, Vronsky felt a need to show off the improvements to a new person, and was genuinely delighted at Darya Alexandrovna's praise.

"If you would care to look at the hospital, and are not tired, indeed, it's not far. Shall we go?" he said, glancing into her face to convince himself that she was not bored. "Are you coming, Anna?" he turned to her.

"We will come, won't we?" she said, addressing Sviazhsky. "*Mais il ne faut pas laisser le pauvre Veslovsky et Tushkevitch se morfondre là dans le bateau.* We must send and tell them."

"Yes, this is a monument he is setting up here," said Anna,

turning to Dolly with that sly smile of comprehension with which she had previously talked about the hospital.

"Oh, it's a work of real importance!" said Sviazhsky. But to show he was not trying to ingratiate himself with Vronsky, he promptly added some slightly critical remarks.

"I wonder, though, count," he said, "that while you do so much for the health of the peasants, you take so little interest in the schools."

"*C'est devenu tellement commun, les écoles,*" said Vronsky. "You understand it's not on that account, but it just happens so, my interest has been diverted elsewhere. This way then to the hospital," he said to Darya Alexandrovna, pointing to a turning out of the avenue.

The ladies put up their parasols and turned into the side-path. After going down several turnings, and going through a little gate, Darya Alexandrovna saw standing on rising ground before her a large pretentious-looking red building, almost finished. The iron roof, which was not yet painted, shone with dazzling brightness in the sunshine. Beside the finished building another had been begun, surrounded by scaffolding. Workmen in aprons, standing on scaffolds, were laying bricks, pouring mortar out of vats, and smoothing it with trowels.

"How quickly work gets done with you!" said Sviazhsky. "When I was here last time the roof was not on."

"By the autumn it will all be ready. Inside almost everything is done," said Anna.

"And what's this new building?"

"That's the house for the doctor and the dispensary," answered Vronsky, seeing the architect in a short jacket coming towards him; and excusing himself to the ladies, he went to meet him.

Going round a hole where the workmen were slaking lime, he stood still with the architect and began talking rather warmly.

"The front is still too low," he said to Anna, who had asked what was the matter.

"I said the foundation ought to be raised," said Anna.

"Yes, of course it would have been much better, Anna Arkadyevna," said the architect, "but now it's too late."

"Yes, I take a great interest in it," Anna answered Sviazhsky, who was expressing his surprise at her knowledge of architecture. "This new building ought to have been in harmony with the hospital. It was an afterthought, and was begun without a plan."

Vronsky, having finished his talk with the architect, joined the ladies, and led them inside the hospital. Although they were still at work on the cornices outside and were painting on the ground-floor, up-stairs almost all the rooms were finished. Going up the broad cast-iron staircase to the landing, they walked into the first large room. The walls were stuccoed to look like marble, the huge plate-glass windows were already in, only the parquet floor was not yet finished, and the carpenters, who were planing a block of it, left their work, taking off the bands that fastened their hair, to greet the gentry.

"This is the reception-room," said Vronsky. "Here there will be a desk, tables, and benches, and nothing more."

"This way; let us go in here. Don't go near the window," said Anna, trying the paint to see if it were dry. "Alexey, the paint's dry already," she added.

From the reception-room they went into the corridor. Here Vronsky showed them the mechanism for ventilation on a novel system. Then he showed them marble baths, and beds with extraordinary springs. Then he showed them the wards one after another, the store-room, the linen-room, then the heating-stove of a new pattern, then the trolleys, which would make no noise as they carried everything needed along the corridors, and many other things. Sviazhsky, as a connoisseur in the latest mechanical improvements, appreciated everything fully. Dolly simply wondered at all she had not seen before, and, anxious to understand it all, made minute inquiries about everything, which gave Vronsky great satisfaction.

"Yes, I imagine that this will be the solitary example of a properly fitted hospital in Russia," said Sviazhsky.

"And won't you have a lying-in ward?" asked Dolly. "That's so much needed in the country. I have often . . ."

In spite of his usual courtesy, Vronsky interrupted her.

"This is not a lying-in home, but a hospital for the sick, and is intended for all diseases, except infectious complaints," he said. "Ah! look at this," and he rolled up to Darya Alexandrovna an invalid-chair that had just been ordered for the convalescents. "Look." He sat down in the chair and began moving it. "The patient can't walk—still too weak, perhaps, or something wrong with his legs, but he must have air, and he moves, rolls himself along. . . ."

Darya Alexandrovna was interested by everything. She liked everything very much, but most of all she liked Vronsky himself with his natural, simple-hearted eagerness. "Yes, he's a very nice, good man," she thought several times, not hearing what he said, but looking at him and penetrating into his expression, while she mentally put herself in Anna's place. She liked him so much just now with his eager interest that she saw how Anna could be in love with him.

CHAPTER XXI

"No, I think the princess is tired, and horses don't interest her," Vronsky said to Anna, who wanted to go on to the stables, where Sviazhsky wished to see the new stallion. "You go on, while I escort the princess home, and we'll have a little talk," he said, "if you would like that?" he added, turning to her.

"I know nothing about horses, and I shall be delighted," answered Darya Alexandrovna, rather astonished.

She saw by Vronsky's face that he wanted something from her. She was not mistaken. As soon as they had passed through the little gate back into the garden, he looked in the direction Anna had taken, and having made sure that she could neither hear nor see them, he began:

"You guess that I have something I want to say to you," he said, looking at her with laughing eyes. "I am not wrong in believing you to be a friend of Anna's." He took off his hat, and taking out his handkerchief, wiped his head, which was growing bald.

Darya Alexandrovna made no answer, and merely stared at him with dismay. When she was left alone with him, she suddenly felt afraid; his laughing eyes and stern expression scared her.

The most diverse suppositions as to what he was about to

speak of to her flashed into her brain. "He is going to beg me to come to stay with them with the children, and I shall have to refuse; or to create a set that will receive Anna in Moscow. . . . Or isn't it Vassenka Veslovsky and his relations with Anna? Or perhaps about Kitty, that he feels he was to blame?" All her conjectures were unpleasant, but she did not guess what he really wanted to talk about to her.

"You have so much influence with Anna, she is so fond of you," he said; "do help me."

Darya Alexandrovna looked with timid inquiry into his energetic face, which under the lime-trees was continually being lighted up in patches by the sunshine, and then passing into complete shadow again. She waited for him to say more, but he walked in silence beside her, scratching with his cane in the gravel.

"You have come to see us, you, the only woman of Anna's former friends—I don't count Princess Varvara—but I know that you have done this not because you regard our position as normal, but because, understanding all the difficulty of the position, you still love her and want to be a help to her. Have I understood you rightly?" he asked, looking round at her.

"Oh, yes," answered Darya Alexandrovna, putting down her sunshade, "but . . ."

"No," he broke in, and unconsciously, oblivious of the awkward position into which he was putting his companion, he stopped abruptly, so that she had to stop short too. "No one feels more deeply and intensely than I do all the difficulty of Anna's position; and that you may well understand, if you do me the honor of supposing I have any heart. I am to blame for that position, and that is why I feel it."

"I understand," said Darya Alexandrovna, involuntarily admiring the sincerity and firmness with which he said this. "But just because you feel yourself responsible, you exaggerate it, I am afraid," she said. "Her position in the world is difficult, I can well understand."

"In the world it is hell!" he brought out quickly, frowning darkly. "You can't imagine moral sufferings greater than what she went through in Petersburg in that fortnight . . . and I beg you to believe it."

"Yes, but here, so long as neither Anna . . . nor you miss society . . ."

"Society!" he said contemptuously, "how could I miss society?"

"So far—and it may be so always—you are happy and at peace. I see in Anna that she is happy, perfectly happy, she has had time to tell me so much already," said Darya Alexandrovna, smiling; and involuntarily, as she said this, at the same moment a doubt entered her mind whether Anna really were happy.

But Vronsky, it appeared, had no doubts on that score.

"Yes, yes," he said, "I know that she has revived after all her sufferings; she is happy. She is happy in the present. But I? . . . I am afraid of what is before us . . . I beg your pardon, you would like to walk on?"

"No, I don't mind."

"Well, then, let us sit here."

Darya Alexandrovna sat down on a garden-seat in a corner of the avenue. He stood up facing her.

"I see that she is happy," he repeated, and the doubt whether she were happy sank more deeply into Darya Alexandrovna's mind. "But can it last? Whether we have acted rightly or wrongly is another question, but the die is cast," he said, passing from Russian to French, "and we are bound together for life. We are united by all the ties of love that we hold most sacred. We have a child, we may have other children. But the law and all the conditions of our position are such that thousands of complications arise which she does not see and does not want to see. And that one can well understand. But I can't help seeing them. My daughter is by law not my daughter, but Karenin's. I cannot bear this falsity!" he said, with a vigorous gesture of refusal, and he looked with gloomy inquiry towards Darya Alexandrovna.

She made no answer, but simply gazed at him. He went on:

"One day a son may be born, my son, and he will be legally a Karenin; he will not be the heir of my name nor of my property, and however happy we may be in our home life and however many children we may have, there will be no real tie between us. They will be Karenins. You can understand the bitterness and horror of this position! I have tried to speak of this to Anna. It irritates her. She does not understand, and to her I cannot speak plainly of all this. Now look at another side. I am happy, happy in her love, but I must have occupation. I have found occupation, and am proud of what I am doing and consider it nobler than the pursuits of my former companions at court and in the army. And most certainly I would not change the work I am doing for theirs. I am working here, settled in my own place, and I am happy and contented, and we need nothing more to make us happy. I love my work here. *Ce n'est pas un pis-aller,* on the contrary . . ."

Darya Alexandrovna noticed that at this point in his explanation he grew confused, and she did not quite understand this digression, but she felt that having once begun to speak of matters near his heart, of which he could not speak to Anna, he was now making a clean breast of everything, and that the question of his pursuits in the country fell into the same category of matters near his heart, as the question of his relations with Anna.

"Well, I will go on," he said, collecting himself. "The great thing is that as I work I want to have a conviction that what I am doing will not die with me, that I shall have heirs to come after me,—and this I have not. Conceive the position of a man who knows that his children, the children of the woman he loves, will not be his, but will belong to some one who hates them and cares nothing about them! It is awful!"

He paused, evidently much moved.

"Yes, indeed, I see that. But what can Anna do?" queried Darya Alexandrovna.

"Yes, that brings me to the object of my conversation," he said, calming himself with an effort. "Anna can, it depends on her. . . . Even to petition the Tsar for legitimization, a divorce is essential. And that depends on Anna. Her husband agreed to a divorce—at that time your husband had arranged it completely. And now, I know, he would not refuse it. It is only a matter of writing to him. He said plainly at that time that if she expressed the desire, he would not refuse. Of course," he said gloomily, "it is one of those Pharisaical cruelties of which only such heartless men are capable. He knows what agony any recollection of him must give her, and knowing her, he must have a letter from her. I can understand that it is agony to her. But the matter is of such importance, that one must *passer par-dessus toutes ces finesses de sentiment. Il y va du bonheur et de l'existence d'Anne et de ses enfants.* I won't speak of myself, though it's hard for me, very hard," he said, with an expression as though he were threatening some one for its being hard for him. "And so it is, princess, that I am shamelessly clutching at you as an anchor of salvation. Help me to persuade her to write to him and ask for a divorce."

"Yes, of course," Darya Alexandrovna said dreamily, as she vividly recalled her last interview with Alexey Alexandrovitch. "Yes, of course," she repeated with decision, thinking of Anna.

"Use your influence with her, make her write. I don't like—I'm almost unable to speak about this to her."

"Very well, I will talk to her. But how is it she does not think of it herself?" said Darya Alexandrovna, and for some reason she suddenly at that point recalled Anna's strange new habit of half-closing her eyes. And she remembered that Anna drooped her eyelids just when the deeper questions of life were touched upon. "Just as though she half-shut her eyes to her own life, so as not to see everything," thought Dolly. "Yes, indeed, for my own sake and for hers I will talk to her," Dolly said in reply to his look of gratitude.

They got up and walked to the house.

CHAPTER XXII

When Anna found Dolly at home before her, she looked intently in her eyes, as though questioning her about the talk she had had with Vronsky, but she made no inquiry in words.

"I believe it's dinner-time," she said. "We've not seen each other at all yet. I am reckoning on the evening. Now I want to go and dress. I expect you do too; we all got splashed at the buildings."

Dolly went to her room and she felt amused. To change her dress was impossible, for she had already put on her best dress. But in order to signify in some way her preparation for dinner, she asked the maid to brush her dress, changed her cuffs and tie, and put some lace on her head.

"This is all I can do," she said with a smile to Anna, who came in to her in a third dress, again of extreme simplicity.

"Yes, we are too formal here," she said, as it were apologizing for her magnificence. "Alexey is delighted at your visit, as he rarely is at anything. He has completely lost his heart to you," she added. "You're not tired?"

There was no time for talking about anything before dinner. Going into the drawing-room they found Princess Varvara already there, and the gentlemen of the party in black frockcoats. The architect wore a swallow-tail coat. Vronsky presented the doctor and the steward to his guest. The architect he had already introduced to her at the hospital.

A stout butler, resplendent with a smoothly shaven round chin and a starched white cravat, announced that dinner was ready, and the ladies got up. Vronsky asked Sviazhsky to take in Anna Arkadyevna, and himself offered his arm to Dolly. Veslovsky was before Tushkevitch in offering his arm to Princess Varvara, so that Tushkevitch with the steward and the doctor walked in alone.

The dinner, the dining-room, the service, the waiting at table, the wine, and the food, were not simply in keeping with the general tone of modern luxury throughout all the house, but seemed even more sumptuous and modern. Darya Alexandrovna watched this luxury which was novel to her, and as a good housekeeper used to managing a household—although she never dreamed of adapting anything she saw to her own household, as it was all in a style of luxury far above her own manner of living—she could not help scrutinizing every detail, and wondering how and by whom it was all done. Vassenka Veslovsky, her husband, and even Sviazhsky, and many other people she knew, would never have considered this question, and would have readily believed what every well-bred host tries to make his guests feel, that is, that all that is well-ordered in his house has cost him, the host, no trouble whatever, but comes of itself. Darya Alexandrovna was well aware that even porridge for the children's breakfast does not come of itself, and that therefore, where so complicated and magnificent a style of luxury was maintained, some one must give earnest attention to its organization. And from the glance with which Alexey Kirillovitch scanned the table, from the way he nodded to the butler, and offered Darya Alexandrovna her choice between cold soup and hot soup, she saw that it was all organized and maintained by the care of the master of the house himself. It was evident that it all rested no more upon Anna than upon Veslovsky. She, Sviazhsky, the princess, and Veslovsky, were equally guests, with light hearts enjoying what had been arranged for them.

Anna was the hostess only in conducting the conversation. The conversation was a difficult one for the lady of the house at a small table with persons present, like the steward and the architect, belonging to a completely different world, struggling not to be overawed by an elegance to which they were unaccustomed, and unable to sustain a large share in the general conversation. But this difficult conversation Anna directed with her usual tact and naturalness, and indeed she did so with actual enjoyment, as Darya Alexandrovna observed. The conversation began about the row Tushkevitch and Veslovsky had taken alone together in the boat, and Tushkevitch began describing the last boat-races in Petersburg at the Yacht Club. But Anna, seizing the first pause, at once turned to the architect to draw him out of his silence.

"Nikolay Ivanitch was struck," she said, meaning Sviazhsky, "at the progress the new building had made since he was here last; but I am there every day, and every day I wonder at the rate at which it grows."

"It's first-rate working with his excellency," said the architect with a smile (he was respectful and composed, though with a sense of his own dignity). "It's a very different matter to have to do with the district authorities. Where one would have to write out sheaves of papers, here I call upon the count, and in three words we settle the business."

"The American way of doing business," said Sviazhsky, with a smile.

"Yes, there they build in a rational fashion . . ."

The conversation passed to the misuse of political power in the United States, but Anna quickly brought it round to another topic, so as to draw the steward into talk.

"Have you ever seen a reaping-machine?" she said, addressing Darya Alexandrovna. "We had just ridden over to look at one when we met. It's the first time I ever saw one."

"How do they work?" asked Dolly.

"Exactly like little scissors. A plank and a lot of little scissors. Like this."

Anna took a knife and fork in her beautiful white hands covered with rings, and began showing how the machine worked. It was clear that she saw nothing would be understood from her explanation; but aware that her talk was pleasant and her hands beautiful she went on explaining.

"More like little penknives," Veslovsky said playfully, never taking his eyes off her.

Anna gave a just perceptible smile, but made no answer. "Isn't it true, Karl Fedoritch, that it's just like little scissors?" she said to the steward.

"*Oh, ja,*" answered the German. "*Es ist ein ganz einfaches Ding,*" and he began to explain the construction of the machine.

"It's a pity it doesn't bind too. I saw one at the Vienna exhibition, which binds with a wire," said Sviazhsky. "They would be more profitable in use."

"*Es kommt drauf an . . . Der Preis vom Draht muss ausgerechnet werden.*" And the German, roused from his taciturnity, turned to Vronsky. "*Das lässt sich ausrechnen, Erlaucht.*" The German was just feeling in the pocket where were his pencil and the note-book he always wrote in, but recollecting that he was at a dinner, and observing Vronsky's chilly glance, he checked himself. "*Zu compliziert, macht zu viel Klopot,*" he concluded.

"*Wünscht man Dorhots, so hat man auch Klopots,*" said Vassenka Veslovsky, mimicking the German. "*J'adore l'allemand,*" he addressed Anna again with the same smile.

"*Cessez,*" she said with playful severity.

"We expected to find you in the fields, Vassily Semyonitch," she said to the doctor, a sickly-looking man; "have you been there?"

"I went there, but I had taken flight," the doctor answered with gloomy jocoseness.

"Then you've taken a good constitutional?"

"Splendid!"

"Well, and how was the old woman? I hope it's not typhus?"

"Typhus it is not, but it's taking a bad turn."

"What a pity!" said Anna, and having thus paid the dues of civility to her domestic circle, she turned to her own friends.

"It would be a hard task, though, to construct a machine from your description, Anna Arkadyevna," Sviazhsky said jestingly.

"Oh, no, why so?" said Anna with a smile that betrayed that she knew there was something charming in her disquisitions upon the machine that had been noticed by Sviazhsky. This new trait of girlish coquettishness made an unpleasant impression on Dolly.

"But Anna Arkadyevna's knowledge of architecture is marvelous," said Tushkevitch.

"To be sure, I heard Anna Arkadyevna talking yesterday about plinths and damp-courses," said Veslovsky. "Have I got it right?"

"There's nothing marvelous about it, when one sees and hears so much of it," said Anna. "But, I dare say, you don't even know what houses are made of?"

Darya Alexandrovna saw that Anna disliked the tone of raillery that existed between her and Veslovsky, but fell in with it against her will.

Vronsky acted in this matter quite differently from Levin. He obviously attached no significance to Veslovsky's chattering; on the contrary, he encouraged his jests.

"Come now, tell us, Veslovsky, how are the stones held together?"

"By cement, of course."

"Bravo! And what is cement?"

"Oh, some sort of paste . . . no, putty," said Veslovsky, raising a general laugh.

The company at dinner, with the exception of the doctor, the architect, and the steward, who remained plunged in gloomy silence, kept up a conversation that never paused, glancing off one subject, fastening on another, and at times stinging one or the other to the quick. Once Darya Alexandrovna felt wounded to the quick, and got so hot that she positively flushed and wondered afterwards whether she had said anything extreme or unpleasant. Sviazhsky began talking of Levin, describing his strange view that machinery is simply pernicious in its effects on Russian agriculture.

"I have not the pleasure of knowing this M. Levin," Vronsky said, smiling, "but most likely he has never seen the machines he condemns; or if he has seen and tried any, it must have been after a queer fashion, some Russian imitation, not a machine from abroad. What sort of views can any one have on such a subject?"

"Turkish views, in general," Veslovsky said, turning to Anna with a smile.

"I can't defend his opinions," Darya Alexandrovna said, firing up; "but I can say that he's a highly cultivated man, and if he were here he would know very well how to answer you, though I am not capable of doing so."

"I like him extremely, and we are great friends," Sviazhsky said, smiling good-naturedly. *"Mais pardon, il est un petit peu toqué;* he maintains, for instance, that district councils and arbitration boards are all of no use, and he is unwilling to take part in anything."

"It's our Russian apathy," said Vronsky, pouring water from an iced decanter into a delicate glass on a high stem; "we've no sense of the duties our privileges impose upon us, and so we refuse to recognize these duties."

"I know no man more strict in the performance of his duties," said Darya Alexandrovna, irritated by Vronsky's tone of superiority.

"For my part," pursued Vronsky, who was evidently for some reason or other keenly affected by this conversation, "such as I am, I am, on the contrary, extremely grateful for the honor they have done me, thanks to Nikolay Ivanitch" (he indicated Sviazhsky), "in electing me a justice of the peace. I consider that for me the duty of being present at the session, of judging some peasants' quarrel about a horse, is as important as anything I can do. And I shall regard it as an honor if they elect me for the district council. It's only in that way I can pay for the advantages I enjoy as a landowner. Unluckily they don't understand the weight that the big landowners ought to have in the state."

It was strange to Darya Alexandrovna to hear how serenely confident he was of being right at his own table. She thought how Levin, who believed the opposite, was just as positive in his opinions at his own table. But she loved Levin, and so she was on his side.

"So we can reckon upon you, count, for the coming elections?" said Sviazhsky. "But you must come a little beforehand, so as to be on the spot by the eighth. If you would do me the honor to stop with me."

"I rather agree with your *beau-frère*," said Anna, "though not quite on the same ground as he," she added with a smile. "I'm afraid that we have too many of these public duties in these latter days. Just as in old days there were so many government functionaries that one had to call in a functionary for every single thing, so now every one's doing some sort of publc duty. Alexey has been here now six months, and he's a member, I do believe, of five or six different public bodies. *Du train que cela va,* the whole time will be wasted on it. And I'm afraid that with such a multiplicity of these bodies, they'll end in being a mere form. How many are you a member of, Nikolay Ivanitch?" she turned to Sviazhsky—"over twenty, I fancy."

Anna spoke lightly, but irritation could be discerned in her tone. Darya Alexandrovna, watching Anna and Vronsky attentively, detected it instantly. She noticed, too, that as she spoke Vronsky's face had immediately taken a serious and obstinate expression. Noticing this, and that Princess Varvara at once made haste to change the conversation by talking of Petersburg acquaintances, and remembering what Vronsky had without apparent connection said in the garden of his work in the country, Dolly surmised that this question of public activity was connected with some deep private disagreement between Anna and Vronsky.

The dinner, the wine, the decoration of the table, was all very good; but it was all like what Darya Alexandrovna had seen at formal dinners and balls which of late years had become quite unfamiliar to her; it all had the same impersonal and constrained character, and so on an ordinary day and in a little circle of friends it made a disagreeable impression on her.

After dinner they sat on the terrace, then they proceeded to play lawn tennis. The players, divided into two parties, stood on opposite sides of a tightly drawn net with gilt poles on the carefully leveled and rolled croquet-ground. Darya Alexandrovna made an attempt to play, but it was a long time before she could understand the game, and by the time she did understand it, she was so tired that she sat down with Princess Varvara and simply looked on at the players. Her partner, Tushkevitch, gave up playing too, but the others kept the game up for a long time. Sviazhsky and Vronsky both played very well and seriously.

They kept a sharp lookout on the balls served to them, and without haste or getting in each other's way, they ran adroitly up to them, waited for the rebound, and neatly and accurately returned them over the net. Veslovsky played worse than the others. He was too eager, but he kept the players lively with his high spirits. His laughter and outcries never paused. Like the other men of the party, with the ladies' permission, he took off his coat, and his solid, comely figure in his white shirt-sleeves, with his red perspiring face and his impulsive movements, made a picture that imprinted itself vividly on the memory.

When Darya Alexandrovna lay in bed that night, as soon as she closed her eyes, she saw Vassenka Veslovsky flying about the croquet-ground.

During the game Darya Alexandrovna was not enjoying herself. She did not like the light tone of raillery that was kept up all the time between Vassenka Veslovsky and Anna, and the unnaturalness altogether of grown-up people, all alone without children, playing at a child's game. But to avoid breaking up the party and to get through the time somehow, after a rest she joined the game again, and pretended to be enjoying it. All that day it seemed to her as though she were acting in a theater with actors cleverer than she, and that her bad acting was spoiling the whole performance. She had come with the intention of staying two days, if all went well. But in the evening, during the game, she made up her mind that she would go home next day. The maternal cares and worries, which she had so hated on the way, now, after a day spent without them, struck her in quite another light, and tempted her back to them.

When, after evening tea and a row by night in the boat, Darya Alexandrovna went alone to her room, took off her dress, and began arranging her thin hair for the night, she had a great sense of relief.

It was positively disagreeable to her to think that Anna was coming to see her immediately. She longed to be alone with her own thoughts.

CHAPTER XXIII

Dolly was wanting to go to bed when Anna came in to see her, attired for the night. In the course of the day Anna had several times begun to speak of matters near her heart, and every time after a few words she had stopped: "Afterwards, by ourselves, we'll talk about everything. I've got so much I want to tell you," she said.

Now they were by themselves, and Anna did not know what to talk about. She sat in the window looking at Dolly, and going over in her own mind all the stores of intimate talk which had seemed so inexhaustible beforehand, and she found nothing. At that moment it seemed to her that everything had been said already.

"Well, what of Kitty?" she said with a heavy sigh, looking penitently at Dolly. "Tell me the truth, Dolly: isn't she angry with me?"

"Angry? Oh, no!" said Darya Alexandrovna, smiling.
"But she hates me, despises me?"
"Oh, no! But you know that sort of thing isn't forgiven."
"Yes, yes," said Anna, turning away and looking out of the open window. "But I was not to blame. And who is to blame? What's the meaning of being to blame? Could it have been otherwise? What do you think? Could it possibly have happened that you didn't become the wife of Stiva?"
"Really, I don't know. But this is what I want you to tell me . . ."
"Yes, yes, but we've not finished about Kitty. Is she happy? He's a very nice man, they say."
"He's much more than very nice. I don't know a better man."
"Ah, how glad I am! I'm so glad! Much more than very nice," she repeated.
Dolly smiled.
"But tell me about yourself. We've a great deal to talk about. And I've had a talk with . . ." Dolly did not know what to call him. She felt it awkward to call him either the count or Alexey Kirillovitch.
"With Alexey," said Anna, "I know what you talked about. But I wanted to ask you directly what you think of me, of my life?"
"How am I to say like that straight off? I really don't know."
"No, tell me all the same. . . . You see my life. But you mustn't forget that you're seeing us in the summer, when you have come to us and we are not alone. . . . But we came here early in the spring, lived quite alone, and shall be alone again, and I desire nothing better. But imagine me living alone without him, alone, and that will be . . . I see by everything that it will often be repeated, that he will be half the time away from home," she said, getting up and sitting down close by Dolly.
"Of course," she interrupted Dolly, who would have answered, "of course I won't try to keep him by force. I don't keep him indeed. The races are just coming, his horses are running, he will go. I'm very glad. But think of me, fancy my position. . . . But what's the use of talking about it?" She smiled. "Well, what did he talk about with you?"
"He spoke of what I want to speak about of myself, and it's

easy for me to be his advocate; of whether there is not a possibility . . . whether you could not . . ." (Darya Alexandrovna hesitated) "correct, improve your position. . . . You know how I look at it. . . . But all the same, if possible, you should get married. . . ."

"Divorce, you mean?" said Anna. "Do you know, the only woman who came to see me in Petersburg was Betsy Tverskaya? You know her, of course? *Au fond, c'est la femme la plus dépravée qui existe.* She had an intrigue with Tushkevitch, deceiving her husband in the basest way. And she told me that she did not care to know me so long as my position was irregular. Don't imagine I would compare . . . I know you, darling. But I could not help remembering . . . Well, so what did he say to you?" she repeated.

"He said that he was unhappy on your account and his own. Perhaps you will say that it's egoism, but what a legitimate and noble egoism. He wants first of all to legitimize his daughter, and to be your husband, to have a legal right to you."

"What wife, what slave can be so utterly a slave as I, in my position?" she put in gloomily.

"The chief thing he desires . . . he desires that you should not suffer."

"That's impossible. Well?"

"Well, and the most legitimate desire—he wishes that your children should have a name."

"What children?" Anna said, not looking at Dolly, and half closing her eyes.

"Annie and those to come . . ."

"He need not trouble on that score; I shall have no more children."

"How can you tell that you won't?"

"I shall not, because I don't wish it." And, in spite of all her emotion, Anna smiled, as she caught the naïve expression of curiosity, wonder, and horror on Dolly's face.

"The doctor told me after my illness . . ."

. . . . . .

"Impossible!" said Dolly, opening her eyes wide.

For her this was one of those discoveries the consequences and deductions from which are so immense that all that one feels for the first instant is that it is impossible to take it all in, and that one will have to reflect a great, great deal upon it.

This discovery, suddenly throwing light on all those families of one or two children, which had hitherto been so incomprehensible to her, aroused so many ideas, reflections, and contradictory emotions, that she had nothing to say, and simply gazed with wide-open eyes of wonder at Anna. This was the very thing she had been dreaming of, but now learning that it was possible, she was horrified. She felt that it was too simple a solution of too complicated a problem.

"*N'est-ce pas immoral?*" was all she said, after a brief pause.

"Why so? Think, I have a choice between two alternatives: either to be with child, that is an invalid, or to be the friend and companion of my husband—practically my husband," Anna said in a tone intentionally superficial and frivolous.

"Yes, yes," said Darya Alexandrovna, hearing the very arguments she had used to herself, and not finding the same force in them as before.

"For you, for other people," said Anna, as though divining her thoughts, "there may be reason to hesitate; but for me . . . You must consider, I am not his wife; he loves me as long as he loves me. And how am I to keep his love? Not like this!"

She moved her white hands in a curve before her waist with extraordinary rapidity, as happens during moments of excitement; ideas and memories rushed into Darya Alexandrovna's head. "I," she thought, "did not keep my attraction for Stiva; he left me for others, and the first woman for whom he betrayed me did not keep him by being always pretty and lively. He deserted her and took another. And can Anna attract and keep Count Vronsky in that way? If that is what he looks for, he will find dresses and manners still more attractive and charming. And however white and beautiful her bare arms are, however beautiful her full figure and her eager face under her black curls, he will find something better still, just as my disgusting, pitiful, and charming husband does."

Dolly made no answer, she merely sighed. Anna noticed this sigh, indicating dissent, and she went on. In her armory she had other arguments so strong that no answer could be made to them.

"Do you say that it's not right? But you must consider," she went on; "you forget my position. How can I desire children? I'm not speaking of the suffering, I'm not afraid of that. Think only, what are my children to be? Ill-fated children, who will have to bear a stranger's name. For the very fact of their birth they will be forced to be ashamed of their mother, their father, their birth."

"But that is just why a divorce is necessary." But Anna did not hear her. She longed to give utterance to all the arguments with which she had so many times convinced herself.

"What is reason given me for, if I am not to use it to avoid bringing unhappy beings into the world!" She looked at Dolly, but without waiting for a reply she went on:

"I should always feel I had wronged these unhappy children," she said. "If they are not, at any rate they are not unhappy; while if they are unhappy, I alone should be to blame for it."

These were the very arguments Darya Alexandrovna had used in her own reflections; but she heard them without understanding them. "How can one wrong creatures that don't exist?" she thought. And all at once the idea struck her: could it possibly, under any circumstances, have been better for her favorite Grisha if he had never existed? And this seemed to her so wild, so strange, that she shook her head to drive away this tangle of whirling, mad ideas.

"No, I don't know; it's not right," was all she said, with an expression of disgust on her face.

"Yes, but you mustn't forget that you and I . . . And besides that," added Anna, in spite of the wealth of her arguments and the poverty of Dolly's objections, seeming still to admit that it was not right, "don't forget the chief point, that I am not now in the same position as you. For you the question is: do you desire not to have any more children; while for me it is: do I desire to have them? And that's a great difference. You must see that I can't desire it in my position."

Darya Alexandrovna made no reply. She suddenly felt that she had got far away from Anna; that there lay between them a barrier of questions on which they could never agree, and about which it was better not to speak.

CHAPTER XXIV

"Then there is all the more reason for you to legalize your position, if possible," said Dolly.

"Yes, if possible," said Anna, speaking all at once in an utterly different tone, subdued and mournful.

"Surely you don't mean a divorce is impossible? I was told your husband had consented to it."

"Dolly, I don't want to talk about that."

"Oh, we won't then," Darya Alexandrovna hastened to say, noticing the expression of suffering on Anna's face. "All I see is that you take too gloomy a view of things."

"I? Not at all! I'm always bright and happy. You see, *je fais des passions*. Veslovsky . . ."

"Yes, to tell the truth, I don't like Veslovsky's tone," said Darya Alexandrovna, anxious to change the subject.

"Oh, that's nonsense! It amuses Alexey, and that's all; but he's a boy, and quite under my control. You know, I turn him as I please. It's just as it might be with your Grisha. . . . Dolly!"—she suddenly changed the subject—"you say I take too gloomy a view of things. You can't understand. It's too awful! I try not to take any view of it at all."

"But I think you ought to. You ought to do all you can."

"But what can I do? Nothing. You tell me to marry Alexey, and say I don't think about it. I don't think about it!" she repeated, and a flush rose into her face. She got up, straightening her chest, and sighed heavily. With her light step she began pacing up and down the room, stopping now and then. "I don't think of it? Not a day, not an hour passes that I don't think of it, and blame myself for thinking of it . . . because thinking of that may drive me mad. Drive me mad!" she repeated. "When I think of it, I can't sleep without morphine. But never mind. Let us talk quietly. They tell me, divorce. In the first place, he won't give me a divorce. He's under the influence of Countess Lidia Ivanovna now."

Darya Alexandrovna, sitting erect on a chair, turned her head, following Anna with a face of sympathetic suffering.

"You ought to make the attempt," she said softly.

"Suppose I make the attempt. What does it mean?" she said, evidently giving utterance to a thought, a thousand times thought over and learned by heart. "It means that I, hating him, but still recognizing that I have wronged him—and I consider him magnanimous—that I humiliate myself to write to him . . . Well, suppose I make the effort; I do it. Either I receive a humiliating refusal or consent . . . Well, I have received his consent, say . . ." Anna was at that moment at the furthest end of the room, and she stopped there, doing something to the curtain at the window . . . "I receive his consent, but my . . . my son? They won't give him up to me. He will grow up despising me, with his father, whom I've abandoned. Do you see, I love . . . equally, I think, but both more than myself—two creatures, Seryozha and Alexey."

She came out into the middle of the room and stood facing Dolly, with her arms pressed tightly across her chest. In her white dressing-gown her figure seemed more than usually grand and broad. She bent her head, and with shining, wet eyes looked from under her brows at Dolly, a thin little pitiful figure in her patched dressing-jacket and night-cap, shaking all over with emotion.

"It is only those two creatures that I love, and one excludes the other. I can't have them together, and that's the only thing I want. And since I can't have that, I don't care about the rest. I don't care about anything, anything. And it will end one way or another, and so I can't, I don't like to talk of it. So don't blame me, don't judge me for anything. You can't with your pure heart understand all that I'm suffering." She went up, sat down beside Dolly, and with a guilty look, peeped into her face and took her hand.

"What are you thinking? What are you thinking about me? Don't despise me. I don't deserve contempt. I'm simply unhappy. If any one is unhappy, I am," she articulated, and turning away, she burst into tears.

Left alone, Darya Alexandrovna said her prayers and went to bed. She had felt for Anna with all her heart while she was speaking to her, but now she could not force herself to think of her. The memories of home and of her children rose up in her imagination with a peculiar charm quite new to her, with a sort of new brilliance. That world of her own seemed to her now so sweet and precious that she would not on any account spend an extra day outside it, and she made up her mind that she would certainly go back next day.

Anna meantime went back to her boudoir, took a wine-glass and dropped into it several drops of a medicine, of which the principal ingredient was morphine. After drinking it off and sitting still a little while, she went into her bedroom in a soothed and more cheerful frame of mind.

When she went into the bedroom, Vronsky looked intently at her. He was looking for traces of the conversation which he knew that, staying so long in Dolly's room, she must have had with her. But in her expression of restrained excitement, and of a sort of reserve, he could find nothing but the beauty that always bewitched him afresh though he was used to it, the consciousness of it, and the desire that it should affect him. He did not want to ask her what they had been talking of, but he hoped that she would tell him something of her own accord. But she only said:

"I am so glad you like Dolly. You do, don't you?"

"Oh, I've known her a long while, you know. She's very good-hearted, I suppose, *mais excessivement terre-à-terre*. Still, I'm very glad to see her."

He took Anna's hand and looked inquiringly into her eyes.

Misinterpreting the look, she smiled to him. Next morning, in spite of the protests of her hosts, Darya Alexandrovna prepared for her homeward journey. Levin's coachman, in his by no means new coat and shabby hat, with his ill-matched horses and his coach with the patched mud-guards, drove with gloomy determination into the covered gravel approach.

Darya Alexandrovna disliked taking leave of Princess Varvara and the gentlemen of the party. After a day spent together, both she and her hosts were distinctly aware that they did not get on together, and that it was better for them not to meet. Only Anna was sad. She knew that now, from Dolly's departure, no one again would stir up within her soul the feelings that had been roused by their conversation. It hurt her to stir up these feelings, but yet she knew that that was the best part of her soul, and that that part of her soul would quickly be smothered in the life she was leading.

As she drove out into the open country, Darya Alexandrovna had a delightful sense of relief, and she felt tempted to ask the two men how they had liked being at Vronsky's, when suddenly the coachman, Philip, expressed himself unasked:

"Rolling in wealth they may be, but three pots of oats was all they gave us. Everything cleared up till there wasn't a grain left by cockcrow. What are three pots? A mere mouthful! And oats now down to forty-five kopecks. At our place, no fear, all comers may have as much as they can eat."

"The master's a screw," put in the counting-house clerk.

"Well, did you like their horses?" asked Dolly.

"The horses!—there's no two opinions about them. And the food was good. But it seemed to me sort of dreary there, Darya Alexandrovna. I don't know what you thought," he said, turning his handsome, good-natured face to her.

"I thought so too. Well, shall we get home by evening?"

"Eh, we must!"

On reaching home and finding every one entirely satisfactory and particularly charming, Darya Alexandrovna began with great liveliness telling them how she had arrived, how warmly they had received her, of the luxury and good taste in which the Vronskys lived, and of their recreations, and she would not allow a word to be said against them.

"One has to know Anna and Vronsky—I have got to know him better now—to see how nice they are, and how touching," she said, speaking now with perfect sincerity, and forgetting the vague feeling of dissatisfaction and awkwardness she had experienced there.

CHAPTER XXV

VRONSKY and Anna spent the whole summer and part of the winter in the country, living in just the same condition, and still taking no steps to obtain a divorce. It was an understood thing between them that they should not go away anywhere; but both felt, the longer they lived alone, especially in the autumn, without guests in the house, that they could not stand this existence, and that they would have to alter it.

Their life was apparently such that nothing better could be desired. They had the fullest abundance of everything; they had a child, and both had occupation. Anna devoted just as much care to her appearance when they had no visitors, and she did a great deal of reading, both of novels and of what serious literature was in fashion. She ordered all the books that were praised in the foreign papers and reviews she received, and read them with that concentrated attention which is only given to what is read in seclusion. Moreover, every subject that was of interest to Vronsky, she studied in books and special journals, so that he often went straight to her with questions relating to agriculture or architecture, sometimes even with questions relating to horse-breeding or sport. He was amazed at her knowledge, her memory, and at first was disposed to doubt it, to ask for confirmation of her facts; and she would find what he asked for in some book, and show it to him.

The building of the hospital, too, interested her. She did not merely assist, but planned and suggested a great deal herself. But her chief thought was still of herself—how far she was dear to Vronsky, how far she could make up to him for all he had given up. Vronsky appreciated this desire not only to please, but to serve him, which had become the sole aim of her existence, but at the same time he wearied of the loving snares in which she tried to hold him fast. As time went on, and he saw himself more and more often held fast in these snares, he had an ever-growing desire, not so much to escape from them, as to try whether they hindered his freedom. Had it not been for this growing desire to be free, not to have scenes every time he wanted to go to the town to a meeting or a race, Vronsky would have been perfectly satisfied with his life. The rôle he had taken up, the rôle of a wealthy landowner, one of that class which ought to be the very heart of the Russian aristocracy, was entirely to his taste; and now, after spending six months in that character, he derived even greater satisfaction from it. And his management of his estate, which occupied and absorbed him more and more, was most successful. In spite of the immense sums cost him by the hospital, by machinery, by cows ordered from Switzerland, and many other things, he was convinced that he was not wasting, but increasing his substance. In all matters affecting income, the sales of timber, wheat, and wool, the letting of lands, Vronsky was hard as a rock, and knew well how to keep up prices. In all operations on a large scale on this and his other estates, he kept to the simplest methods involving no risk, and in trifling details he was careful and exacting to an extreme degree. In spite of all the cunning and ingenuity of the German steward, who would try to tempt him into purchases by making his original estimate always far larger than really required, and then representing to Vronsky that he might get the thing cheaper, and so make a profit, Vronsky did not give in. He listened to his steward, cross-examined him, and only agreed to his suggestions when the implement to be ordered or constructed was the very newest, not yet known in Russia, and likely to excite wonder. Apart from such exceptions, he resolved upon an increased outlay only where there was a surplus, and in making such an outlay he went into the minutest details, and insisted on getting the very best for his money; so that by the method on which he managed his affairs, it was clear that he was not wasting, but increasing his substance.

In October there were the provincial elections in the Kashinsky province, where were the estates of Vronsky, Sviazhsky, Koznishev, Oblonsky, and a small part of Levin's land.

These elections were attracting public attention from several circumstances connected with them, and also from the people taking part in them. There had been a great deal of talk about them, and great preparations were being made for them. Persons who never attended the elections were coming from Moscow, from Petersburg, and from abroad to attend these. Vronsky had long before promised Sviazhsky to go to them. Before the elections Sviazhsky, who often visited Vozdvizhenskoe, drove over to fetch Vronsky. On the day before there had been almost a quarrel between Vronsky and Anna over this proposed expedition. It was the very dullest autumn weather, which is so dreary in the country, and so, preparing himself for a struggle, Vronsky, with a hard and cold expression, informed Anna of his departure as he had never spoken to her before. But, to his surprise, Anna accepted the information with great composure, and merely asked when he would be back. He looked intently at her, at a loss to explain this composure. She smiled at his look. He knew that way she had of withdrawing into herself, and knew that it only happened when she had determined upon something without letting him know her plans. He was afraid of this; but he was so anxious to avoid a scene that he kept up appearances, and half sincerely believed in what he longed to believe in—her reasonableness.

"I hope you won't be dull?"

"I hope not," said Anna. "I got a box of books yesterday from Gautier's. No, I shan't be dull."

"She's trying to take that tone, and so much the better," he thought, "or else it would be the same thing over and over again."

And he set off for the elections without appealing to her for a candid explanation. It was the first time since the beginning of their intimacy that he had parted from her without a full explanation. From one point of view this troubled him, but on the other side he felt that it was better so. "At first there will be, as this time, something undefined kept back, and then she will get used to it. In any case I can give up anything for her, but not my masculine independence," he thought.

CHAPTER XXVI

IN SEPTEMBER Levin moved to Moscow for Kitty's confinement. He had spent a whole month in Moscow with nothing to do, when Sergey Ivanovitch, who had property in the Kashinsky province, and took great interest in the question of the approaching elections, made ready to set off to the elections. He invited his brother, who had a vote in the Seleznevsky district, to come with him. Levin had, moreover, to transact in Kashin some extremely important business relating to the wardship of land and to the receiving of certain redemption-money for his sister, who was abroad.

Levin still hesitated, but Kitty, who saw that he was bored in Moscow, and urged him to go, on her own authority ordered him the proper nobleman's uniform, costing seven pounds. And that seven pounds paid for the uniform was the chief cause that finally decided Levin to go. He went to Kashin. . . .

Levin had been six days in Kashin, visiting the assembly each day, and busily engaged about his sister's business, which still dragged on. The district marshals of nobility were all occupied with the elections, and it was impossible to get the simplest thing done that depended upon the court of wardship. The other matter, the payment of the sums due, was met too by difficulties. After long negotiations over the legal details, the money was at last ready to be paid; but the notary, a most obliging person, could not hand over the order, because it must have the signature of the president, and the president, though he had not given over his duties to a deputy, was at the elections. All these worrying negotiations, this endless going from place to place, and talking with pleasant and excellent people, who quite saw the unpleasantness of the petitioner's position, but were powerless to assist him—all these efforts that yielded no result, led to a feeling of misery in Levin akin to the mortifying helplessness one experiences in dreams when one tries to use physical force. He felt this frequently as he talked to his most good-natured solicitor. This solicitor did, it seemed, everything possible, and strained every nerve to get him out of his difficulties. "I tell you what you might try," he said more than once; "go to so-and-so and so-and-so," and the solicitor drew up a regular plan for getting round the fatal point that hindered everything. But he would add immediately, "It'll mean some delay, anyway, but you might try it." And Levin did try, and did go. Every one was kind and civil, but the point evaded seemed to crop up again in the end, and again to bar the way. What was particularly trying, was that Levin could not make out with whom he was struggling, to whose interest it was that his business should not be done. That no one seemed to know; the solicitor certainly did not know. If Levin could have understood why, just as he saw why one can only approach the booking-office of a railway station in single file, it would not have been so vexatious and tiresome to him. But with the hindrances that confronted him in his business, no one could explain why they existed.

But Levin had changed a good deal since his marriage; he

was patient, and if he could not see why it was all arranged like this, he told himself that he could not judge without knowing all about it, and that most likely it must be so, and he tried not to fret.

In attending the elections, too, and taking part in them, he tried now not to judge, not to fall foul of them, but to comprehend as fully as he could the question which was so earnestly and ardently absorbing honest and excellent men whom he respected. Since his marriage there had been revealed to Levin so many new and serious aspects of life that had previously, through his frivolous attitude to them, seemed of no importance, that in the question of the elections too he assumed and tried to find some serious significance.

Sergey Ivanovitch explained to him the meaning and object of the proposed revolution at the elections. The marshal of the province in whose hands the law had placed the control of so many important public functions—the guardianship of wards (the very department which was giving Levin so much trouble just now), the disposal of large sums subscribed by the nobility of the province, the high schools, female, male, and military, and popular instruction on the new model, and finally, the district council—the marshal of the province, Snetkov, was a nobleman of the old school,—dissipating an immense fortune, a good-hearted man, honest after his own fashion, but utterly without any comprehension of the needs of modern days. He always took, in every question, the side of the nobility; he was positively antagonistic to the spread of popular education, and he succeeded in giving a purely party character to the district council which ought by rights to be of such an immense importance. What was needed was to put in his place a fresh, capable, perfectly modern man, of contemporary ideas, and to frame their policy so as from the rights conferred upon the nobles, not as the nobility, but as an element of the district council, to extract all the powers of self-government that could possibly be derived from them. In the wealthy Kashinsky province, which always took the lead of other provinces in everything, there was now such a preponderance of forces that this policy once carried through properly there, might serve as a model for other provinces for all Russia.

And hence the whole question was of the greatest importance. It was proposed to elect as marshal in place of Snetkov either Sviazhsky, or, better still, Nevyedovsky, a former university professor, a man of remarkable intelligence and a great friend of Sergey Ivanovitch.

The meeting was opened by the governor, who made a speech to the nobles, urging them to elect the public functionaries, not from regard for persons, but for the service and welfare of their fatherland, and hoping that the honorable nobility of the Kashinsky province would, as at all former elections, hold their duty as sacred, and vindicate the exalted confidence of the monarch.

When he had finished with his speech, the governor walked out of the hall, and the noblemen noisily and eagerly — some even enthusiastically — followed him and thronged round him while he put on his fur coat and conversed amicably with the marshal of the province. Levin, anxious to see into everything and not to miss anything, stood there too in the crowd, and heard the governor say: "Please tell Marya Ivanovna my wife is very sorry she couldn't come to the Home." And thereupon the nobles in high good-humor sorted out their fur coats and all drove off to the cathedral. In the cathedral Levin, lifting his hand like the rest and repeating the words of the archdeacon, swore with most terrible oaths to do all the governor had hoped they would do. Church services always affected Levin, and as he uttered the words "I kiss the cross," and glanced round at the crowd of young and old men repeating the same, he felt touched.

On the second and third days there was business relating to the finances of the nobility and the female high school, of no importance whatever, as Sergey Ivanovitch explained, and Levin, busy seeing after his own affairs, did not attend the meetings. On the fourth day the auditing of the marshal's accounts took place at the high table of the marshal of the province. And then there occurred the first skirmish between the new party and the old. The committee who had been deputed to verify the accounts reported to the meeting that all was in order. The marshal of the province got up, thanked the nobility for their confidence, and shed tears. The nobles gave him a loud welcome, and shook hands with him. But at that instant a nobleman of Sergey Ivanovitch's party said that he had heard that the committee had not verified the accounts, considering such a verification an insult to the marshal of the province. One of the members of the committee incautiously admitted this. Then a small gentleman, very young-looking but very malignant, began to say that it would probably be agreeable to the marshal of the province to give an account of his expenditures of the public moneys, and that the misplaced delicacy of the members of the committee was depriving him of this moral satisfaction. Then the members of the committee tried to withdraw their admission, and Sergey Ivanovitch began to prove that they must logically admit either that they had verified the accounts or that they had not, and he developed this dilemma in detail. Sergey Ivanovitch was answered by the spokesman of the opposite party. Then Sviazhsky spoke, and then the malignant gentleman again. The discussion lasted a long time and ended in nothing. Levin was surprised that they should dispute upon this subject so long, especially as, when he asked Sergey Ivanovitch whether he supposed that money had been misappropriated, Sergey Ivanovitch answered:

"Oh, no! He's an honest man. But those old-fashioned methods of paternal family arrangements in the management of provincial affairs must be broken down."

On the fifth day came the elections of the district marshals. It was rather a stormy day in several districts. In the Seleznevsky district Sviazhsky was elected unanimously without a ballot, and he gave a dinner that evening.

CHAPTER XXVII

THE sixth day was fixed for the election of the marshal of the province. The rooms, large and small, were full of noblemen in all sorts of uniforms. Many had come only for that day. Men who had not seen each other for years, some from the Crimea, some from Petersburg, some from abroad, met in the rooms of the Hall of Nobility. There was much discussion around the governor's table under the portrait of the Tsar.

The nobles, both in the larger and the smaller rooms, grouped themselves in camps, and from their hostile and suspicious glances, from the silence that fell upon them when outsiders approached a group, and from the way that some, whispering together, retreated to the further corridor, it was evident that each side had secrets from the other. In appearance the noblemen were sharply divided into two classes: the old and the new. The old were for the most part either in old uniforms of the nobility, buttoned up closely, with spurs and hats, or in their own special naval, cavalry, infantry, or official uniforms. The uniforms of the older men were embroidered in the old-fashioned way with epaulets on their shoulders; they were unmistakably tight and short in the waist, as though their wearers had grown out of them. The younger men wore the uniform of the nobility with long waists and broad shoulders, unbuttoned over white waistcoats, or uniforms with black collars and with the embroidered badges of justices of the peace. To the younger men belonged the court uniforms that here and there brightened up the crowd.

But the division into young and old did not correspond with the division of parties. Some of the young men, as Levin observed, belonged to the old party; and some of the very oldest noblemen, on the contrary, were whispering with Sviazhsky, and were evidently ardent partisans of the new party.

Levin stood in the smaller room, where they were smoking and taking light refreshments, close to his own friends, and listening to what they were saying, he conscientiously exerted all his intelligence trying to understand what was said. Sergey Ivanovitch was the center round which the others grouped themselves. He was listening at that moment to Sviazhsky and Hliustov, the marshal of another district, who belonged to their party. Hliustov would not agree to go with his district to ask Snetkov to stand, while Sviazhsky was persuading him to do so, and Sergey Ivanovitch was approving of the plan. Levin could not make out why the opposition was to ask the marshal to stand whom they wanted to supersede.

Stepan Arkadyevitch, who had just been drinking and taking some lunch, came up to them in his uniform of a gentleman of the bedchamber, wiping his lips with a perfumed handkerchief of bordered batiste.

"We are placing our forces," he said, pulling out his whiskers, "Sergey Ivanovitch!"

And listening to the conversation, he supported Sviazhsky's contention.

"One district's enough, and Sviazhsky's obviously of the opposition," he said, words evidently intelligible to all except Levin.

"Why, Kostya, you here too! I suppose you're converted, eh?" he added, turning to Levin and drawing his arm through his. Levin would have been glad indeed to be converted, but could not make out what the point was, and retreating a few steps from the speakers, he explained to Stepan Arkadyevitch his inability to understand why the marshal of the province should be asked to stand.

"*O sancta simplicitas!*" said Stepan Arkadyevitch, and briefly and clearly he explained it to Levin. If, as at previous elections, all the districts asked the marshal of the province to stand, then he would be elected without a ballot. That must not be. Now eight districts had agreed to call upon him: if two refused to do so, Snetkov might decline to stand at all; and then the old party might choose another of their party, which would throw them completely out in their reckoning. But if only one district, Sviazhsky's, did not call upon him to stand, Snetkov would let himself be balloted for. They were even, some of them, going to vote for him, and purposely to let him get a good many votes, so that the enemy might be thrown off the scent, and when a candidate of the other side was put up, they too might give him some votes. Levin understood to some extent, but not fully, and would have put a few more questions, when suddenly every one began talking and making a noise and they moved towards the big room.

"What is it? eh? whom?" "No guarantee? whose? what?" "They won't pass him?" "No guarantee?" "They won't let Flerov in?" "Eh, because of the charge against him?" "Why, at this rate, they won't admit any one. It's a swindle!" "The law!" Levin heard exclamations on all sides, and he moved into the big room together with the others, all hurrying somewhere and afraid of missing something. Squeezed by the crowding noblemen, he drew near the high table where the marshal of the province, Sviazhsky, and the other leaders were hotly disputing about something.

CHAPTER XXVIII

LEVIN was standing rather far off. A nobleman breathing heavily and hoarsely at his side, and another whose thick boots were creaking, prevented him from hearing distinctly. He could only hear the soft voice of the marshal faintly, then the shrill voice of the malignant gentleman, and then the voice of Sviazhsky. They were disputing, as far as he could make out, as to the interpretation to be put on the act and the exact meaning of the words: "liable to be called up for trial."

The crowd parted to make way for Sergey Ivanovitch approaching the table. Sergey Ivanovitch, waiting till the malignant gentleman had finished speaking, said that he thought the best solution would be to refer to the act itself, and asked the secretary to find the act. The act said that in case of difference of opinion, there must be a ballot.

Sergey Ivanovitch read the act and began to explain its meaning, but at that point a tall, stout, round-shouldered landowner, with dyed whiskers, in a tight uniform that cut the back of his neck, interrupted him. He went up to the table, and striking it with his finger-ring, he shouted loudly: "A ballot! Put it to the vote! No need for more talking!" Then several voices began to talk all at once, and the tall nobleman with the ring, getting more and more exasperated, shouted more and more loudly. But it was impossible to make out what he said.

He was shouting for the very course Sergey Ivanovitch had proposed; but it was evident that he hated him and all his party, and this feeling of hatred spread through the whole party and roused in opposition to it the same vindictiveness, though in a more seemly form, on the other side. Shouts were raised, and for a moment all was confusion, so that the marshal of the province had to call for order.

"A ballot! A ballot! Every nobleman sees it! We shed our blood for our country! . . . The confidence of the monarch. . . . No checking the accounts of the marshal; he's not a cashier. . . . But that's not the point. . . . Votes, please! Beastly! . . ." shouted furious and violent voices on all sides. Looks and faces were even more violent and furious than their words. They expressed the most implacable hatred. Levin did not in the least understand what was the matter, and he marveled at the passion with which it was disputed whether or not the decision about Flerov should be put to the vote. He forgot, as Sergey Ivanovitch explained to him afterwards, this syllogism: that it was necessary for the public good to get rid of the marshal of the province; that to get rid of the marshal it was necessary to have a majority of votes; that to get a majority of votes it was necessary to secure Flerov's right to vote; that to secure the recognition of Flerov's right to vote they must decide on the interpretation to be put on the act.

"And one vote may decide the whole question and one must be serious and consecutive, if one wants to be of use in public life," concluded Sergey Ivanovitch. But Levin forgot all that, and it was painful to him to see all these excellent persons, for whom he had a respect, in such an unpleasant and vicious state of excitement. To escape from this painful feeling he went away into the other room where there was nobody except the waiters at the refreshment-bar. Seeing the waiters busy over washing up the crockery and setting in order their plates and wine-glasses, seeing their calm and cheerful faces, Levin felt an unexpected sense of relief as though he had come out of a stuffy room into the fresh air. He began walking up and down, looking with pleasure at the waiters. He particularly liked the way one gray-whiskered waiter, who showed his scorn for the other younger ones and was jeered at by them, was teaching them how to fold up napkins properly. Levin was just about to enter into conversation with the old waiter, when the secretary of the court of wardship, a little old man whose specialty it was to know all the noblemen of the province by name and patronymic, drew him away.

"Please come, Konstantin Dmitrievitch," he said, "your brother's looking for you. They are voting on the legal point."

Levin walked into the room, received a white ball, and followed his brother, Sergey Ivanovitch, to the table where Sviazhsky was standing with a significant and ironical face, holding his beard in his fist and sniffing at it. Sergey Ivanovitch put his hand into the box, put the ball somewhere, and making room for Levin, stopped. Levin advanced, but utterly forgetting what he was to do, and much embarrassed, he turned to Sergey Ivanovitch with the question, "Where am I to put it?" He asked this softly, at a moment when there was talking going on near, so that he had hoped his question would not be overheard. But the persons speaking paused, and his improper question was overheard. Sergey Ivanovitch frowned.

"That is a matter for each man's own decision," he said severely.

Several people smiled. Levin crimsoned, hurriedly thrust his hand under the cloth, and put the ball to the right as it was in his right hand. Having put it in, he recollected that he ought to have thrust his left hand too, and so he thrust it in though too late, and, still more overcome with confusion, he beat a hasty retreat into the background.

"A hundred and twenty-six for admission! Ninety-eight against!" sang out the voice of the secretary, who could not pronounce the letter *r*. Then there was a laugh; a button and two nuts were found in the box. The nobleman was allowed the right to vote, and the new party had conquered.

But the old party did not consider themselves conquered. Levin heard that they were asking Snetkov to stand, and he saw that a crowd of noblemen was surrounding the marshal, who was saying something. Levin went nearer. In reply Snetkov spoke of the trust the noblemen of the province had placed in him, the affection they had shown him, which he did not deserve, as his only merit had been his attachment to the nobility, to whom he had devoted twelve years of service. Several times he repeated the words: "I have served to the best of my powers with truth and good faith, I value your goodness and thank you," and suddenly he stopped short from the tears that choked him, and went out of the room. Whether these tears came from a sense of the injustice being done him, from his love for the nobility, or from the strain of the position he was placed in, feeling himself surrounded by enemies, his emotion infected the assembly, the majority were touched, and Levin felt a tenderness for Snetkov.

In the doorway the marshal of the province jostled against Levin.

"Beg pardon, excuse me, please," he said as to a stranger, but recognizing Levin, he smiled timidly. It seemed to Levin that he would have liked to say something, but could not speak for emotion. His face and his whole figure in his uniform with the crosses, and white trousers striped with braid, as he moved hurriedly along, reminded Levin of some hunted beast who sees that he is in evil case. This expression in the marshal's face was particularly touching to Levin, because, only the day before, he had been at his house about his trustee business and had seen him in all his grandeur, a kind-hearted, fatherly man. The big house with the old family furniture; the rather dirty, far from stylish, but respectful footmen, unmistakably old house serfs who had stuck to their master; the stout, good-natured wife in a cap with lace and a Turkish shawl, petting her pretty grandchild, her daughter's daughter; the young son, a sixth form high school boy, coming home from school, and greeting his father, kissing his big hand; the genuine, cordial words and gestures of the old man—all this had the day before roused an instinctive feeling of respect and sympathy in Levin. This old man was a touching and pathetic figure to Levin now, and he longed to say something pleasant to him.

"So you're sure to be our marshal again," he said.

"It's not likely," said the marshal, looking round with a scared expression. "I'm worn out, I'm old. If there are men younger and more deserving than I, let them serve."

And the marshal disappeared through a side-door.

The most solemn moment was at hand. They were to proceed immediately to the election. The leaders of both parties were reckoning white and black on their fingers.

The discussion upon Flerov had given the new party not only Flerov's vote, but had also gained time for them, so that they could send to fetch three noblemen who had been rendered unable to take part in the elections by the wiles of the other party. Two noble gentlemen, who had a weakness for strong drink, had been made drunk by the partisans of Snetkov, and a third had been robbed of his uniform.

On learning this, the new party had made haste, during the dispute about Flerov, to send some of their men in a sledge to clothe the stripped gentleman, and to bring along one of the intoxicated to the meeting.

"I've brought one, drenched him with water," said the landowner, who had gone on this errand, to Sviazhsky. "He's all right? he'll do."

"Not too drunk, he won't fall down?" said Sviazhsky, shaking his head.

"No, he's first-rate. If only they don't give him any more here . . . I've told the waiter not to give him anything on any account."

CHAPTER XXIX

The narrow room, in which they were smoking and taking refreshments, was full of noblemen. The excitement grew more intense, and every face betrayed some uneasiness. The excitement was specially keen for the leaders of each party, who knew every detail, and had reckoned up every vote. They were the generals organizing the approaching battle. The rest, like the rank and file before an engagement, though they were getting ready for the fight, sought for other distractions in the interval. Some were lunching, standing at the bar, or sitting at the table; others were walking up and down the long room, smoking cigarettes, and talking with friends whom they had not seen for a long while.

Levin did not care to eat, and he was not smoking; he did not want to join his own friends, that is Sergey Ivanovitch, Stepan

Arkadyevitch, Sviazhsky and the rest, because Vronsky in his equerry's uniform was standing with them in eager conversation. Levin had seen him already at the meeting on the previous day, and he had studiously avoided him, not caring to greet him. He went to the window and sat down, scanning the groups, and listening to what was being said around him. He felt depressed, especially because every one else was, as he saw, eager, anxious, and interested, and he alone, with an old, toothless little man with mumbling lips wearing a naval uniform, sitting beside him, had no interest in it and nothing to do.

"He's such a blackguard! I have told him so, but it makes no difference. Only think of it! He couldn't collect it in three years!" he heard vigorously uttered by a round-shouldered, short, country gentleman, who had pomaded hair hanging on his embroidered collar, and new boots obviously put on for the occasion, with heels that tapped energetically as he spoke. Casting a displeased glance at Levin, this gentleman sharply turned his back.

"Yes, it's a dirty business, there's no denying," a small gentleman assented in a high voice.

Next, a whole crowd of country gentlemen, surrounding a stout general, hurriedly came near Levin. These persons were unmistakably seeking a place where they could talk without being overheard.

"How dare he say I had his breeches stolen! Pawned them for drink, I expect. Damn the fellow, prince indeed! He'd better not say it, the beast!"

"But excuse me! They take their stand on the act," was being said in another group; "the wife must be registered as noble."

"Oh, damn your acts! I speak from my heart. We're all gentlemen, aren't we? Above suspicion."

"Shall we go on, your excellency, *fine champagne?*"

Another group was following a nobleman, who was shouting something in a loud voice; it was one of the three intoxicated gentlemen.

"I always advised Marya Semyonovna to let for a fair rent, for she can never save a profit," he heard a pleasant voice say. The speaker was a country gentleman with gray whiskers, wearing the regimental uniform of an old general staff-officer. It was the very landowner Levin had met at Sviazhsky's. He knew him at once. The landowner too stared at Levin, and they exchanged greetings.

"Very glad to see you! To be sure! I remember you very well. Last year at our district marshal, Nikolay Ivanovitch's."

"Well, and how is your land doing?" asked Levin.

"Oh, still just the same, always at a loss," the landowner answered with a resigned smile, but with an expression of serenity and conviction that so it must be. "And how do you come to be in our province?" he asked. "Come to take part in our *coup d'état?*" he said, confidently pronouncing the French words with a bad accent. "All Russia's here—gentlemen of the bedchamber, and everything short of the ministry." He pointed to the imposing figure of Stepan Arkadyevitch in white trousers and his court uniform, walking by with a general.

"I ought to own that I don't very well understand the drift of the provincial elections," said Levin.

The landowner looked at him.

"Why, what is there to understand? There's no meaning in it at all. It's a decaying institution that goes on running only by the force of inertia. Just look, the very uniforms tell you that it's an assembly of justices of the peace, permanent members of the court, and so on, but not of noblemen."

"Then why do you come?" asked Levin.

"From habit, nothing else. Then, too, one must keep up connections. It's a moral obligation of a sort. And then, to tell the truth, there's one's own interests. My son-in-law wants to stand as a permanent member; they're not rich people, and he must be brought forward. These gentlemen, now, what do they come for?" he said, pointing to the malignant gentleman, who was talking at the high table.

"That's the new generation of nobility."

"New it may be, but nobility it isn't. They're proprietors of a sort, but we're the landowners. As noblemen, they're cutting their own throats."

"But you say it's an institution that's served its time."

"That it may be, but still it ought to be treated a little more respectfully. Snetkov, now . . . We may be of use, or we may not, but we're the growth of a thousand years. If we're laying out a garden, planning one before the house, you know, and there you've a tree that's stood for centuries in the very spot. . . . Old and gnarled it may be, and yet you don't cut down the old fellow to make room for the flowerbeds, but lay out your beds so as to take advantage of the tree. You won't grow him again in a year," he said cautiously, and he immediately changed the conversation. "Well, and how is your land doing?"

"Oh, not very well. I make five per cent."

"Yes, but you don't reckon your own work. Aren't you worth something too? I'll tell you my own case. Before I took to seeing after the land, I had a salary of three hundred pounds from the service. Now I do more work than I did in the service, and like you I get five per cent on the land, and thank God for that. But one's work is thrown in for nothing."

"Then why do you do it, if it's a clear loss?"

"Oh, well, one does it! What would you have? It's habit, and one knows it's how it should be. And what's more," the landowner went on, leaning his elbows on the window and chatting on, "my son, I must tell you, has no taste for it. There's no doubt he'll be a scientific man. So there'll be no one to keep it up. And yet one does it. Here this year I've planted an orchard."

"Yes, yes," said Levin, "that's perfectly true. I always feel there's no real balance of gain in my work on the land, and yet one does it. . . . It's a sort of duty one feels to the land."

"But I tell you what," the landowner pursued; "a neighbor of mine, a merchant, was at my place. We walked about the fields and the garden. 'No,' said he, 'Stepan Vassilievitch, everything's well looked after, but your garden's neglected.' But, as a fact, it's well kept up. 'To my thinking, I'd cut down that lime-tree. Here you've thousands of limes, and each would make two good bundles of bark. And nowadays that bark's worth something. I'd cut down the lot.' "

"And with what he made he'd increase his stock, or buy some land for a trifle, and let it out in lots to the peasants," Levin added, smiling. He had evidently more than once come across those commercial calculations. "And he'd make his fortune. But you and I must thank God if we keep what we've got and leave it to our children."

"You're married, I've heard?" said the landowner.

"Yes," Levin answered, with proud satisfaction. "Yes, it's rather strange," he went on. "So we live without making anything, as though we were ancient vestals set to keep in a fire."

The landowner chuckled under his white mustaches.

"There are some among us, too, like our friend Nikolay Ivanovitch, or Count Vronsky, that's settled here lately, who try to carry on their husbandry as though it were a factory; but so far it leads to nothing but making away with capital on it."

"But why is it we don't do like the merchants? Why don't we cut down our parks for timber?" said Levin, returning to a thought that had struck him.

"Why, as you said, to keep the fire in. Besides that's not work for a nobleman. And our work as noblemen isn't done here at the elections, but yonder, each in our corner. There's a class instinct, too, of what one ought and oughtn't to do. There's the peasants, too, I wonder at them sometimes; any good peasant tries to take all the land he can. However bad the land is, he'll work it. Without a return too. At a simple loss."

"Just as we do," said Levin. "Very, very glad to have met you," he added, seeing Sviazhsky approaching him.

"And here we've met for the first time since we met at your place," said the landowner to Sviazhsky, "and we've had a good talk too."

"Well, have you been attacking the new order of things?" said Sviazhsky with a smile.

"That we're bound to do."

"You've relieved your feelings?"

CHAPTER XXX

Sviazhsky took Levin's arm, and went with him to his own friends.

This time there was no avoiding Vronsky. He was standing with Stepan Arkadyevitch and Sergey Ivanovitch, and looking straight at Levin as he drew near.

"Delighted! I believe I've had the pleasure of meeting you . . . at Princess Shtcherbatskaya's," he said, giving Levin his hand.

"Yes, I quite remember our meeting," said Levin, and blushing crimson, he turned away immediately, and began talking to his brother.

With a slight smile Vronsky went on talking to Sviazhsky, obviously without the slightest inclination to enter into conversation with Levin. But Levin, as he talked to his brother, was continually looking round at Vronsky, trying to think of something to say to him to gloss over his rudeness.

"What are we waiting for now?" asked Levin, looking at Sviazhsky and Vronsky.

"For Snetkov. He has to refuse or to consent to stand," answered Sviazhsky.

"Well, and what has he done, consented or not?"

"That's the point, that he's done neither," said Vronsky.

"And if he refuses, who will stand then?" asked Levin, looking at Vronsky.

"Whoever chooses to," said Sviazhsky.

"Shall you?" asked Levin.

"Certainly not I," said Sviazhsky, looking confused, and turning an alarmed glance at the malignant gentleman, who was standing beside Sergey Ivanovitch.

"Who then? Nevyedovsky?" said Levin, feeling he was putting his foot into it.

But this was worse still. Nevyedovsky and Sviazhsky were the two candidates.

"I certainly shall not, under any circumstances," answered the malignant gentleman.

This was Nevyedovsky himself. Sviazhsky introduced him to Levin.

"Well, you find it exciting too?" said Stepan Arkadyevitch, winking at Vronsky. "It's something like a race. One might bet on it."

"Yes, it is keenly exciting," said Vronsky. "And once taking the thing up, one's eager to see it through. It's a fight!" he said, scowling and setting his powerful jaws.

"What a capable fellow Sviazhsky is! Sees it all so clearly."

"Oh, yes!" Vronsky assented indifferently.

A silence followed, during which Vronsky—since he had to look at something—looked at Levin, at his feet, at his uniform, then at his face, and noticing his gloomy eyes fixed upon him, he said, in order to say something:

"How is it that you, living constantly in the country, are not a justice of the peace? You are not in the uniform of one."

"It's because I consider that the justice of the peace is a silly institution," Levin answered gloomily. He had been all the time looking for an opportunity to enter into conversation with Vronsky, so as to smooth over his rudeness at their first meeting.

"I don't think so, quite the contrary," Vronsky said, with quiet surprise.

"It's a plaything," Levin cut him short. "We don't want justices of the peace. I've never had a single thing to do with them during eight years. And what I have had was decided wrongly by them. The justice of the peace is over thirty miles from me. For some matter of two roubles I should have to send a lawyer, who costs me fifteen."

And he related how a peasant had stolen some flour from the miller, and when the miller told him of it, had lodged a complaint for slander. All this was utterly uncalled for and stupid, and Levin felt it himself as he said it.

"Oh, this is such an original fellow!" said Stepan Arkadyevitch with his most soothing, almond-oil smile. "But come along; I think they're voting. . . ."

And they separated.

"I can't understand," said Sergey Ivanovitch, who had observed his brother's clumsiness, "I can't understand how any one can be so absolutely devoid of political tact. That's where we Russians are so deficient. The marshal of the province is our opponent, and with him you're *ami cochon,* and you beg him to stand. Count Vronsky, now . . . I'm not making a friend of him; he's asked me to dinner, and I'm not going; but he's one of our side—why make an enemy of him? Then you ask Nevyedovsky if he's going to stand. That's not a thing to do."

"Oh, I don't understand it at all! And it's all such nonsense," Levin answered gloomily.

"You say it's all such nonsense, but as soon as you have anything to do with it, you make a muddle."

Levin did not answer, and they walked together into the big room.

The marshal of the province, though he was vaguely conscious in the air of some trap being prepared for him, and though he had not been called upon by all to stand, had still made up his mind to stand. All was silence in the room. The secretary announced in a loud voice that the captain of the guards, Mihail Stepanovitch Snetkov, would now be balloted for as marshal of the province.

The district marshals walked carrying plates, on which were balls, from their tables to the high table, and the election began.

"Put it in the right side," whispered Stepan Arkadyevitch, as with his brother Levin followed the marshal of his district to the table. But Levin had forgotten by now the calculations that had been explained to him, and was afraid Stepan Arkadyevitch might be mistaken in saying "the right side." Surely Snetkov was the enemy. As he went up, he held the ball in his right hand, but thinking he was wrong, just at the box he changed to the left hand, and undoubtedly put the ball to the left. An adept in the business, standing at the box and seeing by the mere action of the elbow where each put his ball, scowled with annoyance. It was no good for him to use his insight.

Everything was still, and the counting of the balls was heard. Then a single voice rose and proclaimed the numbers for and against. The marshal had been voted for by a considerable majority. All was noise and eager movement towards the doors. Snetkov came in, and the nobles thronged round him, congratulating him.

"Well, now is it over?" Levin asked Sergey Ivanovitch.

"It's only just beginning," Sviazhsky said, replying for Sergey Ivanovitch with a smile. "Some other candidate may receive more votes than the marshal."

Levin had quite forgotten about that. Now he could only remember that there was some sort of trickery in it, but he was too bored to think what it was exactly. He felt depressed, and longed to get out of the crowd.

As no one was paying any attention to him, and no one apparently needed him, he quietly slipped away into the little room where the refreshments were, and again had a great sense of comfort when he saw the waiters. The little old waiter pressed him to have something, and Levin agreed. After eating a cutlet with beans and talking to the waiters of their former masters, Levin, not wishing to go back to the hall, where it was all so distasteful to him, proceeded to walk through the galleries. The galleries were full of fashionably dressed ladies, leaning over the balustrade and trying not to lose a single word of what was being said below. With the ladies were sitting and standing smart lawyers, high school teachers in spectacles, and officers. Everywhere they were talking of the election, and of how worried the marshal was, and how splendid the discussions had been. In one group Levin heard his brother's praises. One lady was telling a lawyer:

"How glad I am I heard Koznishev! It's worth losing one's dinner. He's exquisite! So clear and distinct, all of it! There's not one of you in the law-courts that speaks like that. The only one is Meidel, and he's not so eloquent by a long way."

Finding a free place, Levin leaned over the balustrade and began looking and listening.

All the noblemen were sitting railed off behind barriers according to their districts. In the middle of the room stood a man in a uniform, who shouted in a loud, high voice:

"As a candidate for the marshalship of the nobility of the province we call upon staff-captain Yevgeney Ivanovitch Apuhtin!" A dead silence followed, and then a weak old voice was heard: "Declined!"

"We call upon the privy councilor Pyotr Petrovitch Bol," the voice began again.

"Declined!" a high boyish voice replied.

Again it began, and again "Declined." And so it went on for about an hour. Levin, with his elbows on the balustrade, looked and listened. At first he wondered and wanted to know what it meant; then feeling sure that he could not make it out he began to be bored. Then recalling all the excitement and vindictiveness he had seen on all the faces, he felt sad; he made up his mind to go, and went down-stairs. As he passed through the entry to the galleries he met a dejected high school boy walking up and down with tired-looking eyes. On the stairs he met a couple —a lady running quickly on her high heels and the jaunty deputy prosecutor.

"I told you you weren't late," the deputy prosecutor was saying at the moment when Levin moved aside to let the lady pass.

Levin was on the stairs to the way out, and was just feeling in his waistcoat pocket for the number of his overcoat, when the secretary overtook him.

"This way, please, Konstantin Dmitrievitch; they are voting."

The candidate who was being voted on was Nevyedovsky, who had so stoutly denied all idea of standing. Levin went up to the door of the room; it was locked. The secretary knocked, the door opened, and Levin was met by two red-faced gentlemen, who darted out.

"I can't stand any more of it," said one red-faced gentleman.

After them the face of the marshal of the province was poked out. His face was dreadful-looking from exhaustion and dismay.

"I told you not to let any one out!" he cried to the doorkeeper.

"I let some one in, your excellency!"

"Mercy on us!" and with a heavy sigh the marshal of the province walked with downcast head to the high table in the middle of the room, his legs staggering in his white trousers.

Nevyedovsky had scored a higher majority, as they had planned, and he was the new marshal of the province. Many people were amused, many were pleased and happy, many were in ecstasies, many were disgusted and unhappy. The former marshal of the province was in a state of despair, which he could not conceal. When Nevyedovsky went out of the room, the crowd thronged round him and followed him enthusiastically, just as they had followed the governor who had opened the meetings, and just as they had followed Snetkov when he was elected.

CHAPTER XXXI

THE newly elected marshal and many of the successful party dined that day with Vronsky.

Vronsky had come to the elections partly because he was bored in the country and wanted to show Anna his right to independence, and also to repay Sviazhsky by his support at the election for all the trouble he had taken for Vronsky at the district council election, but chiefly in order strictly to perform all those duties of a nobleman and landowner which he had taken upon himself. But he had not in the least expected that the election would so interest him, so keenly excite him, and that he would be so good at this kind of thing. He was quite a new man in the circle of the nobility of the province, but his success was unmistakable, and he was not wrong in supposing that he had already obtained a certain influence. This influence was due to his wealth and reputation, the capital house in the town lent him by his old friend Shirkov, who had a post in the department of finances and was director of a flourishing bank in Kashin, the excellent cook Vronsky had brought from the country, and his friendship with the governor, who was a schoolfellow of Vronsky's—a schoolfellow he had patronized and protected indeed. But what contributed more than all to his success was his direct, equable manner with every one, which very quickly made the majority of the noblemen reverse the current opinion of his supposed haughtiness. He was himself conscious that, except that whimsical gentleman married to Kitty Shtcherbatskaya, who had *à propos de bottes* poured out a stream of irrelevant absurdities with such spiteful fury, every nobleman with whom he had made acquaintance had become his adherent. He saw clearly, and other people recognized it, too, that he had done a great deal to secure the success of Nevyedovsky. And now at his own table, celebrating Nevyedovsky's election, he was experiencing an agreeable sense of triumph over the success of his candidate. The election itself had so fascinated him that, if he could succeed in getting married during the next three years, he began to think of standing himself—much as after winning a race ridden by a jockey, he had longed to ride a race himself.

To-day he was celebrating the success of his jockey. Vronsky sat at the head of the table, on his right hand sat the young governor, a general of high rank. To all the rest he was the chief man in the province, who had solemnly opened the elections with his speech, and aroused a feeling of respect and even of awe in many people, as Vronsky saw; to Vronsky he was little Katka Maslov—that had been his nickname in the Pages' Corps—whom he felt to be shy and tried to *mettre à son aise*. On the left hand sat Nevyedovsky with his youthful, stubborn, and malignant face. With him Vronsky was simple and deferential.

Sviazhsky took his failure very light-heartedly. It was indeed no failure in his eyes, as he said himself, turning, glass in hand, to Nevyedovsky; they could not have found a better representative of the new movement, which the nobility ought to follow. And so every honest person, as he said, was on the side of today's success and was rejoicing over it.

Stepan Arkadyevitch was glad, too, that he was having a good time, and that every one was pleased. The episode of the elections served as a good occasion for a capital dinner. Sviazhsky comically imitated the tearful discourse of the marshal, and observed, addressing Nevyedovsky, that his excellency would have to select another more complicated method of auditing the accounts than tears. Another nobleman jocosely described how footmen in stockings had been ordered for the marshal's ball, and how now they would have to be sent back unless the new marshal would give a ball with footmen in stockings.

Continually during dinner they said of Nevyedovsky: "Our marshal," and "your excellency."

This was said with the same pleasure with which a bride is called "Madame" and her husband's name. Nevyedovsky affected to be not merely indifferent but scornful of this appellation, but it was obvious that he was highly delighted, and had to keep a curb on himself not to betray the triumph which was unsuitable to their new liberal tone.

After dinner several telegrams were sent to people interested in the result of the election. And Stepan Arkadyevitch, who was in high good-humor, sent Darya Alexandrovna a telegram: "Nevyedovsky elected by twenty votes. Congratulations. Tell people." He dictated it aloud, saying: "We must let them share our rejoicing." Darya Alexandrovna, getting the message, simply sighed over the rouble wasted on it, and understood that it was an after-dinner affair. She knew Stiva had a weakness after dining for *faire jouer le télégraphe.*

Everything, together with the excellent dinner and the wine, not from Russian merchants, but imported direct from abroad, was extremely dignified, simple, and enjoyable. The party— some twenty—had been selected by Sviazhsky from among the more active new liberals, all of the same way of thinking, who were at the same time clever and well bred. They drank, also half in jest, to the health of the new marshal of the province, of the governor, of the bank director, and of "our amiable host."

Vronsky was satisfied. He had never expected to find so pleasant a tone in the provinces.

Towards the end of dinner it was still more lively. The governor asked Vronsky to come to a concert for the benefit of the Servians which his wife, who was anxious to make his acquaintance, had been getting up.

"There'll be a ball, and you'll see the belle of the province. Worth seeing, really."

"Not in my line," Vronsky answered. He liked that English phrase. But he smiled, and promised to come.

Before they rose from the table, when all of them were smoking, Vronsky's valet went up to him with a letter on a tray.

"From Vozdvizhenskoe by special messenger," he said with a significant expression.

"Astonishing! how like he is to the deputy prosecutor Sventitsky," said one of the guests in French of the valet, while Vronsky, frowning, read the letter.

The letter was from Anna. Before he read the letter, he knew its contents. Expecting the elections to be over in five days, he had promised to be back on Friday. To-day was Saturday, and he knew that the letter contained reproaches for not being back at the time fixed. The letter he had sent the previous evening had probably not reached her yet.

The letter was what he had expected, but the form of it was unexpected, and particularly disagreeable to him. "Annie is very ill, the doctor says it may be inflammation. I am losing my head all alone. Princess Varvara is no help, but a hindrance. I expected you the day before yesterday, and yesterday, and now I am sending to find out where you are and what are you doing. I wanted to come myself, but thought better of it, knowing you would dislike it. Send some answer, that I may know what to do."

The child ill, yet she had thought of coming herself. Their daughter ill, and this hostile tone.

The innocent festivities over the election, and this gloomy, burdensome love to which he had to return struck Vronsky by their contrast. But he had to go, and by the first train that night he set off home.

CHAPTER XXXII

BEFORE Vronsky's departure for the elections, Anna had reflected that the scenes constantly repeated between them each time he left home, might only make him cold to her instead of attaching him to her, and resolved to do all she could to control herself so as to bear the parting with composure. But the cold, severe glance with which he had looked at her when he came to tell her he was going had wounded her, and before he had started her peace of mind was destroyed.

In solitude afterwards, thinking over that glance which had expressed his right to freedom, she came as she always did, to the same point—the sense of her own humiliation. "He has the right to go away when and where he chooses. Not simply to go away, but to leave me. He has every right, and I have none. But knowing that, he ought not to do it. What has he done, though? . . . He looked at me with a cold, severe expression. Of course that is something indefinable, impalpable, but it has never been so before, and that glance means a great deal," she thought. "That glance shows the beginning of indifference."

And though she felt sure that a coldness was beginning, there was nothing she could do, she could not in any way alter her relations to him. Just as before, only by love and by charm could she keep him. And so, just as before, only by occupation in the day, by morphine at night, could she stifle the fearful thought of what would be if he ceased to love her. It is true there was still one means; not to keep him—for that she wanted nothing more than his love—but to be nearer to him, to be in such a position that he would not leave her. That means was divorce and marriage. And she began to long for that, and made up her mind to agree to it the first time he or Stiva approached her on the subject.

Absorbed in such thoughts, she passed five days without him, the five days that he was to be at the elections.

Walks, conversation with Princess Varvara, visits to the hospital, and, most of all, reading—reading of one book after another—filled up her time. But on the sixth day, when the coachman came back without him, she felt that now she was utterly incapable of stifling the thought of him and of what he was doing there, just at that time her little girl was taken ill. Anna began to look after her, but even that did not distract her mind, especially as the illness was not serious. However hard she tried, she could not love this little child, and to feign love was beyond her powers. Towards the evening of that day, still alone, Anna was in such a panic about him that she decided to start for the town, but on second thoughts wrote him the contradictory letter that Vronsky received, and without reading it through, sent it off by a special messenger. The next morning she received his letter and regretted her own. She dreaded a repetition of the severe look he had flung at her at parting, especially when he knew that the baby was not dangerously ill. But still she was glad she had written to him. At this moment Anna was positively admitting to herself that she was a burden to him, that he would relinquish his freedom regretfully to return to her, and in spite of that she was glad he was coming. Let him weary of her, but he would be here with her, so that she would see him, would know of every action he took.

She was sitting in the drawing-room near a lamp, with a new volume of Taine, and as she read, listening to the sound of the wind outside, and every minute expecting the carriage to arrive. Several times she had fancied she heard the sound of wheels, but she had been mistaken. At last she heard not the sound of wheels, but the coachman's shout and the dull rumble in the covered entry. Even Princess Varvara, playing patience, confirmed this, and Anna, flushing hotly, got up; but instead of going down, as she had done twice before, she stood still. She suddenly felt ashamed of her duplicity, but even more she dreaded how he might meet her. All feeling of wounded pride had passed now; she was only afraid of the expression of his displeasure. She remembered that her child had been perfectly well again for the last two days. She felt positively vexed with her for getting better from the very moment her letter was sent off. Then she thought of him, that he was here, all of him, with his hands, his eyes. She heard his voice. And forgetting everything, she ran joyfully to meet him.

"Well, how is Annie?" he said timidly from below, looking up to Anna as she ran down to him.

He was sitting on a chair, and a footman was pulling off his warm over-boot.

"Oh, she is better."

"And you?" he said, shaking himself.

She took his hand in both of hers, and drew it to her waist, never taking her eyes off him.

"Well, I'm glad," he said, coldly scanning her, her hair, her dress, which he knew she had put on for him. All was charming, but how many times it had charmed him! And the stern, stony expression that she so dreaded settled upon his face.

"Well, I'm glad. And are you well?" he said, wiping his damp beard with his handkerchief and kissing her hand.

"Never mind," she thought, "only let him be here, and so long as he's here he cannot, he dare not, cease to love me."

The evening was spent happily and gaily in the presence of Princess Varvara, who complained to him that Anna had been taking morphine in his absence.

"What am I to do? I couldn't sleep . . . My thoughts prevented me. When he's here I never take it—hardly ever."

He told her about the election, and Anna knew how by adroit questions to bring him to what gave him most pleasure—his own success. She told him of everything that interested him at home; and all that she told him was of the most cheerful description.

But late in the evening, when they were alone, Anna, seeing that she had regained complete possession of him, wanted to erase the painful impression of the glance he had given her for her letter. She said:

"Tell me frankly, you were vexed at getting my letter, and you didn't believe me?"

As soon as she had said it, she felt that however warm his feelings were to her, he had not forgiven her for that.

"Yes," he said, "the letter was so strange. First, Annie ill, and then you thought of coming yourself."

"It was all the truth."

"Oh, I don't doubt it."

"Yes, you do doubt it. You are vexed, I see."

"Not for one moment. I'm only vexed, that's true, that you seem somehow unwilling to admit that there are duties . . ."

"The duty of going to a concert . . ."

"But we won't talk about it," he said.

"Why not talk about it?" she said.

"I only meant to say that matters of real importance may turn up. Now, for instance, I shall have to go to Moscow to arrange about the house. . . . Oh, Anna, why are you so irritable? Don't you know that I can't live without you?"

"If so," said Anna, her voice suddenly changing, "it means that you are sick of this life . . . Yes, you will come for a day and go away, as men do . . ."

"Anna, that's cruel. I am ready to give up my whole life."

But she did not hear him.

"If you go to Moscow, I will go too. I will not stay here. Either we must separate or else live together."

"Why, you know, that's my one desire. But for that . . ."

"We must get a divorce. I will write to him. I see I cannot go on like this . . . But I will come with you to Moscow."

"You talk as if you were threatening me. But I desire nothing so much as never to be parted from you," said Vronsky, smiling.

But as he said these words there gleamed in his eyes not merely a cold look, but the vindictive look of a man persecuted and made cruel.

She saw the look and correctly divined its meaning.

"If so, it's a calamity!" that glance told her. It was a moment's impression, but she never forgot it.

Anna wrote to her husband asking him about a divorce, and towards the end of November, taking leave of Princess Varvara, who wanted to go to Petersburg, she went with Vronsky to Mos-

cow. Expecting every day an answer from Alexey Alexandrovitch, and after that the divorce, they now established themselves together like married people.

Part Seven

CHAPTER I

The Levins had been three months in Moscow. The date had long passed on which, according to the most trustworthy calculations of people learned in such matters, Kitty should have been confined. But she was still about, and there was nothing to show that her time was any nearer than two months ago. The doctor, the monthly nurse, and Dolly and her mother, and most of all Levin, who could not think of the approaching event without terror, began to be impatient and uneasy. Kitty was the only person who felt perfectly calm and happy.

She was distinctly conscious now of the birth of a new feeling of love for the future child, for her to some extent actually existing already, and she brooded blissfully over this feeling. He was not by now altogether a part of herself, but sometimes lived his own life independently of her. Often this separate being gave her pain, but at the same time she wanted to laugh with a strange new joy.

All the people she loved were with her, and all were so good to her, so attentively caring for her, so entirely pleasant was everything presented to her, that if she had not known and felt that it must all soon be over, she could not have wished for a better and pleasanter life. The only thing that spoiled the charm of this manner of life was that her husband was not here as she loved him to be, and as he was in the country.

She liked his serene, friendly, and hospitable manner in the country. In the town he seemed continually uneasy and on his guard, as though he were afraid some one would be rude to him, and still more to her. At home in the country, knowing himself distinctly to be in his right place, he was never in haste to be off elsewhere. He was never unoccupied. Here in town he was in a continual hurry, as though afraid of missing something, and yet he had nothing to do. And she felt sorry for him. To others, she knew, he did not appear an object of pity. On the contrary, when Kitty looked at him in society, as one sometimes looks at those one loves, trying to see him as if he were a stranger, so as to catch the impression he must make on others, she saw with a panic even of jealous fear that he was far indeed from being a pitiable figure, that he was very attractive with his fine breeding, his rather old-fashioned, reserved courtesy with women, his powerful figure, and striking, as she thought, and expressive face. But she saw him not from without, but from within; she saw that here he was not himself; that was the only way she could define his condition to herself. Sometimes she inwardly reproached him for his inability to live in the town; sometimes she recognized that it was really hard for him to order his life here so that he could be satisfied with it.

What had he to do, indeed? He did not care for cards; he did not go to a club. Spending the time with jovial gentlemen of Oblonsky's type—she knew now what that meant . . . it meant drinking and going somewhere after drinking. She could not think without horror of where men went on such occasions. Was he to go into society? But she knew he could only find satisfaction in that if he took pleasure in the society of young women, and that she could not wish for. Should he stay at home with her, her mother and her sisters? But much as she liked and enjoyed their conversations forever on the same subjects—"Aline-Nodine," as the old prince called the sisters' talks—she knew it must bore him. What was there left for him to do? To go on writing at his book he had indeed attempted, and at first he used to go to the library and make extracts and look up references for his book. But, as he told her, the more he did nothing, the less time he had to do anything. And besides, he complained that he had talked too much about his book here, and that consequently all his ideas about it were muddled and had lost their interest for him.

One advantage in this town life was that quarrels hardly ever happened between them here in town. Whether it was that their conditions were different, or that they had both become more careful and sensible in that respect, they had no quarrels in Moscow from jealousy, which they had so dreaded when they moved from the country.

One event, an event of great importance to both from that

point of view, did indeed happen—that was Kitty's meeting with Vronsky.

The old Princess Marya Borissovna, Kitty's godmother, who had always been very fond of her, had insisted on seeing her. Kitty, though she did not go into society at all on account of her condition, went with her father to see the venerable old lady, and there met Vronsky.

The only thing Kitty could reproach herself for at this meeting was that at the instant when she recognized in his civilian dress the features once so familiar to her, her breath failed her, the blood rushed to her heart, and a vivid blush—she felt it—overspread her face. But this lasted only a few seconds. Before her father, who purposely began talking in a loud voice to Vronsky, had finished, she was perfectly ready to look at Vronsky, to speak to him, if necessary, exactly as she spoke to Princess Marya Borissovna, and more than that, to do so in such a way that everything to the faintest intonation and smile would have been approved by her husband, whose unseen presence she seemed to feel about her at that instant.

She said a few words to him, even smiled serenely at his joke about the elections, which he called "our parliament." (She had to smile to show she saw the joke.) But she turned away immediately to Princess Marya Borissovna, and did not once glance at him till he got up to go; then she looked at him, but evidently only because it would be uncivil not to look at a man when he is saying good-bye.

She was grateful to her father for saying nothing to her about their meeting Vronsky, but she saw by his special warmth to her after the visit during their usual walk that he was pleased with her. She was pleased with herself. She had not expected she would have had the power, while keeping somewhere in the bottom of her heart all the memories of her old feeling for Vronsky, not only to seem but to be perfectly indifferent and composed with him.

Levin flushed a great deal more than she when she told him she had met Vronsky at Princess Marya Borissovna's. It was very hard for her to tell him this, but still harder to go on speaking of the details of the meeting, as he did not question her, but simply gazed at her with a frown.

"I am very sorry you weren't there," she said. "Not that you weren't in the room . . . I couldn't have been so natural in your presence . . . I am blushing now much more, much, much more," she said, blushing till the tears came into her eyes. "But that you couldn't see through a crack."

The truthful eyes told Levin that she was satisfied with herself, and in spite of her blushing he was quickly reassured and began questioning her, which was all she wanted. When he had heard everything, even to the detail that for the first second she could not help flushing, but that afterwards she was just as direct and as much at her ease as with any chance acquaintance, Levin was quite happy again and said he was glad of it, and would not now behave as stupidly as he had done at the election, but would try the first time he met Vronsky to be as friendly as possible.

"It's so wretched to feel that there's a man almost an enemy whom it's painful to meet," said Levin. "I'm very, very glad."

CHAPTER II

"Do, PLEASE, go then and call on the Bols," Kitty said to her husband, when he came in to see her at eleven o'clock before going out. "I know you are dining at the club; papa put down your name. But what are you going to do in the morning?"

"I am only going to Katavasov," answered Levin.

"Why so early?"

"He promised to introduce me to Metrov. I wanted to talk to him about my work. He's a distinguished scientific man from Petersburg," said Levin.

"Yes; wasn't it his article you were praising so? Well, and after that?" said Kitty.

"I shall go to the court, perhaps, about my sister's business."

"And the concert?" she queried.

"I shan't go there all alone."

"No? do go; there are going to be some new things. . . . That interested you so. I should certainly go."

"Well, anyway, I shall come home before dinner," he said, looking at his watch.

"Put on your frock-coat, so that you can go straight to call on Countess Bola."

"But is it absolutely necessary?"

"Oh, absolutely! He has been to see us. Come, what is it? You go in, sit down, talk for five minutes of the weather, get up and go away."

"Oh, you wouldn't believe it! I've got so out of the way of all this that it makes me feel positively ashamed. It's such a horrible thing to do! A complete outsider walks in, sits down, stays on with nothing to do, wastes their time and worries himself, and walks away!"

Kitty laughed.

"Why, I suppose you used to pay calls before you were married, didn't you?"

"Yes, I did, but I always felt ashamed, and now I'm so out of the way of it that, by Jove! I'd sooner go two days running without my dinner than pay this call! One's so ashamed! I feel all the while that they're annoyed, that they're saying, 'What has he come for?'"

"No, they won't. I'll answer for that," said Kitty, looking into his face with a laugh. She took his hand. "Well, good-bye. . . . Do go, please."

He was just going out after kissing his wife's hand, when she stopped him.

"Kostya, do you know I've only fifty roubles left?"

"Oh, all right, I'll go to the bank and get some. How much?" he said, with the expression of dissatisfaction she knew so well.

"No, wait a minute." She held his hand. "Let's talk about it, it worries me. I seem to spend nothing unnecessary, but money seems to fly away simply. We don't manage well, somehow."

"Oh, it's all right," he said with a little cough, looking at her from under his brows.

That cough she knew well. It was a sign of intense dissatisfaction, not with her, but with himself. He certainly was displeased not at so much money being spent, but at being reminded of what he, knowing something was unsatisfactory, wanted to forget.

"I have told Sokolov to sell the wheat, and to borrow an advance on the mill. We shall have money enough in any case."

"Yes, but I'm afraid that altogether . . ."

"Oh, it's all right, all right," he repeated. "Well, good-bye, darling."

"No, I'm really sorry sometimes that I listened to mamma. How nice it would have been in the country! As it is, I'm worrying you all, and we're wasting our money."

"Not at all, not at all. Not once since I've been married have I said that things could have been better than they are. . . ."

"Truly?" she said, looking into his eyes.

He had said it without thinking, simply to console her. But when he glanced at her and saw those sweet truthful eyes fastened questioningly on him, he repeated it with his whole heart. "I was positively forgetting her," he thought. And he remembered what was before them, so soon to come.

"Will it be soon? How do you feel?" he whispered, taking her two hands.

"I have so often thought so, that now I don't think about it or know anything about it."

"And you're not frightened?"

She smiled contemptuously.

"Not the least little bit," she said.

"Well, if anything happens, I shall be at Katavasov's."

"No, nothing will happen, and don't think about it. I'm going for a walk on the boulevard with papa. We're going to see Dolly. I shall expect you before dinner. Oh, yes! Do you know that Dolly's position is becoming utterly impossible? She's in debt all round; she hasn't a penny. We were talking yesterday with mamma and Arseny" (this was her sister's husband Lvov), "and we determined to send you with him to talk to Stiva. It's really unbearable. One can't speak to papa about it . . . But if you and he . . ."

"Why, what can we do?" said Levin.

"You'll be at Arseny's, anyway; talk to him, he will tell what we decided."

"Oh, I agree to everything Arseny thinks beforehand. I'll go and see him. By the way, if I do go to the concert, I'll go with Natalia. Well, good-bye."

On the steps Levin was stopped by his old servant Kouzma,

who had been with him before his marriage, and now looked after their household in town.

"Beauty" (that was the left shaft-horse brought up from the country) "has been badly shod and is quite lame," he said. "What does your honor wish to be done?"

During the first part of their stay in Moscow, Levin had used his own horses brought up from the country. He had tried to arrange this part of their expenses in the best and cheapest way possible; but it appeared that their own horses came dearer than hired horses, and they still hired too.

"Send for the veterinary, there may be a bruise."

"And for Katerina Alexandrovna?" asked Kouzma.

Levin was not by now struck as he had been at first by the fact that to get from one end of Moscow to the other he had to have two powerful horses put into a heavy carriage, to take the carriage three miles through the snowy slush and to keep it standing there four hours, paying five roubles every time.

Now it seemed quite natural.

"Hire a pair for our carriage from the jobmaster," said he.

"Yes, sir."

And so, simply and easily, thanks to the facilities of town life, Levin settled a question which, in the country, would have called for so much personal trouble and exertion, and going out onto the steps, he called a sledge, sat down, and drove to Nikitsky. On the way he thought no more of money, but mused on the introduction that awaited him to the Petersburg savant, a writer on sociology, and what he would say to him about his book.

Only during the first days of his stay in Moscow Levin had been struck by the expenditure, strange to one living in the country, unproductive but inevitable, that was expected of him on every side. But by now he had grown used to it. That had happened to him in this matter which is said to happen to drunkards—the first glass sticks in the throat, the second flies down like a hawk, but after the third they're like tiny little birds. When Levin had changed his first hundred-rouble note to pay for liveries for his footmen and hall-porter he could not help reflecting that these liveries were of no use to any one—but they were indubitably necessary, to judge by the amazement of the princess and Kitty when he suggested that they might do without liveries,—that these liveries would cost the wages of two laborers for the summer, that is, would pay for about three hundred working days from Easter to Ash Wednesday, and each a day of hard work from early morning to late evening—and that hundred-rouble note did stick in his throat. But the next note, changed to pay for providing a dinner for their relations, that cost twenty-eight roubles, though it did excite in Levin the reflection that twenty-eight roubles meant nine measures of oats, which men would with groans and sweat have reaped and bound and thrashed and winnowed and sifted and sown,—this next one he parted with more easily. And now the notes he changed no longer aroused such reflections, and they flew off like little birds. Whether the labor devoted to obtaining the money corresponded to the pleasure given by what was bought with it, was a consideration he had long ago dismissed. His business calculation that there was a certain price below which he could not sell certain grain was forgotten too. The rye, for the price of which he had so long held out, had been sold for fifty kopecks a measure cheaper than it had been fetching a month ago. Even the consideration that with such an expenditure he could not go on living for a year without debt, that even had no force. Only one thing was essential: to have money in the bank, without inquiring where it came from, so as to know that one had the wherewithal to buy meat for to-morrow. And this condition had hitherto been fulfilled; he had always had the money in the bank. But now the money in the bank had gone, and he could not quite tell where to get the next installment. And this it was which, at the moment when Kitty had mentioned money, had disturbed him; but he had no time to think about it. He drove off, thinking of Katavasov and the meeting with Metrov that was before him.

CHAPTER III

Levin had on this visit to town seen a great deal of his old friend at the university, Professor Katavasov, whom he had not seen since his marriage. He liked in Katavasov the clearness and simplicity of his conception of life. Levin thought that the clearness of Katavasov's conception of life was due to the poverty of his nature; Katavasov thought that the disconnectedness of Levin's ideas was due to his lack of intellectual discipline; but Levin enjoyed Katavasov's clearness, and Katavasov enjoyed the abundance of Levin's untrained ideas, and they liked to meet and to discuss.

Levin had read Katavasov some parts of his book, and he had liked them. On the previous day Katavasov had met Levin at a public lecture and told him that the celebrated Metrov, whose article Levin had so much liked, was in Moscow, that he had been much interested by what Katavasov had told him about Levin's work, and that he was coming to see him to-morrow at eleven, and would be very glad to make Levin's acquaintance.

"You're positively a reformed character, I'm glad to see," said Katavasov, meeting Levin in the little drawing-room. "I heard the bell and thought: Impossible that it can be he at the exact time! . . . Well, what do you say to the Montenegrins now? They're a race of warriors."

"Why, what's happened?" asked Levin.

Katavasov in a few words told him the last piece of news from the war, and going into his study, introduced Levin to a short, thick-set man of pleasant appearance. This was Metrov. The conversation touched for a brief space on politics and on how recent events were looked at in the higher spheres in Petersburg. Metrov repeated a saying that had reached him through a most trustworthy source, reported as having been uttered on this subject by the Tsar and one of the ministers. Katavasov had heard also on excellent authority that the Tsar had said something quite different. Levin tried to imagine circumstances in which both sayings might have been uttered, and the conversation on that topic dropped.

"Yes, here he's written almost a book on the natural conditions of the laborer in relation to the land," said Katavasov; "I'm not a specialist, but I, as a natural science man, was pleased at his not taking mankind as something outside biological laws; but, on the contrary, seeing his dependence on his surroundings, and in that dependence seeking the laws of his development."

"That's very interesting," said Metrov.

"What I began precisely was to write a book on agriculture; but studying the chief instrument of agriculture, the laborer," said Levin, reddening, "I could not help coming to quite unexpected results."

And Levin began carefully, as it were, feeling his ground, to expound his views. He knew Metrov had written an article against the generally accepted theory of political economy, but to what extent he could reckon on his sympathy with his own new views he did not know and could not guess from the clever and serene face of the learned man.

"But in what do you see the special characteristics of the Russian laborer?" said Metrov; "in his biological characteristics, so to speak, or in the condition in which he is placed?"

Levin saw that there was an idea underlying this question with which he did not agree. But he went on explaining his own idea that the Russian laborer has a quite special view of the land, different from that of other people; and to support this proposition he made haste to add that in his opinion this attitude of the Russian peasant was due to the consciousness of his vocation to people vast unoccupied expanses in the East.

"One may easily be led into error in basing any conclusion on the general vocation of a people," said Metrov, interrupting Levin. "The condition of the laborer will always depend on his relation to the land and to capital."

And without letting Levin finish explaining his idea, Metrov began expounding to him the special point of his own theory.

In what the point of his theory lay, Levin did not understand, because he did not take the trouble to understand. He saw that Metrov, like other people, in spite of his own article, in which he had attacked the current theory of political economy, looked at the position of the Russian peasant simply from the point of view of capital, wages, and rent. He would indeed have been obliged to admit that in the eastern—much the larger—part of Russia rent was as yet *nil,* that for nine-tenths of the eighty millions of the Russian peasants wages took the form simply of food provided for themselves, and that capital does not so far exist except in the form of the most primitive tools. Yet it was only from that point of view that he considered every laborer, though in many points he differed from the economists and had his own theory of the wage-fund, which he expounded to Levin.

Levin listened reluctantly, and at first made objections. He would have liked to interrupt Metrov, to explain his own thought, which in his opinion would have rendered further exposition of Metrov's theories superfluous. But later on, feeling convinced that they looked at the matter so differently, that they could never understand one another, he did not even oppose his statements, but simply listened. Although what Metrov was saying was by now utterly devoid of interest for him, he yet experienced a certain satisfaction in listening to him. It flattered his vanity that such a learned man should explain his ideas to him so eagerly, with such intensity and confidence in Levin's understanding of the subject, sometimes with a mere hint referring him to a whole aspect of the subject. He put this down to his own credit, unaware that Metrov, who had already discussed his theory over and over again with all his intimate friends, talked of it with special eagerness to every new person, and in general was eager to talk to any one of any subject that interested him, even if still obscure to himself.

"We are late though," said Katavasov, looking at his watch directly Metrov had finished his discourse.

"Yes, there's a meeting of the Society of Amateurs to-day in commemoration of the jubilee of Svintitch," said Katavasov in answer to Levin's inquiry. "Pyotr Ivanovitch and I were going. I've promised to deliver an address on his labors in zoology. Come along with us, it's very interesting."

"Yes, and indeed it's time to start," said Metrov. "Come with us, and from there, if you care to, come to my place. I should very much like to hear your work."

"Oh, no! It's no good yet, it's unfinished. But I shall be very glad to go to the meeting."

"I say, friends, have you heard? He has handed in the separate report," Katavasov called from the other room, where he was putting on his frock-coat.

And a conversation sprang up upon the university question, which was a very important event that winter in Moscow. Three old professors in the council had not accepted the opinion of the younger professors. The young ones had registered a separate resolution. This, in the judgment of some people, was monstrous, in the judgment of others it was the simplest and most just thing to do, and the professors were split up into two parties.

One party, to which Katavasov belonged, saw in the opposite party a scoundrelly betrayal and treachery, while the opposite party saw in them childishness and lack of respect for the authorities. Levin, though he did not belong to the university, had several times already during his stay in Moscow heard and talked about this matter, and had his own opinion on the subject. He took part in the conversation that was continued in the street, as they all three walked to the buildings of the old university.

The meeting had already begun. Round the cloth-covered table, at which Katavasov and Metrov seated themselves, there

were some half-dozen persons, and one of these was bending close over a manuscript, reading something aloud. Levin sat down in one of the empty chairs that were standing round the table, and in a whisper asked a student sitting near what was being read. The student, eyeing Levin with displeasure, said:

"Biography."

Though Levin was not interested in the biography, he could not help listening, and learned some new and interesting facts about the life of the distinguished man of science.

When the reader had finished, the chairman thanked him and read some verses of the poet Ment sent him on the jubilee, and said a few words by way of thanks to the poet. Then Katavasov in his loud, ringing voice read his address on the scientific labors of the man whose jubilee was being kept.

When Katavasov had finished, Levin looked at his watch, saw it was past one, and thought that there would not be time before the concert to read Metrov his book, and indeed, he did not now care to do so. During the reading he had thought over their conversation. He saw distinctly now that though Metrov's ideas might perhaps have value, his own ideas had a value too, and their ideas could only be made clear and lead to something if each worked separately in his chosen path, and that nothing would be gained by putting their ideas together. And having made up his mind to refuse Metrov's invitation, Levin went up to him at the end of the meeting. Metrov introduced Levin to the chairman, with whom he was talking of the political news. Metrov told the chairman what he had already told Levin, and Levin made the same remarks on his news that he had already made that morning, but for the sake of variety he expressed also a new opinion which had only just struck him. After that the conversation turned again on the university question. As Levin had already heard it all, he made haste to tell Metrov that he was sorry he could not take advantage of his invitation, took leave, and drove to Lvov's.

CHAPTER IV

Lvov, the husband of Natalia, Kitty's sister, had spent all his life in foreign capitals, where he had been educated, and had been in the diplomatic service.

During the previous year he had left the diplomatic service, not owing to any "unpleasantness" (he never had any "unpleasantness" with any one), and was transferred to the department of the court of the palace in Moscow, in order to give his two boys the best education possible.

In spite of the striking contrast in their habits and views and the fact that Lvov was older than Levin, they had seen a great deal of one another that winter, and had taken a great liking to each other.

Lvov was at home, and Levin went in to him unannounced.

Lvov, in a house coat with a belt and in chamois leather shoes, was sitting in an armchair, and with a pince-nez with blue glasses he was reading a book that stood on a reading-desk, while in his beautiful hand he held a half-burned cigarette daintily away from him.

His handsome, delicate, and still youthful-looking face, to which his curly, glistening silvery hair gave a still more aristocratic air, lighted up with a smile when he saw Levin.

"Capital! I was meaning to send to you. How's Kitty? Sit here, it's more comfortable." He got up and pushed up a rocking-chair. "Have you read the last circular in the *Journal de St. Pétersburg?* I think it's excellent," he said with a slight French accent.

Levin told him what he had heard from Katavasov was being said in Petersburg, and after talking a little about politics, he told him of his interview with Metrov, and the learned society's meeting. To Lvov it was very interesting.

"That's what I envy you, that you are able to mix in these interesting scientific circles," he said. And as he talked, he passed as usual into French, which was easier to him. "It's true I haven't the time for it. My official work and the children leave me no time; and then I'm not ashamed to own that my education has been too defective."

"That I don't believe," said Levin with a smile, feeling, as he always did, touched at Lvov's low opinion of himself, which was not in the least put on from a desire to seem or to be modest, but was absolutely sincere.

"Oh, yes, indeed! I feel now how badly educated I am. To educate my children I positively have to look up a great deal, and in fact simply to study myself. For it's not enough to have teachers, there must be some one to look after them, just as on your land you want laborers and an overseer. See what I'm reading"—he pointed to Buslaev's *Grammar* on the desk—"it's expected of Misha, and it's so difficult . . . Come, explain to me . . . Here he says . . ."

Levin tried to explain to him that it couldn't be understood, but that it had to be taught; but Lvov would not agree with him.

"Oh, you're laughing at it!"

"On the contrary, you can't imagine how, when I look at you, I'm always learning the task that lies before me, that is the education of one's children."

"Well, there's nothing for you to learn," said Lvov.

"All I know," said Levin, "is that I have never seen better brought-up children than yours, and I wouldn't wish for children better than yours."

Lvov visibly tried to restrain the expression of his delight, but he was positively radiant with smiles.

"If only they're better than I! That's all I desire. You don't know yet all the work," he said, "with boys who've been left like mine to run wild abroad."

"You'll catch all that up. They're such clever children. The great thing is the education of character. That's what I learn when I look at your children."

"You talk of the education of character. You can't imagine how difficult that is! You have hardly succeeded in combating one tendency when others crop up, and the struggle begins again. If one had not a support in religion—you remember we talked about that—no father could bring children up relying on his own strength alone without that help."

This subject, which always interested Levin, was cut short by the entrance of the beauty Natalia Alexandrovna, dressed to go out.

"I didn't know you were here," she said, unmistakably feeling no regret, but a positive pleasure, in interrupting this conversation on a topic she had heard so much of that she was by now weary of it. "Well, how is Kitty? I am dining with you to-day. I tell you what, Arseny," she turned to her husband, "you take the carriage."

And the husband and wife began to discuss their arrangements for the day. As the husband had to drive to meet some one on official business, while the wife had to go to the concert and some public meeting of a committee on the Eastern Question, there was a great deal to consider and settle. Levin had to take part in their plans as one of themselves. It was settled that Levin should go with Natalia to the concert and the meeting, and that from there they should send the carriage to the office for Arseny, and he should call for her and take her to Kitty's; or that, if he had not finished his work, he should send the carriage back and Levin would go with her.

"He's spoiling me," Lvov said to his wife: "he assures me that our children are splendid, when I know how much that's bad there is in them."

"Arseny goes to extremes, I always say," said his wife. "If you look for perfection, you will never be satisfied. And it's true, as papa says,—that when we were brought up there was one extreme—we were kept in the basement, while our parents lived in the best rooms; now it's just the other way—the parents are in the wash-house, while the children are in the best rooms. Parents now are not expected to live at all, but to exist altogether for their children."

"Well, what if they like it better?" Lvov said, with his beautiful smile, touching her hand. "Any one who didn't know you would think you were a stepmother, not a true mother."

"No, extremes are not good in anything," Natalia said serenely, putting his paper-knife straight in its proper place on the table.

"Well, come here, you perfect children," Lvov said to the two handsome boys who came in, and after bowing to Levin, went up to their father, obviously wishing to ask him about something.

Levin would have liked to talk to them, to hear what they would say to their father, but Natalia began talking to him, and then Lvov's colleague in the service, Mahotin, walked in, wearing his court uniform, to go with him to meet some one, and a conversation was kept up without a break upon Herzegovina, Princess Korzinskaya, the town council, and the sudden death of Madame Apraksina.

Levin even forgot the commission intrusted to him. He recollected it as he was going into the hall.

"Oh, Kitty told me to talk to you about Oblonsky," he said, as Lvov was standing on the stairs, seeing his wife and Levin off.

"Yes, yes, maman wants us, *les beaux-frères,* to attack him," he said, blushing. "But why should I?"

"Well, then, I will attack him," said Madame Lvova, with a smile, standing in her white sheepskin cape, waiting till they had finished speaking. "Come, let us go."

CHAPTER V

AT THE concert in the afternoon two very interesting things were performed. One was a fantasia, *King Lear;* the other was a quartette dedicated to the memory of Bach. Both were new and in the new style, and Levin was eager to form an opinion of them. After escorting his sister-in-law to her stall, he stood against a column and tried to listen as attentively and conscientiously as possible. He tried not to let his attention be distracted, and not to spoil his impression by looking at the conductor in a white tie, waving his arms, which always disturbed his enjoyment of music so much, or the ladies in bonnets, with strings carefully tied over their ears, and all these people either thinking of nothing at all or thinking of all sorts of things except the music. He tried to avoid meeting musical connoisseurs or talkative acquaintances, and stood looking at the floor straight before him, listening.

But the more he listened to the fantasia of *King Lear* the further he felt from forming any definite opinion of it. There was, as it were, a continual beginning, a preparation of the musical expression of some feeling, but it fell to pieces again directly, breaking into new musical motives, or simply nothing but the whims of the composer, exceedingly complex but disconnected sounds. And these fragmentary musical expressions, though sometimes beautiful, were disagreeable, because they were utterly unexpected and not led up to by anything. Gaiety and grief and despair and tenderness and triumph followed one another without any connection, like the emotions of a madman. And those emotions, like a madman's, sprang up quite unexpectedly.

During the whole of the performance Levin felt like a deaf man watching people dancing, and was in a state of complete bewilderment when the fantasia was over, and felt a great weariness from the fruitless strain on his attention. Loud applause resounded on all sides. Every one got up, moved about, and began talking. Anxious to throw some light on his own perplexity from the impressions of others, Levin began to walk about, looking for connoisseurs, and was glad to see a well-known musical amateur in conversation with Pestsov, whom he knew.

"Marvelous!" Pestsov was saying in his mellow bass. "How are you, Konstantin Dmitrievitch? Particularly sculpturesque and plastic, so to say, and richly colored is that passage where you feel Cordelia's approach, where woman, *das ewig Weibliche,* enters into conflict with fate. Isn't it?"

"You mean . . . what has Cordelia to do with it?" Levin asked timidly, forgetting that the fantasia was supposed to represent King Lear.

"Cordelia comes in . . . see here!" said Pestsov, tapping his finger on the satiny surface of the program he held in his hand and passing it to Levin.

Only then Levin recollected the title of the fantasia, and made haste to read in the Russian translation the lines from Shakespeare that were printed on the back of the program.

"You can't follow it without that," said Pestsov, addressing Levin, as the person he had been speaking to had gone away, and he had no one to talk to.

In the *entr'acte* Levin and Pestsov fell into an argument upon the merits and defects of music of the Wagner school. Levin maintained that the mistake of Wagner and all his followers lay in their trying to take music into the sphere of another art, just as poetry goes wrong when it tries to paint a face as the art of painting ought to do, and as an instance of this mistake he cited the sculptor who carved in marble certain poetic phantasms flitting round the figure of the poet on the pedestal. "These phantoms were so far from being phantoms that they were positively clinging on the ladder," said Levin. The comparison pleased him, but he could not remember whether he had not used the same phrase before, and to Pestsov, too, and as he said it he felt confused.

Pestsov maintained that art is one, and that it can attain its highest manifestations only by conjunction with all kinds of art.

The second piece that was performed Levin could not hear.

Pestsov, who was standing beside him, was talking to him almost all the time, condemning the music for its excessive affected assumption of simplicity, and comparing it with the simplicity of the Pre-Raphaelites in painting. As he went out Levin met many more acquaintances, with whom he talked of politics, of music, and of common acquaintances. Among others he met Count Bol, whom he had utterly forgotten to call upon.

"Well, go at once then," Madame Lvova said, when he told her; "perhaps they'll not be at home, and then you can come to the meeting to fetch me. You'll find me still there."

CHAPTER VI

"PERHAPS they're not at home?" said Levin, as he went into the hall of Countess Bola's house.

"At home; please walk in," said the porter, resolutely removing his overcoat.

"How annoying!" thought Levin with a sigh, taking off one glove and stroking his hat. "What did I come for? What have I to say to them?"

As he passed through the first drawing-room Levin met in the doorway Countess Bola, giving some order to a servant with a care-worn and severe face. On seeing Levin she smiled, and asked him to come into the little drawing-room, where he heard voices. In this room there were sitting in armchairs the two daughters of the countess, and a Moscow colonel, whom Levin knew. Levin went up, greeted them, and sat down beside the sofa with his hat on his knees.

"How is your wife? Have you been at the concert? We couldn't go. Mamma had to be at the funeral service."

"Yes, I heard . . . What a sudden death!" said Levin.

The countess came in, sat down on the sofa, and she too asked after his wife and inquired about the concert.

Levin answered, and repeated an inquiry about Madame Apraksina's sudden death.

"But she was always in weak health."

"Were you at the opera yesterday?"

"Yes, I was."

"Lucca was very good."

"Yes, very good," he said, and as it was utterly of no consequence to him what they thought of him, he began repeating what they had heard a hundred times about the characteristics of the singer's talent. Countess Bol pretended to be listening. Then, when he had said enough and paused, the colonel, who had been silent till then, began to talk. The colonel too talked of the opera, and about culture. At last, after speaking of the proposed *folle journée* at Turin's, the colonel laughed, got up noisily, and went away. Levin too rose, but he saw by the face of the countess that it was not yet time for him to go. He must stay two minutes longer. He sat down.

But as he was thinking all the while how stupid it was, he could not find a subject for conversation, and sat silent.

"You are not going to the public meeting? They say it will be very interesting," began the countess.

"No, I promised my *belle-sœur* to fetch her from it," said Levin.

A silence followed. The mother once more exchanged glances with a daughter.

"Well, now I think the time has come," thought Levin, and he got up. The ladies shook hands with him, and begged him to say *mille choses* to his wife for them.

The porter asked him, as he gave him his coat, "Where is your honor staying?" and immediately wrote down his address in a big handsomely-bound book.

"Of course I don't care, but still I feel ashamed and awfully stupid," thought Levin, consoling himself with the reflection that every one does it. He drove to the public meeting, where he was to find his sister-in-law, so as to drive home with her.

At the public meeting of the committee there were a great many people, and almost all the highest society. Levin was in time for the report which, as every one said, was very interesting. When the reading of the report was over, people moved about, and Levin met Sviazhsky, who invited him very pressingly to come that evening to a meeting of the Society of Agriculture, where a celebrated lecture was to be delivered, and Stepan Arkadyevitch, who had only just come from the races, and many other acquaintances; and Levin heard and uttered various criticisms on the meeting, on the new fantasia, and on a public trial. But, probably from the mental fatigue he was beginning to feel, he made a blunder in speaking of the trial, and this blunder he recalled several times with vexation. Speaking of the sentence upon a foreigner who had been condemned in Russia, and of how unfair it would be to punish him by exile abroad, Levin repeated what he had heard the day before in conversation from an acquaintance.

"I think sending him abroad is much the same as punishing a carp by putting it into the water," said Levin. Then he recollected that this idea, which he had heard from an acquaintance and uttered as his own, came from a fable of Krilov's, and that the acquaintance had picked it up from a newspaper article.

After driving home with his sister-in-law, and finding Kitty in good spirits and quite well, Levin drove to the club.

CHAPTER VII

Levin reached the club just at the right time. Members and visitors were driving up as he arrived. Levin had not been at the club for a very long while—not since he lived in Moscow, when he was leaving the university and going into society. He remembered the club, the external details of its arrangement, but he had completely forgotten the impression it had made on him in old days. But as soon as, driving into the wide semicircular court and getting out of the sledge, he mounted the steps, and the hall-porter, adorned with a crossway scarf, noiselessly opened the door to him with a bow; as soon as he saw in the porter's room the cloaks and goloshes of members who thought it less trouble to take them off downstairs; as soon as he heard the mysterious ringing bell that preceded him as he ascended the easy, carpeted staircase, and saw the statue on the landing, and the third porter at the top doors, a familiar figure grown older, in the club livery, opening the door without haste or delay, and scanning the visitors as they passed in—Levin felt the old impression of the club come back in a rush, an impression of repose, comfort, and propriety.

"Your hat, please," the porter said to Levin, who forgot the club rule to leave his hat in the porter's room. "Long time since you've been. The prince put your name down yesterday. Prince Stepan Arkadyevitch is not here yet."

The porter did not only know Levin, but also all his ties and relationships, and so immediately mentioned his intimate friends.

Passing through the outer hall, divided up by screens, and the room partitioned on the right, where a man sits at the fruit-buffet, Levin overtook an old man walking slowly in, and entered the dining-room full of noise and people.

He walked along the tables, almost all full, and looked at the visitors. He saw people of all sorts, old and young; some he knew a little, some intimate friends. There was not a single cross or worried-looking face. All seemed to have left their cares and anxieties in the porter's room with their hats, and were all deliberately getting ready to enjoy the material blessings of life. Sviazhsky was here and Shtcherbatsky, Nevyedovsky and the old prince, and Vronsky and Sergey Ivanovitch.

"Ah! why are you late?" the prince said smiling, and giving him his hand over his own shoulder. "How's Kitty?" he added, smoothing out the napkin he had tucked in at his waistcoat buttons.

"All right; they are dining at home, all the three of them."

"Ah, 'Aline-Nadine,' to be sure! There's no room with us. Go to that table, and make haste and take a seat," said the prince, and turning away he carefully took a plate of eel soup.

"Levin, this way!" a good-natured voice shouted a little further on. It was Turovtsin. He was sitting with a young officer, and beside them were two chairs turned upside down. Levin gladly went up to them. He had always liked the good-hearted rake, Turovtsin—he was associated in his mind with memories of his courtship—and at that moment, after the strain of intellectual conversation, the sight of Turovtsin's good-natured face was particularly welcome.

"For you and Oblonsky. He'll be here directly."

The young man, holding himself very erect, with eyes forever twinkling with enjoyment, was an officer from Petersburg, Gagin. Turovtsin introduced them.

"Oblonsky's always late."

"Ah, here he is!"

"Have you only just come?" said Oblonsky, coming quickly towards them. "Good-day. Had some vodka? Well, come along then."

Levin got up and went with him to the big table spread with spirits and appetizers of the most various kinds. One would have thought that out of two dozen delicacies one might find something to one's taste, but Stepan Arkadyevitch asked for something special, and one of the liveried waiters standing by immediately brought what was required. They drank a wineglassful and returned to their table.

At once, while they were still at the soup, Gagin was served with champagne, and told the waiter to fill four glasses. Levin did not refuse the wine, and asked for a second bottle. He was very hungry, and ate and drank with great enjoyment, and with still greater enjoyment took part in the lively and simple conversation of his companions. Gagin, dropping his voice, told the last good story from Petersburg, and the story, though improper and stupid, was so ludicrous that Levin broke into roars of laughter so loud that those near looked round.

"That's in the same style as, 'that's a thing I can't endure!' You know the story?" said Stepan Arkadyevitch. "Ah, that's exquisite! Another bottle," he said to the waiter, and he began to relate his good story.

"Pyotr Illyitch Vinovsky invites you to drink with him," a little old waiter interrupted Stepan Arkadyevitch, bringing two delicate glasses of sparkling champagne, and addressing Stepan Arkadyevitch and Levin. Stepan Arkadyevitch took the glass, and looking towards a bald man with red mustaches at the other end of the table, he nodded to him, smiling.

"Who's that?" asked Levin.

"You met him once at my place, don't you remember? A good-natured fellow."

Levin did the same as Stepan Arkadyevitch and took the glass.

Stepan Arkadyevitch's anecdote too was very amusing. Levin told his story, and that too was successful. Then they talked of horses, of the races, of what they had been doing that day, and of how smartly Vronsky's Atlas had won the first prize. Levin did not notice how the time passed at dinner.

"Ah! and here they are!" Stepan Arkadyevitch said towards the end of dinner, leaning over the back of his chair and holding out his hand to Vronsky, who came up with a tall officer of the Guards. Vronsky's face too beamed with the look of good-humored enjoyment that was general in the club. He propped his elbow playfully on Stepan Arkadyevitch's shoulder, whispering something to him, and he held out his hand to Levin with the same good-humored smile.

"Very glad to meet you," he said. "I looked out for you at the election, but I was told you had gone away."

"Yes, I left the same day. We've just been talking of your horse. I congratulate you," said Levin. "It was very rapidly run."

"Yes; you've race-horses too, haven't you?"

"No, my father had; but I remember and know something about it."

"Where have you dined?" asked Stepan Arkadyevitch.

"We were at the second table, behind the columns."

"We've been celebrating his success," said the tall colonel. "It's his second Imperial prize. I wish I might have the luck at cards he has with horses. Well, why waste the precious time? I'm going to the 'infernal regions,'" added the colonel, and he walked away.

"That's Yashvin," Vronsky said in answer to Turovtsin, and he sat down in the vacated seat beside them. He drank the glass offered him, and ordered a bottle of wine. Under the influence of the club atmosphere or the wine he had drunk, Levin chatted away to Vronsky of the best breeds of cattle, and was very glad not to feel the slightest hostility to this man. He even told him, among other things, that he had heard from his wife that she had met him at Princess Marya Borissovna's.

"Ah, Princess Marya Borissovna, she's exquisite!" said Stepan Arkadyevitch, and he told an anecdote about her which set them all laughing. Vronsky particularly laughed with such simple-hearted amusement that Levin felt quite reconciled to him.

"Well, have we finished?" said Stepan Arkadyevitch, getting up with a smile. "Let us go."

CHAPTER VIII

GETTING up from the table, Levin walked with Gagin through the lofty room to the billiard-room, feeling his arms swing as he walked with a peculiar lightness and ease. As he crossed the big room, he came upon his father-in-law.

"Well, how do you like our Temple of Indolence?" said the prince, taking his arm. "Come along, come along!"

"Yes, I wanted to walk about and look at everything. It's interesting."

"Yes, it's interesting for you. But its interest for me is quite different. You look at those little old men now," he said, pointing to a club member with bent back and projecting lip, shuffling towards them in his soft boots, "and imagine that they were *shlupiks* like that from their birth up."

"How *shlupiks?*"

"I see you don't know that name. That's our club designation. You know the game of rolling eggs: when one's rolled a long while it becomes a *shlupik*. So it is with us; one goes on coming and coming to the club, and ends by becoming a *shlupik*. Ah, you laugh! but we look out, for fear of dropping into it ourselves. You know Prince Tchetchensky?" inquired the prince; and Levin saw by his face that he was just going to relate something funny.

"No, I don't know him."

"You don't say so! Well, Prince Tchetchensky is a well-known figure. No matter, though. He's always playing billiards here. Only three years ago he was not a *shlupik* and kept up his spirits and even used to call other people *shlupiks*. But one day he turns up, and our porter . . . you know Vassily? Why, that fat one; he's famous for his *bon mots*. And so Prince Tchetchensky asks him, 'Come, Vassily, who's here? Any *shlupiks* here yet?' And he says, 'You're the third.' Yes, my dear boy, that he did!"

Talking and greeting the friends they met, Levin and the prince walked through all the rooms: the great room where tables had already been set, and the usual partners were playing for small stakes; the divan-room, where they were playing chess, and Sergey Ivanovitch was sitting talking to somebody; the billiard-room, where, about a sofa in a recess, there was a lively party drinking champagne—Gagin was one of them. They peeped into the "infernal regions," where a good many men were crowding round one table, at which Yashvin was sitting. Trying not to make a noise, they walked into the dark reading-room, where under the shaded lamps there sat a young man with a wrathful countenance, turning over one journal after another, and a bald general buried in a book. They went, too, into what the prince called the intellectual room, where three gentlemen were engaged in a heated discussion of the latest political news.

"Prince, please come, we're ready," said one of his card-party, who had come to look for him, and the prince went off. Levin sat down and listened, but recalling all the conversation of the morning he felt all of a sudden fearfully bored. He got up hurriedly, and went to look for Oblonsky and Turovtsin, with whom it had been so pleasant.

Turovtsin was one of the circle drinking in the brilliard-room, and Stepan Arkadyevitch was talking with Vronsky near the door at the farther corner of the room.

"It's not that she's dull; but this undefined, this unsettled position," Levin caught, and he was hurrying away, but Stepan Arkadyevitch called to him.

"Levin!" said Stepan Arkadyevitch; and Levin noticed that his eyes were not full of tears exactly, but moist, which always happened when he had been drinking, or when he was touched. Just now it was due to both causes. "Levin, don't go," he said, and he warmly squeezed his arm above the elbow, obviously not at all wishing to let him go.

"This is a true friend of mine—almost my greatest friend," he said to Vronsky. "You have become even closer and dearer to me. And I want you, and I know you ought, to be friends, and great friends, because you're both splendid fellows."

"Well, there's nothing for us now but to kiss and be friends," Vronsky said, with good-natured playfulness, holding out his hand.

Levin quickly took the offered hand, and pressed it warmly.

"I'm very, very glad," said Levin.

"Waiter, a bottle of champagne," said Stepan Arkadyevitch.

"And I'm very glad," said Vronsky.

But in spite of Stepan Arkadyevitch's desire, and their own desire, they had nothing to talk about, and both felt it.

"Do you know, he has never met Anna?" Stepan Arkadyevitch said to Vronsky. "And I want above everything to take him to see her. Let us go, Levin!"

"Really?" said Vronsky. "She will be very glad to see you. I should be going home at once," he added, "but I'm worried about Yashvin, and I want to stay on till he finishes."

"Why, is he losing?"

"He keeps losing, and I'm the only friend that can restrain him."

"Well, what do you say to pyramids? Levin, will you play? Capital!" said Stepan Arkadyevitch. "Get the table ready," he said to the marker.

"It has been ready a long while," answered the marker, who had already set the balls in a triangle, and was knocking the red one about for his own diversion.

"Well, let us begin."

After the game Vronsky and Levin sat down at Gagin's table, and at Stepan Arkadyevitch's suggestion Levin took a hand in the game.

Vronsky sat down at the table, surrounded by friends, who were incessantly coming up to him. Every now and then he went to the "infernal" to keep an eye on Yashvin. Levin was enjoying a delightful sense of repose after the mental fatigue of the morning. He was glad that all hostility was at an end with Vronsky, and the sense of peace, decorum, and comfort never left him.

When the game was over, Stepan Arkadyevitch took Levin's arm.

"Well, let us go to Anna's, then. At once? Eh? She is at home. I promised her long ago to bring you. Where were you meaning to spend the evening?"

"Oh, nowhere specially. I promised Sviazhsky to go to the Society of Agriculture. By all means, let us go," said Levin.

"Very good; come along. Find out if my carriage is here," Stepan Arkadyevitch said to the waiter.

Levin went up to the table, paid the forty roubles he had lost; paid his bill, the amount of which was in some mysterious way ascertained by the little old waiter who stood at the counter, and swinging his arms he walked through all the rooms to the way out.

CHAPTER IX

"Oblonsky's carriage!" the porter shouted in an angry bass. The carriage drove up and both got in. It was only for the first few moments, while the carriage was driving out of the club-house gates, that Levin was still under the influence of the club atmosphere of repose, comfort, and unimpeachable good form. But as soon as the carriage drove out into the street, and he felt it jolting over the uneven road, heard the angry shout of a sledge-driver coming towards them, saw in the uncertain light the red blind of a tavern and the shops, this impression was dissipated, and he began to think over his actions, and to wonder whether he was doing right in going to see Anna. What would Kitty say? But Stepan Arkadyevitch gave him no time for reflection, and, as though divining his doubts, he scattered them.

"How glad I am," he said, "that you should know her! You know Dolly has long wished for it. And Lvov's been to see her, and often goes. Though she is my sister," Stepan Arkadyevitch pursued, "I don't hesitate to say that she's a remarkable woman. But you will see. Her position is very painful, especially now."

"Why especially now?"

"We are carrying on negotiations with her husband about a divorce. And he's agreed; but there are difficulties in regard to the son, and the business, which ought to have been arranged long ago, has been dragging on for three months past. As soon as the divorce is over, she will marry Vronsky. How stupid these old ceremonies are, that no one believes in, and which only prevent people being comfortable!" Stepan Arkadyevitch put in. "Well, then their position will be as regular as mine, as yours."

"What is the difficulty?" said Levin.

"Oh, it's a long and tedious story! The whole business is in such an anomalous position with us. But the point is she has been for three months in Moscow, where every one knows her, waiting for the divorce; she goes out nowhere, sees no woman except Dolly, because, do you understand, she doesn't care to have people come as a favor. That fool Princess Varvara, even she has left her, considering this a breach of propriety. Well, you see, in such a position any other woman would not have found resources in herself. But you'll see how she has arranged her life—how calm, how dignified she is. To the left, in the crescent opposite the church!" shouted Stepan Arkadyevitch, leaning out of the window. "Phew! how hot it is!" he said, in spite of twelve degrees of frost, flinging his open overcoat still wider open.

"But she has a daughter: no doubt she's busy looking after her?" said Levin.

"I believe you picture every woman simply as a female, *une couveuse,*" said Stepan Arkadyevitch. "If she's occupied, it must be with her children. No, she brings her up capitally, I believe, but one doesn't hear about her. She's busy, in the first place, with what she writes. I see you're smiling ironically, but you're wrong. She's writing a children's book, and doesn't talk about it to any one, but she read it to me and I gave the manuscript to Vorkuev . . . you know the publisher . . . and he's an author himself too, I fancy. He understands those things, and he says it's a remarkable piece of work. But are you fancying she's an authoress?—not a bit of it. She's a woman with a heart, before everything, but you'll see. Now she has a little English girl with her, and a whole family she's looking after."

"Oh, something in a philanthropic way?"

"Why, you will look at everything in the worst light. It's not from philanthropy, it's from the heart. They—that is, Vronsky —had a trainer, an Englishman, first-rate in his own line, but a drunkard. He's completely given up to drink—delirium tremens—and the family were cast on the world. She saw them, helped them, got more and more interested in them, and now the whole family is on her hands. But not by way of patronage, you know, helping with money; she's herself preparing the boys in Russian for the high school, and she's taken the little girl to live with her. But you'll see her for yourself."

The carriage drove into the courtyard, and Stepan Arkadyevitch rang loudly at the entrance where sledges were standing.

And without asking the servant who opened the door whether the lady were at home, Stepan Arkadyevitch walked into the hall. Levin followed him, more and more doubtful whether he was doing right or wrong.

Looking at himself in the glass, Levin noticed that he was red in the face, but he felt certain he was not drunk, and he followed Stepan Arkadyevitch up the carpeted stairs. At the top Stepan Arkadyevitch inquired of the footman, who bowed to him as to an intimate friend, who was with Anna Arkadyevna, and received the answer that it was M. Vorkuev.

"Where are they?"

"In the study."

Passing through the dining-room, a room not very large, with dark, paneled walls, Stepan Arkadyevitch and Levin walked over the soft carpet to the half-dark study, lighted up by a single lamp with a big, dark shade. Another lamp with a reflector was hanging on the wall, lighting up a big full-length portrait of a woman, which Levin could not help looking at. It was the portrait of Anna, painted in Italy by Mihailov. While Stepan Arkadyevitch went behind the *treillage,* and the man's voice which had been speaking paused, Levin gazed at the portrait, which stood out from the frame in the brilliant light thrown on it, and he could not tear himself away from it. He positively forgot where he was, and not even hearing what was said, he could not take his eyes off the marvelous portrait. It was not a picture, but a living, charming woman, with black curling hair, with bare arms and shoulders, with a pensive smile on the lips, covered with soft down; triumphantly and softly she looked at him with eyes that baffled him. She was not living only because she was more beautiful than a living woman can be.

"I am delighted!" He heard suddenly near him a voice, unmistakably addressing him, the voice of the very woman he had been admiring in the portrait. Anna had come from behind the *treillage* to meet him, and Levin saw in the dim light of the study the very woman of the portrait, in a dark blue shot gown, not in the same position nor with the same expression, but with the same perfection of beauty which the artist had caught in the portrait. She was less dazzling in reality, but, on the other hand, there was something fresh and seductive in the living woman which was not in the portrait.

CHAPTER X

She had risen to meet him, not concealing her pleasure at seeing him; and in the quiet ease with which she held out her little vigorous hand, introduced him to Vorkuev and indicated a red-haired, pretty little girl who was sitting at work, calling her her pupil, Levin recognized and liked the manners of a woman of the great world, always self-possessed and natural.

"I am delighted, delighted," she repeated, and on her lips these simple words took for Levin's ears a special significance. "I have known you and liked you for a long while, both from your friendship with Stiva and for your wife's sake. . . . I knew her for a very short time, but she left on me the impression of an exquisite flower, simply a flower. And to think she will soon be a mother!"

She spoke easily and without haste, looking now and then from Levin to her brother, and Levin felt that the impression he was making was good, and he felt immediately at home, simple and happy with her, as though he had known her from childhood.

"Ivan Petrovitch and I settled in Alexey's study," she said in answer to Stepan Arkadyevitch's question whether he might smoke, "just so as to be able to smoke"—and glancing at Levin, instead of asking whether he would smoke, she pulled closer a tortoise-shell cigar-case and took a cigarette.

"How are you feeling to-day?" her brother asked her.

"Oh, nothing. Nerves, as usual."

"Yes, isn't it extraordinarily fine?" said Stepan Arkadyevitch, noticing that Levin was scrutinizing the picture.

"I have never seen a better portrait."

"And extraordinarily like, isn't it?" said Vorkuev.

Levin looked from the portrait to the original. A peculiar brilliance lighted up Anna's face when she felt his eyes on her. Levin flushed, and to cover his confusion would have asked whether she had seen Darya Alexandrovna lately; but at that moment Anna spoke. "We were just talking, Ivan Petrovitch and I, of Vashtchenkov's last pictures. Have you seen them?"

"Yes, I have seen them," answered Levin.

"But, I beg your pardon, I interrupted you . . . you were saying? . . ."

Levin asked if she had seen Dolly lately.

"She was here yesterday. She was very indignant with the high school people on Grisha's account. The Latin teacher, it seems, had been unfair to him."

"Yes, I have seen his pictures. I didn't care for them very much," Levin went back to the subject she had started.

Levin talked now not at all with that purely businesslike attitude to the subject with which he had been talking all the morning. Every word in his conversation with her had a special significance. And talking to her was pleasant; still pleasanter it was to listen to her.

Anna talked not merely naturally and cleverly, but cleverly and carelessly, attaching no value to her own ideas and giving great weight to the ideas of the person she was talking to.

The conversation turned on the new movement in art, on the new illustrations of the Bible by a French artist. Vorkuev attacked the artist for a realism carried to the point of coarseness.

Levin said that the French had carried conventionality further than any one, and that consequently they see a great merit in the return to realism. In the fact of not lying they see poetry.

Never had anything clever said by Levin given him so much pleasure as this remark. Anna's face lighted up at once, as at once she appreciated the thought. She laughed.

"I laugh," she said, "as one laughs when one sees a very true portrait. What you said so perfectly hits off French art now, painting and literature too, indeed—Zola, Daudet. But perhaps it is always so, that men form their conceptions from fictitious, conventional types, and then—all the *combinaisons* made—they are tired of the fictitious figures and begin to invent more natural, true figures."

"That's perfectly true," said Vorkuev.

"So you've been at the club?" she said to her brother.

"Yes, yes, this is a woman!" Levin thought, forgetting himself and staring persistently at her lovely, mobile face, which at that moment was all at once completely transformed. Levin did not hear what she was talking of as she leaned over to her brother, but he was struck by the change of her expression. Her face—so handsome a moment before in its repose—suddenly wore a look of strange curiosity, anger, and pride. But this lasted only an instant. She dropped her eyelids, as though recollecting something.

"Oh, well, but that's of no interest to any one," she said, and she turned to the English girl.

"Please order the tea in the drawing-room," she said in English.

The girl got up and went out.

"Well, how did she get through her examination?" asked Stepan Arkadyevitch.

"Splendidly! She's a very gifted child and a sweet character."

"It will end in your loving her more than your own."

"There a man speaks. In love there's no more nor less. I love my daughter with one love, and her with another."

"I was just telling Anna Arkádyevna," said Vorkuev, "that if she were to put a hundredth part of the energy she devotes to this English girl to the public question of the education of Russian children, she would be doing a great and useful work."

"Yes, but I can't help it; I couldn't do it. Count Alexey Kirillovitch urged me very much" (as she uttered the words *Count Alexey Kirillovitch* she glanced with appealing timidity at Levin, and he unconsciously responded with a respectful and reassuring look); "he urged me to take up the school in the village. I visited it several times. The children were very nice, but I could not feel drawn to the work. You speak of energy.

Energy rests upon love; and come as it will, there's no forcing it. I took to this child—I could not myself say why."

And she glanced again at Levin. And her smile and her glance—all told him that it was to him only she was addressing her words, valuing his good opinion, and at the same time sure beforehand that they understood each other.

"I quite understand that," Levin answered. "It's impossible to give one's heart to a school or such institutions in general, and I believe that that's just why philanthropic institutions always give such poor results."

She was silent for a while, then she smiled.

"Yes, yes," she agreed; "I never could. *Je n'ai pas le cœur assez large* to love a whole asylum of horrid little girls. *Cela ne m'a jamais réussi.* There are so many women who have made themselves *une position sociale* in that way. And now more than ever," she said with a mournful, confiding expression, ostensibly addressing her brother, but unmistakably intending her words only for Levin, "now when I have such need of some occupation, I cannot." And suddenly frowning (Levin saw that she was frowning at herself for talking about herself) she changed the subject. "I know about you," she said to Levin; "that you're not a public-spirited citizen, and I have defended you to the best of my ability."

"How have you defended me?"

"Oh, according to the attacks made on you. But won't you have some tea?" She rose and took up a book bound in morocco.

"Give it to me, Anna Arkadyevna," said Vorkuev, indicating the book. "It's well worth taking up."

"Oh, no, it's all so sketchy."

"I told him about it," Stepan Arkadyevitch said to his sister, nodding at Levin.

"You shouldn't have. My writing is something after the fashion of those little baskets and carving which Liza Mertsalova used to sell me from the prisons. She had the direction of the prison department in that society," she turned to Levin; "and they were miracles of patience, the work of those poor wretches."

And Levin saw a new trait in this woman, who attracted him so extraordinarily. Besides wit, grace, and beauty, she had truth. She had no wish to hide from him all the bitterness of her position. As she said that, she sighed, and her face suddenly taking a hard expression, looked as it were turned to stone. With that expression on her face she was more beautiful than ever; but the expression was new; it was utterly unlike that expression, radiant with happiness and creating happiness, which had been caught by the painter in her portrait. Levin looked more than once at the portrait and at her figure, as taking her brother's arm she walked with him to the high doors and he felt for her a tenderness and pity at which he wondered himself.

She asked Levin and Vorkuev to go into the drawing-room, while she stayed behind to say a few words to her brother. "About her divorce, about Vronsky, and what he's doing at the club, about me?" wondered Levin. And he was so keenly interested by the question of what she was saying to Stepan Arkadyevitch, that he scarcely heard what Vorkuev was telling him of the qualities of the story for children Anna Arkadyevna had written.

At tea the same pleasant sort of talk, full of interesting matter, continued. There was not a single instant when a subject for conversation was to seek; on the contrary, it was felt that one had hardly time to say what one had to say, and eagerly held back to hear what the others were saying. And all that was said, not only by her, but by Vorkuev and Stepan Arkadyevitch—all, so it seemed to Levin, gained peculiar significance from her appreciation and her criticism. While he followed this interesting conversation, Levin was all the time admiring her—her beauty, her intelligence, her culture, and at the same time her directness and genuine depth of feeling. He listened and talked, and all the while he was thinking of her inner life, trying to divine her feelings. And though he had judged her so severely hitherto, now by some strange chain of reasoning he was justifying her and also sorry for her, and afraid that Vronsky did not fully understand her. At eleven o'clock, when Stepan Arkadyevitch got up to go (Vorkuev had left earlier), it seemed to Levin that he had only just come. Regretfully Levin too rose.

"Good-bye," she said, holding his hand and glancing into his face with a winning look. "I am very glad *que la glace est rompue.*"

She dropped his hand, and half closed her eyes.

"Tell your wife that I love her as before, and that if she cannot pardon me my position, then my wish for her is that she may never pardon it. To pardon it, one must go through what I have gone through, and may God spare her that."

"Certainly, yes, I will tell her . . ." Levin said, blushing.

CHAPTER XI

"What a marvelous, sweet and unhappy woman!" he was thinking, as he stepped out into the frosty air with Stepan Arkadyevitch.

"Well, didn't I tell you?" said Stepan Arkadyevitch, seeing that Levin had been completely won over.

"Yes," said Levin dreamily, "an extraordinary woman! It's not her cleverness, but she has such wonderful depth of feeling. I'm awfully sorry for her!"

"Now, please God everything will soon be settled. Well, well, don't be hard on people in future," said Stepan Arkadyevitch, opening the carriage door. "Good-bye; we don't go the same way."

Still thinking of Anna, of everything, even the simplest phrase in their conversation with her, and recalling the most minute changes in her expression, entering more and more into her position, and feeling sympathy for her, Levin reached home.

. . . . . .

At home Kouzma told Levin that Katerina Alexandrovna was quite well, and that her sisters had not long been gone, and he handed him two letters. Levin read them at once in the hall, that he might not overlook them later. One was from Sokolov, his bailiff. Sokolov wrote that the corn could not be sold, that it was fetching only five and a half roubles, and that more than that could not be got for it. The other letter was from his sister. She scolded him for her business being still unsettled.

"Well, we must sell it at five and a half if we can't get more," Levin decided the first question, which had always before seemed such a weighty one, with extraordinary facility on the spot. "It's extraordinary how all one's time is taken up here," he thought, considering the second letter. He felt himself to blame for not having got done what his sister had asked him to do for her. "To-day, again, I've not been to the court, but to-day I've certainly not had time." And resolving that he would not fail to do it next day, he went up to his wife. As he went in, Levin rapidly ran through mentally the day he had spent. All the events of the day were conversations, conversations he had heard and taken part in. All the conversations were upon subjects which, if he had been alone at home, he would never have taken up, but here they were very interesting. And all these conversations were right enough, only in two places there was something not quite right. One was what he had said about the carp, the other was something not "quite the thing" in the tender sympathy he was feeling for Anna.

Levin found his wife low-spirited and dull. The dinner of the three sisters had gone off very well, but then they had waited and waited for him, all of them had felt dull, the sisters had departed, and she had been left alone.

"Well, and what have you been doing?" she asked him, looking straight into his eyes, which shone with rather a suspicious brightness. But that she might not prevent his telling her everything, she concealed her close scrutiny of him, and with an approving smile listened to his account of how he had spent the evening.

"Well, I'm very glad I met Vronsky. I felt quite at ease and natural with him. You understand, I shall try not to see him, but I'm glad that this awkwardness is all over," he said, and remembering that by way of trying not to see him, he had immediately gone to call on Anna, he blushed. "We talk about the peasants drinking; I don't know which drinks most, the peasantry or our own class; the peasants do on holidays, but . . ."

But Kitty took not the slightest interest in discussing the drinking habits of the peasants. She saw that he blushed, and she wanted to know why.

"Well, and then where did you go?"

"Stiva urged me awfully to go and see Anna Arkadyevna."

And as he said this, Levin blushed even more, and his doubts as to whether he had done right in going to see Anna were settled once for all. He knew now that he ought not to have done so.

Kitty's eyes opened in a curious way and gleamed at Anna's

name, but controlling herself with an effort, she concealed her emotion and deceived him.

"Oh!" was all she said.

"I'm sure you won't be angry at my going. Stiva begged me to, and Dolly wished it," Levin went on.

"Oh, no!" she said, but he saw in her eyes a constraint that boded him no good.

"She is a very sweet, very, very unhappy, good woman," he said, telling her about Anna, her occupations, and what she had told him to say to her.

"Yes, of course, she is very much to be pitied," said Kitty, when he had finished. "Whom was your letter from?"

He told her, and believing in her calm tone, he went to change his coat.

Coming back, he found Kitty in the same easy-chair. When he went up to her, she glanced at him and broke into sobs.

"What? what is it?" he asked, knowing beforehand what.

"You're in love with that hateful woman; she has bewitched you! I saw it in your eyes. Yes, yes! What can it all lead to? You were drinking at the club, drinking and gambling, and then you went . . . to her of all people! No, we must go away. . . . I shall go away to-morrow."

It was a long while before Levin could soothe his wife. At last he succeeded in calming her, only by confessing that a feeling of pity, in conjunction with the wine he had drunk, had been too much for him, that he had succumbed to Anna's artful influence, and that he would avoid her. One thing he did with more sincerity confess to was that living so long in Moscow, a life of nothing but conversation, eating and drinking, he was degenerating. They talked till three o'clock in the morning. Only at three o'clock were they sufficiently reconciled to be able to go to sleep.

CHAPTER XII

AFTER taking leave of her guests, Anna did not sit down, but began walking up and down the room. She had unconsciously the whole evening done her utmost to arouse in Levin a feeling of love—as of late she had fallen into doing with all young men —and she knew she had attained her aim, as far as was possible in one evening, with a married and conscientious man. She liked him indeed extremely, and, in spite of the striking difference, from the masculine point of view, between Vronsky and Levin, as a woman she saw something they had in common, which had made Kitty able to love both. Yet as soon as he was out of the room, she ceased to think of him.

One thought, and one only, pursued her in different forms, and refused to be shaken off. "If I have so much effect on others, on this man, who loves his home and his wife, why is it *he* is so cold to me? . . . not cold exactly, he loves me, I know that! But something new is drawing us apart now. Why wasn't he here all the evening? He told Stiva to say he could not leave Yashvin, and must watch over his play. Is Yashvin a child? But supposing it's true. He never tells a lie. But there's something else in it if it's true. He is glad of an opportunity of showing me that he has other duties; I know that, I submit to that. But why prove that to me? He wants to show me that his love for me is not to interfere with his freedom. But I need no proofs, I need love. He ought to understand all the bitterness of this life for me here in Moscow. Is this life? I am not living, but waiting for an event, which is continually put off and put off. No answer again! And Stiva says he cannot go to Alexey Alexandrovitch. And I can't write again. I can do nothing, can begin nothing, can alter nothing; I hold myself in, I wait, inventing amusements for myself—the English family, writing, reading—but it's all nothing but a sham, it's all the same as morphine. He ought to feel for me," she said, feeling tears of self-pity coming into her eyes.

She heard Vronsky's abrupt ring and hurriedly dried her tears—not only dried her tears, but sat down by a lamp and opened a book, affecting composure. She wanted to show him that she was displeased that he had not come home as he had promised —displeased only, and not on any account to let him see her distress, and least of all, her self-pity. She might pity herself, but he must not pity her. She did not want strife, she blamed him for wanting to quarrel, but unconsciously put herself into an attitude of antagonism.

"Well, you've not been dull?" he said, eagerly and good-humoredly, going up to her. "What a terrible passion it is—gambling!"

"No, I've not been dull; I've learned long ago not to be dull. Stiva has been here and Levin."

"Yes, they meant to come and see you. Well, how did you like Levin?" he said, sitting down beside her.

"Very much. They have not long been gone. What was Yashvin doing?"

"He was winning—seventeen thousand. I got him away. He had really started home, but he went back again, and now he's losing."

"Then what did you stay for?" she asked, suddenly lifting her eyes to him. The expression of her face was cold and ungracious. "You told Stiva you were staying on to get Yashvin away. And you have left him there."

The same expression of cold readiness for the conflict appeared on his face too.

"In the first place, I did not ask him to give you any message; and secondly, I never tell lies. But what's the chief point, I wanted to stay, and I stayed," he said, frowning. "Anna, what is it for, why will you?" he said after a moment's silence, bending over towards her, and he opened his hand, hoping she would lay hers in it.

She was glad of this appeal for tenderness. But some strange force of evil would not let her give herself up to her feelings, as though the rules of warfare would not permit her to surrender.

"Of course you wanted to stay, and you stayed. You do everything you want to. But what do you tell me that for? With what object?" she said, getting more and more excited. "Does any one contest your rights? But you want to be right, and you're welcome to be right."

His hand closed, he turned away, and his face wore a still more obstinate expression.

"For you it's a matter of obstinacy," she said, watching him intently and suddenly finding the right word for that expression that irritated her, "simply obstinacy. For you it's a question of whether you keep the upper hand of me, while for me . . ." Again she felt sorry for herself, and she almost burst into tears.

"If you knew what it is for me! When I feel as I do now that you are hostile, yes, hostile to me, if you knew what this means for me! If you knew how I feel on the brink of calamity at this instant, how afraid I am of myself!" And she turned away, hiding her sobs.

"But what are you talking about?" he said, horrified at her expression of despair, and again bending over her, he took her hand and kissed it. "What is it for? Do I seek amusements outside our home? Don't I avoid the society of women?"

"Well, yes! If that were all!" she said.

"Come, tell me what I ought to do to give you peace of mind? I am ready to do anything to make you happy," he said, touched by her expression of despair; "what wouldn't I do to save you from distress of any sort, as now, Anna!" he said.

"It's nothing, nothing!" she said. "I don't know myself whether it's the solitary life, my nerves . . . Come, don't let us talk of it. What about the race? You haven't told me!" she inquired, trying to conceal her triumph at the victory, which had anyway been on her side.

He asked for supper, and began telling her about the races; but in his tone, in his eyes, which became more and more cold, she saw that he did not forgive her for her victory, that the feeling of obstinacy with which she had been struggling had asserted itself again in him. He was colder to her than before, as though he were regretting his surrender. And she, remembering the words that had given her the victory, "how I feel on the brink of calamity, how afraid I am of myself," saw that this weapon was a dangerous one, and that it could not be used a second time. And she felt that beside the love that bound them together there had grown up between them some evil spirit of strife, which she could not exorcise from his, and still less from her own heart.

CHAPTER XIII

There are no conditions to which a man cannot become used, especially if he sees that all around him are living in the same way. Levin could not have believed three months before that he could have gone quietly to sleep in the condition in which he was that day, that leading an aimless, irrational life, living too beyond his means, after drinking to excess (he could not call what happened at the club anything else), forming inappropriately friendly relations with a man with whom his wife had once been in love, and a still more inappropriate call upon a woman who could only be called a lost woman, after being fascinated by that woman and causing his wife distress—he could still go quietly to sleep. But under the influence of fatigue, a sleepless night, and the wine he had drunk, his sleep was sound and untroubled.

At five o'clock the creak of a door opening waked him. He jumped up and looked round. Kitty was not in bed beside him. But there was a light moving behind the screen, and he heard her steps.

"What is it? . . . what is it?" he said, half-asleep. "Kitty! What is it?"

"Nothing," she said, coming from behind the screen with a candle in her hand. "I felt unwell," she said, smiling a particularly sweet and meaning smile.

"What? has it begun?" he said in terror. "We ought to send . . ." and hurriedly he reached after his clothes.

"No, no," she said, smiling and holding his hand. "It's sure to be nothing. I was rather unwell, only a little. It's all over now."

And getting into bed, she blew out the candle, lay down and was still. Though he thought her stillness suspicious, as though she were holding her breath, and still more suspicious the expression of peculiar tenderness and excitement with which, as she came from behind the screen, she said "nothing," he was so sleepy that he fell asleep at once. Only later he remembered the stillness of her breathing, and understood all that must have been passing in her sweet, precious heart while she lay beside him, not stirring, in anticipation of the greatest event in a woman's life. At seven o'clock he was waked by the touch of her hand on his shoulder, and a gentle whisper. She seemed struggling between regret at waking him, and the desire to talk to him.

"Kostya, don't be frightened. It's all right. But I fancy . . . We ought to send for Lizaveta Petrovna."

The candle was lighted again. She was sitting up in bed, holding some knitting, which she had been busy upon during the last few days.

"Please, don't be frightened, it's all right. I'm not a bit afraid," she said, seeing his scared face, and she pressed his hand to her bosom and then to her lips.

He hurriedly jumped up, hardly awake, and kept his eyes fixed on her, as he put on his dressing-gown; then he stopped, still looking at her. He had to go, but he could not tear himself from her eyes. He thought he loved her face, knew her expression, her eyes, but never had he seen it like this. How hateful and horrible he seemed to himself, thinking of the distress he had caused her yesterday. Her flushed face, fringed with soft curling hair under her night-cap, was radiant with joy and courage.

Though there was so little that was complex or artificial in Kitty's character in general, Levin was struck by what was revealed now, when suddenly all disguises were thrown off and the very kernel of her soul shone in her eyes. And in this simplicity and nakedness of her soul, she, the very woman he loved in her, was more manifest than ever. She looked at him, smiling; but all at once her brows twitched, she threw up her head, and going quickly up to him, clutched his hand and pressed close up to him, breathing her hot breath upon him. She was in pain and was, as it were, complaining to him of her suffering. And for the first minute, from habit, it seemed to him that he was to blame. But in her eyes there was a tenderness that told him that she was far from reproaching him, that she loved him for her sufferings.

"If not I, who is to blame for it?" he thought unconsciously, seeking some one responsible for this suffering for him to punish; but there was no one responsible. She was suffering, complaining, and triumphing in her sufferings, and rejoicing in them, and loving them. He saw that something sublime was being accomplished in her soul, but what? He could not make it out. It was beyond his understanding.

"I have sent to mamma. You go quickly to fetch Lizaveta Petrovna . . . Kostya! . . . Nothing, it's over."

She moved away from him and rang the bell.

"Well, go now; Pasha's coming. I am all right."

And Levin saw with astonishment that she had taken up the knitting she had brought in in the night and begun working at it again.

As Levin was going out of one door, he heard the maid-servant come in at the other. He stood at the door and heard Kitty giving exact directions to the maid, and beginning to help her move the bedstead.

He dressed, and while they were putting in his horses, as a hired sledge was not to be seen yet, he ran again up to the bedroom, not on tiptoe, it seemed to him, but on wings. Two maid-servants were carefully moving something in the bedroom.

Kitty was walking about knitting rapidly and giving directions.

"I'm going for the doctor. They have sent for Lizaveta Petrovna, but I'll go on there too. Isn't there anything wanted? Yes, shall I go to Dolly's?"

She looked at him, obviously not hearing what he was saying.

"Yes, yes. Do go," she said quickly, frowning and waving her hand to him.

He had just gone into the drawing-room, when suddenly a plaintive moan sounded from the bedroom, smothered instantly. He stood still, and for a long while he could not understand.

"Yes, that is she," he said to himself, and clutching at his head he ran down-stairs.

"Lord have mercy on us! pardon us! aid us!" he repeated the words that for some reason came suddenly to his lips. And he, an unbeliever, repeated these words not with his lips only. At that instant he knew that all his doubts, even the impossibility of believing with his reason, of which he was aware in himself, did not in the least hinder his turning to God. All of that now floated out of his soul like dust. To whom was he to turn if not to Him in whose hands he felt himself, his soul, and his love?

The horse was not yet ready, but feeling a peculiar concentration of his physical forces and his intellect on what he had to do, he started off on foot without waiting for the horse, and told Kouzma to overtake him.

At the corner he met a night cabman driving hurriedly. In

the little sledge, wrapped in a velvet cloak, sat Lizaveta Petrovna with a kerchief round her head. "Thank God! thank God!" he said, overjoyed to recognize her little fair face which wore a peculiarly serious, even stern expression. Telling the driver not to stop, he ran along beside her.

"For two hours, then? Not more?" she inquired. "You should let Pyotr Dmitrievitch know, but don't hurry him. And get some opium at the chemist's."

"So you think that it may go on well? Lord have mercy on us and help us!" Levin said, seeing his own horse driving out of the gate. Jumping into the sledge beside Kouzma, he told him to drive to the doctor's.

CHAPTER XIV

THE doctor was not yet up, and the footman said that he had been up late, and had given orders not to be waked, but would get up soon. The footman was cleaning the lamp-chimneys, and seemed very busy about them. This concentration of the footman upon his lamps, and his indifference to what was passing in Levin, at first astounded him, but immediately on considering the question he realized that no one knew or was bound to know his feelings, and that it was all the more necessary to act calmly, sensibly, and resolutely to get through this wall of indifference and attain his aim.

"Don't be in a hurry or let anything slip," Levin said to himself, feeling a greater and greater flow of physical energy and attention to all that lay before him to do.

Having ascertained that the doctor was not getting up, Levin considered various plans, and decided on the following one: that Kouzma should go for another doctor, while he himself should go to the chemist's for opium, and if when he came back the doctor had not yet begun to get up, he would either by tipping the footman, or by force, wake the doctor at all hazards.

At the chemist's the lank shopman sealed up a packet of powders for a coachman who stood waiting, and refused him opium with the same callousness with which the doctor's footman had cleaned his lamp-chimneys. Trying not to get flurried or out of temper, Levin mentioned the names of the doctor and midwife, and explaining what the opium was needed for, tried to persuade him. The assistant inquired in German whether he should give it, and receiving an affirmative reply from behind the partition, he took out a bottle and a funnel, deliberately poured the opium from a bigger bottle into a little one, stuck on a label, sealed it up, in spite of Levin's request that he would not do so, and was about to wrap it up too. This was more than Levin could stand; he took the bottle firmly out of his hands, and ran to the big glass doors. The doctor was not even now getting up, and the footman, busy now in putting down the rugs, refused to wake him. Levin deliberately took out a ten-rouble note, and careful to speak slowly, though losing no time over the business, he handed him the note, and explained that Pyotr Dmitrievitch (what a great and important personage he seemed to Levin now, this Pyotr Dmitrievitch, who had been of so little consequence in his eyes before!) had promised to come at any time; that he would certainly not be angry! and that he must therefore wake him at once.

The footman agreed, and went up-stairs, taking Levin into the waiting-room.

Levin could hear through the door the doctor coughing, moving about, washing, and saying something. Three minutes passed; it seemed to Levin that more than an hour had gone by. He could not wait any longer.

"Pyotr Dmitrievitch, Pyotr Dmitrievitch!" he said in an imploring voice at the open door. "For God's sake, forgive me! See me as you are. It's been going on more than two hours already."

"In a minute; in a minute!" answered a voice, and to his amazement Levin heard that the doctor was smiling as he spoke.

"For one instant."

"In a minute."

Two minutes more passed while the doctor was putting on his boots, and two minutes more while the doctor put on his coat and combed his hair.

"Pyotr Dmitrievitch!" Levin was beginning again in a plaintive voice, just as the doctor came in dressed and ready. "These people have no conscience," thought Levin. "Combing his hair, while we're dying!"

"Good-morning!" the doctor said to him, shaking hands, and, as it were, teasing him with his composure. "There's no hurry. Well now?"

Trying to be as accurate as possible Levin began to tell him every unnecessary detail of his wife's condition, interrupting his account repeatedly with entreaties that the doctor would come with him at once.

"Oh, you needn't be in any hurry. You don't understand, you know. I'm certain I'm not wanted, still I've promised, and if you like, I'll come. But there's no hurry. Please sit down; won't you have some coffee?"

Levin stared at him with eyes that asked whether he was laughing at him; but the doctor had no notion of making fun of him.

"I know, I know," the doctor said, smiling; "I'm a married man myself; and at these moments we husbands are very much to be pitied. I've a patient whose husband always takes refuge in the stables on such occasions."

"But what do you think, Pyotr Dmitrievitch? Do you suppose it may go all right?"

"Everything points to a favorable issue."

"So you'll come immediately?" said Levin, looking wrathfully at the servant who was bringing in the coffee.

"In an hour's time."

"Oh, for mercy's sake!"

"Well, let me drink my coffee, anyway."

The doctor started upon his coffee. Both were silent.

"The Turks are really getting beaten, though. Did you read yesterday's telegrams?" said the doctor, munching some roll.

"No, I can't stand it!" said Levin, jumping up. "So you'll be with us in a quarter of an hour."

"In half an hour."

"On your honor?"

When Levin got home, he drove up at the same time as the princess, and they went up to the bedroom door together. The princess had tears in her eyes, and her hands were shaking. Seeing Levin, she embraced him, and burst into tears.

"Well, my dear Lizaveta Petrovna?" she queried, clasping the hand of the midwife, who came out to meet them with a beaming and anxious face.

"She's going on well," she said: "persuade her to lie down. She will be easier so."

From the moment when he had waked up and understood what was going on, Levin had prepared his mind to bear resolutely what was before him, and without considering or anticipating anything, to avoid upsetting his wife, and on the contrary to soothe her and keep up her courage. Without allowing himself even to think of what was to come, of how it would end, judging from his inquiries as to the usual duration of these ordeals, Levin had in his imagination braced himself to bear up and to keep a tight rein on his feelings for five hours, and it had seemed to him he could do this. But when he came back from the doctor's and saw her sufferings again, he fell to repeating more and more frequently: "Lord, have mercy on us, and succor us!" He sighed, and flung his head up, and began to feel afraid he could not bear it, that he would burst into tears or run away. Such agony it was to him. And only one hour had passed.

But after that hour there passed another hour, two hours, three, the full five hours he had fixed as the furthest limit of his sufferings, and the position was still unchanged; and he was still bearing it because there was nothing to be done but bear it; every instant feeling that he had reached the utmost limits of his endurance, and that his heart would break with sympathy and pain.

But still the minutes passed by and the hours, and still hours more, and his misery and horror grew and were more and more intense.

All the ordinary conditions of life, without which one can form no conception of anything, had ceased to exist for Levin. He lost all sense of time. Minutes—those minutes when she sent for him and he held her moist hand, that would squeeze his hand with extraordinary violence and then push it away—seemed to him hours, and hours seemed to him minutes. He was surprised when Lizaveta Petrovna asked him to light a candle behind a screen, and he found that it was five o'clock in the afternoon. If he had been told it was only ten o'clock in the morning he would not have been more surprised. Where he was all this time, he knew as little as the time of anything. He saw her swollen face, sometimes bewildered and in agony, sometimes smiling and trying to reassure him. He saw the old princess too, flushed and overwrought, with her gray curls in disorder, forcing herself to gulp down her tears, biting her lips; he saw Dolly too and the doctor, smoking fat cigarettes, and Lizaveta Petrovna with a firm, resolute, reassuring face, and the old prince walking up and down the hall with a frowning face. But why they came in and went out, where they were, he did not know. The princess was with the doctor in the bedroom, then in the study, where a table set for dinner suddenly appeared; then she was not there, but Dolly was. Then Levin remembered he had been sent somewhere. Once he had been sent to move a table and sofa. He had done this eagerly, thinking it had to be done for her sake, and only later on he found it was his own bed he had been getting ready. Then he had been sent to the study to ask the doctor something. The doctor had answered and then had said something about the irregularities in the municipal council. Then he had been sent to the bedroom to help the old princess to move the holy picture in its silver and gold setting, and with the princess's old waiting-maid he had clambered on a shelf to reach it and had broken the little lamp, and the old servant had tried to reassure him about the lamp and about his wife, and he carried the holy picture and set it at Kitty's head, carefully tucking it in behind the pillow. But where, when, and why all this had happened, he could not tell. He did not understand why the old princess took his hand, and looking compassionately at him, begged him not to worry himself, and Dolly persuaded him to eat something and led him out of the room, and even the doctor looked seriously and with commiseration at him and offered him a drop of something.

All he knew and felt was that what was happening was what had happened nearly a year before in the hotel of the country town at the deathbed of his brother Nikolay. But that had been grief—this was joy. Yet that grief and this joy were alike outside all the ordinary conditions of life; they were loopholes, as it were, in that ordinary life through which there came glimpses of something sublime. And in the contemplation of this sublime something the soul was exalted to inconceivable heights of which it had before had no conception, while reason lagged behind, unable to keep up with it.

"Lord, have mercy on us, and succor us!" he repeated to himself incessantly, feeling, in spite of his long and, as it seemed, complete alienation from religion, that he turned to God just as trustfully and simply as he had in his childhood and first youth.

All this time he had two distinct spiritual conditions. One was away from her, with the doctor, who kept smoking one fat cigarette after another and extinguishing them on the edge of a full ash-tray, with Dolly, and with the old prince, where there was talk about dinner, about politics, about Marya Petrovna's illness, and where Levin suddenly forgot for a minute what was happening, and felt as though he had waked up from sleep; the other was in her presence, at her pillow, where his heart seemed breaking and still did not break from sympathetic suffering, and he prayed to God without ceasing. And every time he was brought back from a moment of oblivion by a scream reaching him from the bedroom, he fell into the same strange terror that had come upon him the first minute. Every time he heard a shriek, he jumped up, ran to justify himself, remembered on the way that he was not to blame, and he longed to defend her, to help her. But as he looked at her, he saw again that help was impossible, and he was filled with terror and prayed: "Lord, have mercy on us, and help us!" And as time went on, both these conditions became more intense; the calmer he became away from her, completely forgetting her, the more agonizing became both her sufferings and his feeling of helplessness before them. He jumped up, would have liked to run away, but ran to her.

Sometimes, when again and again she called upon him, he blamed her; but seeing her patient, smiling face, and hearing the words, "I am worrying you," he threw the blame on God; but thinking of God, at once he fell to beseeching God to forgive him and have mercy.

CHAPTER XV

He did not know whether it was late or early. The candles had all burned out. Dolly had just been in the study and had suggested to the doctor that he should lie down. Levin sat listening to the doctor's stories of a quack mesmerizer and looking at the ashes of his cigarette. There had been a period of repose, and he had sunk into oblivion. He had completely forgotten what was going on now. He heard the doctor's chat and understood it. Suddenly there came an unearthly shriek. The shriek was so awful that Levin did not even jump up, but holding his breath, gazed in terrified inquiry at the doctor. The doctor put his head on one side, listened, and smiled approvingly. Everything was so extraordinary that nothing could strike Levin as strange. "I suppose it must be so," he thought, and still sat where he was. Whose scream was this? He jumped up, ran on tiptoe to the bedroom, edged round Lizaveta Petrovna and the princess, and took up his position at Kitty's pillow. The scream had subsided, but there was some change now. What it was he did not see and did not comprehend, and he had no wish to see or comprehend. But he saw it by the face of Lizaveta Petrovna. Lizaveta Petrovna's face was stern and pale, and still as resolute, though her jaws were twitching, and her eyes were fixed intently on Kitty. Kitty's swollen and agonized face, a tress of hair clinging to her moist brow, was turned to him and sought his eyes. Her lifted hands asked for his hands. Clutching his chill hands in her moist ones, she began squeezing them to her face.

"Don't go, don't go! I'm not afraid, I'm not afraid!" she said rapidly. "Mamma, take my earrings. They bother me. You're not afraid? Quick, quick, Lizaveta Petrovna . . ."

She spoke quickly, very quickly, and tried to smile. But suddenly her face was drawn, she pushed him away.

"Oh, this is awful! I'm dying, I'm dying! Go away!" she shrieked, and again he heard that unearthly scream.

Levin clutched at his head and ran out of the room.

"It's nothing, it's nothing, it's all right," Dolly called after him.

But they might say what they liked, he knew now that all was over. He stood in the next room, his head leaning against the door-post, and heard shrieks, howls such as he had never heard before, and he knew that what had been Kitty was uttering these shrieks. He had long ago ceased to wish for the child. By now he loathed this child. He did not even wish for her life now, all he longed for was the end of this awful anguish.

"Doctor! what is it? What is it? By God!" he said, snatching at the doctor's hand as he came up.

"It's the end," said the doctor. And the doctor's face was so grave as he said it that Levin took *the end* as meaning her death.

Beside himself, he ran into the bedroom. The first thing he saw was the face of Lizaveta Petrovna. It was even more frowning and stern. Kitty's face he did not know. In the place where it had been was something that was fearful in its strained distortion and in the sounds that came from it. He fell down with his head on the wooden framework of the bed, feeling that his heart was bursting. The awful scream never paused, it became still more awful, and as though it had reached the utmost limit of terror, suddenly it ceased. Levin could not believe his ears, but there could be no doubt; the scream had ceased and he heard a subdued stir and bustle, and hurried breathing, and her voice, gasping, alive, tender, and blissful, uttered softly, "It's over!"

He lifted his head. With her hands hanging exhausted on the quilt, looking extraordinarily lovely and serene, she looked at him in silence and tried to smile, and could not.

And suddenly, from the mysterious and awful far-away world in which he had been living for the last twenty-two hours, Levin felt himself all in an instant borne back to the old every-day world, glorified though now, by such a radiance of happiness that he could not bear it. The strained chords snapped, sobs and tears of joy which he had never foreseen rose up with such violence that his whole body shook, that for long they prevented him from speaking.

Falling on his knees before the bed, he held his wife's hand before his lips and kissed it, and the hand, with a weak movement of the fingers, responded to his kiss. And meanwhile, there at the foot of the bed, in the deft hands of Lizaveta Petrovna, like a flickering light in a lamp, lay the life of a human creature, which had never existed before, and which would now with the same right, with the same importance to itself, live and create in its own image.

"Alive! alive! And a boy too! Set your mind at rest!" Levin heard Lizaveta Petrovna saying, as she slapped the baby's back with a shaking hand.

"Mamma, is it true?" said Kitty's voice.

The princess's sobs were all the answers she could make. And in the midst of the silence there came in unmistakable reply to the mother's question, a voice quite unlike the subdued voices speaking in the room. It was the bold, clamorous, self-assertive squall of the new human being, who had so incomprehensibly appeared.

If Levin had been told before that Kitty was dead, and that he had died with her, and that their children were angels, and that God was standing before him, he would have been surprised at nothing. But now, coming back to the world of reality, he had to make great mental efforts to take in that she was alive and well, and that the creature squalling so desperately was his son. Kitty was alive, her agony was over. And he was unutterably happy. That he understood; he was completely happy in it. But the baby? Whence, why, who was he? . . . He could not get used to the idea. It seemed to him something extraneous, superfluous, to which he could not accustom himself.

CHAPTER XVI

At ten o'clock the old prince, Sergey Ivanovitch, and Stepan Arkadyevitch were sitting at Levin's. Having inquired after Kitty, they had dropped into conversation upon other subjects. Levin heard them, and unconsciously, as they talked, going over the past, over what had been up to that morning, he thought of himself as he had been yesterday till that point. It was as though a hundred years had passed since then. He felt himself exalted to unattainable heights, from which he studiously lowered himself so as not to wound the people he was talking to. He talked, and was all the time thinking of his wife, of her condition now, of his son, in whose existence he tried to school himself into believing. The whole world of woman, which had taken for him since his marriage a new value he had never suspected before, was now so exalted that he could not take it in in his imagination. He heard them talk of yesterday's dinner at the club, and thought: "What is happening with her now? Is she asleep? How is she? What is she thinking of? Is he crying, my son Dmitri?" And in the middle of the conversation, in the middle of a sentence, he jumped up and went out of the room.

"Send me word if I can see her," said the prince.

"Very well, in a minute," answered Levin, and without stopping, he went to her room.

She was not asleep, she was talking gently with her mother, making plans about the christening.

Carefully set to rights, with hair well-brushed, in a smart little cap with some blue in it, her arms out on the quilt, she was lying on her back. Meeting his eyes, her eyes drew him to her. Her face, bright before, brightened still more as he drew near her. There was the same change in it from earthly to unearthly that is seen in the face of the dead. But then it means farewell, here it meant welcome. Again a rush of emotion, such as he had felt at the moment of the child's birth, flooded his heart. She took his hand and asked him if he had slept. He could not answer, and turned away, struggling with his weakness.

"I have had a nap, Kostya!" she said to him; "and I am so comfortable now."

She looked at him, but suddenly her expression changed.

"Give him to me," she said, hearing the baby's cry. "Give him to me, Lizaveta Petrovna, and he shall look at him."

"To be sure, his papa shall look at him," said Lizaveta Petrovna, getting up and bringing something red, and queer, and wriggling. "Wait a minute, we'll make him tidy first," and Lizaveta Petrovna laid the red wobbling thing on the bed, began untrussing and trussing up the baby, lifting it up and turning it over with one finger and powdering it with something.

Levin, looking at the tiny, pitiful creature, made strenuous efforts to discover in his heart some traces of fatherly feeling for it. He felt nothing towards it but disgust. But when it was undressed and he caught a glimpse of wee, wee, little hands, little feet, saffron-colored, with little toes, too, and positively with a little big toe different from the rest, and when he saw Lizaveta Petrovna closing the wide-open little hands, as though they were soft springs, and putting them into linen garments, such pity for the little creature came upon him, and such terror that she would hurt it, that he held her hand back.

Lizaveta Petrovna laughed.

"Don't be frightened, don't be frightened!"

When the baby had been put to rights and transformed into a firm doll, Lizaveta Petrovna dandled it as though proud of her handiwork, and stood a little away so that Levin might see his son in all his glory.

Kitty looked sideways in the same direction, never taking her eyes off the baby. "Give him to me! give him to me!" she said, and even made as though she would sit up.

"What are you thinking of, Katerina Alexandrovna, you mustn't move like that! Wait a minute. I'll give him to you. Here we're showing papa what a fine fellow we are!"

And Lizaveta Petrovna, with one hand supporting the wobbling head, lifted up on the other arm the strange, limp, red creature, whose head was lost in its swaddling-clothes. But it had a nose, too, and slanting eyes and smacking lips.

"A splendid baby!" said Lizaveta Petrovna.

Levin sighed with mortification. This splendid baby excited in him no feeling but disgust and compassion. It was not at all the feeling he had looked forward to.

He turned away while Lizaveta Petrovna put the baby to the unaccustomed breast.

Suddenly laughter made him look round. The baby had taken the breast.

"Come, that's enough, that's enough!" said Lizaveta Petrovna, but Kitty would not let the baby go. He fell asleep in her arms.

"Look, now," said Kitty, turning the baby so that he could see it. The aged-looking little face suddenly puckered up still more and the baby sneezed.

Smiling, hardly able to restrain his tears, Levin kissed his wife and went out of the dark room. What he felt towards this little creature was utterly unlike what he had expected. There was nothing cheerful and joyous in the feeling; on the contrary, it was a new torture of apprehension. It was the consciousness of a new sphere of liability to pain. And this sense was so painful at first, the apprehension lest this helpless creature should suffer was so intense, that it prevented him from noticing the strange thrill of senseless joy and even pride that he had felt when the baby sneezed.

CHAPTER XVII

STEPAN ARKADYEVITCH's affairs were in a very bad way.

The money for two-thirds of the forest had all been spent already, and he had borrowed from the merchant in advance at ten per cent discount almost all the remaining third. The merchant would not give more, especially as Darya Alexandrovna, for the first time that winter insisting on her right to her own property, had refused to sign the receipt for the payment of the last third of the forest. All his salary went on household expenses and in payment of petty debts that could not be put off. There was positively no money.

This was unpleasant and awkward, and in Stepan Arkadyevitch's opinion things could not go on like this. The explanation of the position was, in his view, to be found in the fact that his salary was too small. The post he filled had been unmistakably very good five years ago, but it was so no longer.

Petrov, the bank director, had twelve thousand; Sventitsky, a company director, had seventeen thousand; Mitin, who had founded a bank, received fifty thousand.

"Clearly I've been napping, and they've overlooked me," Stepan Arkadyevitch thought about himself. And he began keeping his eyes and ears open, and towards the end of the winter he had discovered a very good berth and had formed a plan of attack upon it, at first from Moscow through aunts, uncles, and friends, and then, when the matter was well advanced, in the spring, he went himself to Petersburg. It was one of those snug, lucrative berths of which there are so many more nowadays than there used to be, with incomes ranging from one thousand to fifty thousand roubles. It was the post of secretary of the committee of the amalgamated agency of the southern railways, and of certain banking companies. This position, like all such appointments, called for such immense energy and such varied qualifications, that it was difficult for them to be found united in any one man. And since a man combining all the qualifications was not to be found, it was at least better that the post be filled by an honest than by a dishonest man. And Stepan Arkadyevitch was not merely an honest man—unemphatically—in the common acceptation of the words, he was an honest man—emphatically—in that special sense which the word has in Moscow, when they talk of an "honest" politician, an "honest" writer, an "honest" newspaper, an "honest" institution, an "honest" tendency, meaning not simply that the man or the institution is not dishonest, but that they are capable on occasion of taking a line of their own in opposition to the authorities.

Stepan Arkadyevitch moved in those circles in Moscow in which that expression had come into use, was regarded there as an honest man, and so had more right to this appointment than others.

The appointment yielded an income of from seven to ten thousand a year, and Oblonsky could fill it without giving up his government position. It was in the hands of two ministers, one lady, and two Jews, and all these people, though the way had been paved already with them, Stepan Arkadyevitch had to see in Petersburg. Besides this business, Stepan Arkadyevitch had promised his sister Anna to obtain from Karenin a definite answer on the question of divorce. And begging fifty roubles from Dolly, he set off for Petersburg.

Stepan Arkadyevitch sat in Karenin's study listening to his report on the causes of the unsatisfactory position of Russian finance, and only waiting for the moment when he would finish to speak about his own business or about Anna.

"Yes, that's very true," he said, when Alexey Alexandrovitch took off the pince-nez, without which he could not read now, and looked inquiringly at his former brother-in-law, "that's very true in particular cases, but still the principle of our day is freedom."

"Yes, but I lay down another principle, embracing the principle of freedom," said Alexey Alexandrovitch, with emphasis on the word "embracing," and he put on his pince-nez again, so as to read the passage in which this statement was made. And turning over the beautifully written, wide-margined manuscript, Alexey Alexandrovitch read aloud over again the conclusive passage.

"I don't advocate protection for the sake of private interests, but for the public weal, and for the lower and upper classes equally," he said, looking over his pince-nez at Oblonsky. "But *they* cannot grasp that, *they* are taken up now with personal interests, and carried away by phrases."

Stepan Arkadyevitch knew that when Karenin began to talk of what *they* were doing and thinking, the persons who would not accept his report and were the cause of everything wrong in Russia, that it was coming near the end. And so now he eagerly abandoned the principle of free-trade, and fully agreed. Alexey Alexandrovitch paused, thoughtfully turning over the pages of his manuscript.

"Oh, by the way," said Stepan Arkadyevitch, "I wanted to ask you, some time when you see Pomorsky, to drop him a hint that I should be very glad to get that new appointment of secretary of the committee of the amalgamated agency of the Southern Railways and banking companies." Stepan Arkadyevitch was familiar by now with the title of the post he coveted, and he brought it out rapidly without mistake.

Alexey Alexandrovitch questioned him as to the duties of this new committee, and pondered. He was considering whether the new committee would not be acting in some way contrary to the views he had been advocating. But as the influence of the new committee was of a very complex nature, and his views were of very wide application, he could not decide this straight off, and taking off his pince-nez, he said:

"Of course, I can mention it to him; but what is your reason precisely for wishing to obtain the appointment?"

"It's a good salary, rising to nine thousand, and my means . . ."

"Nine thousand!" repeated Alexey Alexandrovitch, and he frowned. The high figure of the salary made him reflect that on that side Stepan Arkadyevitch's proposed position ran counter to the main tendency of his own projects of reform, which always leaned towards economy.

"I consider, and I have embodied my views in a note on the subject, that in our day these immense salaries are evidence of the unsound economic *assiette* of our finances."

"But what's to be done?" said Stepan Arkadyevitch. "Suppose a bank director gets ten thousand—well, he's worth it; or an engineer gets twenty thousand—after all, it's a growing thing, you know!"

"I assume that a salary is the price paid for a commodity, and it ought to conform with the law of supply and demand. If the salary is fixed without any regard for that law, as, for instance, when I see two engineers leaving college together, both equally well trained and efficient, and one getting forty thousand while the other is satisfied with two; or when I see lawyers and hussars, having no special qualifications, appointed directors of banking companies with immense salaries, I conclude that the salary is not fixed in accordance with the law of supply and demand, but simply through personal interest. And this is an abuse of great gravity in itself, and one that reacts injuriously on the government service. I consider . . ."

Stepan Arkadyevitch made haste to interrupt his brother-in-law.

"Yes; but you must agree that it's a new institution of undoubted utility that's being started. After all, you know, it's a growing thing! What they lay particular stress on is the thing being carried on honestly," said Stepan Arkadyevitch with emphasis.

But the Moscow significance of the word "honest" was lost on Alexey Alexandrovitch.

"Honesty is only a negative qualification," he said.

"Well, you'll do me a great service, anyway," said Stepan Arkadyevitch, "by putting in a word to Pomorsky—just in the way of conversation. . . ."

"But I fancy it's more in Volgarinov's hands," said Alexey Alexandrovitch.

"Volgarinov has fully assented, as far as he's concerned," said Stepan Arkadyevitch, turning red. Stepan Arkadyevitch reddened at the mention of that name, because he had been that morning at the Jew Volgarinov's, and the visit had left an unpleasant recollection.

Stepan Arkadyevitch believed most positively that the committee in which he was trying to get an appointment was a new, genuine, and honest public body, but that morning when Volgarinov had—intentionally, beyond a doubt—kept him two hours waiting with other petitioners in his waiting-room, he had suddenly felt uneasy.

Whether he was uncomfortable that he, a descendant of Rurik, Prince Oblonsky, had been kept for two hours waiting to see a Jew, or that for the first time in his life he was not following the example of his ancestors in serving the government, but was turning off into a new career, anyway he was very uncomfortable. During those two hours in Volgarinov's waiting-room Stepan Arkadyevitch, stepping jauntily about the room, pulling his whiskers, entering into conversation with the other petitioners, and inventing an epigram on his position, assiduously concealed from others, and ever from himself, the feeling he was experiencing.

But all the time he was uncomfortable and angry, he could not have said why—whether because he could not get his epigram just right, or from some other reason. When at last Volgarinov had received him with exaggerated politeness and unmistakable triumph at his humiliation, and had all but refused the favor asked of him, Stepan Arkadyevitch had made haste to forget it all as soon as possible. And now, at the mere recollection, he blushed.

CHAPTER XVIII

"Now there is something I want to talk about, and you know what it is. About Anna," Stepan Arkadyevitch said, pausing for a brief space, and shaking off the unpleasant impression.

As soon as Oblonsky uttered Anna's name, the face of Alexey Alexandrovitch was completely transformed; all the life was gone out of it, and it looked weary and dead.

"What is it exactly that you want from me?" he said, moving in his chair and snapping his pince-nez.

"A definite settlement, Alexey Alexandrovitch, some settlement of the position. I'm appealing to you" ("not as an injured husband," Stepan Arkadyevitch was going to say, but afraid of wrecking his negotiation by this, he changed the words) "not as a statesman" (which did not sound *à propos*), "but simply as a man, and a good-hearted man and a Christian. You must have pity on her," he said.

"That is, in what way precisely?" Karenin said softly.

"Yes, pity on her. If you had seen her as I have!—I have been spending all the winter with her—you would have pity on her. Her position is awful, simply awful!"

"I had imagined," answered Alexey Alexandrovitch in a higher, almost shrill voice, "that Anna Arkadyevna had everything she had desired for herself."

"Oh, Alexey Alexandrovitch, for heaven's sake, don't let us indulge in recriminations! What is past is past, and you know what she wants and is waiting for—divorce."

"But I believe Anna Arkadyevna refuses a divorce, if I make it a condition to leave me my son. I replied in that sense, and supposed that the matter was ended. I consider it at an end," shrieked Alexey Alexandrovitch.

"But, for heaven's sake, don't get hot!" said Stepan Arkadyevitch, touching his brother-in-law's knee. "The matter is not ended. If you will allow me to recapitulate, it was like this: when you parted, you were as magnanimous as could possibly be; you were ready to give her everything—freedom, divorce even. She appreciated that. No, don't think that. She did appreciate it—to such a degree that at the first moment, feeling how she had wronged you, she did not consider and could not consider everything. She gave up everything. But experience, time, have shown that her position is unbearable, impossible."

"The life of Anna Arkadyevna can have no interest for me," Alexey Alexandrovitch put in, lifting his eyebrows.

"Allow me to disbelieve that," Stepan Arkadyevitch replied gently. "Her position is intolerable for her, and of no benefit to any one whatever. She has deserved it, you will say. She knows that and asks you for nothing; she says plainly that she dare not ask you. But I, all of us, her relatives, all who love her, beg you, entreat you. Why should she suffer? Who is any the better for it?"

"Excuse me, you seem to put me in the position of the guilty party," observed Alexey Alexandrovitch.

"Oh, no, oh, no, not at all! please understand me," said Stepan Arkadyevitch, touching his hand again, as though feeling sure this physical contact would soften his brother-in-law. "All I say is this: her position is intolerable, and it might be alleviated by you, and you will lose nothing by it. I will arrange it all for you, so that you'll not notice it. You did promise it, you know."

"The promise was given before. And I had supposed that the question of my son had settled the matter. Besides, I had hoped that Anna Arkadyevna had enough generosity . . ." Alexey Alexandrovitch articulated with difficulty, his lips twitching and his face white.

"She leaves it all to your generosity. She begs, she implores one thing of you—to extricate her from the impossible position in which she is placed. She does not ask for her son now. Alexey Alexandrovitch, you are a good man. Put yourself in her position for a minute. The question of divorce for her in her position is a question of life and death. If you had not promised it once, she would have reconciled herself to her position, she would have gone on living in the country. But you promised it, and she wrote to you, and moved to Moscow. And here she's been for six months in Moscow, where every chance meeting cuts her to the heart, every day expecting an answer. Why, it's like keeping a condemned criminal for six months with the rope round his neck, promising him perhaps death, perhaps mercy. Have pity on her, and I will undertake to arrange everything. *Vos scrupules* . . ."

"I am not talking about that, about that . . ." Alexey Alexandrovitch interrupted with disgust. "But, perhaps, I promised what I had no right to promise."

"So you go back from your promise?"

"I have never refused to do all that is possible, but I want time to consider how much of what I promised is possible."

"No, Alexey Alexandrovitch!" cried Oblonsky, jumping up, "I won't believe that! She's unhappy as only an unhappy woman can be, and you cannot refuse in such . . ."

"As much of what I promised as is possible. *Vous professez d'être libre penseur*. But I as a believer cannot, in a matter of such gravity, act in opposition to the Christian law."

"But in Christian societies and among us, as far as I'm aware, divorce is allowed," said Stepan Arkadyevitch. "Divorce is sanctioned even by our church. And we see . . ."

"It is allowed, but not in the sense . . ."

"Alexey Alexandrovitch, you are not like yourself," said Oblonsky, after a brief pause. "Wasn't it you (and didn't we all appreciate it in you?) who forgave everything, and moved simply by Christian feeling was ready to make any sacrifice? You said yourself: 'if a man take thy coat, give him thy cloak also,' and now . . ."

"I beg," said Alexey Alexandrovitch shrilly, getting suddenly onto his feet, his face white and his jaws twitching, "I beg you to drop this . . . to drop . . . this subject!"

"Oh, no! Oh, forgive me, forgive me if I have wounded you," said Stepan Arkadyevitch, holding out his hand with a smile of embarrassment; "but like a messenger I have simply performed the commission given me."

Alexey Alexandrovitch gave him his hand, pondered a little, and said:

"I must think it over and seek for guidance. The day after tomorrow I will give you a final answer," he said, after considering a moment.

CHAPTER XIX

STEPAN ARKADYEVITCH was about to go away when Korney came in to announce:

"Sergey Alexeitch!"

"Who's Sergey Alexeitch?" Stepan Arkadyevitch was beginning, but he remembered immediately.

"Ah, Seryozha!" he said aloud. "Sergey Alexeitch! I thought it was the director of a department. Anna asked me to see him too," he thought.

And he recalled the timid, piteous expression with which Anna had said to him at parting: "Anyway, you will see him. Find out exactly where he is, who is looking after him. And Stiva . . . if it were possible! Could it be possible?" Stepan Arkadyevitch knew what was meant by that "if it were possible,"—if it were possible to arrange the divorce so as to let her have her son. . . . Stepan Arkadyevitch saw now that it was no good to dream of that, but still he was glad to see his nephew.

Alexey Alexandrovitch reminded his brother-in-law that they never spoke to the boy of his mother, and he begged him not to mention a single word about her.

"He was very ill after that interview with his mother, which we had not foreseen," said Alexey Alexandrovitch. "Indeed, we feared for his life. But with rational treatment, and sea-bathing in the summer, he regained his strength, and now, by the doctor's advice, I have let him go to school. And certainly the companionship of school has had a good effect on him, and he is perfectly well, and making good progress."

"What a fine fellow he's grown! He's not Seryozha now, but quite full-fledged Sergey Alexeitch!" said Stepan Arkadyevitch, smiling, as he looked at the handsome, broad-shouldered lad in blue coat and long trousers, who walked in alertly and confidently. The boy looked healthy and good-humored. He bowed to his uncle as to a stranger, but recognizing him, he blushed and turned hurriedly away from him, as though offended and irritated at something. The boy went up to his father and handed him a note of the marks he had gained in school.

"Well, that's very fair," said his father, "you can go."

"He's thinner and taller, and has grown out of being a child into a boy; I like that," said Stepan Arkadyevitch. "Do you remember me?"

The boy looked back quickly at his uncle.

"Yes, *mon oncle,*" he answered, glancing at his father, and again he looked downcast.

His uncle called him to him, and took his hand.

"Well, and how are you getting on?" he said, wanting to talk to him, and not knowing what to say.

The boy, blushing and making no answer, cautiously drew his hand away. As soon as Stepan Arkadyevitch let go his hand, he glanced doubtfully at his father, and like a bird set free, he darted out of the room.

A year had passed since the last time Seryozha had seen his mother. Since then he had heard nothing more of her. And in the course of that year he had gone to school, and made friends among his schoolfellows. The dreams and memories of his mother, which had made him ill after seeing her, did not occupy his thoughts now. When they came back to him, he studiously drove them away, regarding them as shameful and girlish, below the dignity of a boy and a schoolboy. He knew that his father and mother were separated by some quarrel, he knew that he had to remain with his father, and he tried to get used to that idea.

He disliked seeing his uncle, so like his mother, for it called up those memories which he was ashamed of. He disliked it all the more as from some words he had caught as he waited at the study door, and still more from the faces of his father and uncle, he guessed that they must have been talking of his mother. And to avoid condemning the father with whom he lived and on whom he was dependent, and, above all, to avoid giving way to sentimentality, which he considered so degrading, Seryozha tried not to look at his uncle who had come to disturb his peace of mind, and not to think of what he recalled to him.

But when Stepan Arkadyevitch, going out after him, saw him on the stairs, and calling to him, asked him how he spent his playtime at school, Seryozha talked more freely to him away from his father's presence.

"We have a railway now," he said in answer to his uncle's

question. "It's like this, do you see: two sit on a bench—they're the passengers; and one stands up straight on the bench. And all are harnessed to it by their arms or by their belts, and they run through all the rooms—the doors are left open beforehand. Well, and it's pretty hard work being the conductor!"

"That's the one that stands?" Stepan Arkadyevitch inquired, smiling.

"Yes, you want pluck for it, and cleverness too, especially when they stop all of a sudden, or some one falls down."

"Yes, that must be a serious matter," said Stepan Arkadyevitch, watching with mournful interest the eager eyes, like his mother's; not childish now—no longer fully innocent. And though he had promised Alexey Alexandrovitch not to speak of Anna, he could not restrain himself.

"Do you remember your mother?" he asked suddenly.

"No, I don't," Seryozha said quickly. He blushed crimson, and his face clouded over. And his uncle could get nothing more out of him. His tutor found his pupil on the staircase half an hour later, and for a long while he could not make out whether he was ill-tempered or crying.

"What is it? I expect you hurt yourself when you fell down?" said the tutor. "I told you it was a dangerous game. And we shall have to speak to the director."

"If I had hurt myself, nobody should have found it out, that's certain."

"Well, what is it, then?"

"Leave me alone! If I remember, or if I don't remember? . . . what business is it of his? Why should I remember? Leave me in peace!" he said, addressing not his tutor, but the whole world.

CHAPTER XX

STEPAN ARKADYEVITCH, as usual, did not waste his time in Petersburg. In Petersburg, besides business, his sister's divorce, and his coveted appointment, he wanted, as he always did, to freshen himself up, as he said, after the mustiness of Moscow.

In spite of its *cafés chantants* and its omnibuses, Moscow was yet a stagnant bog. Stepan Arkadyevitch always felt it. After living for some time in Moscow, especially in close relations with his family, he was conscious of a depression of spirits. After being a long time in Moscow without a change, he reached a point when he positively began to be worrying himself over his wife's ill-humor and reproaches, over his children's health and education, and the petty details of his official work; even the fact of being in debt worried him. But he had only to go and stay a little while in Petersburg, in the circle there in which he moved, where people lived—really lived—instead of vegetating as in Moscow, and all such ideas vanished and melted away at once, like wax before the fire. His wife? . . . Only that day he had been talking to Prince Tchetchensky. Prince Tchetchensky had a wife and family, grown-up pages in the corps, . . . and he had another illegitimate family of children also. Though the first family was very nice too, Prince Tchetchensky felt happier in his second family; and he used to take his eldest son with him to his second family, and told Stepan Arkadyevitch that he thought it good for his son, enlarging his ideas. What would have been said to that in Moscow?

His children? In Petersburg children did not prevent their parents from enjoying life. The children were brought up in schools, and there was no trace of the wild idea that prevailed in Moscow, in Lvov's household, for instance, that all the luxuries of life were for the children, while the parents have nothing but work and anxiety. Here people understood that a man is in duty bound to live for himself, as every man of culture should live.

His official duties? Official work here was not the stiff, hopeless drudgery that it was in Moscow. Here there was some interest in official life. A chance meeting, a service rendered, a happy phrase, a knack of facetious mimicry, and a man's career might be made in a trice. So it had been with Bryantsev, whom Stepan Arkadyevitch had met the previous day, and who was one of the highest functionaries in government now. There was some interest in official work like that.

The Petersburg attitude on pecuniary matters had an especially soothing effect on Stepan Arkadyevitch. Bartnyansky, who must spend at least fifty thousand to judge by the style he lived in, had made an interesting comment the day before on that subject.

As they were talking before dinner, Stepan Arkadyevitch said to Bartnyansky:

"You're friendly, I fancy, with Mordvinsky; you might do me a favor: say a word to him, please, for me. There's an appointment I should like to get—secretary of the agency . . ."

"Oh, I shan't remember all that, if you tell it to me . . . But what possesses you to have to do with railways and Jews? . . . Take it as you will, it's a low business."

Stepan Arkadyevitch did not say to Bartnyansky that it was a "growing thing"—Bartnyansky would not have understood that.

"I want the money, I've nothing to live on."

"You're living, aren't you?"

"Yes, but in debt."

"Are you, though? Heavily?" said Bartnyansky sympathetically.

"Very heavily: twenty thousand."

Bartnyansky broke into good-humored laughter.

"Oh, lucky fellow!" said he. "My debts mount up to a million and a half, and I've nothing, and still I can live, as you see!"

And Stepan Arkadyevitch saw the correctness of this view not in words only but in actual fact. Zhivahov owed three hundred thousand, and hadn't a farthing to bless himself with, and he lived, and in style too! Count Krivtsov was considered a hopeless case by every one, and yet he kept two mistresses. Petrovsky had run through five millions, and still lived in just the same style, and was even a manager in the financial department with a salary of twenty thousand. But besides this, Petersburg had physically an agreeable effect on Stepan Arkadyevitch. It made him younger. In Moscow he sometimes found a gray hair in his head, dropped asleep after dinner, stretched, walked slowly upstairs, breathing heavily, was bored by the society of young women, and did not dance at balls. In Petersburg he always felt ten years younger.

His experience in Petersburg was exactly what had been described to him on the previous day by Prince Pyotr Oblonsky, a man of sixty, who had just come back from abroad:

"We don't know the way to live here," said Pyotr Oblonsky. "I spent the summer in Baden, and you wouldn't believe it, I felt quite a young man. At a glimpse of a pretty woman, my thoughts . . . One dines and drinks a glass of wine, and feels strong and ready for anything. I came home to Russia—had to see my wife, and, what's more, go to my country place; and there, you'd hardly believe it, in a fortnight I'd got into a dressing-gown and given up dressing for dinner. Needn't say I had no thoughts left for pretty women. I became quite an old gentleman. There was nothing left for me but to think of my eternal salvation. I went off to Paris—I was as right as could be at once."

Stepan Arkadyevitch felt exactly the difference that Pyotr Oblonsky described. In Moscow he degenerated so much that if he had had to be there for long together, he might in good earnest have come to considering his salvation; in Petersburg he felt himself a man of the world again.

Between Princess Betsy Tverskaya and Stepan Arkadyevitch there had long existed rather curious relations. Stepan Arkadyevitch always flirted with her in jest, and used to say to her, also in jest, the most unseemly things, knowing that nothing delighted her so much. The day after his conversation with Karenin, Stepan Arkadyevitch went to see her, and felt so youthful that in this jesting flirtation and nonsense he recklessly went so far that he did not know how to extricate himself, as unluckily he was so far from being attracted by her that he thought her positively disagreeable. What made it hard to change the conversation was the fact that he was very attractive to her. So that he was considerably relieved at the arrival of Princess Myakaya, which cut short their *tête-à-tête*.

"Ah, so you're here!" said she when she saw him. "Well, and what news of your poor sister? You needn't look at me like that," she added. "Ever since they've all turned against her, all those who're a thousand times worse than she, I've thought she did a very fine thing. I can't forgive Vronsky for not letting me know when she was in Petersburg. I'd have gone to see her and gone about with her everywhere. Please give her my love. Come, tell me about her."

"Yes, her position is very difficult; she . . ." began Stepan Arkadyevitch, in the simplicity of his heart accepting as sterling coin Princess Myakaya's words "tell me about her." Princess Myakaya interrupted him immediately, as she always did, and began talking herself.

"She's done what they all do, except me—only they hide it. But she wouldn't be deceitful, and she did a fine thing. And she did better still in throwing up that crazy brother-in-law of yours. You must excuse me. Everybody used to say he was so clever, so very clever; I was the only one that said he was a fool. Now that he's so thick with Lidia Ivanovna and Landau, they all say he's crazy, and I should prefer not to agree with everybody, but this time I can't help it."

"Oh, do please explain," said Stepan Arkadyevitch; "what does it mean? Yesterday I was seeing him on my sister's behalf, and I asked him to give me a final answer. He gave me no answer, and said he would think it over. But this morning, instead of an answer, I received an invitation from Countess Lidia Ivanovna for this evening."

"Ah, so that's it, that's it!" said Princess Myakaya gleefully, "they're going to ask Landau what he's to say."

"Ask Landau? What for? Who or what's Landau?"

"What! you don't know Jules Landau, *le fameux Jules Landau, le clairvoyant?* He's crazy too, but on him your sister's fate depends. See what comes of living in the provinces—you know nothing about anything. Landau, do you see, was a *commis* in a shop in Paris, and he went to a doctor's; and in the doctor's waiting-room he fell asleep, and in his sleep he began giving advice to all the patients. And wonderful advice it was! Then the wife of Yury Meledinsky—you know, the invalid?—heard of this Landau, and had him to see her husband. And he cured her husband, though I can't say that I see he did him much good, for he's just as feeble a creature as ever he was, but they believed in him, and took him along with them and brought him to Russia. Here there's been a general rush to him, and he's begun doctoring every one. He cured Countess Bezzubova, and she took such a fancy to him that she adopted him."

"Adopted him?"

"Yes, as her son. He's not Landau any more now, but Count Bezzubov. That's neither here nor there, though; but Lidia—I'm very fond of her, but she has a screw loose somewhere—has lost her heart to this Landau now, and nothing is settled now in her house or Alexey Alexandrovitch's without him, and so your sister's fate is now in the hands of Landau, *alias* Count Bezzubov."

CHAPTER XXI

AFTER a capital dinner and a great deal of cognac drunk at Bartnyansky's, Stepan Arkadyevitch, only a little later than the appointed time, went in to Countess Lidia Ivanovna's.

"Who else is with the countess?—a Frenchman?" Stepan Arkadyevitch asked the hall-porter, as he glanced at the familiar overcoat of Alexey Alexandrovitch and a queer, rather artless-looking overcoat with clasps.

"Alexey Alexandrovitch Karenin and Count Bezzubov," the porter answered severely.

"Princess Myakaya guessed right," thought Stepan Arkadyevitch, as he went up-stairs. "Curious! It would be quite as well, though, to get on friendly terms with her. She has immense influence. If she would say a word to Pomorsky, the thing would be a certainty."

It was still quite light out-of-doors, but in Countess Lidia Ivanovna's little drawing-room the blinds were drawn and the lamps lighted. At a round table under a lamp sat the countess and Alexey Alexandrovitch, talking softly. A short, thinnish man, very pale and handsome, with feminine hips and knock-kneed legs, with fine brilliant eyes and long hair lying on the collar of his coat, was standing at the other end of the room gazing at the portraits on the wall. After greeting the lady of the house and Alexey Alexandrovitch, Stepan Arkadyevitch could not resist glancing once more at the unknown man.

"Monsieur Landau!" the countess addressed him with a softness and caution that impressed Oblonsky. And she introduced them.

Landau looked round hurriedly, came up, and smiling, laid his moist, lifeless hand in Stepan Arkadyevitch's outstretched hand and immediately walked away and fell to gazing at the portraits again. The countess and Alexey Alexandrovitch looked at each other significantly.

"I am very glad to see you, particularly to-day," said Countess Lidia Ivanovna, pointing Stepan Arkadyevitch to a seat beside Karenin.

"I introduced you to him as Landau," she said in a soft voice, glancing at the Frenchman and again immediately after at Alexey Alexandrovitch, "but he is really Count Bezzubov, as you're probably aware. Only he does not like the title."

"Yes, I heard so," answered Stepan Arkadyevitch; "they say he completely cured Countess Bezzubova."

"She was here to-day, poor thing!" the countess said, turning to Alexey Alexandrovitch. "This separation is awful for her. It's such a blow to her!"

"And he positively is going?" queried Alexey Alexandrovitch.

"Yes, he's going to Paris. He heard a voice yesterday," said Countess Lidia Ivanovna, looking at Stepan Arkadyevitch.

"Ah, a voice!" repeated Oblonsky, feeling that he must be as circumspect as he possibly could in this society, where something peculiar was going on, or was to go on, to which he had not the key.

A moment's silence followed, after which Countess Lidia Ivanovna, as though approaching the main topic of conversation, said with a fine smile to Oblonsky:

"I've known you for a long while, and am very glad to make a closer acquaintance with you. *Les amis de nos amis sont nos amis.* But to be a true friend, one must enter into the spiritual state of one's friend, and I fear that you are not doing so in the case of Alexey Alexandrovitch. You understand what I mean?" she said, lifting her fine pensive eyes.

"In part, countess, I understand the position of Alexey Alexandrovitch. . . ." said Oblonsky. Having no clear idea what they were talking about, he wanted to confine himself to generalities.

"The change is not in his external position," Countess Lidia Ivanovna said sternly, following with eyes of love the figure of Alexey Alexandrovitch as he got up and crossed over to Landau; "his heart is changed, a new heart has been vouchsafed him, and I fear you don't fully apprehend the change that has taken place in him."

"Oh, well, in general outlines I can conceive the change. We have always been friendly, and now . . ." said Stepan Arkadyevitch, responding with a sympathetic glance to the expression of the countess, and mentally balancing the question with which of the two ministers she was most intimate, so as to know about which to ask her to speak for him.

"The change that has taken place in him cannot lessen his love for his neighbors; on the contrary, that change can only intensify love in his heart. But I am afraid you do not understand me. Won't you have some tea?" she said, with her eyes indicating the footman, who was handing round tea on a tray.

"Not quite, countess. Of course, his misfortune . . ."

"Yes, a misfortune which has proved the highest happiness, when his heart was made new, was filled full of it," she said, gazing with eyes full of love at Stepan Arkadyevitch.

"I do believe I might ask her to speak to both of them," thought Stepan Arkadyevitch.

"Oh, of course, countess," he said; "but I imagine such changes are a matter so private that no one, even the most intimate friend, would care to speak of them."

"On the contrary! We ought to speak freely and help one another."

"Yes, undoubtedly so, but there is such a difference of convictions, and besides . . ." said Oblonsky with a soft smile.

"There can be no difference where it is a question of holy truth."

"Oh, no, of course; but . . ." and Stepan Arkadyevitch paused in confusion. He understood at last that they were talking of religion.

"I fancy he will fall asleep immediately," said Alexey Alexandrovitch in a whisper full of meaning, going up to Lidia Ivanovna.

Stepan Arkadyevitch looked round. Landau was sitting at the window, leaning on his elbow and the back of his chair, his head drooping. Noticing that all eyes were turned on him he raised his head and smiled a smile of childlike artlessness.

"Don't take any notice," said Lidia Ivanovna, and she lightly moved a chair up for Alexey Alexandrovitch. "I have observed . . ." she was beginning, when a footman came into the room with a letter. Lidia Ivanovna rapidly ran her eyes over the note, and excusing herself, wrote an answer with extraordinary rapidity, handed it to the man, and came back to the table. "I have observed," she went on, "that Moscow people, especially the men, are more indifferent to religion than any one."

"Oh, no, countess, I thought Moscow people had the reputation of being the firmest in the faith," answered Stepan Arkadyevitch.

"But as far as I can make out, you are unfortunately one of the indifferent ones," said Alexey Alexandrovitch, turning to him with a weary smile.

"How any one can be indifferent!" said Lidia Ivanovna.

"I am not so much indifferent on that subject as I am waiting in suspense," said Stepan Arkadyevitch, with his most deprecating smile. "I hardly think that the time for such questions has come yet for me."

Alexey Alexandrovitch and Lidia Ivanovna looked at each other.

"We can never tell whether the time has come for us or not," said Alexey Alexandrovitch severely. "We ought not to think whether we are ready or not ready. God's grace is not guided by human considerations: sometimes it comes not to those that strive for it, and comes to those that are unprepared, like Saul."

"No, I believe it won't be just yet," said Lidia Ivanovna, who had been meanwhile watching the movements of the Frenchman. Landau got up and came to them.

"Do you allow me to listen?" he asked.

"Oh, yes; I did not want to disturb you," said Lidia Ivanovna, gazing tenderly at him; "sit here with us."

"One has only not to close one's eyes to shut out the light," Alexey Alexandrovitch went on.

"Ah, if you knew the happiness we know, feeling His presence ever in our hearts!" said Countess Lidia Ivanovna with a rapturous smile.

"But a man may feel himself unworthy sometimes to rise to that height," said Stepan Arkadyevitch, conscious of hypocrisy in admitting this religious height, but at the same time unable to bring himself to acknowledge his free-thinking views before a person who, by a single word to Pomorsky, might procure him the coveted appointment.

"That is, you mean that sin keeps him back?" said Lidia Ivanovna. "But that is a false idea. There is no sin for believers, their sin has been atoned for. *Pardon,*" she added, looking at the footman, who came in again with another letter. She read it and gave a verbal answer: "To-morrow at the Grand Duchess's, say." "For the believer sin is not," she went on.

"Yes, but faith without works is dead," said Stepan Arkadyevitch, recalling the phrase from the catechism, and only by his smile clinging to his independence.

"There you have it—from the epistle of St. James," said Alexey Alexandrovitch, addressing Lidia Ivanovna, with a certain reproachfulness in his tone. It was unmistakably a subject they had discussed more than once before. "What harm has been done by the false interpretation of that passage! Nothing holds men back from belief like that misinterpretation. 'I have not works, so I cannot believe,' though all the while that is not said. But the very opposite is said."

"Striving for God, saving the soul by fasting," said Countess Lidia Ivanovna, with disgusted contempt, "those are the crude ideas of our monks. . . . Yet that is nowhere said. It is far simpler and easier," she added, looking at Oblonsky with the same encouraging smile with which at court she encouraged youthful maids of honor, disconcerted by the new surroundings of the court.

"We are saved by Christ who suffered for us. We are saved by faith," Alexey Alexandrovitch chimed in, with a glance of approval at her words.

"*Vous comprenez l'anglais?*" asked Lidia Ivanovna, and receiving a reply in the affirmative, she got up and began looking through a shelf of books.

"I want to read him 'Safe and Happy,' or 'Under the Wing,'" she said, looking inquiringly at Karenin. And finding the book, and sitting down again in her place, she opened it. "It's very short. In it is described the way by which faith can be reached, and the happiness, above all earthly bliss, with which it fills the soul. The believer cannot be unhappy because he is not alone. But you will see." She was just settling herself to read when the footman came in again. "Madame Borozdina? Tell her, to-morrow at two o'clock. Yes," she said, putting her finger in the place in the book, and gazing before her with her fine pensive eyes, "that is how true faith acts. You know Marie Sanina? You know about her trouble? She lost her only child. She was in despair. And what happened? She found this comforter, and she thanks God now for the death of her child. Such is the happiness faith brings!"

"Oh, yes, that is most . . ." said Stepan Arkadyevitch, glad they were going to read, and let him have a chance to collect his faculties. "No, I see I'd better not ask her about anything to-day," he thought. "If only I can get out of this without putting my foot in it!"

"It will be dull for you," said Countess Lidia Ivanovna, addressing Landau; "you don't know English, but it's short."

"Oh, I shall understand," said Landau, with the same smile, and he closed his eyes. Alexey Alexandrovitch and Lidia Ivanovna exchanged meaning glances, and the reading began.

CHAPTER XXII

STEPAN ARKADYEVITCH felt completely nonplussed by the strange talk which he was hearing for the first time. The complexity of Petersburg, as a rule, had a stimulating effect on him, rousing him out of his Moscow stagnation. But he liked these complications, and understood them only in the circles he knew and was at home in. In these unfamiliar surroundings he was puzzled and disconcerted, and could not get his bearings. As he listened to Countess Lidia Ivanovna, aware of the beautiful, artless—or perhaps artful, he could not decide which—eyes of Landau fixed upon him, Stepan Arkadyevitch began to be conscious of a peculiar heaviness in his head.

The most incongruous ideas were in confusion in his head. "Marie Sanina is glad her child's dead . . . How good a smoke would be now! . . . To be saved, one need only believe, and the monks don't know how the thing's to be done, but Countess Lidia Ivanovna does know . . . And why is my head so heavy?

Is it the cognac, or all this being so queer? Anyway, I fancy I've done nothing unsuitable so far. But anyway, it won't do to ask her now. They say they make one say one's prayers. I only hope they won't make me! That'll be too imbecile. And what stuff it is she's reading! but she has a good accent. Landau—Bezzubov—what's he Bezzubov for?" All at once Stepan Arkadyevitch became aware that his lower jaw was uncontrollably forming a yawn. He pulled his whiskers to cover the yawn, and shook himself together. But soon after he became aware that he was dropping asleep and on the very point of snoring. He recovered himself at the very moment when the voice of Countess Lidia Ivanovna was saying "he's asleep." Stepan Arkadyevitch started with dismay, feeling guilty and caught. But he was reassured at once by seeing that the words "he's asleep" referred not to him, but to Landau. The Frenchman was asleep as well as Stepan Arkadyevitch. But Stepan Arkadyevitch's being asleep would have offended them, as he thought (though even this, he thought, might not be so, as everything seemed so queer), while Landau's being asleep delighted them extremely, especially Countess Lidia Ivanovna.

"*Mon ami,*" said Lidia Ivanovna, carefully holding the folds of her silk gown so as not to rustle, and in her excitement calling Karenin not Alexey Alexandrovitch, but *"mon ami," "donnez-lui la main. Vous voyez?* Sh!" she hissed at the footman as he came in again. "Not at home."

The Frenchman was asleep, or pretending to be asleep, with his head on the back of his chair, and his moist hand, as it lay on his knee, made faint movements, as though trying to catch something. Alexey Alexandrovitch got up, tried to move carefully, but stumbled against the table, went up and laid his hand in the Frenchman's hand. Stepan Arkadyevitch got up too, and opening his eyes wide, trying to wake himself up if he was asleep, he looked first at one and then at the other. It was all real. Stepan Arkadyevitch felt that his head was getting worse and worse.

"*Que la personne qui est arrivée la dernière, celle qui demande, qu'elle sorte! Qu'elle sorte!*" articulated the Frenchman, without opening his eyes.

"*Vous m'excuserez, mais vous voyez . . . Revenez vers dix heures, encore mieux demain.*"

"*Qu'elle sorte!*" repeated the Frenchman impatiently.

"*C'est moi, n'est-ce pas?*" And receiving an answer in the affirmative, Stepan Arkadyevitch, forgetting the favor he had meant to ask of Lidia Ivanovna, and forgetting his sister's affairs, caring for nothing, but filled with the sole desire to get away as soon as possible, went out on tiptoe and ran out into the street as though from a plague-stricken house. For a long while he chatted and joked with his cab-driver, trying to recover his spirits.

At the French theater where he arrived for the last act, and afterwards at the Tatar restaurant after his champagne, Stepan Arkadyevitch felt a little refreshed in the atmosphere he was used to. But still he felt quite unlike himself all that evening.

On getting home to Pyotr Oblonsky's, where he was staying, Stepan Arkadyevitch found a note from Betsy. She wrote to him that she was very anxious to finish their interrupted conversation, and begged him to come next day. He had scarcely read this note, and frowned at its contents, when he heard below the ponderous tramp of the servants, carrying something heavy.

Stepan Arkadyevitch went out to look. It was the rejuvenated Pyotr Oblonsky. He was so drunk that he could not walk upstairs; but he told them to set him on his legs when he saw Stepan Arkadyevitch, and clinging to him, walked with him into his room and there began telling him how he had spent the evening, and fell asleep doing so.

Stepan Arkadyevitch was in very low spirits, which happened rarely with him, and for a long while he could not go to sleep. Everything he could recall to his mind, everything was disgusting; but most disgusting of all, as if it were something shameful, was the memory of the evening he had spent at Countess Lidia Ivanovna's.

Next day he received from Alexey Alexandrovitch a final answer, refusing to grant Anna's divorce, and he understood that this decision was based on what the Frenchman had said in his real or pretended trance.

CHAPTER XXIII

IN ORDER to carry through any undertaking in family life, there must necessarily be either complete division between the husband and wife, or loving agreement. When the relations of a couple are vacillating and neither one thing nor the other, no sort of enterprise can be undertaken.

Many families remain for years in the same place, though both husband and wife are sick of it, simply because there is neither complete division nor agreement between them.

Both Vronsky and Anna felt life in Moscow insupportable in the heat and dust, when the spring sunshine was followed by the glare of summer, and all the trees in the boulevards had long since been in full leaf, and the leaves were covered with dust. But they did not go back to Vozdvizhenskoe, as they had arranged to do long before; they went staying on in Moscow, though they both loathed it, because of late there had been no agreement between them.

The irritability that kept them apart had no external cause, and all efforts to come to an understanding intensified it, instead of removing it. It was an inner irritation, grounded in her mind on the conviction that his love had grown less; in his, on regret that he had put himself for her sake in a difficult position, which she, instead of lightening, made still more difficult. Neither of them gave full utterance to their sense of grievance, but they considered each other in the wrong, and tried on every pretext to prove this to one another.

In her eyes the whole of him, with all his habits, ideas, desires, with all his spiritual and physical temperament, was one thing—love for women, and that love, she felt, ought to be entirely concentrated on her alone. That love was less; consequently, as she reasoned, he must have transferred part of his love to other women or to another woman—and she was jealous. She was jealous not of any particular woman but of the decrease of his love. Not having got an object for her jealousy, she was on the lookout for it. At the slightest hint she transferred her jealousy from one object to another. At one time she was jealous of those low women with whom he might so easily renew his old bachelor ties; then she was jealous of the society women he might meet; then she was jealous of the imaginary girl whom he might want to marry, for whose sake he would break with her. And this last form of jealousy tortured her most of all, especially as he had unwarily told her, in a moment of frankness, that his mother knew him so little that she had had the audacity to try and persuade him to marry the young Princess Sorokina.

And being jealous of him, Anna was indignant against him and found grounds for indignation in everything. For everything that was difficult in her position she blamed him. The agonizing condition of suspense she had passed at Moscow, the tardiness and indecision of Alexey Alexandrovitch, her solitude—she put it all down to him. If he had loved her he would have seen all the bitterness of her position, and would have rescued her from it. For her being in Moscow and not in the country, he was to blame too. He could not live buried in the country as she would have liked to do. He must have society, and he had put her in this awful position, the bitterness of which he would not see. And again, it was his fault that she was forever separated from her son.

Even the rare moments of tenderness that came from time to time did not soothe her; in his tenderness now she saw a shade of complacency, of self-confidence, which had not been of old and which exasperated her.

It was dusk. Anna was alone, and waiting for him to come back from a bachelor dinner. She walked up and down in his study (the room where the noise from the street was least heard), and thought over every detail of their yesterday's quarrel. Going back from the well-remembered, offensive words of the quarrel to what had been the ground of it, she arrived at last at its origin. For a long while she could hardly believe that their dissension had arisen from a conversation so inoffensive, of so little moment to either. But so it actually had been. It all arose from his laughing at the girls' high schools, declaring they were useless, while she defended them. He had spoken slightingly of women's education in general, and had said that Hannah, Anna's English protégée, had not the slightest need to know anything of physics.

This irritated Anna. She saw in this a contemptuous reference to her occupations. And she bethought her of a phrase to pay him back for the pain he had given her. "I don't expect you to understand me, my feelings, as any one who loved me might, but simple delicacy I did expect," she said.

And he had actually flushed with vexation, and had said something unpleasant. She could not recall her answer, but at that point, with an unmistakable desire to wound her too, he had said:

"I feel no interest in your infatuation over this girl, that's true, because I see it's unnatural."

The cruelty with which he shattered the world she had built up for herself so laboriously to enable her to endure her hard life, the injustice with which he had accused her of affectation, of artificiality, aroused her.

"I am very sorry that nothing but what's coarse and material is comprehensible and natural to you," she said and walked out of the room.

When he had come in to her yesterday evening, they had not referred to the quarrel, but both felt that the quarrel had been smoothed over, but was not at an end.

To-day he had not been at home all day, and she felt so lonely and wretched in being on bad terms with him that she wanted to forget it all, to forgive him, and be reconciled with him; she wanted to throw the blame on herself and to justify him.

"I am myself to blame. I'm irritable, I'm insanely jealous. I will make it up with him, and we'll go away to the country, there I shall be more at peace."

"Unnatural!" She suddenly recalled the word that had stung her most of all, not so much the word itself as the intent to wound her with which it was said. "I know what he meant; he meant—unnatural, not loving my own daughter, to love another person's child. What does he know of love for children, of my love for Seryozha, whom I've sacrificed for him? But that wish to wound me! No, he loves another woman, it must be so."

And perceiving that, while trying to regain her peace of mind, she had gone round the same circle that she had been round so often before, and had come back to her former state of exasperation, she was horrified at herself. "Can it be impossible? Can it be beyond me to control myself?" she said to herself, and began again from the beginning. "He's truthful, he's honest, he loves me. I love him, and in a few days the divorce will come. What more do I want? I want peace of mind and trust, and I will take the blame on myself. Yes, now when he comes in, I will tell him I was wrong, though I was not wrong, and we will go away to-morrow."

And to escape thinking any more, and being overcome by irritability, she rang, and ordered the boxes to be brought up for packing their things for the country.

At ten o'clock Vronsky came in.

CHAPTER XXIV

"WELL, was it nice?" she asked, coming out to meet him with a penitent and meek expression.

"Just as usual," he answered, seeing at a glance that she was in one of her good moods. He was used by now to these transitions, and he was particularly glad to see it to-day, as he was in a specially good-humor himself.

"What do I see? Come, that's good!" he said, pointing to the boxes in the passage.

"Yes, we must go. I went out for a drive, and it was so fine I longed to be in the country. There's nothing to keep you, is there?"

"It's the one thing I desire. I'll be back directly, and we'll talk it over; I only want to change my coat. Order some tea."

And he went into his room.

There was something mortifying in the way he had said "Come, that's good," as one says to a child when it leaves off being naughty, and still more mortifying was the contrast between her penitent and his self-confident tone; and for one instant she felt the lust of strife rising up in her again, but making an effort she conquered it, and met Vronsky as good-humoredly as before.

When he came in she told him, partly repeating phrases she had prepared beforehand, how she had spent the day, and her plans for going away.

"You know it came to me almost like an inspiration," she said. "Why wait here for the divorce? Won't it be just the same in the country? I can't wait any longer! I don't want to go on hoping, I don't want to hear anything about the divorce. I have made up my mind it shall not have any more influence on my life. Do you agree?"

"Oh, yes!" he said, glancing uneasily at her excited face.

"What did you do? Who was there?" she said, after a pause.

Vronsky mentioned the names of the guests. "The dinner was first-rate, and the boat race, and it was all pleasant enough, but in Moscow they can never do anything without something *ridicule*. A lady of a sort appeared on the scene, teacher of swimming to the Queen of Sweden, and gave us an exhibition of her skill."

"How? did she swim?" asked Anna, frowning.

"In an absurd red *costume de natation;* she was old and hideous too. So when shall we go?"

"What an absurd fancy! Why, did she swim in some special way, then?" said Anna, not answering.

"There was absolutely nothing in it. That's just what I say, it was awfully stupid. Well, then, when do you think of going?"

Anna shook her head as though trying to drive away some unpleasant idea.

"When? Why, the sooner the better! By to-morrow we shan't be ready. The day after to-morrow."

"Yes . . . oh, no, wait a minute! The day after to-morrow's Sunday, I have to be at maman's," said Vronsky, embarrassed, because as soon as he uttered his mother's name he was aware of her intent, suspicious eyes. His embarrassment confirmed her suspicion. She flushed hotly and drew away from him. It was now not the Queen of Sweden's swimming-mistress who filled Anna's imagination, but the young Princess Sorokina. She was staying in a village near Moscow with Countess Vronskaya.

"Can't you go to-morrow?" she said.

"Well, no! The deeds and the money for the business I'm going there for I can't get by to-morrow," he answered.

"If so, we won't go at all."

"But why so?"

"I shall not go later. Monday or never!"

"What for?" said Vronsky, as though in amazement. "Why, there's no meaning in it!"

"There's no meaning in it to you, because you care nothing for me. You don't care to understand my life. The one thing that I cared for here was Hannah. You say it's affectation. Why, you said yesterday that I don't love my daughter, that I love this English girl, that it's unnatural. I should like to know what life there is for me that could be natural!"

For an instant she had a clear vision of what she was doing, and was horrified at how she had fallen away from her resolution. But even though she knew it was her own ruin, she could not restrain herself, could not keep herself from proving to him that he was wrong, could not give way to him.

"I never said that; I said I did not sympathize with this sudden passion."

"How is it, though you boast of your straightforwardness, you don't tell the truth?"

"I never boast, and I never tell lies," he said slowly, restraining his rising anger. "It's a great pity if you can't respect . . ."

"Respect was invented to cover the empty place where love should be. And if you don't love me any more, it would be better and more honest to say so."

"No, this is becoming unbearable!" cried Vronsky, getting up from his chair; and stopping short, facing her, he said, speaking deliberately: "What do you try my patience for?" looking as though he might have said much more, but was restraining himself. "It has limits."

"What do you mean by that?" she cried, looking with terror at the undisguised hatred in his whole face, and especially in his cruel, menacing eyes.

"I mean to say . . ." he was beginning, but he checked himself. "I must ask what it is you want of me?"

"What I can want? All I can want is that you should not desert me, as you think of doing," she said, understanding all he had not uttered. "But that I don't want; that's secondary. I want love, and there is none. So then all is over."

She turned towards the door.

"Stop! sto—op!" said Vronsky, with no change in the gloomy

lines of his brows, though he held her by the hand. "What is it all about? I said that we must put off going for three days, and on that you told me I was lying, that I was not an honorable man."

"Yes, and I repeat that the man who reproaches me with having sacrificed everything for me," she said, recalling the words of a still earlier quarrel, "that he's worse than a dishonorable man—he's a heartless man."

"Oh, there are limits to endurance!" he cried, and hastily let go her hand.

"He hates me, that's clear," she thought, and in silence, without looking round, she walked with faltering steps out of the room. "He loves another woman, that's even clearer," she said to herself as she went into her own room. "I want love, and there is none. So, then, all is over." She repeated the words she had said, "and it must be ended."

"But how?" she asked herself, and she sat down in a low chair before the looking-glass.

Thoughts of where she would go now, whether to the aunt who had brought her up, to Dolly, or simply alone abroad, and of what *he* was doing now alone in his study; whether this was the final quarrel, or whether reconciliation were still possible; and of what all her old friends at Petersburg would say of her now; and of how Alexey Alexandrovitch would look at it, and many other ideas of what would happen now after this rupture, came into her head; but she did not give herself up to them with all her heart. At the bottom of her heart was some obscure idea that alone interested her, but she could not get clear sight of it. Thinking once more of Alexey Alexandrovitch, she recalled the time of her illness after her confinement, and the feeling which never left her at that time. "Why didn't I die?" and the words and the feeling of that time came back to her. And all at once she knew what was in her soul. Yes, it was that idea which alone solved all. "Yes, to die! . . . And the shame and disgrace of Alexey Alexandrovitch and of Seryozha, and my awful shame, it will all be saved by death. To die! and he will feel remorse; will be sorry; will love me; he will suffer on my account." With the trace of a smile of commiseration for herself she sat down in the armchair, taking off and putting on the rings on her left hand, vividly picturing from different sides his feelings after her death.

Approaching footsteps—his steps—distracted her attention. As though absorbed in the arrangement of her rings, she did not even turn to him.

He went up to her, and taking her by the hand, said softly:

"Anna, we'll go the day after to-morrow, if you like. I agree to everything."

She did not speak.

"What is it?" he urged.

"You know," she said, and at the same instant, unable to restrain herself any longer, she burst into sobs.

"Cast me off!" she articulated between her sobs. "I'll go away to-morrow . . . I'll do more. What am I? An immoral woman! A stone round your neck. I don't want to make you wretched; I don't want to! I'll set you free. You don't love me; you love some one else!"

Vronsky besought her to be calm, and declared that there was no trace of foundation for her jealousy; that he had never ceased, and never would cease, to love her; that he loved her more than ever.

"Anna, why distress yourself and me so?" he said to her, kissing her hands. There was tenderness now in his face, and she fancied she caught the sound of tears in his voice, and she felt them wet on her hand. And instantly Anna's despairing jealousy changed to a despairing passion of tenderness. She put her arms round him, and covered with kisses his head, his neck, his hands.

CHAPTER XXV

FEELING that the reconciliation was complete, Anna set eagerly to work in the morning preparing for their departure. Though it was not settled whether they should go on Monday or Tuesday, as they had each given way to the other, Anna packed busily, feeling absolutely indifferent whether they went a day earlier or later. She was standing in her room over an open box, taking things out of it, when he came in to see her earlier than usually, dressed to go out.

"I'm going off at once to see maman; she can send me the money by Yegorov. And I shall be ready to go to-morrow," he said.

Though she was in such a good mood, the thought of his visit to his mother's gave her a pang.

"No, I shan't be ready by then myself," she said; and at once reflected, "so then it was possible to arrange to do as I wished."

"No, do as you meant to do. Go into the dining-room, I'm coming directly. It's only to turn out those things that aren't wanted," she said, putting something more on the heap of frippery that lay in Annushka's arms.

Vronsky was eating his beefsteak when she came into the dining-room.

"You wouldn't believe how distasteful these rooms have become to me," she said, sitting down beside him to her coffee. "There's nothing more awful than these *chambres garnies*. There's no individuality in them, no soul. These clocks, and curtains, and, worst of all, the wall-papers—they're a nightmare. I think of Vozdvizhenskoe as the promised land. You're not sending the horses off yet?"

"No, they will come after us. Where are you going to?"

"I wanted to go to Wilson's to take some dresses to her. So it's really to be to-morrow?" she said in a cheerful voice; but suddenly her face changed.

Vronsky's valet came in to ask him to sign a receipt for a telegram from Petersburg. There was nothing out of the way in Vronsky's getting a telegram, but he said, as though anxious to conceal something from her, that the receipt was in his study, and he turned hurriedly to her.

"By to-morrow, without fail, I will finish it all."

"From whom is the telegram?" she asked, not hearing him.

"From Stiva," he answered reluctantly.

"Why didn't you show it to me? What secret can there be between Stiva and me?"

Vronsky called the valet back, and told him to bring the telegram.

"I didn't want to show it to you, because Stiva has such a passion for telegraphing: why telegraph when nothing is settled?"

"About the divorce?"

"Yes; but he says he has not been able to come at anything yet. He has promised a decisive answer in a day or two. But here it is; read it."

With trembling hands Anna took the telegram, and read what Vronsky had told her. At the end was added: "Little hope; but I will do everything possible and impossible."

"I said yesterday that it's absolutely nothing to me when I get, or whether I never get, a divorce," she said, flushing crimson. "There was not the slightest necessity to hide it from me." "So he may hide and does hide his correspondence with women from me," she thought.

"Yashvin meant to come this morning with Voytov," said Vronsky; "I believe he's won from Pyevtsov all and more than he can pay, about sixty thousand."

"No," she said, irritated by his so obviously showing by this change of subject that he was irritated, "why did you suppose that this news would affect me so, that you must even try to hide it? I said I don't want to consider it, and I should have liked you to care as little about it as I do."

"I care about it because I like definiteness," he said.

"Definiteness is not in the form but the love," she said, more and more irritated, not by his words, but by the tone of cool composure in which he spoke. "What do you want it for?"

"My God! love again," he thought, frowning.

"Oh, you know what for; for your sake and your children's in the future."

"There won't be children in the future."

"That's a great pity," he said.

"You want it for the children's sake, but you don't think of me?" she said, quite forgetting or not having heard that he had said, *"for your sake* and the children's."

The question of the possibility of having children had long been a subject of dispute and irritation to her. His desire to have children she interpreted as a proof he did not prize her beauty.

"Oh, I said: for your sake. Above all for your sake," he repeated, frowning as though in pain, "because I am certain that the greater part of your irritability comes from the indefiniteness of the position."

"Yes, now he has laid aside all pretense, and all his cold hatred for me is apparent," she thought, not hearing his words, but watching with terror the cold, cruel judge who looked mocking her out of his eyes.

"The cause is not that," she said, "and, indeed, I don't see how the cause of my irritability, as you call it, can be that I am completely in your power. What indefiniteness is there in the position? on the contrary . . ."

"I am very sorry that you don't care to understand," he interrupted, obstinately anxious to give utterance to his thought. "The indefiniteness consists in your imagining that I am free."

"On that score you can set your mind quite at rest," she said, and turning away from him, she began drinking her coffee.

She lifted her cup, with her little finger held apart, and put it to her lips. After drinking a few sips she glanced at him, and by his expression, she saw clearly that he was repelled by her hand, and her gesture, and the sound made by her lips.

"I don't care in the least what your mother thinks, and what match she wants to make for you," she said, putting the cup down with a shaking hand.

"But we are not talking about that."

"Yes, that's just what we are talking about. And let me tell you that a heartless woman, whether she's old or not old, your mother or any one else, is of no consequence to me, and I would not consent to know her."

"Anna, I beg you not to speak disrespectfully of my mother."

"A woman whose heart does not tell her where her son's happiness and honor lie has no heart."

"I repeat my request that you will not speak disrespectfully of my mother, whom I respect," he said, raising his voice and looking sternly at her.

She did not answer. Looking intently at him, at his face, his hands, she recalled all the details of their reconciliation the previous day, and his passionate caresses. "There, just such caresses he has lavished, and will lavish, and longs to lavish on other women!" she thought.

"You don't love your mother. That's all talk, and talk, and talk!" she said, looking at him with hatred in her eyes.

"Even if so, you must . . ."

"Must decide, and I have decided," she said, and she would have gone away, but at that moment Yashvin walked into the room. Anna greeted him and remained.

Why, when there was a tempest in her soul, and she felt she was standing at a turning-point in her life, which might have fearful consequences—why, at that minute, she had to keep up appearances before an outsider, who sooner or later must know it all—she did not know. But at once quelling the storm within her, she sat down and began talking to their guest.

"Well, how are you getting on? Has your debt been paid you?" she asked Yashvin.

"Oh, pretty fair; I fancy I shan't get it all, but I shall get a good half. And when are you off?" said Yashvin, looking at Vronsky, and unmistakably guessing at a quarrel.

"The day after to-morrow, I think," said Vronsky.

"You've been meaning to go so long, though."

"But now it's quite decided," said Anna, looking Vronsky straight in the face with a look which told him not to dream of the possibility of reconciliation.

"Don't you feel sorry for that unlucky Pyevtsov?" she went on, talking to Yashvin.

"I've never asked myself the question, Anna Arkadyevna, whether I'm sorry for him or not. You see, all my fortune's here"—he touched his breast-pocket—"and just now I'm a wealthy man. But to-day I'm going to the club, and I may come out a beggar. You see, whoever sits down to play with me—he wants to leave me without a shirt to my back, and so do I him. And so we fight it out, and that's the pleasure of it."

"Well, but suppose you were married," said Anna, "how would it be for your wife?"

Yashvin laughed.

"That's why I'm not married, and never mean to be."

"And Helsingfors?" said Vronsky, entering into the conversation and glancing at Anna's smiling face. Meeting his eyes, Anna's face instantly took a coldly severe expression as though she were saying to him: "It's not forgotten. It's all the same."

"Were you really in love?" she said to Yashvin.

"Oh heavens! ever so many times! But you see, some men can play but only so that they can always lay down their cards when the hour comes of a *rendezvous,* while I can take up love, but only so as not to be late for my cards in the evening. That's how I manage things."

"No, I didn't mean that, but the real thing." She would have said *Helsingfors,* but would not repeat the word used by Vronsky.

Voytov, who was buying the horse, came in. Anna got up and went out of the room.

Before leaving the house, Vronsky went into her room. She would have pretended to be looking for something on the table, but ashamed of making a pretense, she looked straight in his face with cold eyes.

"What do you want?" she asked in French.

"To get the guarantee for Gambetta, I've sold him," he said, in a tone which said more clearly than words, "I've no time for discussing things, and it would lead to nothing."

"I'm not to blame in any way," he thought. "If she will punish herself, *tant pis pour elle.*" But as he was going he fancied that she said something, and his heart suddenly ached with pity for her.

"Eh, Anna?" he queried.

"I said nothing," she answered just as coldly and calmly.

"Oh, nothing, *tant pis* then," he thought, feeling cold again, and he turned and went out. As he was going out he caught a glimpse in the looking-glass of her face, white, with quivering lips. He even wanted to stop and to say some comforting word to her, but his legs carried him out of the room before he could think what to say. The whole of that day he spent away from home, and when he came in late in the evening the maid told him that Anna Arkadyevna had a headache and begged him not to go in to her.

CHAPTER XXVI

NEVER before had a day been passed in quarrel. To-day was the first time. And this was not a quarrel. It was the open acknowledgment of complete coldness. Was it possible to glance at her as he had glanced when he came into the room for the guarantee?—to look at her, see her heart was breaking with despair, and go out without a word with that face of callous composure? He was not merely cold to her, he hated her because he loved another woman—that was clear.

And remembering all the cruel words he had said, Anna supplied, too, the words that he had unmistakably wished to say and could have said to her, and she grew more and more exasperated.

"I won't prevent you," he might say. "You can go where you like. You were unwilling to be divorced from your husband, no doubt so that you might go back to him. Go back to him. If you want money, I'll give it to you. How many roubles do you want?"

All the most cruel words that a brutal man could say, he said to her in her imagination, and she could not forgive him for them, as though he had actually said them.

"But didn't he only yesterday swear he loved me, he, a truthful and sincere man? Haven't I despaired for nothing many times already?" she said to herself afterwards.

All that day, except for the visit to Wilson's, which occupied two hours, Anna spent in doubts whether everything were over or whether there were still hope of reconciliation, whether she should go away at once or see him once more. She was expecting him the whole day, and in the evening, as she went to her own room, leaving a message for him that her head ached, she said to herself, "If he comes in spite of what the maid says, it means that he loves me still. If not, it means that all is over, and then I will decide what I'm to do! . . ."

In the evening she heard the rumbling of his carriage stop at the entrance, his ring, his steps and his conversation with the servant; he believed what was told him, did not care to find out more, and went to his own room. So then everything was over.

And death rose clearly and vividly before her mind as the sole means of bringing back love for her in his heart, of punishing him and of gaining the victory in that strife which the evil spirit in possession of her heart was waging with him.

Now nothing mattered: going or not going to Vozdvizhenskoe, getting or not getting a divorce from her husband—all that did not matter. The one thing that mattered was punishing him.

When she poured herself out her usual dose of opium, and thought that she had only to drink off the whole bottle to die, it seemed to her so simple and easy, that she began musing with enjoyment on how he would suffer, and repent and love her memory when it would be too late. She lay in bed with open eyes, by the light of a single burned-down candle, gazing at the carved cornice of the ceiling and at the shadow of the screen that covered part of it, while she vividly pictured to herself how he would feel when she would be no more, when she would be only a memory to him. "How could I say such cruel things to her?" he would say. "How could I go out of the room without saying anything to her? But now she is no more. She has gone away from us forever. She is . . ." Suddenly the shadow of the screen wavered, pounced on the whole cornice, the whole ceiling; other shadows from the other side swooped to meet it, for an instant the shadows flitted back, but then with fresh swiftness they darted forward, wavered, commingled, and all was darkness. "Death!" she thought. And such horror came upon her that for a long while she could not realize where she was, and for a long while her trembling hands could not find the matches and light another candle, instead of the one that had burned down and gone out. "No, anything—only to live! Why, I love him! Why, he loves me! This has been before and will pass," she said, feeling that tears of joy at the return to life were trickling down her cheeks. And to escape from her panic she went hurriedly to his room.

He was asleep there, and sleeping soundly. She went up to him, and holding the light above his face, she gazed a long while at him. Now when he was asleep, she loved him so that at the sight of him she could not keep back tears of tenderness. But she knew that if he waked up he would look at her with cold eyes, convinced that he was right, and that before telling him of her love, she would have to prove to him that he had been wrong in his treatment of her. Without waking him, she went back, and after a second dose of opium she fell towards morning into a heavy, incomplete sleep, during which she never quite lost consciousness.

In the morning she was waked by a horrible nightmare, which had recurred several times in her dreams, even before her connection with Vronsky. A little old man with unkempt beard was doing something bent down over some iron, muttering meaningless French words, and she, as she always did in this nightmare (it was what made the horror of it), felt that this peasant was taking no notice of her, but was doing something horrible with the iron—over her. And she waked up in a cold sweat.

When she got up, the previous day came back to her as though veiled in mist.

"There was a quarrel. Just what has happened several times. I said I had a headache, and he did not come in to see me. Tomorrow we're going away; I must see him and get ready for the journey," she said to herself. And learning that he was in his study, she went down to him. As she passed through the drawing-room she heard a carriage stop at the entrance, and looking out of the window she saw the carriage, from which a young girl in a lilac hat was leaning out giving some direction to the footman ringing the bell. After a parley in the hall, some one came upstairs, and Vronsky's steps could be heard passing the drawing-room. He went rapidly down-stairs. Anna went again to the window. She saw him come out onto the steps without his hat and go up to the carriage. The young girl in the lilac hat handed him a parcel. Vronsky, smiling, said something to her. The carriage drove away, he ran rapidly up-stairs again.

The mists that had shrouded everything in her soul parted suddenly. The feelings of yesterday pierced the sick heart with a fresh pang. She could not understand now how she could have lowered herself by spending a whole day with him in his house. She went into his room to announce her determination.

"That was Madame Sorokina and her daughter. They came and brought me the money and the deeds from maman. I couldn't get them yesterday. How is your head, better?" he said quietly, not wishing to see and to understand the gloomy and solemn expression of her face.

She looked silently, intently at him, standing in the middle of the room. He glanced at her, frowned for a moment, and went on reading a letter. She turned, and went deliberately out of the room. He still might have turned her back, but she had reached the door, he was still silent, and the only sound audible was the rustling of the note-paper as he turned it.

"Oh, by the way," he said at the very moment she was in the doorway, "we're going to-morrow for certain, aren't we?"

"You, but not I," she said, turning round to him.

"Anna, we can't go on like this . . ."

"You, but not I," she repeated.

"This is getting unbearable!"

"You . . . you will be sorry for this," she said, and went out.

Frightened by the desperate expression with which these words were uttered, he jumped up and would have run after her, but on second thoughts he sat down and scowled, setting his teeth. This vulgar—as he thought it—threat of something vague exasperated him. "I've tried everything," he thought; "the only thing left is not to pay attention," and he began to get ready to drive into town, and again to his mother's to get her signature to the deeds.

She heard the sound of his steps about the study and the dining-room. At the drawing-room he stood still. But he did not turn in to see her, he merely gave an order that the horse should be given to Voytov if he came while he was away. Then she heard the carriage brought round, the door opened, and he came out again. But he went back into the porch again, and some one was running up-stairs. It was the valet running up for his gloves that had been forgotten. She went to the window and saw him take the gloves without looking, and touching the coachman on the back he said something to him. Then without looking up at the window he settled himself in his usual attitude in the carriage, with his legs crossed, and drawing on his gloves he vanished round the corner.

CHAPTER XXVII

"He has gone! It is over!" Anna said to herself, standing at the window; and in answer to this question the impression of the darkness when the candle had flickered out, and of her fearful dream mingling into one, filled her heart with cold terror.

"No, that cannot be!" she cried, and crossing the room she rang the bell. She was so afraid now of being alone, that without waiting for the servant to come in, she went out to meet him.

"Inquire where the count has gone," she said. The servant answered that the count had gone to the stable.

"His honor left word that if you cared to drive out, the carriage would be back immediately."

"Very good. Wait a minute. I'll write a note at once. Send Mihail with the note to the stables. Make haste."

She sat down and wrote:

"I was wrong. Come back home; I must explain. For God's sake come! I'm afraid."

She sealed it up and gave it to the servant.

She was afraid of being left alone now; she followed the servant out of the room, and went to the nursery.

"Why, this isn't it, this isn't he! Where are his blue eyes, his sweet, shy smile?" was her first thought when she saw her chubby rosy little girl with her black, curly hair instead of Seryozha, whom in the tangle of her ideas she had expected to see in the nursery. The little girl sitting at the table was obstinately and violently battering on it with a cork, and staring aimlessly at her mother with her pitch-black eyes. Answering the English nurse that she was quite well, and that she was going to the country to-morrow, Anna sat down by the little girl and began spinning the cork to show her. But the child's loud, ringing laugh, and the motion of her eyebrows, recalled Vronsky so vividly that she got up hurriedly, restraining her sobs, and went away. "Can it be all over? No, it cannot be!" she thought. "He will come back. But how can he explain that smile, that excitement after he had been talking to her? But even if he doesn't explain, I will believe. If I don't believe, there's only one thing left for me, and I can't."

She looked at her watch. Twenty minutes had passed. "By now he has received the note and is coming back. Not long, ten minutes more. . . . But what if he doesn't come? No, that cannot be. He mustn't see me with tear-stained eyes. I'll go and wash. Yes, yes; did I do my hair or not?" she asked herself. And she could not remember. She felt her head with her hand. "Yes, my hair has been done, but when I did it I can't in the least remember." She could not believe the evidence of her hand, and went up to the pier-glass to see whether she really had done her hair. She certainly had, but she could not think when she had done it. "Who's that?" she thought, looking in the looking-glass at the swollen face with strangely glittering eyes, that looked in a scared way at her. "Why, it's I!" she suddenly understood, and looking round, she seemed all at once to feel his kisses on her, and twitched her shoulders, shuddering. Then she lifted her hand to her lips and kissed it.

"What is it? Why, I'm going out of my mind!" and she went into her bedroom, where Annushka was tidying the room.

"Annushka," she said, coming to a standstill before her, and she stared at the maid, not knowing what to say to her.

"You meant to go and see Darya Alexandrovna," said the girl, as though she understood.

"Darya Alexandrovna? Yes, I'll go."

"Fifteen minutes there, fifteen minutes back. He's coming, he'll be here soon." She took out her watch and looked at it. "But how could he go away, leaving me in such a state? How can he live, without making it up with me?" She went to the window and began looking into the street. Judging by the time, he might be back now. But her calculations might be wrong, and she began once more to recall when he had started and to count the minutes.

At the moment when she had moved away to the big clock to compare it with her watch, some one drove up. Glancing out of the window, she saw his carriage. But no one came up-stairs, and voices could be heard below. It was the messenger who had come back in the carriage. She went down to him.

"We didn't catch the count. The count had driven off on the lower city road."

"What do you say? What! . . ." she said to the rosy, good-humored Mihail, as he handed her back her note.

"Why, then, he has never received it!" she thought.

"Go with this note to Countess Vronskaya's place, you know? and bring an answer back immediately," she said to the messenger.

"And I, what am I going to do?" she thought. "Yes, I'm going to Dolly's, that's true or else I shall go out of my mind. Yes, and I can telegraph, too." And she wrote a telegram. "I absolutely must talk to you; come at once." After sending off the telegram, she went to dress. When she was dressed and in her hat, she glanced again into the eyes of the plump, comfortable-looking Annushka. There was unmistakable sympathy in those good-natured little gray eyes.

"Annushka, dear, what am I to do?" said Anna, sobbing and sinking helplessly into a chair.

"Why fret yourself so, Anna Arkadyevna? Why, there's nothing out of the way. You drive out a little, and it'll cheer you up," said the maid.

"Yes, I'm going," said Anna, rousing herself and getting up. "And if there's a telegram while I'm away, send it on to Darya Alexandrovna's . . . but no, I shall be back myself."

"Yes, I mustn't think, I must do something, drive somewhere, and most of all, get out of this house," she said, feeling with terror the strange turmoil going on in her own heart, and she made haste to go out and get into the carriage.

"Where to?" asked Pyotr before getting onto the box.

"To Znamenka, the Oblonskys'."

CHAPTER XXVIII

IT WAS bright and sunny. A fine rain had been falling all the morning, and now it had not long cleared up. The iron roofs, the flags of the roads, the flints of the pavements, the wheels and leather, the brass and the tinplate of the carriages—all glistened brightly in the May sunshine. It was three o'clock, and the very liveliest time in the streets.

As she sat in a corner of the comfortable carriage, that hardly swayed on its supple springs, while the grays trotted swiftly, in the midst of the unceasing rattle of wheels and the changing impressions in the pure air, Anna ran over the events of the last days, and she saw her position quite differently from how it had seemed at home. Now the thought of death seemed no longer so terrible and so clear to her, and death itself no longer seemed so inevitable. Now she blamed herself for the humiliation to which she had lowered herself. "I entreat him to forgive me. I have given in to him. I have owned myself in fault. What for? Can't I live without him?" And leaving unanswered the question how she was going to live without him, she fell to reading the signs on the shops. "Office and warehouse. Dental surgeon. Yes, I'll tell Dolly all about it. She doesn't like Vronsky. I shall be sick and ashamed, but I'll tell her. She loves me, and I'll follow her advice. I won't give in to him; I won't let him train me as he pleases. Filippov, bun-shop. They say they send their dough to Petersburg. The Moscow water is so good for it. Ah, the springs at Mitishtchen, and the pancakes!"

And she remembered how, long, long ago, when she was a girl of seventeen, she had gone with her aunt to Troitsa. "Riding, too. Was that really me, with red hands? How much that seemed to me then splendid and out of reach has become worthless, while what I had then has gone out of my reach forever! Could I ever have believed then that I could come to such humiliation? How conceited and self-satisfied he will be when he gets my note! But I will show him. . . . How horrid that paint smells! Why is it they're always painting and building? *Modes et robes,*" she read. A man bowed to her. It was Annushka's husband. "Our parasites"; she remembered how Vronsky had said that. "Our? Why our? What's so awful is that one can't tear up the past by its roots. One can't tear it out, but one can hide one's memory of it. And I'll hide it." And then she thought of her past with Alexey Alexandrovitch, of how she had blotted the memory of it out of her life. "Dolly will think I'm leaving my second husband, and so I certainly must be in the wrong. As if I cared to be right! I can't help it!" she said, and she wanted to cry. But at once she fell to wondering what those two girls could be smiling about. "Love, most likely. They don't know how dreary it is, how low . . . The boulevard and the children. Three boys running, playing at horses. Seryozha! And I'm losing everything and not getting him back. Yes, I'm losing everything, if he doesn't return. Perhaps he was late for the train and has come back by now. Longing for humiliation again!" she said to herself. "No, I'll go to Dolly, and say straight out to her, I'm unhappy, I deserve this, I'm to blame, but still I'm unhappy, help me. These horses, this carriage—how loathsome I am to myself in this carriage—all his; but I won't see them again."

Thinking over the words in which she would tell Dolly, and mentally working her heart up to great bitterness, Anna went up-stairs.

"Is there any one with her?" she asked in the hall.

"Katerina Alexandrovna Levin," answered the footman.

"Kitty! Kitty, whom Vronsky was in love with!" thought Anna, "the girl he thinks of with love. He's sorry he didn't marry her. But me he thinks of with hatred, and is sorry he had anything to do with me."

The sisters were having a consultation about nursing when Anna called. Dolly went down alone to see the visitor who had interrupted their conversation.

"Well, so you've not gone away yet? I meant to have come to you," she said; "I had a letter from Stiva to-day."

"We had a telegram too," answered Anna, looking round for Kitty.

"He writes that he can't make out quite what Alexey Alexandrovitch wants, but he won't go away without a decisive answer."

"I thought you had some one with you. Can I see the letter?"

"Yes; Kitty," said Dolly, embarrassed. "She stayed in the nursery. She has been very ill."

"So I heard. May I see the letter?"

"I'll get it directly. But he doesn't refuse; on the contrary, Stiva has hopes," said Dolly, stopping in the doorway.

"I haven't, and indeed I don't wish it," said Anna.

"What's this? Does Kitty consider it degrading to meet me?" thought Anna when she was alone. "Perhaps she's right, too. But it's not for her, the girl who was in love with Vronsky, it's not for her to show me that, even if it is true. I know that in my position I can't be received by any decent woman. I knew that from the first moment I sacrificed everything to him. And this is my reward! Oh, how I hate him! And what did I come here for? I'm worse here, more miserable." She heard from the next room the sisters' voices in consultation. "And what am I going to say to Dolly now? Amuse Kitty by the sight of my wretchedness, submit to her patronizing? No; and besides, Dolly wouldn't understand. And it would be no good my telling her. It would only be interesting to see Kitty, to show her how I despise every one and everything, how nothing matters to me now."

Dolly came in with the letter. Anna read it and handed it back in silence.

"I knew all that," she said, "and it doesn't interest me in the least."

"Oh, why so? On the contrary, I have hopes," said Dolly, looking inquisitively at Anna. She had never seen her in such a strangely irritable condition. "When are you going away?" she asked.

Anna, half-closing her eyes, looked straight before her and did not answer.

"Why does Kitty shrink from me?" she said, looking at the door and flushing red.

"Oh, what nonsense! She's nursing, and things aren't going right with her, and I've been advising her. . . . She's delighted. She'll be here in a minute," said Dolly awkwardly, not clever at lying. "Yes, here she is."

Hearing that Anna had called, Kitty had wanted not to appear, but Dolly persuaded her. Rallying her forces, Kitty went in, walked up to her, blushing, and shook hands.

"I am so glad to see you," she said with a trembling voice.

Kitty had been thrown into confusion by the inward conflict between her antagonism to this bad woman and her desire to be nice to her. But as soon as she saw Anna's lovely and attractive face, all feeling of antagonism disappeared.

"I should not have been surprised if you had not cared to meet me. I'm used to everything. You have been ill? Yes, you are changed," said Anna.

Kitty felt that Anna was looking at her with hostile eyes. She ascribed this hostility to the awkward position in which Anna, who had once patronized her, must feel with her now, and she felt sorry for her.

They talked of Kitty's illness, of the baby, of Stiva, but it was obvious that nothing interested Anna.

"I came to say good-bye to you," she said, getting up.

"Oh, when are you going?"

But again not answering, Anna turned to Kitty.

"Yes, I am very glad to have seen you," she said with a smile. "I have heard so much of you from every one, even from your husband. He came to see me, and I liked him exceedingly," she said, unmistakably with malicious intent. "Where is he?"

"He has gone back to the country," said Kitty, blushing.

"Remember me to him, be sure you do."

"I'll be sure to!" Kitty said naïvely, looking compassionately into her eyes.

"So good-bye, Dolly." And kissing Dolly and shaking hands with Kitty, Anna went out hurriedly.

"She's just the same and just as charming! She's very lovely!" said Kitty, when she was alone with her sister. "But there's something piteous about her. Awfully piteous!"

"Yes, there's something unusual about her to-day," said Dolly. "When I went with her into the hall, I fancied she was almost crying."

CHAPTER XXIX

ANNA got into the carriage again in an even worse frame of mind than when she set out from home. To her previous tortures was added now that sense of mortification and of being an outcast which she had felt so distinctly on meeting Kitty.

"Where to? Home?" asked Pyotr.

"Yes, home," she said, not even thinking now where she was going.

"How they looked at me as something dreadful, incomprehensible, and curious! What can he be telling the other with such warmth?" she thought, staring at two men who walked by. "Can one ever tell any one what one is feeling? I meant to tell Dolly, and it's a good thing I didn't tell her. How pleased she would have been at my misery! She would have concealed it, but her chief feeling would have been delight at my being punished for the happiness she envied me for. Kitty, she would have been even more pleased. How I can see through her! She knows I was more than usually sweet to her husband. And she's jealous and hates me. And she despises me. In her eyes I'm an immoral woman. If I were an immoral woman I could have made her husband fall in love with me . . . if I'd cared to. And, indeed, I did care to. There's some one who's pleased with himself," she thought, as she saw a fat, rubicund gentleman coming towards her. He took her for an acquaintance, and lifted his glossy hat above his bald, glossy head, and then perceived his mistake. "He thought he knew me. Well, he knows me as well as any one in the world knows me. I don't know myself. I know my appetites, as the French say. They want that dirty ice-cream, that they do know for certain," she thought, looking at two boys stopping an ice-cream seller, who took a barrel off his head and began wiping his perspiring face with a towel. "We all want what is sweet and nice. If not sweetmeats, then a dirty ice. And Kitty's the same—if not Vronsky, then Levin. And she envies me, and hates me. And we all hate each other. I Kitty, Kitty me. Yes, that's the truth. *'Tiutkin, coiffeur.' Je me fais coiffer par Tiutkin.* . . . I'll tell him that when he comes," she thought and smiled. But the same instant she remembered, that she had no one now to tell anything amusing to. "And there's nothing amusing, nothing mirthful, really. It's all hateful. They're singing for vespers, and how carefully that merchant crosses himself! as if he were afraid of missing something. Why these churches and this singing and this humbug? Simply to conceal that we all hate each other like these cab-drivers who are abusing each other so angrily. Yashvin says, 'He wants to strip me of my shirt, and I him of his.' Yes, that's the truth!"

She was plunged in these thoughts, which so engrossed her that she left off thinking of her own position, when the carriage drew up at the steps of her house. It was only when she saw the porter running out to meet her that she remembered she had sent the note and the telegram.

"Is there an answer?" she inquired.

"I'll see this minute," answered the porter, and glancing into his room, he took out and gave her the thin square envelope of a telegram. "I can't come before ten o'clock.—Vronsky," she read.

"And hasn't the messenger come back?"

"No," answered the porter.

"Then, since it's so, I know what I must do," she said, and feeling a vague fury and craving for revenge rising up within her, she ran up-stairs. "I'll go to him myself. Before going away forever, I'll tell him all. Never have I hated any one as I hate that man!" she thought. Seeing his hat on the rack, she shuddered with aversion. She did not consider that his telegram was an answer to her telegram and that he had not yet received her note. She pictured him to herself as talking calmly to his mother and Princess Sorokina and rejoicing at her sufferings. "Yes, I must go quickly," she said, not knowing yet where she was going. She longed to get away as quickly as possible from the feelings she had gone through in that awful house. The servants, the walls, the things in that house—all aroused repulsion and hatred in her and lay like a weight upon her.

"Yes, I must go to the railway station, and if he's not there, then go there and catch him." Anna looked at the railway time-table in the newspapers. An evening train went at two minutes past eight. "Yes, I shall be in time." She gave orders for the other horses to be put in the carriage, and packed in a traveling-bag the things needed for a few days. She knew she would never come back here again.

Among the plans that came into her head she vaguely determined that after what would happen at the station or at the countess's house, she would go as far as the first town on the Nizhni road and stop there.

Dinner was on the table; she went up, but the smell of the bread and cheese was enough to make her feel that all food was disgusting. She ordered the carriage and went out. The house threw a shadow now right across the street, but it was a bright evening and still warm in the sunshine. Annushka, who came down with her things, and Pyotr, who put the things in the carriage, and the coachman, evidently out of humor, were all hateful to her, and irritated her by their words and actions.

"I don't want you, Pyotr."

"But how about the ticket?"

"Well, as you like, it doesn't matter," she said crossly.

Pyotr jumped on the box, and putting his arms akimbo, told the coachman to drive to the booking-office.

CHAPTER XXX

"Here it is again! Again I understand it all!" Anna said to herself, as soon as the carriage had started and swaying lightly, rumbled over the tiny cobbles of the paved road, and again one impression followed rapidly upon another.

"Yes; what was the last thing I thought of so clearly?" she tried to recall it. " *'Tiutkin, coiffeur?'*—no, not that. Yes, of what Yashvin says, the struggle for existence and hatred is the one thing that holds men together. No, it's a useless journey you're making," she said, mentally addressing a party in a coach and four, evidently going for an excursion into the country. "And the dog you're taking with you will be no help to you. You can't get away from yourselves." Turning her eyes in the direction Pyotr had turned to look, she saw a factory-hand almost dead-drunk, with hanging head, being led away by a policeman. "Come, he's found a quicker way," she thought. "Count Vronsky and I did not find that happiness either, though we expected so much from it." And now for the first time Anna turned that glaring light in which she was seeing everything on to her relations with him, which she had hitherto avoided thinking about. "What was it he sought in me? Not love so much as the satisfaction of vanity." She remembered his words, the expression of his face, that recalled an abject setter-dog, in the early days of their connection. And everything now confirmed this. "Yes, there was the triumph of success in him. Of course there was love too, but the chief element was the pride of success. He boasted of me. Now that's over. There's nothing to be proud of. Not to be proud of, but to be ashamed of. He has taken from me all he could, and now I am no use to him. He is weary of me and is trying not to be dishonorable in his behavior to me. He let that out yesterday—he wants divorce and marriage so as to burn his ships. He loves me, but how? The zest is gone, as the English say. That fellow wants every one to admire him and is very much pleased with himself," she thought, looking at a red-faced clerk, riding on a riding-school horse. "Yes, there's not the same flavor about me for him now. If I go away from him, at the bottom of his heart he will be glad."

This was not mere supposition, she saw it distinctly in the piercing light, which revealed to her now the meaning of life and human relations.

"My love keeps growing more passionate and egoistic, while his is waning and waning, and that's why we're drifting apart." She went on musing. "And there's no help for it. He is everything for me, and I want him more and more to give himself up to me entirely. And he wants more and more to get away from me. We walked to meet each other up to the time of our love, and then we have been irresistibly drifting in different directions. And there's no altering that. He tells me I'm insanely jealous, and I have told myself that I am insanely jealous; but it's not true. I'm not jealous, but I'm unsatisfied. But . . ." she opened her lips, and shifted her place in the carriage in the excitement, aroused by the thought that suddenly struck her. "If I could be anything but a mistress, passionately caring for nothing but his caresses; but I can't and I don't care to be anything else. And by that desire I rouse aversion in him, and he rouses fury in me, and it cannot be different. Don't I know that he wouldn't deceive me, that he has no schemes about Princess Sorokina, that he's not in love with Kitty, that he won't desert me! I know all that, but it makes it no better for me. If without loving me, from *duty* he'll be good and kind to me, without what I want, that's a thousand times worse than unkindness! That's—hell! And that's just how it is. For a long while now he hasn't loved me. And where love ends, hate begins. I don't know these streets at all. Hills it seems, and still houses, and houses . . . And in the houses always people and people . . . How many of them, no end, and all hating each other! Come, let me try and think what I want, to make me happy. Well? Suppose I am divorced, and Alexey Alexandrovitch lets me have Seryozha, and I marry Vronsky." Thinking of Alexey Alexandrovitch, she at once pictured him with extraordinary vividness as though he were alive before her, with his mild, lifeless, dull eyes, the blue veins in his white hands, his intonations and the cracking of his fingers, and remembering the feeling which had existed between them, and which was also called love, she shuddered with loathing. "Well, I'm divorced, and become Vronsky's wife. Well, will Kitty cease looking at me as she looked at me to-day? No. And will Seryozha leave off asking and wondering about my two husbands? And is there any new feeling I can awaken between Vronsky and me? Is there possible, if not happiness, some sort of ease from misery? No, no!" she answered now without the slightest hesitation. "Impossible! We are drawn apart by life, and I make his unhappiness, and he mine, and there's no altering him or me. Every attempt has been made, the screw has come unscrewed. Oh, a beggar-woman with a baby. She thinks I'm sorry for her. Aren't we all flung into the world only to hate each other, and so to torture ourselves and each other? Schoolboys coming—laughing—Seryozha?" she thought. "I thought, too, that I loved him, and used to be touched by my own tenderness. But I have lived without him, I gave him up for another love, and did not regret the exchange till that love was satisfied." And with loathing she thought of what she meant by that love. And the clearness with which she saw life now, her own and all men's, was a pleasure to her. "It's so with me and Pyotr, and the coachman, Fyodor, and that merchant, and all the people living along the Volga, where those placards invite one to go, and everywhere and always," she thought when she had driven under the low-pitched roof of the Nizhigorod station, and the porters ran to meet her.

"A ticket to Obiralovka?" said Pyotr.

She had utterly forgotten where and why she was going, and only by a great effort she understood the question.

"Yes," she said, handing him her purse, and taking a little red bag in her hand, she got out of the carriage.

Making her way through the crowd to the first-class waiting-room, she gradually recollected all the details of her position, and the plans between which she was hesitating. And again at the old sore places, hope and then despair poisoned the wounds of her tortured, fearfully throbbing heart. As she sat on the star-shaped sofa waiting for the train, she gazed with aversion at the people coming and going (they were all hateful to her), and thought how she would arrive at the station, would write him a note, and what she would write to him, and how he was at this moment complaining to his mother of his position, not understanding her sufferings, and how she would go into the room, and what she would say to him. Then she thought that life might still be happy, and how miserably she loved and hated him, and how fearfully her heart was beating.

CHAPTER XXXI

A BELL rang, some young men, ugly and impudent, and at the same time careful of the impression they were making, hurried by. Pyotr, too, crossed the room in his livery and top-boots, with his dull, animal face, and came up to her to take her to the train. Some noisy men were quiet as she passed them on the platform, and one whispered something about her to another—something vile, no doubt. She stepped up on the high step, and sat down in a carriage by herself on a dirty seat that had been white. Her bag lay beside her, shaken up and down by the springiness of the seat. With a foolish smile Pyotr raised his hat, with its colored band, at the window, in token of farewell; an impudent conductor slammed the door and the latch. A grotesque-looking lady wearing a bustle (Anna mentally undressed the woman, and was appalled at her hideousness), and a little girl laughing affectedly ran down the platform.

"Katerina Andreevna, she's got them all, *ma tante!*" cried the girl.

"Even the child's hideous and affected," thought Anna. To avoid seeing any one, she got up quickly and seated herself at the opposite window of the empty carriage. A misshapen-looking peasant covered with dirt, in a cap from which his tangled hair stuck out all round, passed by that window, stooping down to the carriage wheels. "There's something familiar about that hideous peasant," thought Anna. And remembering her dream, she moved away to the opposite door, shaking with terror. The conductor opened the door and let in a man and his wife.

"Do you wish to get out?"

Anna made no answer. The conductor and her two fellow-passengers did not notice under her veil her panic-stricken face. She went back to her corner and sat down. The couple seated themselves on the opposite side, and intently but surreptitiously scrutinized her clothes. Both husband and wife seemed repulsive to Anna. The husband asked, would she allow him to smoke, obviously not with a view to smoking but to getting into conversation with her. Receiving her assent, he said to his wife in French something about caring less to smoke than to talk. They made inane and affected remarks to one another, entirely for her benefit. Anna saw clearly that they were sick of each other, and hated each other. And no one could have helped hating such miserable monstrosities.

A second bell sounded, and was followed by moving of luggage, noise, shouting and laughter. It was so clear to Anna that there was nothing for any one to be glad of, that this laughter irritated her agonizingly, and she would have liked to stop up her ears not to hear it. At last the third bell rang, there was a whistle and a hiss of steam, and a clank of chains, and the man in her carriage crossed himself. "It would be interesting to ask him what meaning he attaches to that," thought Anna, looking angrily at him. She looked past the lady out of the window at the people who seemed whirling by as they ran beside the train or stood on the platform. The train, jerking at regular intervals at the junctions of the rails, rolled by the platform, past a stone wall, a signal-box, past other trains; the wheels, moving more smoothly and evenly, resounded with a slight clang on the rails. The window was lighted up by the bright evening sun, and a slight breeze fluttered the curtain. Anna forgot her fellow-passengers, and to the light swaying of the train she fell to thinking again, as she breathed the fresh air.

"Yes, what did I stop at? That I couldn't conceive a position in which life would not be a misery, that we are all created to be miserable, and that we all know it, and all invent means of deceiving each other. And when one sees the truth, what is one to do?"

"That's what reason is given man for, to escape from what worries him," said the lady in French, lisping affectedly, and obviously pleased with her phrase.

The words seemed an answer to Anna's thoughts.

"To escape from what worries him," repeated Anna. And glancing at the red-cheeked husband and the thin wife, she saw that the sickly wife considered herself misunderstood, and the husband deceived her and encouraged her in that idea of herself. Anna seemed to see all their history and all the crannies of their souls, as it were turning a light upon them. But there was nothing interesting in them, and she pursued her thought.

"Yes, I'm very much worried, and that's what reason was given me for, to escape; so then one must escape: why not put out the light when there's nothing more to look at, when it's sickening to look at it all? But how? Why did the conductor run along the footboard, why are they shrieking, those young men in that train? why are they talking, why are they laughing? It's all falsehood, all lying, all humbug, all cruelty! . . ."

When the train came into the station, Anna got out into the crowd of passengers, and moving apart from them as if they were lepers, she stood on the platform, trying to think what she had come here for, and what she meant to do. Everything that had seemed to her possible before was now so difficult to consider, especially in this noisy crowd of hideous people who would not leave her alone. One moment porters ran up to her proffering their services, then young men clacking their heels on the planks of the platform and talking loudly, stared at her; people meeting her dodged past on the wrong side. Remembering that she had meant to go on further if there was no answer, she stopped a porter and asked if her coachman were not here with a note from Count Vronsky.

"Count Vronsky? They sent up here from the Vronskys just this minute, to meet Princess

Sorokina and her daughter. And what is the coachman like?"

Just as she was talking to the porter, the coachman Mihail, red and cheerful in his smart blue coat and chain, evidently proud of having so successfully performed his commission, came up to her and gave her a letter. She broke it open, and her heart ached before she had read it.

"I am very sorry your note did not reach me. I will be home at ten," Vronsky had written carelessly. . . .

"Yes, that's what I expected!" she said to herself with an evil smile.

"Very good, you can go home then," she said softly, addressing Mihail. She spoke softly because the rapidity of her heart's beating hindered her breathing. "No, I won't let you make me miserable," she thought menacingly, addressing not him, not herself, but the power that made her suffer, and she walked along the platform.

Two maid-servants walking along the platform turned their heads, staring at her and making some remarks about her dress. "Real," they said of the lace she was wearing. The young men would not leave her in peace. Again they passed by, peering into her face, and with a laugh shouting something in an unnatural voice. The station-master coming up asked her whether she was going by train. A boy selling kvas never took his eyes off her. "My God! where am I to go?" she thought, going farther and farther along the platform. At the end she stopped. Some ladies and children, who had come to meet a gentleman in spectacles, paused in their loud laughter and talking, and stared at her as she reached them. She quickened her pace and walked away from them to the edge of the platform. A luggage train was coming in. The platform began to sway, and she fancied she was in the train again.

And all at once she thought of the man crushed by the train the day she had first met Vronsky, and she knew what she had to do. With a rapid, light step she went down the steps that led from the tank to the rails and stopped quite near the approaching train.

She looked at the lower part of the carriages, at the screws and chains, and the tall cast-iron wheel of the first carriage slowly moving up, and trying to measure the middle between the front and back wheels, and the very minute when that middle point would be opposite her.

"There," she said to herself, looking into the shadow of the carriage, at the sand and coal-dust which covered the sleepers— "there, in the very middle, and I will punish him and escape from every one and from myself."

She tried to fling herself below the wheels of the first carriage as it reached her; but the red bag which she tried to drop out of her hand delayed her, and she was too late; she missed the moment. She had to wait for the next carriage. A feeling such as she had known when about to take the first plunge in bathing came upon her, and she crossed herself. That familiar gesture brought back into her soul a whole series of girlish and childish memories, and suddenly the darkness that had covered everything for her was torn apart, and life rose up before her for an instant with all its bright past joys. But she did not take her eyes from the wheels of the second carriage. And exactly at the moment when the space between the wheels came opposite her, she dropped the red bag, and drawing her head back into her shoulders, fell on her hands under the carriage, and lightly, as though she would rise again at once, dropped on to her knees. And at the same instant she was terror-stricken at what she was doing. "Where am I? What am I doing? What for?" She tried to get up, to drop backwards; but something huge and merciless struck her on the head and rolled her on her back. "Lord, forgive me all!" she said, feeling it impossible to struggle. A peasant muttering something was working at the iron above her. And the light by which she had read the book filled with troubles, falsehoods, sorrow, and evil, flared up more brightly than ever before, lighted up for her all that had been in darkness, flickered, began to grow dim, and was quenched forever.

Part Eight

CHAPTER I

ALMOST two months had passed. The hot summer was half over, but Sergey Ivanovitch was only just preparing to leave Moscow.

Sergey Ivanovitch's life had not been uneventful during this time. A year ago he had finished his book, the fruit of six years' labor, "Sketch of a Survey of the Principles and Forms of Government in Europe and Russia." Several sections of this book and its introduction had appeared in periodical publications, and other parts had been read by Sergey Ivanovitch to persons of his circle, so that the leading ideas of the work could not be completely novel to the public. But still Sergey Ivanovitch had expected that on its appearance his book would be sure to make a serious impression on society, and if it did not cause a revolution in social science it would, at any rate, make a great stir in the scientific world.

After the most conscientious revision the book had last year been published, and had been distributed among the booksellers.

Though he asked no one about it, reluctantly and with feigned indifference answered his friends' inquiries as to how the book was going, and did not even inquire of the booksellers how the book was selling, Sergey Ivanovitch was all on the alert, with strained attention, watching for the first impression his book would make in the world and in literature.

But a week passed, a second, a third, and in society no impression whatever could be detected. His friends who were specialists and savants, occasionally—unmistakably from politeness—alluded to it. The rest of his acquaintances, not interested in a book on a learned subject, did not talk of it at all. And society generally—just now especially absorbed in other things—was absolutely indifferent. In the press, too, for a whole month there was not a word about his book.

Sergey Ivanovitch had calculated to a nicety the time necessary for writing a review, but a month passed, and a second, and still there was silence.

Only in the *Northern Beetle,* in a comic article on the singer Drabanti, who had lost his voice, there was a contemptuous allusion to Koznishev's book, suggesting that the book had been long ago seen through by every one, and was a subject of general ridicule.

At last in the third month a critical article appeared in a serious review. Sergey Ivanovitch knew the author of the article. He had met him once at Golubtsov's.

The author of the article was a young man, an invalid, very bold as a writer, but extremely deficient in breeding and shy in personal relations.

In spite of his absolute contempt for the author, it was with complete respect that Sergey Ivanovitch set about reading the article. The article was awful.

The critic had undoubtedly put an interpretation upon the book which could not possibly be put on it. But he had selected quotations so adroitly that for people who had not read the book (and obviously scarcely any one had read it) it seemed absolutely clear that the whole book was nothing but a medley of high-flown phrases, not even—as suggested by marks of interrogation—used appropriately, and that the author of the book was a person absolutely without knowledge of the subject. And all this was so wittingly done that Sergey Ivanovitch would not have disowned such wit himself. But that was just what was so awful.

In spite of the scrupulous conscientiousness with which Sergey Ivanovitch verified the correctness of the critic's arguments, he did not for a minute stop to ponder over the faults and mistakes which were ridiculed; but unconsciously he began immediately trying to recall every detail of his meeting and conversation with the author of the article.

"Didn't I offend him in some way?" Sergey Ivanovitch wondered.

And remembering that when they met he had corrected the young man about something he had said that betrayed ignorance, Sergey Ivanovitch found the clue to explain the article.

This article was followed by a deadly silence about the book both in the press and in conversation, and Sergey Ivanovitch saw that his six years' task, toiled at with such love and labor, had gone, leaving no trace.

Sergey Ivanovitch's position was still more difficult from the fact that, since he had finished his book, he had had no more literary work to do, such as had hitherto occupied the greater part of his time.

Sergey Ivanovitch was clever, cultivated, healthy, and energetic, and he did not know what use to make of his energy. Conversations in drawing-rooms, in meetings, assemblies, and committees — everywhere where talk was possible — took up part of his time. But being used for years to town life, he did not waste all his energies in talk, as his less experienced younger brother did, when he was in Moscow. He had a great deal of leisure and intellectual energy still to dispose of.

Fortunately for him, at this period so difficult for him from the failure of his book, the various public questions of the dissenting sects, of the American alliance, of the Samara famine, of exhibitions, and of spiritualism, were definitely replaced in public interest by the Slavonic question, which had hitherto rather languidly interested society, and Sergey Ivanovitch, who had been one of the first to raise this subject, threw himself into it heart and soul.

In the circle to which Sergey Ivanovitch belonged, nothing was talked of or written about just now but the Servian War. Everything that the idle crowd usually does to kill time was done now for the benefit of the Slavonic States. Balls, concerts, dinners, matchboxes, ladies' dresses, beer, restaurants—everything testified to sympathy with the Slavonic peoples.

From much of what was spoken and written on the subject, Sergey Ivanovitch differed on various points. He saw that the Slavonic question had become one of those fashionable distractions which succeed one another in providing society with an object and an occupation. He saw, too, that a great many people were taking up the subject from motives of self-interest and self-advertisement. He recognized that the newspapers published a great deal that was superfluous and exaggerated, with the sole aim of attracting attention and outbidding one another. He saw that in this general movement those who thrust themselves most forward and shouted the loudest were men who had failed and were smarting under a sense of injury—generals without armies, ministers not in the ministry, journalists not on any paper, party leaders without followers. He saw that there was a great deal in it that was frivolous and absurd. But he saw and recognized an unmistakable growing enthusiasm, uniting all classes, with which it was impossible not to sympathize. The massacre of men who were fellow-Christians, and of the same Slavonic race, excited sympathy for the sufferers and indignation against the oppressors. And the heroism of the Servians and Montenegrins struggling for a great cause begot in the whole people a longing to help their brothers not in word but in deed.

But in this there was another aspect that rejoiced Sergey Ivanovitch. That was the manifestation of public opinion. The public had definitely expressed its desire. The soul of the people had, as Sergey Ivanovitch said, found expression. And the more he worked in this cause, the more incontestable it seemed to him that it was a cause destined to assume vast dimensions, to create an epoch.

He threw himself heart and soul into the service of this great cause, and forgot to think about his book. His whole time now was engrossed by it, so that he could scarcely manage to answer all the letters and appeals addressed to him. He worked the whole spring and part of the summer, and it was only in July that he prepared to go away to his brother's in the country.

He was going both to rest for a fortnight, and in the very heart of the people, in the farthest wilds of the country, to enjoy the sight of that uplifting of the spirit of the people, of which, like all residents in the capital and big towns, he was fully persuaded. Katavasov had long been meaning to carry out his promise to stay with Levin, and so he was going with him.

CHAPTER II

Sergey Ivanovitch and Katavasov had only just reached the station of the Kursk line, which was particularly busy and full of people that day, when, looking round for the groom who was following with their things, they saw a party of volunteers driving up in four cabs. Ladies met them with bouquets of flowers, and followed by the rushing crowd they went into the station.

One of the ladies, who had met the volunteers, came out of the hall and addressed Sergey Ivanovitch.

"You too come to see them off?" she asked in French.

"No, I'm going away myself, princess. To my brother's for a holiday. Do you always see them off?" said Sergey Ivanovitch with a hardly perceptible smile.

"Oh, that would be impossible!" answered the princess. "Is it true that eight hundred have been sent from us already? Malvinsky wouldn't believe me."

"More than eight hundred. If you reckon those who have been sent not directly from Moscow, over a thousand," answered Sergey Ivanovitch.

"There! That's just what I said!" exclaimed the lady. "And it's true too, I suppose, that more than a million has been subscribed?"

"Yes, princess."

"What do you say to to-day's telegram? Beaten the Turks again."

"Yes, so I saw," answered Sergey Ivanovitch. They were speaking of the last telegram stating that the Turks had been for three days in succession beaten at all points and put to flight, and that to-morrow a decisive engagement was expected.

"Ah, by the way, a splendid young fellow has asked leave to go, and they've made some difficulty, I don't know why. I meant to ask you; I know him; please write a note about his case. He's being sent by Countess Lidia Ivanovna."

Sergey Ivanovitch asked for all the details the princess knew about the young man, and going into the first-class waiting-room, wrote a note to the person on whom the granting of leave of absence depended, and handed it to the princess.

"You know Count Vronsky, the notorious one . . . is going by this train?" said the princess with a smile full of triumph and meaning, when he found her again and gave her the letter.

"I had heard he was going, but I did not know when. By this train?"

"I've seen him. He's here: there's only his mother seeing him off. It's the best thing, anyway, that he could do."

"Oh, yes, of course."

While they were talking the crowd streamed by them into the dining-room. They went forward too, and heard a gentleman with a glass in his hand delivering a loud discourse to the volunteers. "In the service of religion, humanity, and our brothers," the gentleman said, his voice growing louder and louder; "to this great cause mother Moscow dedicates you with her blessing. *Jivio!*" he concluded, loudly and tearfully.

Every one shouted *Jivio!* and a fresh crowd dashed into the hall, almost carrying the princess off her legs.

"Ah, princess! that was something like!" said Stepan Arkadyevitch, suddenly appearing in the middle of the crowd and beaming upon them with a delighted smile. "Capitally, warmly said, wasn't it? Bravo! And Sergey Ivanovitch! Why, you ought to have said something—just a few words, you know, to encourage them; you do that so well," he added with a soft, respectful, and discreet smile, moving Sergey Ivanovitch forward a little by the arm.

"No, I'm just off."

"Where to?"

"To the country, to my brother's," answered Sergey Ivanovitch.

"Then you'll see my wife. I've written to her, but you'll see her first. Please tell her that they've seen me and that it's 'all right,' as the English say. She'll understand. Oh, and be so good as to tell her I'm appointed secretary of the committee. . . . But she'll understand! You know, *les petites misères de la vie humaine,*" he said, as it were apologizing to the princess. "And Princess Myakaya—not Liza, but Bibish—is sending a thousand guns and twelve nurses. Did I tell you?"

"Yes, I heard so," answered Koznishev indifferently.

"It's a pity you're going away," said Stepan Arkadyevitch. "To-morrow we're giving a dinner to two who're setting off— Dimer-Bartnyansky from Petersburg and our Veslovsky, Grisha. They're both going. Veslovsky's only lately married. There's a fine fellow for you! Eh, princess?" he turned to the lady.

The princess looked at Koznishev without replying. But the fact that Sergey Ivanovitch and the princess seemed anxious to get rid of him did not in the least disconcert Stepan Arkadyevitch. Smiling, he stared at the feather in the princess's hat, and then about him as though he were going to pick something up. Seeing a lady approaching with a collecting-box, he beckoned her up and put in a five-rouble note.

"I can never see these collecting-boxes unmoved while I've money in my pocket," he said. "And how about to-day's telegram? Fine chaps those Montenegrins!"

"You don't say so!" he cried, when the princess told him that Vronsky was going by this train. For an instant Stepan Arkadyevitch's face looked sad, but a minute later, when, stroking his mustaches and swinging as he walked, he went into the hall where Vronsky was, he had completely forgotten his own despairing sobs over his sister's corpse, and he saw in Vronsky only a hero and an old friend.

"With all his faults one can't refuse to do him justice," said the princess to Sergey Ivanovitch as soon as Stepan Arkadyevitch had left them. "What a typically Russian, Slav nature! Only, I'm afraid it won't be pleasant for Vronsky to see him. Say what you will, I'm touched by that man's fate. Do talk to him a little on the way," said the princess.

"Yes, perhaps, if it happens so."

"I never liked him. But this atones for a great deal. He's not merely going himself, he's taking a squadron at his own expense."

"Yes, so I heard."

A bell sounded. Every one crowded to the doors. "Here he is!" said the princess, indicating Vronsky, who with his mother on his arm walked by, wearing a long overcoat and wide-brimmed black hat. Oblonsky was walking beside him, talking eagerly of something.

Vronsky was frowning and looking straight before him, as though he did not hear what Stepan Arkadyevitch was saying.

Probably on Oblonsky's pointing them out, he looked round in the direction where the princess and Sergey Ivanovitch were standing, and without speaking lifted his hat. His face, aged and worn by suffering, looked stony.

Going on to the platform, Vronsky left his mother and disappeared into a compartment.

On the platform there rang out "God save the Tsar," then shouts of "hurrah!" and *"jivio!"* One of the volunteers, a tall, very young man with a hollow chest, was particularly conspicuous, bowing and waving his felt hat and a nosegay over his head. Then two officers emerged, bowing too, and a stout man with a big beard, wearing a greasy forage-cap.

CHAPTER III

SAYING good-bye to the princess, Sergey Ivanovitch was joined by Katavasov; together they got into a carriage full to overflowing, and the train started.

At Tsaritsino station the train was met by a chorus of young men singing "Hail to Thee!" Again the volunteers bowed and poked their heads out, but Sergey Ivanovitch paid no attention to them. He had had so much to do with the volunteers that the type was familiar to him and did not interest him. Katavasov, whose scientific work had prevented his having a chance of observing them hitherto, was very much interested in them and questioned Sergey Ivanovitch.

Sergey Ivanovitch advised him to go into the second-class and

talk to them himself. At the next station Katavasov acted on this suggestion.

At the first stop he moved into the second-class and made the acquaintance of the volunteers. They were sitting in a corner of the carriage, talking loudly and obviously aware that the attention of the passengers and Katavasov as he got in was concentrated upon them. More loudly than all talked the tall, hollow-chested young man. He was unmistakably tipsy, and was relating some story that had occurred at his school. Facing him sat a middle-aged officer in the Austrian military jacket of the Guards uniform. He was listening with a smile to the hollow-chested youth, and occasionally pulling him up. The third, in an artillery uniform, was sitting on a box beside them. A fourth was asleep.

Entering into conversation with the youth, Katavasov learned that he was a wealthy Moscow merchant who had run through a large fortune before he was two-and-twenty. Katavasov did not like him, because he was unmanly and effeminate and sickly. He was obviously convinced, especially now after drinking, that he was performing a heroic action, and he bragged of it in the most unpleasant way.

The second, the retired officer, made an unpleasant impression too upon Katavasov. He was, it seemed, a man who had tried everything. He had been on a railway, had been a land-steward, and had started factories, and he talked, quite without necessity, of all he had done, and used learned expressions quite inappropriately.

The third, the artilleryman, on the contrary, struck Katavasov very favorably. He was a quiet, modest fellow, unmistakably impressed by the knowledge of the officer and the heroic self-sacrifice of the merchant and saying nothing about himself. When Katavasov asked him what had impelled him to go to Servia, he answered modestly:

"Oh, well, every one's going. The Servians want help, too. I'm sorry for them."

"Yes, you artillerymen especially are scarce there," said Katavasov.

"Oh, I wasn't long in the artillery; maybe they'll put me into the infantry or the cavalry."

"Into the infantry when they need artillery more than anything?" said Katavasov, fancying from the artilleryman's apparent age that he must have reached a fairly high grade.

"I wasn't long in the artillery; I'm a cadet retired," he said, and he began to explain how he had failed in his examination.

All of this together made a disagreeable impression on Katavasov, and when the volunteers got out at a station for a drink, Katavasov would have liked to compare his unfavorable impression in conversation with some one. There was an old man in the carriage, wearing a military overcoat, who had been listening all the while to Katavasov's conversation with the volunteers. When they were left alone, Katavasov addressed him.

"What different positions they come from, all those fellows who are going off there," Katavasov said vaguely, not wishing to express his own opinion, and at the same time anxious to find out the old man's views.

The old man was an officer who had served on two campaigns. He knew what makes a soldier, and judging by the appearance and the talk of those persons, by the swagger with which they had recourse to the bottle on the journey, he considered them poor soldiers. Moreover, he lived in a district town, and he was longing to tell how one soldier had volunteered from his town, a drunkard and a thief whom no one would employ as a laborer. But knowing by experience that in the present condition of the public temper it was dangerous to express an opinion opposed to the general one, and especially to criticize the volunteers unfavorably, he too watched Katavasov without committing himself.

"Well, men are wanted there," he said, laughing with his eyes. And they fell to talking of the last war news, and each concealed from the other his perplexity as to the engagement expected next day, since the Turks had been beaten, according to the latest news, at all points. And so they parted, neither giving expression to his opinion.

Katavasov went back to his own carriage, and with reluctant hypocrisy reported to Sergey Ivanovitch his observations of the volunteers, from which it would appear that they were capital fellows.

At a big station at a town the volunteers were again greeted with shouts and singing, again men and women with collecting-boxes appeared, and provincial ladies brought bouquets to the volunteers and followed them into the refreshment-room; but all this was on a much smaller and feebler scale than in Moscow.

CHAPTER IV

WHILE the train was stopping at the provincial town, Sergey Ivanovitch did not go to the refreshment-room, but walked up and down the platform.

The first time he passed Vronsky's compartment he noticed that the curtain was drawn over the window; but as he passed it the second time he saw the old countess at the window. She beckoned to Koznishev.

"I'm going, you see, taking him as far as Kursk," she said.

"Yes, so I heard," said Sergey Ivanovitch, standing at her window and peeping in. "What a noble act on his part!" he added, noticing that Vronsky was not in the compartment.

"Yes, after his misfortune, what was there for him to do?"

"What a terrible thing it was!" said Sergey Ivanovitch.

"Ah, what I have been through! But do get in. . . . Ah, what I have been through!" she repeated, when Sergey Ivanovitch had got in and sat down beside her. "You can't conceive it! For six weeks he did not speak to any one, and would not touch food except when I implored him. And not for one minute could we leave him alone. We took away everything he could have used against himself. We lived on the ground-floor, but there was no reckoning on anything. You know, of course, that he had shot himself once already on her account," she said, and the old lady's eyelashes twitched at the recollection. "Yes, hers was the fitting end for such a woman. Even the death she chose was low and vulgar."

"It's not for us to judge, countess," said Sergey Ivanovitch; "but I can understand that it has been very hard for you."

"Ah, don't speak of it! I was staying on my estate, and he was with me. A note was brought him. He wrote an answer and sent it off. We hadn't an idea that she was close by at the station. In the evening I had only just gone to my room, when my Mary told me a lady had thrown herself under the train. Something seemed to strike me at once. I knew it was she. The first thing I said was, he was not to be told. But they'd told him already. His coachman was there and saw it all. When I ran into his room, he was beside himself—it was fearful to see him. He didn't say a word, but galloped off there. I don't know to this day what happened there, but he was brought back at death's door. I shouldn't have known him. *Prostration complète,* the doctor said. And that was followed almost by madness. Oh, why talk of it!" said the countess with a wave of her hand. "It was an awful time! No, say what you will, she was a bad woman. Why, what is the meaning of such desperate passions? It was all to show herself something out of the way. Well, and that she did do. She brought herself to ruin and two good men—her husband and my unhappy son."

"And what did her husband do?" asked Sergey Ivanovitch.

"He has taken her daughter. Alexey was ready to agree to anything at first. Now it worries him terribly that he should have given his own child away to another man. But he can't take back his word. Karenin came to the funeral. But we tried to prevent his meeting Alexey. For him, for her husband, it was easier, anyway. She had set him free. But my poor son was utterly given up to her. He had thrown up everything, his career, me, and even then she had no mercy on him, but of set purpose she made his ruin complete. No, say what you will, her very death was the death of a vile woman, of no religious feeling. God forgive me, but I can't help hating the memory of her, when I look at my son's misery!"

"But how is he now?"

"It was a blessing from Providence for us—this Servian war. I'm old, and I don't understand the rights and wrongs of it, but it's come as a providential blessing to him. Of course for me, as his mother, it's terrible; and what's worse, they say, *ce n'est pas très bien vu à Pétersbourg.* But it can't be helped! It was the one thing that could rouse him. Yashvin—a friend of his—he had lost all he had at cards and he was going to Servia. He came to see him and persuaded him to go. Now it's an interest for him. Do please talk to him a little. I want to distract his mind. He's so low-spirited. And as bad luck would have it, he has toothache too. But he'll be delighted to see you. Please do talk to him; he's walking up and down on that side."

Sergey Ivanovitch said he would be very glad to, and crossed over to the other side of the station.

CHAPTER V

IN THE slanting evening shadows cast by the baggage piled up on the platform, Vronsky in his long overcoat and slouch hat, with his hands in his pockets, strode up and down, like a wild beast in a cage, turning sharply after twenty paces. Sergey Ivanovitch fancied, as he approached him, that Vronsky saw him but was pretending not to see. This did not affect Sergey Ivanovitch in the slightest. He was above all personal considerations with Vronsky.

At that moment Sergey Ivanovitch looked upon Vronsky as a man taking an important part in a great cause, and Koznishev thought it his duty to encourage him and express his approval. He went up to him.

Vronsky stood still, looked intently at him, recognized him, and going a few steps forward to meet him, shook hands with him very warmly.

"Possibly you didn't wish to see me," said Sergey Ivanovitch, "but couldn't I be of use to you?"

"There's no one I should less dislike seeing than you," said Vronsky. "Excuse me; and there's nothing in life for me to like."

"I quite understand, and

I merely meant to offer you my services," said Sergey Ivanovitch, scanning Vronsky's face, full of unmistakable suffering. "Wouldn't it be of use to you to have a letter to Ristitch—to Milan?"

"Oh, no!" Vronsky said, seeming to understand him with difficulty. "If you don't mind, let's walk on. It's so stuffy among the carriages. A letter? No, thank you; to meet death one needs no letters of introduction. Nor for the Turks . . ." he said, with a smile that was merely of the lips. His eyes still kept their look of angry suffering.

"Yes; but you might find it easier to get into relations, which are after all essential, with any one prepared to see you. But that's as you like. I was very glad to hear of your intention. There have been so many attacks made on the volunteers, and a man like you raises them in public estimation."

"My use as a man," said Vronsky, "is that life's worth nothing to me. And that I've enough bodily energy to cut my way into their ranks, and to trample on them or fall—I know that. I'm glad there's something to give my life for, for it's not simply useless but loathsome to me. Any one's welcome to it." And his jaw twitched impatiently from the incessant gnawing toothache, that prevented him from even speaking with a natural expression.

"You will become another man, I predict," said Sergey Ivanovitch, feeling touched. "To deliver one's brother-men from bondage is an aim worth death and life. God grant you success outwardly—and inwardly peace," he added, and he held out his hand. Vronsky warmly pressed his outstretched hand.

"Yes, as a weapon I may be of some use. But as a man, I'm a wreck," he jerked out.

He could hardly speak for the throbbing ache in his strong teeth, that were like rows of ivory in his mouth. He was silent, and his eyes rested on the wheels of the tender, slowly and smoothly rolling along the rails.

And all at once a different pain, not an ache, but an inner trouble, that set his whole being in anguish, made him for an instant forget his toothache. As he glanced at the tender and the rails, under the influence of the conversation with a friend he had not met since his misfortune, he suddenly recalled *her*—that is, what was left of her when he had run like one distraught into the cloak-room of the railway-station—on the table, shamelessly sprawling out among strangers, the bloodstained body so lately full of life; the head unhurt dropping back with its weight of hair, and the curling tresses about the temples, and the exquisite face, with red, half-opened mouth, the strange, fixed expression, piteous on the lips and awful in the still open eyes, that seemed to utter that fearful phrase—that he would be sorry for it—that she had said when they were quarreling.

And he tried to think of her as she was when he met her the first time, at a railway-station too, mysterious, exquisite, loving, seeking and giving happiness, and not cruelly revengeful as he remembered her on that last moment. He tried to recall his best moments with her, but those moments were poisoned forever. He could only think of her as triumphant, successful in her menace of a wholly useless remorse never to be effaced. He lost all consciousness of toothache, and his face worked with sobs.

Passing twice up and down beside the baggage in silence and regaining his self-possession, he addressed Sergey Ivanovitch calmly:

"You have had no telegrams since yesterday's? Yes, driven back for a third time, but a decisive engagement expected for to-morrow."

And after talking a little more of King Milan's proclamation, and the immense effect it might have, they parted, going to their carriages on hearing the second bell.

CHAPTER VI

SERGEY IVANOVITCH had not telegraphed to his brother to send to meet him, as he did not know when he should be able to leave Moscow. Levin was not at home when Katavasov and Sergey Ivanovitch in a fly hired at the station drove up to the steps of the Pokrovskoe house, as black as niggers from the dust of the road. Kitty, sitting on the balcony with her father and sister, recognized her brother-in-law, and ran down to meet him.

"What a shame not to have let us know," she said, giving her hand to Sergey Ivanovitch, and putting her forehead up for him to kiss.

"We drove here capitally, and have not put you out," answered Sergey Ivanovitch. "I'm so dirty. I'm afraid to touch you. I've been so busy, I didn't know when I should be able to tear myself away. And so you're still as ever enjoying your peaceful, quiet happiness," he said, smiling, "out of the reach of the current in your peaceful backwater. Here's our friend Fyodor Vassilievitch who has succeeded in getting here at last."

"But I'm not a negro, I shall look like a human being when I wash," said Katavasov in his jesting fashion, and he shook hands and smiled, his teeth flashing white in his black face.

"Kostya will be delighted. He has gone to his settlement. It's time he should be home."

"Busy as ever with his farming. It really is a peaceful backwater," said Katavasov; "while we in town think of nothing but the Servian war. Well, how does our friend look at it? He's sure not to think like other people."

"Oh, I don't know, like everybody else," Kitty answered, a little embarrassed, looking round at Sergey Ivanovitch. "I'll send to fetch him. Papa's staying with us. He's only just come home from abroad."

And making arrangements to send for Levin and for the guests to wash, one in his room and the other in what had been Dolly's, and giving orders for their luncheon, Kitty ran out onto the balcony, enjoying the freedom, and rapidity of movement, of which she had been deprived during the months of her pregnancy.

"It's Sergey Ivanovitch and Katavasov, a professor," she said.

"Oh, that's a bore in this heat," said the prince.

"No, papa, he's very nice, and Kostya's very fond of him," Kitty said, with a deprecating smile, noticing the irony on her father's face.

"Oh, I didn't say anything."

"You go to them, darling," said Kitty to her sister, "and entertain them. They saw Stiva at the station; he was quite well. And I must run to Mitya. As ill-luck would have it, I haven't fed him since tea. He's awake now, and sure to be screaming." And feeling a rush of milk, she hurried to the nursery.

This was not a mere guess; her connection with the child was still so close, that she could gauge by the flow of her milk his need of food, and knew for certain he was hungry.

She knew he was crying before she reached the nursery. And he was indeed crying. She heard him and hastened. But the faster she went, the louder he screamed. It was a fine healthy scream, hungry and impatient.

"Has he been screaming long, nurse, very long?" said Kitty hurriedly, seating herself on a chair, and preparing to give the baby the breast. "But give me him quickly. Oh, nurse, how tiresome you are! There, tie the cap afterwards, do!"

The baby's greedy scream was passing into sobs.

"But you can't manage so, ma'am," said Agafea Mihalovna, who was almost always to be found in the nursery. "He must be put straight. A-oo! a-oo!" she chanted over him, paying no attention to the mother.

The nurse brought the baby to his mother. Agafea Mihalovna followed him with a face dissolving with tenderness.

"He knows me, he knows me. In God's faith, Katerina Alexandrovna, ma'am, he knew me!" Agafea Mihalovna cried above the baby's screams.

But Kitty did not hear her words. Her impatience kept growing, like the baby's.

Their impatience hindered things for a while. The baby could not get hold of the breast right, and was furious.

At last, after despairing, breathless screaming, and vain sucking, things went right, and mother and child felt simultaneously soothed, and both subsided into calm.

"But poor darling, he's all in perspiration!" said Kitty in a whisper, touching the baby.

"What makes you think he knows you?" she added, with a sidelong glance at the baby's eyes, that peered roguishly, as she fancied, from under his cap, at his rhythmically puffing cheeks, and the little red-palmed hand he was waving.

"Impossible! If he knew any one, he would have known me," said Kitty, in response to Agafea Mihalovna's statement, and she smiled.

She smiled because, though she said he could not know her, in her heart she was sure that he knew not merely Agafea Mihalovna, but that he knew and understood everything, and knew and understood a great deal too that no one else knew, and that she, his mother, had learned and come to understand only through him. To Agafea Mihalovna, to the nurse, to his grandfather, to his father even, Mitya was a living being, requiring only material care, but for his mother he had long been a mortal being, with whom there had been a whole series of spiritual relations already.

"When he wakes up, please God, you shall see for yourself. Then when I do like this, he simply beams on me, the darling! Simply beams like a sunny day!" said Agafea Mihalovna.

"Well, well; then we shall see," whispered Kitty. "But now go away, he's going to sleep."

CHAPTER VII

AGAFEA MIHALOVNA went out on tiptoe; the nurse let down the blind, chased a fly out from under the muslin canopy of the crib, and a humblebee struggling on the window-frame, and sat down waving a faded branch of birch over the mother and the baby.

"How hot it is! if God would send a drop of rain," she said.

"Yes, yes, sh—sh—sh——" was all Kitty answered, rocking a little, and tenderly squeezing the plump little arm, with rolls of fat at the wrist, which Mitya still waved feebly as he opened and shut his eyes. That hand worried Kitty; she longed to kiss the little hand, but was afraid to for fear of waking the baby. At last the little hand ceased waving, and the eyes closed. Only from time to time, as he went on sucking, the baby raised his long, curly eyelashes and peeped at his mother with wet eyes, that looked black in the twilight. The nurse had left off fanning, and was dozing. From above came the peals of the old prince's voice, and the chuckle of Katavasov.

"They have got into talk without me," thought Kitty, "but still it's vexing that Kostya's out. He's sure to have gone to the bee-house again. Though it's a pity he's there so often, still I'm glad. It distracts his mind. He's become altogether happier and better now than in the spring. He used to be so gloomy and worried that I felt frightened for him. And how absurd he is!" she whispered, smiling.

She knew what worried her husband. It was his unbelief. Although, if she had been asked whether she supposed that in the future life, if he did not believe, he would be damned, she would have had to admit that he would be damned, his unbelief did not cause her unhappiness. And she, confessing that for an unbeliever there can be no salvation, and loving her husband's soul more than anything in the world, thought with a smile of his unbelief, and told herself that he was absurd.

"What does he keep reading philosophy of some sort for all this year?" she wondered. "If it's all written in those books, he can understand them. If it's all wrong, why does he read them? He says himself that he would like to believe. Then why is it he doesn't believe? Surely from his thinking so much? And he thinks so much from being solitary. He's always alone, alone. He can't talk about it all to us. I fancy he'll be glad of these visitors, especially Katavasov. He likes discussions with them," she thought, and passed instantly to the consideration of where it would be more convenient to put Katavasov, to sleep alone or to share Sergey Ivanovitch's room. And then an idea suddenly struck her, which made her shudder and even disturb Mitya, who glanced severely at her. "I do believe the laundress hasn't sent the washing yet, and all the best sheets are in use. If I don't see to it, Agafea Mihalovna will give Sergey Ivanovitch the wrong sheets," and at the very idea of this the blood rushed to Kitty's face.

"Yes, I will arrange it," she decided, and going back to her former thoughts, she remembered that some spiritual question of importance had been interrupted, and she began to recall what. "Yes, Kostya, an unbeliever," she thought again with a smile.

"Well, an unbeliever then! Better let him always be one than like Madame Stahl, or what I tried to be in those days abroad. No, he won't ever sham anything."

And a recent instance of his goodness rose vividly to her mind. A fortnight ago a penitent letter had come from Stepan

Arkadyevitch to Dolly. He besought her to save his honor, to sell her estate to pay his debts. Dolly was in despair, she detested her husband, despised him, pitied him, resolved on a separation, resolved to refuse, but ended by agreeing to sell part of her property. After that, with an irrepressible smile of tenderness, Kitty recalled her husband's shamefaced embarrassment, his repeated awkward efforts to approach the subject, and how at last, having thought of the one means of helping Dolly without wounding her pride, he had suggested to Kitty—what had not occurred to her before—that she should give up her share of the property.

"He an unbeliever indeed! With his heart, his dread of offending any one, even a child! Everything for others, nothing for himself. Sergey Ivanovitch simply considers it as Kostya's duty to be his steward. And it's the same with his sister. Now Dolly and her children are under his guardianship; all these peasants who come to him every day, as though he were bound to be at their service."

"Yes, only be like your father, only like him," she said, handing Mitya over to the nurse, and putting her lips to his cheek.

CHAPTER VIII

EVER since, by his beloved brother's deathbed, Levin had first glanced into the questions of life and death in the light of these new convictions, as he called them, which had during the period from his twentieth to his thirty-fourth year imperceptibly replaced his childish and youthful beliefs—he had been stricken with horror, not so much of death, as of life, without any knowledge of whence, and why, and how, and what it was. The physical organization, its decay, the indestructibility of matter, the law of the conservation of energy, evolution, were the words which usurped the place of his old belief. These words and the ideas associated with them were very well for intellectual purposes. But for life they yielded nothing, and Levin felt suddenly like a man who has changed his warm fur cloak for a muslin garment, and going for the first time into the frost is immediately convinced, not by reason, but by his whole nature that he is as good as naked, and that he must infallibly perish miserably.

From that moment, though he did not distinctly face it, and still went on living as before, Levin had never lost this sense of terror at his lack of knowledge.

He vaguely felt, too, that what he called his new convictions were not merely lack of knowledge, but that they were part of a whole order of ideas, in which no knowledge of what he needed was possible.

At first, marriage, with the new joys and duties bound up with it, had completely crowded out these thoughts. But of late, while he was staying in Moscow after his wife's confinement, with nothing to do, the question that clamored for solution had more and more often, more and more insistently, haunted Levin's mind.

The question was summed up for him thus: "If I do not accept the answers Christianity gives to the problems of my life, what answers do I accept?" And in the whole arsenal of his convictions, so far from finding any satisfactory answers, he was utterly unable to find anything at all like an answer.

He was in the position of a man seeking food in toy-shops and tool-shops.

Instinctively, unconsciously, with every book, with every conversation, with every man he met, he was on the lookout for light on these questions and their solution.

What puzzled and distracted him above everything was that the majority of men of his age and circle had, like him, exchanged their old beliefs for the same new convictions, and yet saw nothing to lament in this, and were perfectly satisfied and serene. So that, apart from the principal question, Levin was tortured by other questions too. Were these people sincere? he asked himself, or were they playing a part? or was it that they understood the answers science gave to these problems in some different, clearer sense than he did? And he assiduously studied both these men's opinions and the books which treated of these scientific explanations.

One fact he had found out since these questions had engrossed his mind, was that he had been quite wrong in supposing from the recollections of the circle of his young days at college, that religion had outlived its day, and that it was now practically non-existent. All the people nearest to him who were good in their lives were believers. The old prince, and Lvov, whom he liked so much, and Sergey Ivanovitch, and all the women believed, and his wife believed as simply as he had believed in his earliest childhood, and ninety-nine hundredths of the Russian people, all the working-people for whose life he felt the deepest respect, believed.

Another fact of which he became convinced, after reading many scientific books, was that the men who shared his views had no other construction to put on them, and that they gave no explanation of the questions which he felt he could not live without answering, but simply ignored their existence and attempted to explain other questions of no possible interest to him, such as the evolution of organisms, the materialistic theory of consciousness, etc.

Moreover, during his wife's confinement, something had happened that seemed extraordinary to him. He, an unbeliever, had fallen into praying, and at the moment he prayed, he believed. But that moment had passed, and he could not make his state of mind at that moment fit into the rest of his life.

He could not admit that at that moment he knew the truth, and that now he was wrong; for as soon as he began thinking calmly about it, it all fell to pieces. He could not admit that he was mistaken then, for his spiritual condition then was precious to him, and to admit that it was a proof of weakness would have been to desecrate those moments. He was miserably divided against himself, and strained all his spiritual forces to the utmost to escape from this condition.

CHAPTER IX

These doubts fretted and harassed him, growing weaker or stronger from time to time, but never leaving him. He read and thought, and the more he read and the more he thought, the further he felt from the aim he was pursuing.

Of late in Moscow and in the country, since he had become convinced that he would find no solution in the materialists, he had read and reread thoroughly Plato, Spinoza, Kant, Schelling,

Hegel, and Schopenhauer, the philosophers who gave a non-materialistic explanation of life.

Their ideas seemed to him fruitful when he was reading or was himself seeking arguments to refute other theories, especially those of the materialists; but as soon as he began to read or sought for himself a solution of problems, the same thing always happened. As long as he followed the fixed definition of obscure words such as *spirit, will, freedom, essence,* purposely letting himself go into the snare of words the philosophers set for him, he seemed to comprehend something. But he had only to forget the artificial train of reasoning, and to turn from life itself to what had satisfied him while thinking in accordance with the fixed definitions, and all this artificial edifice fell to pieces at once like a house of cards, and it became clear that the edifice had been built up out of those transposed words, apart from anything in life more important than reason.

At one time, reading Schopenhauer, he put in place of his *will* the word *love,* and for a couple of days this new philosophy charmed him, till he removed a little away from it. But then, when he turned from life itself to glance at it again, it fell away too, and proved to be the same muslin garment with no warmth in it.

His brother Sergey Ivanovitch advised him to read the theological works of Homiakov. Levin read the second volume of Homiakov's works, and in spite of the elegant, epigrammatic, argumentative style which at first repelled him, he was impressed by the doctrine of the church he found in them. He was struck at first by the idea that the apprehension of divine truths had not been vouchsafed to man, but to a corporation of men bound together by love—to the church. What delighted him was the thought how much easier it was to believe in a still existing living church, embracing all the beliefs of men, and having God at its head, and therefore holy and infallible, and from it to accept the faith in God, in the creation, the fall, the redemption, than to begin with God, a mysterious, far-away God, the creation, etc. But afterwards, on reading a Catholic writer's history of the church, and then a Greek orthodox writer's history of the church, and seeing that the two churches, in their very conception infallible, each deny the authority of the other, Homiakov's doctrine of the church lost all its charm for him, and this edifice crumbled into dust like the philosophers' edifices.

All that spring he was not himself, and went through fearful moments of horror.

"Without knowing what I am and why I am here, life's impossible; and that I can't know, and so I can't live," Levin said to himself.

"In infinite time, in infinite matter, in infinite space, is formed a bubble-organism, and that bubble lasts a while and bursts, and that bubble is Me."

It was an agonizing error, but it was the sole logical result of ages of human thought in that direction.

This was the ultimate belief on which all the systems elaborated by human thought in almost all their ramifications rested. It was the prevalent conviction, and of all other explanations Levin had unconsciously, not knowing when or how, chosen it, as any way the clearest, and made it his own.

But it was not merely a falsehood, it was the cruel jeer of some wicked power, some evil, hateful power, to whom one could not submit.

He must escape from this power. And the means of escape every man had in his own hands. He had but to cut short this dependence on evil. And there was one means—death.

And Levin, a happy father and husband, in perfect health, was several times so near suicide that he hid the cord that he might not be tempted to hang himself, and was afraid to go out with his gun for fear of shooting himself.

But Levin did not shoot himself, and did not hang himself; he went on living.

CHAPTER X

WHEN Levin thought what he was and what he was living for, he could find no answer to the questions and was reduced to despair, but he left off questioning himself about it. It seemed as though he knew both what he was and for what he was living, for he acted and lived resolutely and without hesitation. Indeed, in these latter days he was far more decided and unhesitating in life than he had ever been.

When he went back to the country at the beginning of June, he went back also to his usual pursuits. The management of the estate, his relations with the peasants and the neighbors, the care of his household, the management of his sister's and brother's property, of which he had the direction, his relations with his wife and kindred, the care of his child, and the new bee-keeping hobby he had taken up that spring, filled all his time.

These things occupied him now, not because he justified them to himself by any sort of general principles, as he had done in former days; on the contrary, disappointed by the failure of his former efforts for the general welfare, and too much occupied with his own thought and the mass of business with which he was burdened from all sides, he had completely given up thinking of the general good, and he busied himself with all this work simply because it seemed to him that he must do what he was doing—that he could not do otherwise. In former days—almost from childhood, and increasingly up to full manhood—when he had tried to do anything that would be good for all, for humanity, for Russia, for the whole village, he had noticed that the idea of it had been pleasant, but the work itself had always been incoherent, that then he had never had a full conviction of its absolute necessity, and that the work that had begun by seeming so great, had grown less and less, till it vanished into nothing. But now, since his marriage, when he had begun to confine himself more and more to living for himself, though he experienced no delight at all at the thought of the work he was doing, he felt a complete conviction of its necessity, saw that it succeeded far better than in old days, and that it kept on growing more and more.

Now, involuntarily it seemed, he cut more and more deeply into the soil like a plough, so that he could not be drawn out without turning aside the furrow.

To live the same family life as his father and forefathers— that is, in the same condition of culture—and to bring up his children in the same, was incontestably necessary. It was as necessary as dining when one was hungry. And to do this, just as it was necessary to cook dinner, it was necessary to keep the mechanism of agriculture at Pokrovskoe going so as to yield an income. Just as incontestably as it was necessary to repay a debt was it necessary to keep the property in such a condition that his son, when he received it as a heritage, would say "thank you" to his father as Levin had said "thank you" to his grandfather for all he built and planted. And to do this it was necessary to look after the land himself, not to let it, and to breed cattle, manure the fields, and plant timber.

It was impossible not to look after the affairs of Sergey Ivanovitch, of his sister, of the peasants who came to him for advice and were accustomed to do so—as impossible as to fling down a child one is carrying in one's arms. It was necessary to look after the comfort of his sister-in-law and her children, and of his wife and baby, and it was impossible not to spend with them at least a short time each day.

And all this, together with shooting and his new bee-keeping, filled up the whole of Levin's life, which had no meaning at all for him, when he began to think.

But besides knowing thoroughly what he had to do, Levin knew in just the same way *how* he had to do it all, and what was more important than the rest.

He knew he must hire laborers as cheaply as possible; but to hire men under bond, paying them in advance at less than the current rate of wages, was what he must not do, even though it was very profitable. Selling straw to the peasants in times of scarcity of provender was what he might do, even though he felt sorry for them; but the tavern and the pot-house must be put down, though they were a source of income. Felling timber must be punished as severely as possible, but he could not exact forfeits for cattle being driven onto his fields; and though it annoyed the keeper and made the peasants not afraid to graze their cattle on his land, he could not keep their cattle as a punishment.

To Pyotr, who was paying a money-lender ten per cent a month, he must lend a sum of money to set him free. But he could not let off peasants who did not pay their rent, nor let them fall into arrears. It was impossible to overlook the bailiff's not having mown the meadows and letting the hay spoil; and it was equally impossible to mow those acres where a young copse had been planted. It was impossible to excuse a laborer who had gone home in the busy season because his father was dying, however sorry he might feel for him, and he must subtract from his pay those costly months of idleness. But it was impossible not to allow monthly rations to the old servants who were of no use for anything.

Levin knew that when he got home he must first of all go to his wife, who was unwell, and that the peasants who had been waiting for three hours to see him could wait a little longer. He knew too that, regardless of all the pleasure he felt in taking a swarm, he must forego that pleasure, and leave the old man to see to the bees alone, while he talked to the peasants who had come after him to the bee-house.

Whether he were acting rightly or wrongly he did not know, and far from trying to prove that he was, nowadays he avoided all thought or talk about it.

Reasoning had brought him to doubt, and prevented him from seeing what he ought to do and what he ought not. When he did not think, but simply lived, he was continually aware of the presence of an infallible judge in his soul, determining which of two possible courses of action was the better and which was the worse, and as soon as he did not act rightly, he was at once aware of it.

So he lived, not knowing and not seeing any chance of knowing what he was and what he was living for, and harassed at this lack of knowledge to such a point that he was afraid of suicide, and yet firmly laying down his own individual definite path in life.

CHAPTER XI

The day on which Sergey Ivanovitch came to Pokrovskoe was one of Levin's most painful days. It was the very busiest working-time, when all the peasantry show an extraordinary intensity of self-sacrifice in labor, such as is never shown in any other conditions of life, and would be highly esteemed if the men who showed these qualities themselves thought highly of them, and if it were not repeated every year, and if the results of this intense labor were not so simple.

To reap and bind the rye and oats and to carry it, to mow the meadows, turn over the fallows, thrash the seed and sow the winter corn—all this seems so simple and ordinary; but to succeed in getting through it all every one in the village, from the old man to the young child, must toil incessantly for three or four weeks, three times as hard as usual, living on rye-beer, onions, and black bread, thrashing and carrying the sheaves at night, and not giving more than two or three hours in the twenty-four to sleep. And every year this is done all over Russia.

Having lived the greater part of his life in the country and in the closest relations with the peasants, Levin always felt in this busy time that he was infected by this general quickening of energy in the people.

In the early morning he rode over to the first sowing of the rye, and to the oats, which were being carried to the stacks, and returning home at the time his wife and sister-in-law were getting up, he drank coffee with them and walked to the farm, where a new thrashing-machine was to be set working to get ready the seed-corn.

He was standing in the cool granary, still fragrant with the leaves of the hazel branches interlaced on the freshly peeled aspen beams of the new thatch roof. He gazed through the open door in which the dry bitter dust of the thrashing whirled and played, at the grass of the thrashing-floor in the sunlight and the fresh straw that had been brought in from the barn, then at the speckly-headed, white-breasted swallows that flew chirping in under the roof and, fluttering their wings, settled in the crevices of the doorway, then at the peasants bustling in the dark, dusty barn, and he thought strange thoughts.

"Why is it all being done?" he thought. "Why am I standing here, making them work? What are they all so busy for, trying to show their zeal before me? What is that old Matrona, my old friend, toiling for? (I doctored her, when the beam fell on her in the fire)" he thought, looking at a thin old woman who was raking up the grain, moving painfully with her bare, sun-blackened feet over the uneven, rough floor. "Then she recovered, but to-day or to-morrow or in ten years she won't; they'll bury her, and nothing will be left either of her or of that smart girl in the red jacket, who with that skilful, soft action shakes the ears out of their husks. They'll bury her and this piebald horse, and very soon too," he thought, gazing at the heavily moving, panting horse that kept walking up the wheel that turned under him. "And they will bury her and Fyodor the thrasher with his curly beard full of chaff and his shirt torn on his white shoulders—they will bury him. He's untying the sheaves, and giving orders, and shouting to the women, and quickly setting straight the strap on the moving wheel. And what's more, it's not them alone—me they'll bury too, and nothing will be left. What for?"

He thought this, and at the same time looked at his watch to reckon how much they thrashed in an hour. He wanted to know this so as to judge by it the task to set for the day.

"It'll soon be one, and they're only beginning the third sheaf," thought Levin. He went up to the man that was feeding the machine, and shouting over the roar of the machine he told him to put it in more slowly. "You put in too much at a time, Fyodor. Do you see—it gets choked, that's why it isn't getting on. Do it evenly."

Fyodor, black with the dust that clung to his moist face, shouted something in response, but still went on doing it as Levin did not want him to.

Levin, going up to the machine, moved Fyodor aside, and began feeding the corn in himself. Working on till the peasants' dinner-hour, which was not long in coming, he went out of the barn with Fyodor and fell into talk with him, stopping beside a neat yellow sheaf of rye laid on the thrashing-floor for seed.

Fyodor came from a village at some distance from the one in which Levin had once allotted land to his coöperative association. Now it had been let to a former house-porter.

Levin talked to Fyodor about this land and asked whether Platon, a well-to-do peasant of good character belonging to the same village, would not take the land for the coming year.

"It's a high rent; it wouldn't pay Platon, Konstantin Dmitrievitch," answered the peasant, picking the ears off his sweat-drenched shirt.

"But how does Kirillov make it pay?"

"Mituh!" (so the peasant called the house-porter, in a tone of contempt), "you may be sure he'll make it pay, Konstantin

Dmitrievitch! He'll get his share, however he has to squeeze to get it! He's no mercy on a Christian. But Uncle Fokanitch" (so he called the old peasant Platon), "do you suppose he'd flay the skin off a man? Where there's debt, he'll let any one off. And he'll not wring the last penny out. He's a man too."

"But why will he let any one off?"

"Oh, well, of course, folks are different. One man lives for his own wants and nothing else, like Mituh, he only thinks of filling his belly, but Fokanitch is a righteous man. He lives for his soul. He does not forget God."

"How thinks of God? How does he live for his soul?" Levin almost shouted.

"Why, to be sure, in truth, in God's way. Folks are different. Take you now, you wouldn't wrong a man. . . ."

"Yes, yes, good-bye!" said Levin, breathless with excitement, and turning round he took his stick and walked quickly away towards home. At the peasant's words that Fokanitch lived for his soul, in truth, in God's way, undefined but significant ideas seemed to burst out as though they had been locked up, and all striving towards one goal, they thronged whirling through his head, blinding him with their light.

CHAPTER XII

LEVIN strode along the highroad, absorbed not so much in his thoughts (he could not yet disentangle them) as in his spiritual condition, unlike anything he had experienced before.

The words uttered by the peasant had acted on his soul like an electric shock, suddenly transforming and combining into a single whole the whole swarm of disjointed, impotent, separate thoughts that incessantly occupied his mind. These thoughts had unconsciously been in his mind even when he was talking about the land.

He was aware of something new in his soul, and joyfully tested this new thing, not yet knowing what it was.

"Not living for his own wants, but for God? For what God? And could one say anything more senseless than what he said? He said that one must not live for one's own wants, that is, that one must not live for what we understand, what we are attracted by, what we desire, but must live for something incomprehensible, for God, whom no one can understand nor even define. What of it? Didn't I understand those senseless words of Fyodor's? And understanding them, did I doubt of their truth? Did I think them stupid, obscure, inexact? No, I understood him, and exactly as he understands the words. I understood them more fully and clearly than I understand anything in life, and never in my life have I doubted nor can I doubt about it. And not only I, but every one, the whole world understands nothing fully but this, and about this only they have no doubt and are always agreed.

"And I looked out for miracles, complained that I did not see a miracle which would convince me. A material miracle would have persuaded me. And here is a miracle, the sole miracle possible, continually existing, surrounding me on all sides, and I never noticed it!

"Fyodor says that Kirillov lives for his belly. That's comprehensible and rational. All of us as rational beings can't do anything else but live for our belly. And all of a sudden the same Fyodor says that one mustn't live for one's belly, but must live for truth, for God, and at a hint I understand him! And I and millions of men, men who lived ages ago and men living now—peasants, the poor in spirit and the learned, who have thought and written about it, in their obscure words saying the same thing—we are all agreed about this one thing: what we must live for and what is good. I and all men have only one firm, incontestable, clear knowledge, and that knowledge cannot be explained by the reason—it is outside it, and has no causes and can have no effects.

"If goodness has causes, it is not goodness; if it has effects, a reward, it is not goodness either. So goodness is outside the chain of cause and effect.

"And yet I know it, and we all know it.

"What could be a greater miracle than that?

"Can I have found the solution of it all? can my sufferings be over?" thought Levin, striding along the dusty road, not noticing the heat nor his weariness, and experiencing a sense of relief from prolonged suffering. This feeling was so delicious that it seemed to him incredible. He was breathless with emotion and incapable of going farther; he turned off the road into the forest and lay down in the shade of an aspen on the uncut grass. He took his hat off his hot head and lay propped on his elbow in the lush, feathery, woodland grass.

"Yes, I must make it clear to myself and understand," he thought, looking intently at the untrampled grass before him, and following the movements of a green beetle, advancing along a blade of couch-grass and lifting up in its progress a leaf of goat-weed. "What have I discovered?" he asked himself, bending aside the leaf of goat-weed out of the beetle's way and twisting another blade of grass above for the beetle to cross over onto it. "What is it makes me glad? What have I discovered?

"I have discovered nothing. I have only found out what I knew. I understand the force that in the past gave me life, and now too gives me life. I have been set free from falsity, I have found the Master.

"Of old I used to say that in my body, that in the body of this grass and of this beetle (there, she didn't care for the grass, she's opened her wings and flown away), there was going on a transformation of matter in accordance with physical, chemical, and physiological laws. And in all of us, as well as in the aspens and the clouds and the misty patches, there was a process of evolution. Evolution from what? into what?—Eternal evolution and struggle. . . . As though there could be any sort of tendency and struggle in the eternal! And I was astonished that in spite of the utmost effort of thought along that road I could not discover the meaning of life, the meaning of my impulses and yearnings. Now I say that I know the meaning of my life: 'To live for God, for my soul.' And this meaning, in spite of its clearness, is mysterious and marvelous. Such, indeed, is the meaning of everything existing. Yes, pride," he said to himself, turning over on his stomach and beginning to tie a noose of blades of grass, trying not to break them.

"And not merely pride of intellect, but dulness of intellect. And most of all, the deceitfulness; yes, the deceitfulness of intellect. The cheating knavishness of intellect, that's it," he said to himself.

And he briefly went through, mentally, the whole course of

his ideas during the last two years, the beginning of which was the clear confronting of death at the sight of his dear brother hopelessly ill.

Then, for the first time, grasping that for every man, and himself too, there was nothing in store but suffering, death, and forgetfulness, he had made up his mind that life was impossible like that, and that he must either interpret life so that it would not present itself to him as the evil jest of some devil, or shoot himself.

But he had not done either, but had gone on living, thinking, and feeling, and had even at that very time married, and had had many joys and had been happy, when he was not thinking of the meaning of his life.

What did this mean? It meant that he had been living rightly, but thinking wrongly.

He had lived (without being aware of it) on those spiritual truths that he had sucked in with his mother's milk, but he had thought, not merely without recognition of these truths, but studiously ignoring them.

Now it was clear to him that he could only live by virtue of the beliefs in which he had been brought up.

"What should I have been, and how should I have spent my life, if I had not had these beliefs, if I had not known that I must live for God and not for my own desires? I should have robbed and lied and killed. Nothing of what makes the chief happiness of my life would have existed for me." And with the utmost stretch of imagination he could not conceive the brutal creature he would have been himself, if he had not known what he was living for.

"I looked for an answer to my question.

And thought could not give an answer to my question—it is incommensurable with my question. The answer has been given me by life itself, in my knowledge of what is right and what is wrong. And that knowledge I did not arrive at in any way, it was given to me as to all men, *given,* because I could not have got it from anywhere.

"Where could I have got it? By reason could I have arrived at knowing that I must love my neighbor and not oppress him? I was told that in my childhood, and I believed it gladly, for they told me what was already in my soul. But who discovered it? Not reason. Reason discovered the struggle for existence, and the law that requires us to oppress all who hinder the satisfaction of our desires. That is the deduction of reason. But loving one's neighbor reason could never discover, because it's irrational."

CHAPTER XIII

AND Levin remembered a scene he had lately witnessed between Dolly and her children. The children, left to themselves, had begun cooking raspberries over the candles and squirting milk into each other's mouths with a syringe. Their mother, catching them at these pranks, began reminding them in Levin's presence of the trouble their mischief gave to the grown-up people, and that this trouble was all for their sake, and that if they smashed the cups they would have nothing to drink their tea out of, and that if they wasted the milk, they would have nothing to eat, and die of hunger.

And Levin had been struck by the passive, weary incredulity with which the children heard what their mother said to them. They were simply annoyed that their amusing play had been interrupted, and did not believe a word of what their mother was saying. They could not believe it indeed, for they could not take in the immensity of all they habitually enjoyed, and so could not conceive that what they were destroying was the very thing they lived by.

"That all comes of itself," they thought, "and there's nothing interesting or important about it because it has always been so, and always will be so. And it's all always the same. We've no need to think about that, it's all ready. But we want to invent something of our own, and new. So we thought of putting raspberries in a cup, and cooking them over a candle, and squirting milk straight into each other's mouths. That's fun, and something new, and not a bit worse than drinking out of cups."

"Isn't it just the same that we do, that I did, searching by the aid of reason for the significance of the forces of nature and the meaning of the life of man?" he thought.

"And don't all the theories of philosophy do the same, trying by the path of thought, which is strange and not natural to man, to bring him to a knowledge of what he has known long ago, and knows so certainly that he could not live at all without it? Isn't it distinctly to be seen in the development of each philosopher's theory, that he knows what is the chief significance of life beforehand, just as positively as the peasant Fyodor, and not a bit more clearly than he, and is simply trying by a dubious intellectual path to come back to what every one knows?

"Now then, leave the children to themselves to get things alone and make their crockery, get the milk from the cows, and so on. Would they be naughty then? Why, they'd die of hunger! Well, then, leave us with our passions and thoughts, without any idea of the one God, of the Creator, or without any idea of what is right, without any idea of moral evil.

"Just try and build up anything without those ideas!

"We only try and destroy them, because we're spiritually provided for. Exactly like the children!

"Whence have I that joyful knowledge, shared with the peasant, that alone gives peace to my soul? Whence did I get it?

"Brought up with an idea of God, a Christian, my whole life filled with the spiritual blessings Christianity has given me, full of them, and living on those blessings, like the children I did not understand them, and destroy, that is try to destroy, what I live by. And as soon as an important moment of life comes, like the children when they are cold and hungry, I turn to Him, and even less than the children when their mother scolds them for their childish mischief, do I feel that my childish efforts at wanton madness are reckoned against me.

"Yes, what I know, I know not by reason, but it has been

given to me, revealed to me, and I know it with my heart, by faith in the chief thing taught by the church.

"The church! the church!" Levin repeated to himself. He turned over on the other side, and leaning on his elbow, fell to gazing into the distance at a herd of cattle crossing over to the river.

"But can I believe in all the church teaches?" he thought, trying himself, and thinking of everything that could destroy his present peace of mind. Intentionally he recalled all those doctrines of the church which had always seemed most strange and had always been a stumbling-block to him.

"The Creation? But how did I explain existence? By existence? By nothing? The devil and sin. But how do I explain evil? . . . The atonement? . . .

"But I know nothing, nothing, and I can know nothing but what has been told to me and all men."

And it seemed to him that there was not a single article of faith of the church which could destroy the chief thing—faith in God, in goodness, as the one goal of man's destiny.

Under every article of faith of the church could be put the faith in the service of truth instead of one's desires. And each doctrine did not simply leave that faith unshaken, each doctrine seemed essential to complete that great miracle, continually manifest upon earth, that made it possible for each man and millions of different sorts of men, wise men and imbeciles, old men and children—all men, peasants, Lvov, Kitty, beggars and kings to understand perfectly the same one thing, and to build up thereby that life of the soul which alone is worth living, and which alone is precious to us.

Lying on his back, he gazed up now into the high, cloudless sky. "Do I not know that that is infinite space, and that it is not a round arch? But, however I screw up my eyes and strain my sight, I cannot see it not round and not bounded, and in spite of my knowing about infinite space, I am incontestably right when I see a solid blue dome, and more right than when I strain my eyes to see beyond it."

Levin ceased thinking, and only, as it were, listened to mysterious voices that seemed talking joyfully and earnestly within him.

"Can this be faith?" he thought, afraid to believe in his happiness. "My God, I thank Thee!" he said, gulping down his sobs, and with both hands brushing away the tears that filled his eyes.

CHAPTER XIV

Levin looked before him and saw a herd of cattle, then he caught sight of his trap with Raven in the shafts, and the coachman, who, driving up to the herd, said something to the herdsman. Then he heard the rattle of the wheels and the snort of the sleek horse close by him. But he was so buried in his thoughts that he did not even wonder why the coachman had come for him.

He only thought of that when the coachman had driven quite up to him and shouted to him. "The mistress sent me. Your brother has come, and some gentleman with him."

Levin got into the trap and took the reins. As though just roused out of sleep, for a long while Levin could not collect his faculties. He stared at the sleek horse flecked with lather between his haunches and on his neck, where the harness rubbed, stared at Ivan the coachman sitting beside him, and remembered that he was expecting his brother, thought that his wife was most likely uneasy at his long absence, and tried to guess who was the visitor who had come with his brother. And his brother and his wife and the unknown guest seemed to him now quite different from before. He fancied that now his relations with all men would be different.

"With my brother there will be none of that aloofness there always used to be between us, there will be no disputes; with Kitty there shall never be quarrels; with the visitor, whoever he may be, I will be friendly and nice; with the servants, with Ivan, it will all be different."

Pulling the stiff rein and holding in the good horse that snorted with impatience and seemed begging to be let go, Levin looked round at Ivan sitting beside him, not knowing what to do with his unoccupied hand, continually pressing down his shirt as it puffed out, and he tried to find something to start a conversation about with him. He would have said that Ivan had pulled the saddle-girth up too high, but that was like blame, and he longed for friendly, warm talk. Nothing else occurred to him.

"Your honor must keep to the right and mind that stump," said the coachman, pulling the rein Levin held.

"Please don't touch and don't teach me!" said Levin, angered by this interference. Now, as always, interference made him angry, and he felt sorrowfully at once how mistaken had been his supposition that his spiritual condition could immediately change him in contact with reality.

He was not a quarter of a mile from home when he saw Grisha and Tanya running to meet him.

"Uncle Kostya! mamma's coming, and grandfather, and Sergey Ivanovitch, and some one else," they said, clambering up into the trap.

"Who is he?"

"An awfully terrible person! And he does like this with his arms," said Tanya, getting up in the trap and mimicking Katavasov.

"Old or young?" asked Levin, laughing, reminded of some one, he did not know whom, by Tanya's performance.

"Oh, I hope it's not a tiresome person!" thought Levin.

As soon as he turned, at a bend in the road, and saw the party coming, Levin recognized Katavasov in a straw hat, walking along swinging his arms just as Tanya had shown him. Katavasov was very fond of discussing metaphysics, having derived his notions from natural science writers who had never studied metaphysics, and in Moscow Levin had had many arguments with him of late.

And one of these arguments, in which Katavasov had obviously considered that he came off victorious, was the first thing Levin thought of as he recognized him.

"No, whatever I do, I won't argue and give utterance to my ideas lightly," he thought.

Getting out of the trap and greeting his brother and Katavasov, Levin asked about his wife.

"She has taken Mitya to Kolok" (a copse near the house). "She meant to have him out there because it's so hot indoors," said Dolly. Levin had always advised his wife not to take the baby to the wood, thinking it unsafe, and he was not pleased to hear this.

"She rushes about from place to place with him," said the prince, smiling. "I advised her to try putting him in the ice cellar."

"She meant to come to the bee-house. She thought you would be there. We are going there," said Dolly.

"Well, and what are you doing?" said Sergey Ivanovitch, falling back from the rest and walking beside him.

"Oh, nothing special. Busy as usual with the land," answered Levin. "Well, and what about you? Come for long? We have been expecting you for such a long time."

"Only for a fortnight. I've a great deal to do in Moscow."

At these words the brothers' eyes met, and Levin, in spite of the desire he always had, stronger than ever just now, to be on affectionate and still more open terms with his brother, felt an awkwardness in looking at him. He dropped his eyes and did not know what to say.

Casting over the subjects of conversation that would be pleasant to Sergey Ivanovitch, and would keep him off the subject of the Servian war and the Slavonic question, at which he had hinted by the allusion to what he had to do in Moscow, Levin began to talk of Sergey Ivanovitch's book.

"Well, have there been reviews of your book?" he asked.

Sergey Ivanovitch smiled at the intentional character of the question.

"No one is interested in that now, and I less than any one," he said. "Just look, Darya Alexandrovna, we shall have a shower," he added, pointing with a sunshade at the white rainclouds that showed above the aspen tree-tops.

And these words were enough to reëstablish again between the brothers that tone—hardly hostile, but chilly—which Levin had been so longing to avoid.

Levin went up to Katavasov.

"It was jolly of you to make up your mind to come," he said to him.

"I've been meaning to a long while. Now we shall have some discussion, we'll see to that. Have you been reading Spencer?"

"No, I've not finished reading him," said Levin. "But I don't need him now."

"How's that? that's interesting. Why so?"

"I mean that I'm fully convinced that the solution of the problems that interest me I shall never find in him and his like. Now . . ."

But Katavasov's serene and good-humored expression suddenly struck him, and he felt such tenderness for his own happy mood, which he was unmistakably disturbing by this conversation, that he remembered his resolution and stopped short.

"But we'll talk later on," he added. "If we're going to the bee-house, it's this way, along this little path," he said, addressing them all.

Going along the narrow path to a little uncut meadow covered on one side with thick clumps of brilliant heart's-ease among which stood up here and there tall, dark green tufts of hellebore, Levin settled his guests in the dense, cool shade of the young aspens on a bench and some stumps purposely put there for visitors to the bee-house who might be afraid of the bees, and he went off himself to the hut to get bread, cucumbers, and fresh honey, to regale them with.

Trying to make his movements as deliberate as possible, and listening to the bees that buzzed more and more frequently past him, he walked along the little path to the hut. In the very entry one bee hummed angrily, caught in his beard, but he carefully extricated it. Going into the shady outer room, he took down from the wall his veil, that hung on a peg, and putting it on, and thrusting his hands into his pockets, he went into the fenced-in bee-garden, where there stood in the midst of a closely mown space in regular rows, fastened with bast on posts, all the hives he knew so well, the old stocks, each with its own history, and along the fences the younger swarms hived that year. In front of the openings of the hives, it made his eyes giddy to watch the bees and drones whirling round and round about the same spot, while among them the working bees flew in and out with spoils or in search of them, always in the same direction into the wood to the flowering lime-trees and back to the hives.

His ears were filled with the incessant hum in various notes, now the busy hum of the working bee flying quickly off, then the blaring of the lazy drone, and the excited buzz of the bees on guard protecting their property from the enemy and preparing to sting. On the farther side of the fence the old bee-keeper was shaving a hoop for a tub, and he did not see Levin. Levin stood still in the midst of the beehives and did not call him.

He was glad of a chance to be alone to recover from the influence of ordinary actual life, which had already depressed his happy mood. He thought that he had already had time to lose his temper with Ivan, to show coolness to his brother, and to talk flippantly with Katavasov.

"Can it have been only a momentary mood, and will it pass and leave no trace?" he thought. But the same instant, going back to his mood, he felt with delight that something new and important had happened to him. Real life had only for a time overcast the spiritual peace he had found, but it was still untouched within him.

Just as the bees, whirling round him, now menacing him and distracting his attention, prevented him from enjoying complete physical peace, forced him to restrain his movements to avoid them, so had the petty cares that had swarmed about him from the moment he got into the trap, restricted his spiritual freedom; but that lasted only so long as he was among them. Just as his bodily strength was still unaffected, in spite of the bees, so too was the spiritual strength that he had just become aware of.

CHAPTER XV

"Do you know, Kostya, with whom Sergey Ivanovitch traveled on his way here?" said Dolly, doling out cucumbers and honey to the children; "with Vronsky! He's going to Servia."

"And not alone; he's taking a squadron out with him at his own expense," said Katavasov.

"That's the right thing for him," said Levin. "Are volunteers still going out then?" he added, glancing at Sergey Ivanovitch.

Sergey Ivanovitch did not answer. He was carefully with a blunt knife getting a live bee covered with sticky honey out of a cup full of white honeycomb.

"I should think so! You should have seen what was going on

at the station yesterday!" said Katavasov, biting with a juicy sound into a cucumber.

"Well, what is one to make of it? For mercy's sake, do explain to me, Sergey Ivanovitch, where are all those volunteers going, whom are they fighting with?" asked the old prince, unmistakably taking up a conversation that had sprung up in Levin's absence.

"With the Turks," Sergey Ivanovitch answered, smiling serenely, as he extricated the bee, dark with honey and helplessly kicking, and put it with the knife on a stout aspen leaf.

"But who has declared war on the Turks?—Ivan Ivanovitch Ragozov and Countess Lidia Ivanovna, assisted by Madame Stahl?"

"No one has declared war, but people sympathize with their neighbors' sufferings and are eager to help them," said Sergey Ivanovitch.

"But the prince is not speaking of help," said Levin, coming to the assistance of his father-in-law, "but of war. The prince says that private persons cannot take part in war without the permission of the government."

"Kostya, mind, that's a bee! Really, they'll sting us!" said Dolly, waving away a wasp.

"But that's not a bee, it's a wasp," said Levin.

"Well now, well, what's your own theory?" Katavasov said to Levin with a smile, distinctly challenging him to a discussion. "Why have not private persons the right to do so?"

"Oh, my theory's this: war is on one side such a beastly, cruel, and awful thing, that no one man, not to speak of a Christian, can individually take upon himself the responsibility of beginning wars; that can only be done by a government, which is called upon to do this, and is driven inevitably into war. On the other hand, both political science and common sense teach us that in matters of state, and especially in the matter of war, private citizens must forego their personal individual will."

Sergey Ivanovitch and Katavasov had their replies ready, and both began speaking at the same time.

"But the point is, my dear fellow, that there may be cases when the government does not carry out the will of the citizens and then the public asserts its will," said Katavasov.

But evidently Sergey Ivanovitch did not approve of this answer. His brows contracted at Katavasov's words and he said something else.

"You don't put the matter in its true light. There is no question here of a declaration of war, but simply the expression of a human Christian feeling. Our brothers, one with us in religion and in race, are being massacred. Even supposing they were not our brothers nor fellow-Christians, but simply children, women, old people, feeling is aroused and Russians go eagerly to help in stopping these atrocities. Fancy, if you were going along the street and saw drunken men beating a woman or a child—I imagine you would not stop to inquire whether war had been declared on the men, but would throw yourself on them, and protect the victim."

"But I should not kill them," said Levin.

"Yes, you would kill them."

"I don't know. If I saw that, I might give way to my impulse of the moment, but I can't say beforehand. And such a momentary impulse there is not, and there cannot be, in the case of the oppression of the Slavonic peoples."

"Possibly for you there is not; but for others there is," said Sergey Ivanovitch, frowning with displeasure. "There are traditions still extant among the people of Slavs of the true faith suffering under the yoke of the 'unclean sons of Hagar.' The people have heard of the sufferings of their brethren and have spoken."

"Perhaps so," said Levin evasively; "but I don't see it. I'm one of the people myself, and I don't feel it."

"Here am I too," said the old prince. "I've been staying abroad and reading the papers, and I must own, up to the time of the Bulgarian atrocities, I couldn't make out why it was all the Russians were all of a sudden so fond of their Slavonic brethren, while I didn't feel the slightest affection for them. I was very much upset, thought I was a monster, or that it was the influence of Carlsbad on me. But since I have been here, my mind's been set at rest. I see that there are people besides me who're only interested in Russia, and not in their Slavonic brethren. Here's Konstantin too."

"Personal opinions mean nothing in such a case," said Sergey

Ivanovitch; "it's not a matter of personal opinions when all Russia—the whole people—has expressed its will."

"But excuse me, I don't see that. The people don't know anything about it, if you come to that," said the old prince.

"Oh, papa! . . . how can you say that? And last Sunday in church?" said Dolly, listening to the conversation. "Please give me a cloth," she said to the old man, who was looking at the children with a smile. "Why, it's not possible that all . . ."

"But what was it in church on Sunday? The priest had been told to read that. He read it. They didn't understand a word of it. Then they were told that there was to be a collection for a pious object in church; well, they pulled out their halfpence and gave them, but what for they couldn't say."

"The people cannot help knowing; the sense of their own destinies is always in the people, and at such moments as the present that sense finds utterance," said Sergey Ivanovitch with conviction, glancing at the old bee-keeper.

The handsome old man, with black grizzled beard and thick silvery hair, stood motionless, holding a cup of honey, looking down from the height of his tall figure with friendly serenity at the gentlefolk, obviously understanding nothing of their conversation and not caring to understand it.

"That's so, no doubt," he said, with a significant shake of his head at Sergey Ivanovitch's words.

"Here, then, ask him. He knows nothing about it and thinks nothing," said Levin. "Have you heard about the war, Mihalitch?" he said, turning to him. "What they read in the church? What do you think about it? Ought we to fight for the Christians?"

"What should we think? Alexander Nikolaevitch our Emperor has thought for us; he thinks for us indeed in all things. It's clearer for him to see. Shall I bring a bit more bread? Give the little lad some more?" he said addressing Darya Alexandrovna and pointing to Grisha, who had finished his crust.

"I don't need to ask," said Sergey Ivanovitch, "we have seen and are seeing hundreds and hundreds of people who give up everything to serve a just cause, come from every part of Russia, and directly and clearly express their thought and aim. They bring their halfpence or go themselves and say directly what for. What does it mean?"

"It means, to my thinking," said Levin, who was beginning to get warm, "that among eighty millions of people there can always be found not hundreds, as now, but tens of thousands of people who have lost caste, ne'er-do-weels, who are always ready to go anywhere—to Pogatchev's bands, to Khiva, to Servia . . ."

"I tell you that it's not a case of hundreds or of ne'er-do-weels, but the best representatives of the people!" said Sergey Ivanovitch, with as much irritation as if he were defending the last penny of his fortune. "And what of the subscriptions? In this case it is a whole people directly expressing their will."

"That word 'people' is so vague," said Levin. "Parish clerks, teachers, and one in a thousand of the peasants, maybe, know what it's all about. The rest of the eighty millions, like Mihalitch, far from expressing their will, haven't the faintest idea what there is for them to express their will about. What right have we to say that this is the people's will?"

CHAPTER XVI

Sergey Ivanovitch, being practised in argument, did not reply, but at once turned the conversation to another aspect of the subject.

"Oh, if you want to learn the spirit of the people by arithmetical computation, of course it's very difficult to arrive at it. And voting has not been introduced among us and cannot be introduced, for it does not express the will of the people; but there are other ways of reaching that. It is felt in the air, it is felt by the heart. I won't speak of those deep currents which are astir in the still ocean of the people, and which are evident to every unprejudiced man; let us look at society in the narrow sense. All the most diverse sections of the educated public, hostile before, are merged in one. Every division is at an end, all the public organs say the same thing over and over again, all feel the mighty torrent that has overtaken them and is carrying them in one direction."

"Yes, all the newspapers do say the same thing," said the prince. "That's true. But so it is the same thing that all the frogs croak before a storm. One can hear nothing for them."

"Frogs or no frogs, I'm not the editor of a paper and I don't want to defend them; but I am speaking of the unanimity in the intellectual world," said Sergey Ivanovitch, addressing his brother. Levin would have answered, but the old prince interrupted him.

"Well, about that unanimity, that's another thing, one may say," said the prince. "There's my son-in-law, Stepan Arkadyevitch, you know him. He's got a place now on the committee of a commission and something or other, I don't remember. Only there's nothing to do in it—why, Dolly, it's no secret!—and a salary of eight thousand. You try asking him whether his post is of use, he'll prove to you that it's most necessary. And he's a truthful man too, but there's no refusing to believe in the utility of eight thousand roubles."

"Yes, he asked me to give a message to Darya Alexandrovna about the post," said Sergey Ivanovitch reluctantly, feeling the prince's remark to be ill-timed.

"So it is with the unanimity of the press. That's been explained to me: as soon as there's war their incomes are doubled. How can they help believing in the destinies of the people and the Slavonic races . . . and all that?"

"I don't care for many of the papers, but that's unjust," said Sergey Ivanovitch.

"I would only make one condition," pursued the old prince. "Alphonse Karr said a capital thing before the war with Prussia: 'You consider war to be inevitable? Very good. Let every one who advocates war be enrolled in a special regiment of advance-guards, for the front of every storm, of every attack, to lead them all!'"

"A nice lot the editors would make!" said Katavasov, with a loud roar, as he pictured the editors he knew in this picked legion.

"But they'd run," said Dolly, "they'd only be in the way."

"Oh, if they ran away, then we'd have grape-shot or Cossacks with whips behind them," said the prince.

"But that's a joke, and a poor one too, if you'll excuse my saying so, prince," said Sergey Ivanovitch.

"I don't see that it was a joke, that . . ." Levin was beginning, but Sergey Ivanovitch interrupted him.

"Every member of society is called upon to do his own special work," said he. "And men of thought are doing their work when they express public opinion. And the single-hearted and full expression of public opinion is the service of the press and a phenomenon to rejoice us at the same time. Twenty years ago we should have been silent, but now we have heard the voice of the Russian people, which is ready to rise as one man and ready to sacrifice itself for its oppressed brethren; that is a great step and a proof of strength."

"But it's not only making a sacrifice, but killing Turks," said Levin timidly. "The people make sacrifices and are ready to make sacrifices for their soul, but not for murder," he added, instinctively connecting the conversation with the ideas that had been absorbing his mind.

"For their soul? That's a most puzzling expression for a natural science man, do you understand? What sort of thing is the soul?" said Katavasov, smiling.

"Oh, you know!"

"No, by God, I haven't the faintest idea!" said Katavasov with a loud roar of laughter.

" 'I bring not peace, but a sword,' says Christ," Sergey Ivanovitch rejoined for his part, quoting as simply as though it were the easiest thing to understand the very passage that had always puzzled Levin most.

"That's so, no doubt," the old man repeated again. He was standing near them and responded to a chance glance turned in his direction.

"Ah, my dear fellow, you're defeated, utterly defeated!" cried Katavasov good-humoredly.

Levin reddened with vexation, not at being defeated, but at having failed to control himself and being drawn into argument.

"No, I can't argue with them," he thought; "they wear impenetrable armor, while I'm naked."

He saw that it was impossible to convince his brother and

Katavasov, and he saw even less possibility of himself agreeing with them. What they advocated was the very pride of intellect that had almost been his ruin. He could not admit that some dozens of men, among them his brother, had the right, on the ground of what they were told by some hundreds of glib volunteers swarming to the capital, to say that they and the newspapers were expressing the will and feeling of the people, and a feeling which was expressed in vengeance and murder. He could not admit this, because he neither saw the expression of such feelings in the people among whom he was living, nor found them in himself (and he could not but consider himself one of the persons making up the Russian people), and most of all because he, like the people, did not know and could not know what is for the general good, though he knew beyond a doubt that this general good could be attained only by the strict observance of that law of right and wrong which has been revealed to every man, and therefore he could not wish for war or advocate war for any general objects whatever. He said as Mihalitch did and the people, who had expressed their feeling in the traditional invitations of the Varyagi: "Be princes and rule over us. Gladly we promise complete submission. All the labor, all humiliations, all sacrifices we take upon ourselves; but we will not judge and decide." And now, according to Sergey Ivanovitch's account, the people had foregone this privilege they had bought at such a costly price.

He wanted to say too that if public opinion were an infallible guide, then why were not revolutions and the commune as lawful as the movement in favor of the Slavonic peoples? But these were merely thoughts that could settle nothing. One thing could be seen beyond doubt—that was that at the actual moment the discussion was irritating Sergey Ivanovitch, and so it was wrong to continue it. And Levin ceased speaking and then called the attention of his guests to the fact that the storm-clouds were gathering, and that they had better be going home before it rained.

CHAPTER XVII

The old prince and Sergey Ivanovitch got into the trap and drove off; the rest of the party hastened homewards on foot.

But the storm-clouds, turning white and then black, moved down so quickly that they had to quicken their pace to get home before the rain. The foremost clouds, lowering and black as soot-laden smoke, rushed with extraordinary swiftness over the sky. They were still two hundred paces from home and a gust of wind had already blown up, and every second the downpour might be looked for.

The children ran ahead with frightened and gleeful shrieks. Darya Alexandrovna, struggling painfully with her skirts that clung round her legs, was not walking, but running, her eyes fixed on the children. The men of the party, holding their hats on, strode with long steps beside her. They were just at the steps when a big drop fell splashing on the edge of the iron guttering. The children and their elders after them ran into the shelter of the house, talking merrily.

"Katerina Alexandrovna?" Levin asked of Agafea Mihalovna, who met them with kerchiefs and rugs in the hall.

"We thought she was with you," she said.

"And Mitya?"

"In the copse, he must be, and the nurse with him."

Levin snatched up the rugs and ran towards the copse.

In that brief interval of time the storm-clouds had moved on, covering the sun so completely that it was dark as an eclipse. Stubbornly, as though insisting on its rights, the wind stopped Levin, and tearing the leaves and flowers off the lime-trees and stripping the white birch branches into strange unseemly nakedness, it twisted everything on one side—acacias, flowers, burdocks, long grass, and tall tree-tops. The peasant girls working in the garden ran shrieking into shelter in the servants' quarters. The streaming rain had already flung its white veil over all the distant forest and half the fields close by, and was rapidly swooping down upon the copse. The wet of the rain spurting up in tiny drops could be smelt in the air.

Holding his head bent down before him, and struggling with the wind that strove to tear the wraps away from him, Levin was moving up to the copse and had just caught sight of something white behind the oak-tree, when there was a sudden flash, the whole earth seemed on fire, and the vault of heaven seemed crashing overhead. Opening his blinded eyes, Levin gazed through the thick veil of rain that separated him now from the copse, and to his horror the first thing he saw was the green crest of the familiar oak-tree in the middle of the copse uncannily changing its position. "Can it have been struck?" Levin hardly

had time to think when, moving more and more rapidly, the oak-tree vanished behind the other trees, and he heard the crash of the great tree falling upon the others.

The flash of lightning, the crash of thunder, and the instantaneous chill that ran through him were all merged for Levin in one sense of terror.

"My God! my God! not on them!" he said.

And though he thought at once how senseless was his prayer that they should not have been killed by the oak which had fallen now, he repeated it, knowing that he could do nothing better than utter this senseless prayer.

Running up to the place where they usually went, he did not find them there.

They were at the other end of the copse under an old lime-tree; they were calling him. Two figures in dark dresses (they had been light summer dresses when they started out) were standing bending over something. It was Kitty with the nurse. The rain was already ceasing, and it was beginning to get light when Levin reached them. The nurse was not wet on the lower part of her dress, but Kitty was drenched through, and her soaked clothes clung to her. Though the rain was over, they still stood in the same position in which they had been standing when the storm broke. Both stood bending over a perambulator with a green umbrella.

"Alive? Unhurt? Thank God!" he said, splashing with his soaked boots through the standing water and running up to them.

Kitty's rosy wet face was turned towards him, and she smiled timidly under her shapeless sopped hat.

"Aren't you ashamed of yourself? I can't think how you can be so reckless!" he said angrily to his wife.

"It wasn't my fault, really. We were just meaning to go, when he made such a to-do that we had to change him. We were just . . ." Kitty began defending herself.

Mitya was unharmed, dry, and still fast asleep.

"Well, thank God! I don't know what I'm saying!"

They gathered up the baby's wet belongings; the nurse picked up the baby and carried it. Levin walked beside his wife, and, penitent for having been angry, he squeezed her hand when the nurse was not looking.

CHAPTER XVIII

During the whole of that day, in the extremely different conversations in which he took part, only as it were with the top layer of his mind, in spite of the disappointment of not finding the change he expected in himself, Levin had been all the while joyfully conscious of the fulness of his heart.

After the rain it was too wet to go for a walk; besides, the storm-clouds still hung about the horizon, and gathered here and there, black and thundery, on the rim of the sky. The whole party spent the rest of the day in the house.

No more discussions sprang up; on the contrary, after dinner every one was in the most amiable frame of mind.

At first Katavasov amused the ladies by his original jokes, which always pleased people on their first acquaintance with him. Then Sergey Ivanovitch induced him to tell them about the very interesting observations he had made on the habits and characteristics of common house-flies, and their life. Sergey Ivanovitch, too, was in good spirits, and at tea his brother drew him on to explain his views of the future of the Eastern question, and he spoke so simply and so well, that every one listened eagerly.

Kitty was the only one who did not hear it all—she was summoned to give Mitya his bath.

A few minutes after Kitty had left the room she sent for Levin to come to the nursery.

Leaving his tea, and regretfully interrupting the interesting conversation, and at the same time uneasily wondering why he had been sent for, as this only happened on important occasions, Levin went to the nursery.

Although he had been much interested by Sergey Ivanovitch's views of the new epoch in history that would be created by the emancipation of forty millions of men of Slavonic race acting with Russia, a conception quite new to him, and although he was disturbed by uneasy wonder at being sent for by Kitty, as soon as he came out of the drawing-room and was alone, his mind reverted at once to the thoughts of the morning. And all the theories of the significance of the Slav element in the history of the world seemed to him so trivial compared with what was passing in his own soul, that he instantly forgot it all and dropped back into the same frame of mind that he had been in that morning.

He did not, as he had done at other times, recall the whole train of thought—that he did not need. He fell back at once into the feeling which had guided him, which was connected with those thoughts, and he found that feeling in his soul even stronger and more definite than before. He did not, as he had

had to do with previous attempts to find comforting arguments, need to revive a whole chain of thought to find the feeling. Now, on the contrary, the feeling of joy and peace was keener than ever, and thought could not keep pace with feeling.

He walked across the terrace and looked at two stars that had come out in the darkening sky, and suddenly he remembered. "Yes, looking at the sky, I thought that the dome that I see is not a deception, and then I thought something, I shirked facing something," he mused. "But whatever it was, there can be no disproving it! I have but to think, and all will come clear!"

Just as he was going into the nursery he remembered what it was he had shirked facing. It was that if the chief proof of the Divinity was His revelation of what is right, how is it this revelation is confined to the Christian church alone? What relation to this revelation have the beliefs of the Buddhists, Mohammedans, who preached and did good too?

It seemed to him that he had an answer to this question; but he had not time to formulate it to himself before he went into the nursery.

Kitty was standing with her sleeves tucked up over the baby in the bath. Hearing her husband's footstep, she turned towards him, summoning him to her with her smile. With one hand she was supporting the fat baby that lay floating and sprawling on its back, while with the other she squeezed the sponge over him.

"Come, look, look!" she said, when her husband came up to her. "Agafea Mihalovna's right. He knows us!"

Mitya had on that day given unmistakable, incontestable signs of recognizing all his friends.

As soon as Levin approached the bath, the experiment was tried, and it was completely successful. The cook, sent for with this object, bent over the baby. He frowned and shook his head disapprovingly. Kitty bent down to him, he gave her a beaming smile, propped his little hands on the sponge and chirruped, making such a queer little contented sound with his lips, that Kitty and the nurse were not alone in their admiration. Levin, too, was surprised and delighted.

The baby was taken out of the bath, drenched with water, wrapped in towels, dried, and after a piercing scream, handed to his mother.

"Well, I am glad you are beginning to love him," said Kitty to her husband, when she had settled herself comfortably in her usual place, with the baby at her breast. "I am so glad! It had begun to distress me. You said you had no feeling for him."

"No; did I say that? I only said I was disappointed."

"What! disappointed in him?"

"Not disappointed in him, but in my own feeling; I had expected more. I had expected a rush of new delightful emotion to come as a surprise. And then instead of that—disgust, pity . . ."

She listened attentively, looking at him over the baby, while she put back on her slender fingers the rings she had taken off while giving Mitya his bath.

"And most of all, at there being far more apprehension and pity than pleasure. To-day, after that fright during the storm, I understand how I love him."

Kitty's smile was radiant.

"Were you very much frightened?" she said. "So was I too, but I feel it more now that it's over. I'm going to look at the oak. How nice Katavasov is! And what a happy day we've had altogether. And you're so nice with Sergey Ivanovitch, when you care to be. . . . Well, go back to them. It's always so hot and steamy here after the bath."

CHAPTER XIX

Going out of the nursery and being again alone, Levin went back at once to the thought, in which there was something not clear.

Instead of going into the drawing-room, where he heard voices, he stopped on the terrace, and leaning his elbows on the parapet, he gazed up at the sky.

It was quite dark now, and in the south, where he was looking, there were no clouds. The storm had drifted on to the opposite side of the sky, and there were flashes of lightning and distant thunder from that quarter. Levin listened to the monotonous drip from the lime-trees in the garden, and looked at the triangle of stars he knew so well, and the Milky Way with its branches that ran through its midst. At each flash of lightning the Milky Way, and even the bright stars, vanished, but as soon as the lightning died away, they reappeared in their places as though some hand had flung them back with careful aim.

"Well, what is it perplexes me?" Levin said to himself, feeling beforehand that the solution of his difficulties was ready in his soul, though he did not know it yet. "Yes, the one unmistakable, incontestable manifestation of the Divinity is the law of right and wrong, which has come into the world by revelation, and which I feel in myself, and in the recognition of which—I don't make myself, but whether I will or not—I am made one with other men in one body of believers, which is called the church. Well, but the Jews, the Mohammedans, the Confucians, the Buddhists—what of them?" he put to himself the question he had feared to face. "Can these hundreds of millions of men be deprived of that highest blessing without which life has no meaning?" He pondered a moment, but immediately corrected himself. "But what am I questioning?" he said to himself. "I am questioning the relation to Divinity of all the different religions of all mankind. I am questioning the universal manifestation of God to all the world with all those misty blurs. What am I about? To me individually, to my heart has been revealed a knowledge beyond all doubt, and unattainable by reason, and here I am obstinately trying to express that knowledge in reason and words.

"Don't I know that the stars don't move?" he asked himself, gazing at the bright planet which had shifted its position up to the topmost twig of the birch-tree. "But looking at the movements of the stars, I can't picture to myself the rotation of the earth, and I'm right in saying that the stars move.

"And could the astronomers have understood and calculated anything, if they had taken into account all the complicated and varied motions of the earth? All the marvelous conclusions they have reached about the distances, weights, movements, and deflections of the heavenly bodies are only founded on the apparent motions of the heavenly bodies about a stationary earth, on that very motion I see before me now, which has been so for millions of men during long ages, and was and will be always alike, and can always be trusted. And just as the conclusions of the astronomers would have been vain and uncertain if not founded on observations of the seen heavens, in relation to a single meridian and a single horizon, so would my conclusions be vain and uncertain if not founded on that conception of right, which has been and will be always alike for all men, which has been revealed to me as a Christian, and which can always be trusted in my soul. The question of other religions and their relations to Divinity I have no right to decide, and no possibility of deciding."

"Oh, you haven't gone in then?" he heard Kitty's voice all at once, as she came by the same way to the drawing-room.

"What is it? you're not worried about anything?" she said, looking intently at his face in the starlight.

But she could not have seen his face if a flash of lightning had not hidden the stars and revealed it. In that flash she saw his face distinctly, and seeing him calm and happy, she smiled at him.

"She understands," he thought; "she knows what I'm thinking about. Shall I tell her or not? Yes, I'll tell her." But at the moment he was about to speak, she began speaking.

"Kostya! do something for me," she said; "go into the corner room and see if they've made it all right for Sergey Ivanovitch. I can't very well. See if they've put the new wash-stand in it."

"Very well, I'll go directly," said Levin, standing up and kissing her.

"No, I'd better not speak of it," he thought, when she had gone in before him. "It is a secret for me alone, of vital importance for me, and not to be put into words.

"This new feeling has not changed me, has not made me happy and enlightened all of a sudden, as I had dreamed, just like the feeling for my child. There was no surprise in this either. Faith—or not faith—I don't know what it is—but this feeling has come just as imperceptibly through suffering, and has taken firm root in my soul.

"I shall go on in the same way, losing my temper with Ivan the coachman, falling into angry discussions, expressing my opinions tactlessly; there will be still the same wall between the holy of holies of my soul and other people, even my wife; I shall still go on scolding her for my own terror, and being remorseful for it; I shall still be as unable to understand with my reason why I pray, and I shall still go on praying; but my life now, my whole life apart from anything that can happen to me, every minute of it is no more meaningless, as it was before, but it has the positive meaning of goodness, which I have the power to put into it."